SLINGELANDT'S EFFORTS
TOWARDS EUROPEAN PEACE

SLINGELANDT'S EFFORTS TOWARDS EUROPEAN PEACE

BY

DR. A. GOSLINGA

PART I

THE HAGUE
MARTINUS NIJHOFF
1915

GEDRUKT BIJ H. J. VAN DE GARDE & CO. — ZALTBOMMEL.

ISBN 978-94-015-0315-0   ISBN 978-94-015-0853-7 (eBook)
DOI 10.1007/978-94-015-0853-7

CONTENTS.

CHAPTER I.

SIMON VAN SLINGELANDT.

HIS LIFE, CHARACTER AND POSITION.

I.

The town of Dordt has deserved well of its country, for in
it two men of signal greatness were born, John de Witt and
Simon van Slingelandt. Both of them were Grand Pensionaries
of Holland. They are classed together because they are fellow
townsmen and for another reason: the rise of the Slingelandts
to the highest positions in the state is closely connected with
the administration of John de Witt. In an early period the
activities of the Slingelandt family were confined to the town
of Dordt, where for at least three centuries they took part, in
some degree, in local government. It is known that a Jan van
Slingelandt became councillor in 1385, alderman in the
next year and afterwards burgomaster. He is said to have
derived his name from his maternal grandfather, the knight
Herbaren van Arkel who held the manor of Slingelandt near
Gorkum, [1]) and therefore he would seem to have been the
first to bear his name in Dordt. After him there were several members of his family who from time to time had a share in the government of their birthplace, [2]) but this seems to have been the
limit of their power until the days of John de Witt. He it was who
changed such condition. In the course of his endeavour to
strengthen his own position in the Republic, he did all in his power to favour men on whom he could rely, of whom his own relatives were first. Among these his cousin and intimate friend,
Govert van Slingelandt, was distinguished in that he was steeped

---

[1]) *Navorscher* XIII. 379. A "dominus Otto de Slinghelandt" is mentioned in the time
of Count Floris V. Cf. Van den Bergh, *Oorkondenboek* II. N°. 331. This may be the first
mention of the name.

[2]) Cf. J. L. van Dalen, *Inventaris van het Archief der gemeente Dordrecht*, 76, 122.

in his ideas. Therefore when De Witt forsook the Pensionaryship of Dordt for that of Holland he chose Slingelandt as fit to succeed him, and induced the regents of Dordt to give him the vacant office. He made yet further use of him. Between 1655 and 1660, when the Republic was taking a decisive part in the struggle against Swedish imperialism, he made that Slingelandt should twice be appointed envoy extraordinary to the Northern courts. Finally in 1664 he succeeded in procuring for him a high government employment, the post of Secretary to the Council of State. [1]

In consequence Slingelandt was obliged to leave Dordt for the Hague. Shortly before his departure, on the 14th of January 1664, the hero of this book was born, Simon van Slingelandt, son of Govert by his second wife, Arnoldina van Beaumont. She, like her husband, belonged to an old aristocratic Dordt family. Her grandfather was the poet Simon van Beaumont, and her brother, who bore the same Christian name, served his country in several important posts, notably as Secretary to the States of Holland. His nephew, who was probably called after him, is said to have owed to him his introduction to statesmanship. [2]

There is no evidence as to whether his father had an equal part in his education. It is possible, however, for the elder Slingelandt lacked none of the requisite qualifications. He passed for one of the most learned regents and ministers of his century, a character which, apart from all other evidence, is revealed in a description of Simon as "a still greater genius than his father and equally learned." [3] For part of his learning Simon was indebted to Leyden University. The evidence as to his studies is slight and somewhat discrepant, but it is likely that he enrolled himself as a student in 1681 at the age of seventeen and remained three years at the university, reading both law and philosophy. There is no ground for even a surmise as to where he graduated, probably not at Leyden. His industry is however placed beyond doubt, judging by results. He was remarkably conversant with the classic languages, especially Greek: according to Van Haren few Greek scholars

---

[1] In 1660 Ruysch, greffier to the States General, was very ill. According to Van Haren, De Witt intended to help Slingelandt to obtain the post in case it fell vacant. *Leven en Werken*, 416 (ed. Van Vloten).

[2] Scheltema, *Staatkundig Nederland*, I. 69.

[3] Van Haren, *op. cit.* 416, 417.

have surpassed him.[1]) He had a no less command of French which he was able both to write and speak with the utmost ease. His study of history is proved by his knowledge of its facts which were always at his disposal. Thus when in 1735 England and the Republic wished to intervene between the powers engaged in the war of the Polish Succession, he gained a starting point for his observations on the existing situation to Fénelon, the French ambassador, by reading to him two passages from the letters of Sir William Temple bearing on the famous Triple Alliance of 1668. His knowledge of the constitutional law of his country had never before been equalled, as it has seldom been since. His great skill in finance may be ascribed to his study of philosophy, of which branch of science mathematics were at that time accounted a part. But however extensive and profound his studies were, his education was not all obtained from this source. He was the son of one high official and the nephew of another; he grew up at the Hague, the seat of the States General and the States of Holland, and moreover a principal centre of European diplomacy in the glorious days of John de Witt and William III. It was inevitable that, with his penetrating mind, he should gather in the sphere of his daily life an abundant treasure of knowledge and of judgment. Only thus can he have acquired the unrivalled thoroughness of his knowledge of the intricate Dutch constitution and the breadth of his outlook on European politics.

His opportunity of using the great gifts at his disposal came early. After the death of his father on July 3rd 1690 he was appointed to succeed him as Secretary to the Council of State. That this appointment was suffered by William III. seems at first sight strange; for Govert had always supported the party opposed to the Stadtholder and had used his influence in the Council to thwart William's designs, [2]) and the younger Slingelandt, highly gifted as he was, was only twenty-six years old. There is an answer to the riddle. At this very time, on July 31st 1690, Simon entered into a contract of marriage with Susanna de Wildt, daughter of Job de Wildt, the Secretary to the Admiralty of Amsterdam. And Job, of whom it was related that he had but one eye, and with it saw further in public affairs than others did with two, [3]) was in

---

[1]) Ibid: 417.
[2]) Blok, *Geschiedenis van het Nederlandsche volk*, V. 405 and quotation.
[3]) John Drummond to the Earl of Oxford, 18 Aug. 1713. *Hist. Mss. Com. Rep.* Portland Mss. V. 319.

high favour with the King-Stadtholder. It is to him that William is said first to have entrusted the secret of the Revolution, [1]) and it was he whom he appointed in 1691 as his representative in the Admiralties of Holland, Zealand and West Friesland. [2])

For no less than thirty-five years, from 1690 to 1725, Slingelandt filled this office of Secretary to the Council of State. As to the first years of his service there is hardly any information; later, knowledge is less scanty but still insufficient. In the war of the Spanish Succession he seems to have played an important part, but one which it is quite impossible to define without answering many questions and making many researches. Slingelandt has been highly praised [3]) for the eloquent introductions to the annual petitions delivered by the Council of State to the States General, but there is no certainty that he really was their author. He kept up a correspondence with the Duke of Marlborough for several years, which doubtless contains valuable particulars as to the mutual relations of the Maritime Powers during the War of the Spanish Succession, but which, save for a few letters, is as yet unpublished and even unexamined. [4]) It is therefore necessary to fall back on

---

[1]) John Drummond to the Earl of Oxford, 18 Aug. 1713. *Hist. Mss. Com. Rep.* Portland Mss. V. 319.

[2]) Elias, *De Vroedschap van Amsterdam*, I. 393.

[3]) Siegenbeek, *Lofrede* 34—6; Collot d'Escury, *Hollands Roem* II, 410, 599; IV², 451—2.

[4]) George Murray in his *Letters and Dispatches of John Churchill, First Duke of Marlborough, from 1702—1712* (5 vols. 1845) has published several letters from Marlborough to Slingelandt, the first of which is dated 8th May 1703. Unpublished letters from the Duke to him during the years 1702, 1703, 1704, 1705, 1706, 1707, 1710 and 1711 are to be found in R. A., Raad van State 1898.

The same bundle contains letters from Slingelandt to the Duke in the years 1706 and '07. Others from Slingelandt to the Duke during the years 1705, '07, '08, '09 and '15 are still to be found among the Marlborough papers, cf *Hist. Mss. Comm. Report VIII* Part I, pp. 31, 32, 36, 37, 40. The letters mentioned on p. 31 of the year 1689 and '90 are probably from Slingelandt's father.

It may perhaps be helpful to add to these remarks others which we have gathered with reference to Slingelandt's correspondence prior to his entering upon the office of Grand Pensionary.

Of this only a single letter of his to Townshend has been published (Coxe, *R. W. II*, 157) The oldest which we have found from his pen is one written to William Blathwayt, Secretary for War 1691—1705, and is dated January 24th 1702 (B. M. Add. 21552 f. 32).

Letters from Athlone to him during 1702, in the above mentioned bundle Raad van State 1898, R. A. Letters from Halifax (1706, '07, '08 and '14), Cardonnel, Marlborough's Secretary, (1711), Albemarle (1712) and from Townshend to him (1714—'17) in R. A. Hl. 2996; this bundle also contains letters of his to Halifax (1706) and to Townshend (1714—'17). Other letters from Slingelandt to Townshend, together a dozen, of the years 1722—'27 are to be found R. O. Hl. 280 and 297. The corresponding letters from Townshend to him are contained in the same bundle, there is one letter from Townshend (1726) in R. A. Hl. 2994.

generalities, which however leave no doubt that during the war, and especially in its latter years, he was a man of much consequence. He exchanged letters not only with Marlborough and his secretary Cardonnel, but also with Halifax, Athlone and Albemarle. [1]) Townshend, who was sent to the Hague in 1709, became his intimate friend. He was accounted one of "the chief men" of the Dutch government, and "one of the greatest and best men in the Republic who with the Grand Pensionary (Heinsius) and the Greffier Fagel do the great affairs." And this testimony is not that of a friend, but is found in the letters of John Drummond, a Scottish merchant, sent to the Republic by the Tory cabinet of the last years of Queen Anne, whose enmity and fear are clearly shewn in another passage. "Secretary Slingelandt," he wrote, "has a correspondence of his own in England, and I look upon him and his correspondence to be the most dangerous of all; he was my lord Townshend's inseparable favourite and no less the confidant of the Captain General (the Duke of Marlborough), and if anyone maintains that correspondence, it is through and by him. He is the Greffier Fagel's near relation and most intimate friend, and to the best of my judgment and information the chief government of this state is managed by the Grand Pensionary, the Greffier Fagel and the Secretary Slingelandt." [2])

The French ambassador who came to the Hague immediately

Since 1697, Slingelandt kept up a correspondence with the Frisian Statesman Goslinga. This correspondence has been drawn upon by Slothouwer in his life of Goslinga. On page 2 of this work he gives his references for this. A part of this correspondence, letters from Goslinga to Slingelandt bearing dates in 1714, '15, '16, '18 and '26 as well as letters from Slingelandt to Goslinga of 1716 and '18, will be found in R. A. Hl. 2996. Unfortunately the letters which Slingelandt received from Goslinga were for the greatest part burnt by the former, cf Slingelandt to Goslinga, May 7th 1724, F. G.

It is not improbable that sooner or later other correspondence of Slingelandt's will be discovered. Tydeman, editor of Bilderdijk's *Geschiedenis des Vaderlands* tells in this work (vol. XI, 214) that he had bought two volumes full of documents dealing with the period 1705—1712, among which there were a great number of original and autograph letters belonging to Heinsius, Slingelandt and other statesman of that period. On Tydeman's death these volumes were bought by the Dutch Government for the R. A. but have since been lost.

Some "very important" correspondence between Slingelandt and Visscher has been referred to in *Verhandeling over den geest van het plakkaat van* 31 *Juli* 1725 (Amsterdam 1816) p. 17 about a new scale of import and export duties. Unfortunately the author forgot to tell us where this correspondence was to be found.

[1]) See the preceding note.

[2]) John Drummond to Robert Harley, Earl of Oxford, 1 Oct. (n. s.) 1712; 9 Dec. (n. s.) 1710; 18 August. (n. s.) 1713. *Hist. Mss. Com. Rep.* Portland Mss. V. 226, IV. 637, V. 318.

after the conclusion of peace, the Marquis de Châteauneuf, thought no less of Slingelandt. "Il était", he wrote, "le chef du parti impérial le plus redoutable par sa place, par son esprit, et par son crédit sur son beau-frère Fagel." [1]) The grounds of Slingelandt's influence are thus well summarized. The first of them was indeed his place. The Council of State, of which the principal cares were the supervision of the militia and of finance, was especially important in time of war. Yet its sphere of action was limited, for it had no direct concern with foreign affairs; and had Slingelandt strictly confined himself to his secretarial duties, his name would not have been regularly mentioned in the same breath as those of Heinsius and Fagel. [2]) It was on account of his "esprit" that these men, on whom, much more than on him, the government of the Republic devolved, habitually took counsel with him, especially Fagel, who as his sister's husband was most intimately bound to him.

II.

After the peace of Utrecht Slingelandt still took part in foreign politics, but most of his time and attention were given to home affairs. Within the Republic the situation was very critical: the state of finance was appalling and the inadequacy of the constitution cried out for remedy. Slingelandt strained every nerve to save his country from present and future dangers; and his efforts deserve attention, for they give an idea of the nature of the Dutch constitution, essential to the right understanding of this book, and also give what is even more important, an aspect of Slingelandt's character.

There were serious defects in the machinery of government which dated from the very beginning of the Republic. Properly speaking, there had never been a formal constitution, for the Union of Utrecht, which since 1579 had bound together the northern provinces, was no more than a defensive treaty against Spain. It had not been called upon to provide for the central government and had not done so. There was at the time of its

---

[1]) A. E. Mem. et Doc. Hl. 60. fol. 22. 13 Nov. 1713.

[2]) cf. for instance Lamberty, *Mémoires pour servir à l'histoire du dix-huitième siècle,* VII, 158: "Heinsius, Slingelandt et Fagel étaient trois des plus sages et des plus solides piliers de la République."

inception an understanding that ruling power would be vested either in a governor aided by a council of state, or directly in such a council, which should have as members the Stadtholders of the provinces. And this had indeed been for some years the case, until Leicester's abuse of the power entrusted to him as governor caused important alterations. Soon after his departure from the country, in 1588, a new instruction to the Council of State greatly limited their powers, which was still further curtailed, when in 1593 the States General became from an occasional assembly a permanent body, and assumed the management of many affairs which would have been better left to the Council. The change was an indirect result of the treaty made with Elizabeth in 1585 which provided that two Englishmen should have a seat in the Council: the dislike of foreign influence caused the body in which it was necessarily strong to be deprived of their principal functions. There was another and special reason for this: the province of Holland had in an independent council far less power than in the States General, which were constituted by the States of the provinces and responsible to them. It was thus that finally there came to be two governing bodies in the Republic, the much restrained Council of State, and the assembly of the States General. The duality of authority gave rise to much trouble and confusion, yet since, on the whole, the States were predominant, there would have been a working condition had they been equal to their task. But their scope of action was small; in all matters of importance they were obliged to consult their constituents, the States of the provinces. And Holland, by far the most important among the provinces, was ever intent on imposing her will on the others who were often little disposed to submit to her dictation. The resultant discord was the more serious because unanimity was generally compulsory in matters of importance. And in such cases it some-times became next to impossible to take action, for, there were no efficient means for the coercion of unwilling provinces, nor when a resolution had been laboriously passed, was there any guarantee of its being carried out.

This condition had the gravest effects: the course of affairs was hampered in manifold ways and the most necessary measures were frequently neglected. There had been several attempts to remedy one or more of the defects of the constitution but all had

failed. To a certain extent however, weaknesses were counterbalanced. In time of war, and many have been the wars of the
Republic, fear of a common enemy, whether Spain or France,
often brought the desired harmony. But the unity of action without which seven small provinces could never have played their
remarkable part in the world's history was principally induced
by the Princes of Orange, not so much by virtue of their position
in the Republic as a whole, which they served as Captains General
and Admirals General, as by reason of their position within the
provinces. In four or five of these they were Stadtholders, and
thus becoming in a way interprovincial authorities, and, strengthening their authority with their personal influence, they were
often able to establish unity and suppress differences.

The defects however, though thus partially neutralised, were
not removed, and as counterpoises to them were withdrawn, they
were increasingly manifest. They were instanced after the peace of
Utrecht. William III. had been almost absolute master of the
Republic, and had exercised a greater power than any of his predecessors. He had not however, used this extraordinary authority
for the remedy of the underlying defects and abuses of the republican institutions, whether original or otherwise, but had
only by its means brought the regents to a condition of dependence which in the opinion of many was inconsistent with the
liberty of the State. Whether we blame him with Slingelandt; or
with Fruin, think his course was forced on him by the necessity
of saving Europe from the supremacy of France and Roman
Catholicism, it is indisputable that after his death the flaws in the
constitution were more apparent than before. This was less the
case during the war of the Spanish Succession; after its cessation
they became immediately and alarmingly distinct. A chronic ill
which had been latent had grown acute. For the time being there
was no danger from outside; and there was not a Stadtholder left
who could bring the provinces into harmony, for the Stadtholder of
Friesland, afterwards William IV, was a young child, at this
moment of no account. In this state of affairs Holland attempted to
exert too much power over the other provinces, which however
were more jealous than ever of her ascendancy. Moreover she herself
had lost that unity, which she had enjoyed at least to some extent
in the first period of government without a Stadtholder, the days of

John de Witt. The condition of the country at large was repeated within every province. The States General depended on the provincial States, but these in their turn were dependent on the towns which gave them their mandate, and who quarrelled among themselves, even as did the provinces. Within the provinces, as in the country, public spirit was lost. Each man upheld his particular opinions with the perseverance peculiar to the narrow-minded and self-conceited, epithets which may justly be applied to the eighteenth century Dutch regents. Decentralization and discord had progressed so far that, in the words of Slingelandt's famous epigram, the survival of the Republic was more of a marvel than her decline.

All this would have been less serious had the public exchequer been well filled. "A rich household can stand against disorders by which one that is poor is overthrown." [1]) The condition of finance was, however, appalling. Since the accession of William III, three expensive wars had accumulated debts of unprecedented magnitude. The war of the English Succession cost the province of Holland no less than twenty-eight million guilders, that of the Spanish Succession one hundred million. [2]) After the peace, relief was first sought in a reduction of military expenses. The army was reduced from 130,000 to 50,000 men immediately, and soon afterwards to 40,000. Some provinces made their poverty an excuse to disband more than their due proportion, which they had no right to do, this power over the militia pertaining legally only to the central government. The other provinces thus found themselves unequally burdened, but their protests were vain, and all efforts to bring about an agreement miscarried. Then the province of Overijsel, led by the Count van Rechteren, proposed that an extra-ordinary assembly should be held, as at the beginning of the first period of government without a Stadtholder, in 1651. It was resolved, in accordance with this proposal, that the provinces should return representatives to this assembly sufficiently empowered to put matters in order, and bound by oath to subordinate all provincial interests to the well-being and the preservation of the commonwealth.

The supervision of finance and the militia belonged to the

---

[1]) Slingelandt, *Staatkundige Geschriften*, II. 14.
[2]) Secr. Res. Hl. VII. 835—6.

Council of State, whose advice had therefore to be taken. Their whole-hearted consent to Overijsel's proposal was a matter of course, but they went beyond this and did their utmost to ensure the success of the assembly. Slingelandt, their eminent and zealous secretary, would not miss such an opportunity, and in a letter of advice he went to the very root of the matter. First he emphasized the necessity that this extraordinary assembly should have a character other than the ordinary meetings of the States General, that its members should come to it fully instructed and empowered by the provinces, and so pass resolutions without further reference to their constituents. He went so far as to state that in his opinion it would be better not to hold the proposed assembly, than to suffer the deputies who composed it to lack full authority. Secondly he gave warning of the danger of allowing them first to occupy themselves with the disbanding of the militia, the immediate occasion of their meeting, for once this matter were settled, he feared that others might be entirely neglected. It was those others which seemed to Slingelandt the more important. The problem of how to obtain a decision when voting by majority had been excluded, and that of the means of executing a resolution which had been passed, were of such primordial interest, that he wished to see all others subordinated to them. He closed with an earnest exhortation to the assembly to strengthen the central government and set aside all private objects.

Exhortations by themselves however, were of little avail; if practical measures were to be expected of the assembly, the path along which they should pass must be chalked out, and this task also was undertaken by Slingelandt, who was more fitted for it than anyone else. By serious study he had broadened and deepened that knowledge of the machinery of the Republic's government which he had acquired by long service. There was hardly any literature on the subject, however he had not failed to examine the original sources, principally the resolutions of the States General, the States of Holland and the Council of State, and had given his few spare hours to this work. It bore fruit in a series of treatises, which are still indispensable to any student of the constitution of the Republic. But it was not as text books that they were written: their author was not a scholar, but a statesman; and he wrote "not to give a systematic and complete description of the constitution, but merely to explain those parts thereof, of which a thorough knowledge is necessary before the successful restoration of the reduced fortunes of the state can be undertaken." [1]) Such profound study enabled him to trace the causes of weaknesses, and suggested means of reform to his fertile mind.

To dwell on those means is beyond our plan. We only ask how he faced the problems, and, for a reason which will afterwards be clear, we wish to emphasize that it was not as a doctrinaire. He did not desire to reform the Republic by a new system, invented in his study and unrelated to actual conditions; but made the established constitution his starting-point. First he showed how in given cases, they acted in the early days, then the defects, whether original or of late growth; and finally he pointed out the means of correction, giving due regard both to the intentions of the past and the needs of the present. He was above all, zealous for accomplishment; he went to extreme lengths in yielding to circumstances, so long only as thereby an end was attained. His attitude towards the Council of State is typical. He was convinced that it would be advantageous for the Republic that the Council should regain its old authority and place in the machinery of government, and that the States General should content themselves with short annual meetings for the discussion of the budget and of bills prepared by the Council. But he knew that the States were incapable of so much self-restraint, and therefore he was willing, in order to secure resolutions and their execution, to sacrifice this authority of the Council, in spite of their historical claims, and even in so doing to strengthen their ancient rival. He was prepared to accept a chamber which could quickly and regularly pass resolutions, and a Council able to execute them effectively.

Eternal shame attaches to the regents of the eighteenth century, for all Slingelandt's work was in vain. Despite his earnest warning the disbanding of the militia was first considered, and it took up all the attention of the assembly. Other business was treated only in a cursory and intermittent fashion, much to the mortification of Slingelandt, who frankly told the assembly that it was useless to provide means for executing resolutions while, since

[1]) Slingelandt, *op. cit.* I. p. VI. This work, published about half a century after the author's death (2 volumes. Amsterdam, 1784) contains many political writings of varied character. Some other writings of Slingelandt are still unpublished (cf. catalogue of the Slingelandt Collection at the Rijks-Archief at the Hague).

the matter of obtaining a decision had not been settled, any province could prevent their passage, and while nobody had been vested with sufficient executive authority. It was but "to give a tool to a lame hand."

His words were sharp, but in his chagrin at seeing people fritter their time away in empty talk, he took no pains to conceal his opinion or palliate the truth. While hope remained he adjured the assembly to undertake the reform of the constitution. "It was," he said, summarizing all his message, "inexcusable before God, and before the world, always to trust to miracles."[1]

He had reason to speak of miracles. The student of this time wonders again and again how desperate disorder was avoided. It is true that in 1715 the public pay-office was closed for nine months, yet on the whole the machinery of the state was kept in motion. Two years later the prospect of another suspension was very near, and the danger was averted in a manner hardly intelligible. The credit belongs to some extent to the excellent administration of Slingelandt and of Hop, the Treasurer General. [2] To them also is ascribed the responsibility for saving the state from the financial disasters which about 1720 overtook both France and England.

III.

Slingelandt put forth all his strength for the sake of his country but did not obtain due recognition. He was disliked by most of the regents because he laid his finger on the vital malady of the state and because of his downright language. As he himself complained, his words, too like the oracles of Cassandra, [3] frequently had little effect, and there was no disposition to promote him to that place to which his merits and his parts gave him an undisputable right. In 1720 the Grand Pensionary Heinsius died. Slingelandt's friends were zealous on his behalf; the majority however,

---

[1] This passage, pp. 6 to 12, as to the defects in the constitution and the extraordinary assembly is founded on Slingelandt's political writings mentioned above.

[2] Van Wijn, *Nalezingen*, II. 351—2.

[3] Slingelandt to Goslinga. 14 Sep. 1726. F. G. Goslinga had written that his intended marriage with his servant would lose him all his reputation. Slingelandt answered as follows: "Au reste mes peines et mon travail pour le bien de la patrie et les avis que j'ai pris la liberté de donner à ceux qui sont dans les postes à s'en servir ont été si inutiles et les derniers ressemblent si fort aux oracles de Cassandre que certainement la perte sera très médiocre, s'il était demontré que je me rends inutile au public."

who were more or less worked upon by French diplomacy, feared his so-called "tyranny," and the possibility that he would subordinate the interests of Holland to those of the Republic as a whole. [1]) He was passed over in favour of a man in every respect his inferior, Isaac van Hoornbeek.

This was not the first rebuff which he had met in the course of his public career, for in 1699 he had stood vainly for the office of Treasurer General.[2]) In his private life and with regard to his health he was not fortunate either, he being a martyr to gout for many years.[3]) He suffered most cruelly from this complaint, which often affected his whole body so that he could stir neither hand nor foot. In later years, when he was a Pensionary, he was again and again unable for weeks to leave his house or even his bed: often it was necessary to carry him to the assembly of the States. Attacks were sometimes brought on by misfortunes. At a later date many attacks were caused by the actions of the States of Holland, but at this time they must be ascribed to the conduct of his only daughter.

Of his six children by Susanna de Wildt, four did not reach maturity. One son, Job, died as a student at Leyden University, at the age of nineteen. The sole survivors were Govert and Susanna. The latter was sought in marriage by a Baron Spörker, a boorish country gentleman of Hanover. Her father would not allow the match, and she eloped with her suitor to Cleves. Slingelandt then wisely let her have her way, but his grief brought on several attacks of gout. Shortly after the marriage he lost his wife, and his insolent son-in-law then accused him of depriving his daughter of part of her mother's inheritance. There ensued a new disagreement, which was finally settled by Lord Townshend when he stayed for some days at the Hague on his way to Hanover. [4])

These years were sad, but at length fortune turned. On the death of Hop in 1725 Slingelandt was appointed Treasurer General

---

[1]) R. O. Hl. 274. Whitworth to Sunderland, 19 August 1720. An instance of very bad treatment is in Slothouwer, *Sicco van Goslinga*, 117—8.

[2]) *Archives de la Maison d'Orange*, Ser. III, II. 505. Heinsius to William III. 10 Nov. 1699.

[3]) At least since 1713. *Hist Mss. Com. Rep.* Portland Mss. V. 316. Matthew Decker to Oxford, 18 Aug. 1713.

[4]) Slothouwer, *op. cit.* 118—9. Townshend's stay at the Hague was in 1723. Baron Spörker had meanwhile been appointed envoy extra-ordinary at the Hague to George I. as elector of Hanover.

in his stead. He accepted the office chiefly in the belief that in it
he would find his repeated attacks of gout less hampering than
he had done as Secretary. [1]

In the next year he resolved to marry again. After his wife's
death his house was kept by a woman who had been for years in
his service, Johanna van Coesveld. On account of his age and his
recurrent complaint he tried to persuade her to promise that, as her
late mistress had wished, she would stay with him for the rest of
his life. She refused to commit herself and then, after careful
consideration, he proposed to her. He acted in opposition to his
friends; Goslinga especially strenuously disapproved of his resolution. He seems to have judged too hardly, for Slingelandt,
since his children were married, was alone in the world; he was
sixty-two years old and suffered much from gout. In the circumstances it was pardonable that he should, in spite of her lower
class, marry a woman to whose society he had been accustomed
for years. As he wrote to Goslinga he did it for the rest and comfort of his life. [2] In so far Jorissen was right in his surmise:
"Slingelandt has at last been bent by life and takes his place in
that large company whom deception and physical suffering
cause to break with the ideals of their youth and who learn to
submit to the inevitable." [3] This is true as regards his private
life, but where his career as a statesman is concerned, it is utterly
false, as is proved by his conduct as Grand Pensionary of Holland.

He was called to this office, the first place in the Republic, in
1727. It is with Slingelandt as Grand Pensionary that this book is
more particularly concerned, and therefore we shall dwell no
longer on his private life. We shall leave the part he played in home
affairs, and treat of his foreign policy, of his efforts for the pacification of Europe. Properly speaking the title of this book covers a
larger period than the years, from 1727 to 1736, in which he was
Pensionary. As early as the time of the Quadruple Alliance he
seems to have striven for this great purpose. But his earlier participation in foreign affairs was only private and indirect, and will

---

[1] Slingelandt to Townshend. 14 Nov. 1725. R. O. Hl. 280.
[2] Slingelandt to Goslinga. 10 Sep. 1726. F. G. Neither this letter nor the other on this
subject is ridiculous as Slothouwer (*op. cit.* 119—20) would have us believe, but the
way he interprets them is ridiculous. There is no question of any amorousness of Slingelandt.
[3] *Historische Bladen.* (Popular ed.) II, 54.

perhaps never be exactly determined. We have therefore confined ourselves to the period in which he was the recognised and unrivalled leader of the foreign policy of his country, able to exert all the influence of which his position allowed.

It is necessary to closely examine that position as it was conditioned by his office and his environment; but first it is necessary more particularly to portray his gifts and character, which hitherto have been shewn only incidentally.

IV.

As to his gifts there is no difference of opinion: his friends and foes are in agreement. [1]) Goslinga called him "the first man of the Republic," and added "I doubt even whether she has ever before produced one who combined so many rare talents." This sentence occurs in a letter which is anything but favourable to Slingelandt. [2]) Another testimony has still greater value. At the end of the year 1726 the Grand Pensionary Hoornbeek was losing strength, and the French ambassador at the Hague, the Marquis de Fénelon, thought it opportune to send to his court his conclusions as to the choice of a successor. Slingelandt was naturally among those whom he passed in review. "It is superfluous," he wrote, "to dwell on the superior talents of Mr. Slingelandt. If the choice were to be made for ability he could not fail to carry off the honours." As he strongly objected to the election of Slingelandt he was happier in expatiating on obstacles to it which might be contrived, yet at the end of his letter he again praised the minister's talents, both inborn and acquired. [3])

---

[1]) Even Bilderdijk, who had not a good word for him only because he believed him opposed to the revival of the stadtholdership (*Geschiedenis des Vaderlands*, XI. 78, 232).

[2]) Goslinga to Vegelin van Claerbergen. 7 June, 1725. F. G. The part of this letter which regards Slingelandt is too remarkable not to quote. "Je vois que mes craintes d'une rechute de notre digne ami n'ont été que trop bien fondées; il y contribue, moralement parlant, en lachant trop la bride à ces humeurs acres, qui animent son naturel sévère et trop peu charitable; au reste le premier homme de la République, je doute même qu'elle en ait jamais produit avec tant de rares talents à la fois. Son malheureux penchant pour la continuation d'une guerre, qu'il voyait devoir ruiner la Rep. est *l'unique crime* qu'on peut lui imputer, je dis crime car il ne peut avoir (éclairé et au fait des finances comme il l'étoit) pesché par ignorance; je ne puis pas me guérir du soupçon (soit dit, mon cher, entre nous) que l'ambition et les grands gains que lui produisoit la guerre n'y ayent influé, avec ces principes contre la France, que trois guerres avoient inspirés à tous les vieux regents."

[3]) A. E. Hl. 366. Mémoire sur le choix d'un pensionaire en Hollande. 14 Dec. 1724. The

Besides these generalities Fortune has given us some particulars. Bentinck states that Slingelandt "had an intense penetration, so that he at once laid hold of the core of an affair and could view it from all sides." Chesterfield's opinion was much the same for he ascribed to him "a quick, intuitive sagacity." [1]) This was accompanied by an extensive and many sided knowledge and a long experience: his memory was a very chronicle of all events which had befallen the Republic. He was an untiring worker, although he managed public affairs with equal ease and celerity. The remonstrances to the States General which it fell to him to draw up in the name of the Council of State have been praised as masterpieces, as eloquent as they are skilful in demonstrating the interests of the state. The same is true of his letters and remarks as Pensionary: all are clear and terse and so compare most favourably with the writings of average eighteenth century diplomats, such as the prolix and tedious productions of Horace Walpole, Robert's brother, and of Fénelon. Slingelandt could distinguish between the important and the unimportant, and "did not approve", as he once said, [2]) "of making mountains of molehills and a business of nothing."

To all this was added his practical sense. He saw clearly the limits of the attainable, as is proved sufficiently by his letter of advice to the extraordinary assembly. His conduct as Pensionary, when he undertook the reform of the finances of Holland, was consistent with the attitude shewn in that letter, and it met with no more success. [3]) One of his few achievements however was the edict of 1725 as to import and export duties, for which, although it was not solely his work, he may fairly receive the chief credit. It has been praised as clear, simple, well-considered and well-arranged; it had the further merit of hampering trade only a little, and of leaving details to be arranged to suit local conditions. It promoted commerce as much as is possible for such an edict; and it is indeed regrettable that it was never well enforced. [4])

---

last words are as follows: "D'ailleurs c'est un ministre qui ne laisse rien du coté des talents superieurs, des connaissances acquises, d'une trempe d'esprit forte et nerveuse et sur la manière de traiter les affaires."

[1]) *Letters* (ed. Bradshaw) II. 622 note.
[2]) In a conversation with Finch. Finch to Harrington, 2 Oct. 1733, R. O. Hl. 324.
[3]) Siegenbeek, *Lofrede*, 94—105.
[4]) *Verhandeling over den geest van het plakkaat van 31 Juli 1725* (Amsterdam, 1816) 15—29.

Practical sense and thoroughness are seldom found together, yet both characterized Slingelandt. He was thorough but not a doctrinaire; and for all his practicality, he never took appearance for reality, as do so many to whom the quality is ascribed. It is no wonder that he is described as a thinker whose thoughts sometimes quite absorbed him. Before he made up his mind, he looked at a question from all sides and gauged its every merit and defect. We are so fortunate as to possess a letter which illustrates this quality of his mind. It is on a theological subject, which, in view of the predilection of the Dutch for theology, is not remarkable. "Je ne suis nullement surpris", he wrote to Goslinga, "que vous ayez été charmé de la morale de Ciceron dans les traités *De Officiis* et autres, et que vous vous êtes questionné s'il est possible que des gens d'une morale si pure soient damnés pour ne pas avoir embrassé une revélation dont ils n'ont pas eu la moindre connaissance. On s'y perd, soit qu'on raisonne sur les idées des perfections divines ou qu'on raisonne sur ce que l'écriture nous en dit et nommément St. Paul dans plus d'un endroit. Si vous voulez savoir ce que d'autres, aussi ignorants que nous, en ont dit, vous pourrez vous satisfaire en lisant ce qu'en a écrit Lamothe-le-Vayer. [1]) Mais je sais si bien que ce n'est pas ce que vous souhaitez de savoir. Pour mes petites pensées je vous les dirai au coin du feu, ne pouvant pas le faire dans une lettre avec l'étendue et en même temps avec la précision que la matière demande." [2]) It is clear from this letter that Slingelandt was familiar with St. Paul's epistles: he told Van Haren that of Greek text they were his favourite reading. Probably he was attracted by St. Paul's thoroughness in dealing with his subjects. In Slingelandt thoroughness was so developed that it may be called his most outstanding characteristic.

Little is known of his religious life apart from what has been quoted. He seems to have been firmly convinced of man's high destiny in general, and of his own vocation by Providence, to his office in particular. Religion and morality appear to have been closely connected in his mind, for he repeatedly grouped them together. [3])

---

[1]) French philosopher and historian (1588—1672), teacher of Louis XIV.
[2]) Slingelandt to Goslinga. 7 May 1724. F. G.
[3]) Slingelandt to Goslinga. N°. 50; 10 and 14 Sep. 1726. F. G.; address on entering into office, Slingelandt Collection. 142. R. A.

That he was a moral man has never been disputed. His second marriage caused much talk for a time, but Slingelandt was felt to be above certain suspicion. [1] This is to take morality in its limited sense; if it be given the wider meaning there is less unanimity. Slingelandt's honesty has been questioned in more than one quarter. Fénelon, suspecting all his words and actions, was convinced that "personne n'a plus que lui l'artifice à la main." But Fénelon was himself so much of an intriguer that it was natural to him to discern plots and schemes where none existed and to mistake Slingelandt's frank dealing for the most malicious and premeditated hypocrisy. The Dutchman had of course wisdom to withhold some of his knowledge from the ambassador of a court which never was a real friend to the Republic, but no real doubt can be thrown on his honesty by the fancies of one cruelly prejudiced against him, who shows in all his despatches how totally he failed to understand his intentions. More weight is to be attached to a statement by Goslinga, in a letter to an intimate friend; that ambition and avarice would have induced Slingelandt to promote the continuation of the War of the Spanish Succession, which he saw would ruin the Republic. [2] This charge seems to prove that Slingelandt was greedy of money, a fault the more reprehensible because he was a well-to-do man.[3] Others as well as Goslinga called him ambitious, and that, according to Fénelon, to the sacrifice of his principles. The accusation was made especially with regard to the restoration of the Stadtholder's office. If he were chosen Grand Pensionary it was said that he would hinder the restoration, if he saw a fair chance of becoming absolute himself; and promote it, if he met with much opposition, and so desired to have the support of a Stadtholder whose youth and obligations should make him a mere instrument. [4] History has neither confirmed nor belied these suppositions, for before his election Slingelandt was compelled to promise not to advance in

---

[1] A. E. Hl. 366. Mémoire sur le choix d'un pensionaire. Dec. 1731. Haack, director to the admiralty of Enkhuizen, is here said to have injured himself considerably by marrying his servant, and the same is asserted of Slingelandt but "il n'est pas donné à tout le monde de se mettre au dessus de certains reproches."

[2] Goslinga to Vegelin van Claerbergen. 7 June, 1725. F. G. cf. note on p. 15.

[3] According to Bentinck his income during the war reached 40,000, even 70,000 guilders. Cf. for his wealth Elias, *De Vroedschap van Amsterdam*, I. 393; and Slothouwer, *op. cit.* 121.

[4] A. E. Hl. 366. Mémoire 14 Dec. 1726. Cf. Bilderdijk, *Geschiedenis*, XI. 78.

any way a change in the constitution. As to his attitude during the war of the Spanish Succession, it is to be remembered that Goslinga was the great advocate of peace, and consequently not the most fit judge of the motives of those who desired to continue the war. Slingelandt may have had ambition, but that he sacrificed his principles to it, is untenable. There is the contrary evidence of Lord Chesterfield, who during his embassy was in the closest relations with him and who called him "the ablest minister and honestest man I ever knew." [1]) There is the contrary evidence of his whole life, in which, far from seeking personal success, he often stood in his own light.

It was not personal triumph, but the welfare of his country which was his dearest object. When he entered on his great office he had the promise of several prominent men to help him in the work of financial reform; but a year later nothing had been accomplished. His pretended allies excused themselves on the plea of shortness of time. He retaliated that there was a great difference between doing all in one year, and doing nothing for a whole year; and added that he was willing to risk his gouty body and his reputation gained during thirty-eight years' service, but dared not be found guilty of dereliction of duty. [2]) He cared for the dignity of the Republic, as much as for her welfare, and could not suffer her to lack respect. Although in no real sense a formalist, he insisted on the due observation of forms, which he held to be essential to the right transaction of affairs. He was tenacious of the honour due to his position and is even said to have been a little jealous of the Greffier, his brother-in-law Fagel. It was generally known that to apply first to Fagel was not the way to succeed with Slingelandt. [3]) Yet Slingelandt was a humble man, averse to all flattery. On one occasion he sharply reproved Townshend for showering praise on him in his letters; for thus, he said, the frankness which he regarded as one of the principal charms of their correspondence would be ended. He begged ear-

---

[1]) *Letters* (ed. Bradshaw) II. 621 note. Cf. the testimonies at his death: "the Grand Pensionary is much lamented, for he was esteemed to be a gentleman of great probity", Sir Redmond Everard to Hamilton. 4 Dec. 1736; "the Grand Pensionary is extremely lamented; he was allowed to be a gentleman of great abilities and great integrity", Hamilton to Ormond. 3 Dec. 1736. *Hist. Mss. Com. Rep.* X. (1). 466.

[2]) Vreede, *Voorouderlijke Wijsheid*, 13.

[3]) Chesterfield to Townshend. 18 May 1728. R. O. Hl. 300.

nestly that compliments should be left to professional courtiers. [1])

A man who loved his country more than himself, a man of many rare talents, yet he often met with scanty success. The explanation seems hard to seek. A prominent Dutch historian believed that he lacked the tenacity and resolution necessary to the execution of his designs; [2]) but his contemporaries considered him tenacious, and not irresolute, but rather endowed with too much determination. [3]) Two men have observed, probably independently, that Slingelandt would have been perfect as minister of a kingdom, but was too strong for a republic. It was the practice of the Grand Pensionary Heinsius to sound the principal members of the government, before he introduced a measure; but Slingelandt revealed his projects exactly as they had been prepared in his study, and attempted to carry them out unmodified.[4]) Until he lifted the veil, no one had an inkling of their nature; not even Fagel, who at Slingelandt's death complained "that notwithstanding their near relationship and forty years of uninterrupted harmony and intimacy, he found himself at the last, left ignorant of the real issue and end to which his brother-in-law intended or wished to bring any public business then in treaty." [5]) Conscious of superiority and wholly self-reliant he endeavoured, as soon as he himself had made up his mind, to effect what had cost him careful deliberation. [6]) Yet he often received checks, for the rulers of the commonwealth had no desire to be led: they esteemed themselves able to find the way unaided, and the very thought of guidance was hateful to them. To succeed with them it was necessary "to be last of all and minister of all" but such was not Slingelandt's method. He did not lack persuasive powers which unfailingly prevailed upon the intelligent, but he could not brook contradiction. It irritated him and aroused his passions.

---

[1]) Jorissen, *Lord Chesterfield en de Republiek der Vereenigde Nederlanden*, Historische Studiën (2nd, popular ed.) V, 59.

[2]) De Bosch Kemper, *Staatkundige Geschiedenis van Nederland tot* 1830, 190.

[3]) A contemporary describes him as follows: "welcher von der mehristen Resolution und eines sehr geschwinden Begriffs ist."A. Rosenlehner, *Kurfürst Karl Philipp von der Pfalz und die julichsche Frage*, 1725—9. (Munich 1906) 224.

[4]) Fénelon, *Mémoire Instructif pour M. De La Baune* (25 March 1728) edited by Bussemaker (*Bijdragen en Mededeelingen van het Historisch Genootschap* XXX, 96—197) 165; note of Bentinck on Slingelandt in Bilderdijk, *op. cit.* XI, 233.

[5]) Trevor to Horace Walpole. 1 Dec. 1736. R. O. Hl. 360.

[6]) He was reputed to be fond of his own productions, so that once when Horace Walpole got him to lay down his pen and acquiesce in another's words Trevor spoke of "clavam extorquere Herculi."

His temper was indeed most imperfect. He was often impatient and brusque, and sometimes fretful;[1]) faults which were probably innate in him. It was said of his father that he "sometimes added much passion to excellent gifts."[2]) Slingelandt's weaknesses must however have been aggravated by his lack of success and especially by his attacks of gout. His mind remained clear, except when he was suffering from the most violent attacks and he often astonished the foreign ambassadors by his ability to discuss affairs when he was in extreme pain. "Toute émotion", Fagel once wrote,[3]) "est nuisible à sa santé, mais la tête est toujours bonne." His temper however was less invulnerable than his powers of thought; and on the other hand his gout was often brought on by fits of anger. According to Goslinga, he contributed to his own ill health "en lachant trop la bride à ces humeurs acres qui animent son naturel sévère et trop peu charitable." [4]) The implied criticism of his disposition is harsh; for Slingelandt was susceptible to the emotions of generosity and friendship. He behaved with all possible moderation and generosity to his daughter and her husband, who caused him so much pain.[5]) His friends were few, but greatly beloved. One of them, Lord Chesterfield, has in a few expressive words summed op his memories of Slingelandt's affection: "I may justly call him my Friend, my Master and my

---

[1]) It is particularly Horace Walpole who complains strongly of Slingelandt's temper. Once after receiving a peevish letter from him he wrote to his secretary Trevor: "It is a great pity the Pensionary, who is otherwise so great a man, will on any occasion that does not please him fret himself so much." In another letter to Trevor he contrasted, as he also did elsewhere, Slingelandt's temper with the gentle disposition of Fagel: "The Greffier is so mild in his temper that he dreads the effect of the least step taken in their distracted government that is not agreeable to you all: the Pensionary is so rough that he cannot give his real or imaginary reasons, upon a point where he is particularly to act the minister, with common decency. What a pity that such a Billingsgate tongue and temper should belong to such an excellent understanding." (Coxe, *H. W.* 176 note.) This is strongly said, but we must bear in mind that the speaker is Horace Walpole, of whom in his turn Slingelandt says, "no visits of any ambassador are so prolix, and consequently to a man who is in pain, so tedious as his" (Slingelandt to H. Hop. 27 Aug. 1735.) In his correspondence with Queen Caroline, Horace Walpole also complained, but in this great woman's answers a different note is struck: "I entreat you to propose to the Pensionary my ptisan as a remedy for the gout with which he is so grievously afflicted. I cannot but interest myself for the life and health of a person of his merit".... "I pity the poor Pensionary more because his disorder gives him lowness of spirits as well as bodily pain. In short it is necessary to take men as God has made them, and overlook their frailties as we hope God will overlook ours." Coxe, *op. cit.* 194.*

[2]) Van Haren, *op. cit.* 416; Notes of Bentinck (MS. Univ. Library, Leyden) i. v. Govert van Slingelandt.

[3]) to Goslinga. 23 Jan. 1722. F. G.

[4]) to Vegelin van Claerbergen. 7 June 1725. F. G. cf. p. 15 note.

[5]) Fagel to Goslinga, *passim.* F. G.

Guide, for I was then quite new in business; he instructed me, he loved, he trusted me." [1]) Chesterfield apparently knew him to be superior and appreciated him accordingly, which was not the case with every one with whom he had to deal during his time of office. Who they were we shall treat of later, but first it is necessary to treat of his office itself in so far as it was concerned with foreign affairs. In its domestic aspect it may be neglected. [2])

V.

It appears strange that, although virtually the first minister of the Republic, the Grand Pensionary was an officer of the province of Holland. If the Pensionary of Holland had not been actually foreign secretary to the Republic, the change to this office would to Slingelandt, who all his life had served the central government, have been not promotion but a step backwards. To account for the anomaly it is necessary to revert to the beginning of the revolt against Spain. At that time Holland and Zealand had for several years formed one state, having its own diplomatic service over which the Pensionary, then called the Advocate, of Holland presided. The Union of Utrecht, which joined to these two provinces five others, left the arrangement unaltered, and foreign affairs remained in the hands of the Pensionary of Holland, until the end of the Republic. To deprive him of competence to deal with them, anomalous as was the position, would have been injurious to the country, for it would have rendered almost unattainable the necessary harmony between the central government and the powerful province of Holland. The link would have been broken. How inevitable this was, will appear on an examination of the method of dealing with foreign affairs.

Foreign affairs belonged to the sphere of the States General. The official despatches of ambassadors abroad were sent to their Greffier, who read them at their session; and their subsequent resolutions determined the attitude of the Republic to foreign courts. There was however little permanence in the composition of

---

[1]) *Letters* (ed. Bradshaw) II. 621 note Cf. Jorissen, *op. cit.* 137—40.
[2]) This description of Slingelandt is principally drawn from Fénelon, *Mémoire instructif*, 165—7, from Bentinck's Notes, the annotations to Van Haren's *Geuzen* and the *Mémoires de Monsieur de B. (Bijdragen en Mededeelingen van het Historisch Genootschap* XIX. 119—20.)

the States General, for members were returned by the States of the provinces, for fixed periods, at the end of which others replaced them. But whosoever came and went, the Greffier and the Grand Pensionary always remained. They were, it is true, excluded from voting, and from the presidency, which was held in turn by the different provinces; but the fixity of tenure of their office naturally enabled them to have much influence over the members of the States, who lacked their experience. This influence was strengthened by their similar position in the committee, which was composed of themselves as the only permanent members and of a member from each province. In the committee all business relative to foreign affairs was prepared before it was introduced into the larger assembly.

Up to this point the Pensionary shared his powers with the Greffier and even gave precedence to him; for while the Pensionary sat in the States General and the Committee for Foreign Affairs only as a deputy of Holland the Greffier was there *ex officio*, and it was the Greffier who received the official despatches of ambassadors abroad, and who sent them their instructions in resolutions or letters formulated by himself. So fart herefore the Greffier was certainly not inferior to the Pensionary. He was however the official of a body who could not act on its own authority, for sovereignty was virtually vested, not in the central government but in the provinces. Properly speaking they should always have been consulted on current business, but this was quite impracticable, for even in that little country distances were then great, and the provincial States met only at intervals. Unless therefore a very important matter, as for example the conclusion of a treaty, was at stake, the deputies took it upon themselves to consent to measures so long as they felt sure of the support of their constituents. But the case of Holland was exceptional: the States of Holland also met at the Hague, and could easily be convoked at short notice; thus it was that they were consulted before a resolution of any interest was taken. At their meeting the Grand Pensionary laid before them the foreign situation as it had developed since they had last assembled, and before them his position was quite other than that which he held in the States General. He took the chair, and recorded the votes; he stated the result of discussions, and drew up the resolutions. They were, it is true, resolutions which had no validity in respect of foreign affairs, but as a rule they were accepted and adopted by the States General. The formal and regular procedure was that Holland should pass a resolution which the deputy of the province on the Committee for Foreign Affairs should introduce there, that the Committee should then advise the States General, who should finally pass the decisive resolution. But there were variations. Sometimes pressing business allowed no time for a convocation of the States of Holland; then the States General passed resolutions without their co-operation, but not without private consultation with some of their leading members, in order to ensure the sanction at the next meeting of the unauthorized action of the representatives. This expedient, however, could only occasionally be resorted to, for the States of Holland were most jealous of their powers.

Apart from his position in the assembly of Holland the Grand Pensionary had an advantage over the Greffier in the greater scope of action allowed to him. The Greffier was obliged to lay all communications made to him before the assembly of his masters or at least before the committee. The Pensionary was under no such restriction: ambassadors might write to him, on whatever subjects they judged to be of moment to the state, without the caution necessary in their official despatches; foreign secretaries of other countries could safely write to him, when they wished for a correspondence with the leaders of his country, shorn of the dangers to secrecy which belong to a government by many. Again the Greffier could give no instructions, except by order of the States; but the Pensionary was answerable to none, as to his correspondence. It had not a final character: Slingelandt always begged his correspondents not to look upon his letters as binding the States in any way, or even himself, if the States did not concur in his policy; he said of what he wrote that it "ne tire pas à conséquence."[1] Yet, although its strictly private character prevented it from being decisive, the correspondence of the Pensionary was far more important than that of the Greffier. For the Pensionary could give the ambassadors abroad all the information they desired; he could give them provisional indications as to business

---

[1] For instance Slingelandt wrote to Goslinga that he expected him not to reprove his conduct without knowing its motives, because a minister of the Republic "n'est rien moins que maître des délibérations, mais l'exécuteur des sentiments d'autres." 22 July 1727. F. G.

which, for the sake of secrecy or for other reasons, was not yet ripe enough to be brought before the States for their decision.

VI.

It is clear from the foregoing, how important it was to a Pensionary, that he should be on good terms with those who held the right of ultimate decision. All his activities, his conversations with foreign ambassadors at home and his letters to the ambassadors of his own country abroad, were of a provisional and to some degree of a private character, and needed confirmation and justification from the States. Their reversion of what he had done injured his authority, and thus he was always obliged to keep in touch with their leaders.

And of these the Greffier was first. The office was filled at this period by François Fagel who lived from 1659 to 1746. He was the son of the Greffier Henri Fagel, with whom he served his apprenticeship and whom he succeeded on the latter's death in 1690. Ever since that date, he had retained the position, which he was to hold almost until the end of his life. "By this long experience and by his simple and modest character he had gained the confidence of the States General to such an extent that whenever an important matter had to be decided he was their oracle." [1]) Men did not know which to praise more, his character, or his abilities. He was, said an unknown contemporary, "un de ces trésors cachés qu'il faut découvrir pour en connaître la valeur. Sous un exterieur modeste et humble vous trouverez un esprit fin et subtil, infatigable dans le travail, toujours présent, jamais étourdi par les grandes affaires; il les manie, il les développe, et en fait un précis dans l'assemblée qui en abrégeant des longueurs ennuyantes les fait comprendre à tous les membres qui la composent, en dresse les résolutions avec une netteté laconique, qui en exposant le sujet justifie le sentiment des Etats." [2]) Chesterfield's opinion is not less favourable: "he had the deepest knowledge of business and the soundest judgement of any man I ever knew in my life, but", he added, "he had not that quick, that intuitive sagacity which the Pensionary Slingelandt had." [3])

---

[1]) Fénelon, *Mémoire Instructif*, 168.
[2]) *Mémoires de Monsieur de B.* (*loc. cit.*) 118—9.
[3]) *Letters* (ed. Bradshaw) II, 622 note.

Fagel himself would readily have subscribed to these last words; he heartily acknowledged the Pensionary's superiority. Foreign ministers complained of his "deference and devotion to Slingelandt," [1]) after consulting whom he would change his mind having "resigned his own sense to the will of Slingelandt." [2]) The latter's ascendancy over him was regretted by none more than by the French ministers. They, notwithstanding his predilection for the stadtholdership, and his pro-English sympathies, gave the highest praise to his character, to his simplicity and integrity, his modesty and moderation, his self-command and constancy, his affability and kind-heartedness. They judged him worthy of a large confidence, and would not have objected to his elevation to the office of Pensionary. Had he himself desired such promotion he would infallibly have gained it in 1720 and 1727, but he insisted that he should be passed over in favour of Slingelandt, whom he esteemed more fit than himself, and to whom he was bound as a relative and an intimate friend. To Slingelandt, since he never failed to support his policy, he was an unrivalled co-operator. It was by no means the rule, that Slingelandt carried through his schemes in the assembly of Holland, but he met with much more success, in the Committee for Foreign Affairs and the States General, where he had the assistance of Fagel's strong influence.

Had Slingelandt been able to dispense with the province of Holland, he would indubitably have done so; but it was impossible: he must consult, if not the States themselves, at least the leading members.

The assembly of Holland was composed of the nobles and of the representatives of the towns. The towns had a vote each, the nobles only one vote among them. Yet the nobles were no negligible section, for to them belonged the first vote, and one of the seats which Holland had in the States General. Their leader at this time was Van den Boetzelaer, a man of distinguished birth, whose many offices had gained him great credit and who was able; yet on account of his selfishness and his brusque manners he was little liked. Another prominent noble was the Count of Obdam who belonged to the Wassenaer family and who occupied the

---

[1]) Trevor to Horace Walpole. 30 Sep. 1736. R. O. Hl. 359.
[2]) Horace Walpole to Harrington. 3 Sep. 1734. R. O. Hl. 331.

seat of his section in the States General. He was a man of consequence, by reason of his birth and offices; and was further a man of
undisputed honesty; but his conceit exceeded his self-command,
and lack of popularity detracted from his influence.

The members of the States of Holland other than the nobles
were the delegates of town councils. Eighteen towns contributed
each of them a deputation which usually included the Burgomaster and the Pensionary. The relation of these delegates to the
municipalities was like that of the members of the States General
to the provincial States: they acted on the authority of their
constituents; were responsible to them; and were obliged to consult them on matters of importance, with which they had not been
empowered to deal. Thus ultimately the government of the provinces rested in the towns, and since the Republic depended largely on the province of Holland, the actual rulers of the commonwealth might be said to have been the authorities of the towns of
Holland. After all, the members of the States, whether General or
Provincial, were no more than mandatories; the town councillors
formed independent bodies who themselves filled up the vacan-
cies which occurred in their numbers; they were the mandators.

This is true in general, but there was a remarkable exception. In
Amsterdam the town council was only theoretically vested with the
highest authority. It virtually belonged to the four Burgomasters,
who owing to a peculiar mode of election, were almost |wholly in-
dependent of the council. Power was thus concentrated in a few
hands, and next to other agencies, in particular the town's extraordinary wealth, this has contributed to the very great inflence
exercised by Amsterdam on the policy of Holland, and, by means
of Holland, on that of the Republic. Both De Witt and William III.
experienced the impossibility of asserting their will against the
Burgomasters of Amsterdam. [1]) These officers had included in the
17th century remarkable men, but at this period, though emphat-

---

[1]) In a letter dated 1679 the English Ambassador, Henry Sidney, has testified to the power of one of the greatest amongst them, Valckenier, in these words "I assure you, the
Great Turk hath not more absolute dominion and power over any of his countrymen
than he hath at Amsterdam. What he saith is ever done without contradiction; he turns
out and puts in who he likes: raises what money he pleases, does whatever he has a mind
to, and yet he walks about the streets just like an ordinary shopkeeper." *Diary*, vol. 1
p. 66, quoted by Fruin in his *"Bijdrage tot de Geschiedenis van het Burgemeesterschap van
Amsterdam tijdens de Republiek"* (*Verspreide Geschriften IV* 305 et seq.), from which
article we have borrowed these particulars about the peculiar place which Amsterdam
occupied among the towns of Holland.

ically still to be reckoned with, their abilities were not distinguished, and they were of less consequence. The most prominent member of their deputation to the Hague was the Pensionary De la Bassecour, a man of sense but of only average powers. His predecessor Buys, had no longer any share in the government of Amsterdam, as in 1726 he had been appointed secretary to the States of Holland; but he still kept in touch with the leading men of his town, and always promoted its interests as far as he could. "He did not found the greatness of Amsterdam on that of the Republic, but on the contrary, the greatness of the Republic on that of Amsterdam." [1]) Had he been able he would have "ruled Holland by Amsterdam and the Republic by Holland." [2]) He had often had employment in embassies and had an adequate knowledge of foreign affairs, but he was markedly opinionative and conceited. Yet although he was generally disliked he often succeeded in attaining his ends.

During the early part of Slingelandt's administration, a somewhat important part in the States of Holland was played by Visscher, the Pensionary of Haarlem. Hoornbeek wished this man to be his successor, and he would have stood a fair chance of attaining to the office, had he not yielded to Slingelandt. He was a capable man and considered most ambitious. He was however very unsteady and never contented with the position in which he found himself. By one change of office, when he left Haarlem for the Admiralty of Rotterdam, he lost his seat in the States.

One of the most distinguished men, especially in the latter years of Slingelandt's office, was Halewijn, the Pensionary of Dordt, whose influence in the States of Holland came to be second only to that of the Grand Pensionary himself. His reading had given him a fair amount of knowledge, which however was speculative rather than practical. He was honest, but was not well disposed to Slingelandt and Fagel, prejudiced perhaps by the close relations they had with Heinsius. For Halewijn, according to Bentinck, believed that his father had been wronged by Heinsius, and disliked all that statesman's friends in consequence. [3])

All these men belonged to Holland. Slingelandt naturally had

---

[1]) Fénelon. Mémoire 14 Dec. 1726. A. E. Hl. 366.
[2]) Fénelon. Mémoire Dec. 1731. *ibid:*
[3]) Bentinck's Notes i. v. Halewijn. Cf. Horace Walpole to Harrington. 20 Aug. 1734. R. O. Hl. 330; 15 Oct. 1734. ibid: 333.

dealings also with deputies of other provinces, in the States General and in the Committee, but their influence on the course of affairs was as a rule inferior to that of the men of Holland; the more so, because in this period the most capable men were seldom sent to the Hague. Of this evil sign of the times Slingelandt complained in a letter to Goslinga, apparently in reference to the latter's recommendation of a certain Schuurman, a new deputy of Friesland. "M. Schuurman, honnête homme tant qu'il vous plaira, peutil juger des affaires? peut-il se charger de la moindre chose? peutil se répondre de rien? En vérité l'assemblée des Etats Généraux est presque rendue inutile et les meilleures têtes quand elles sont dans les provinces ne sont informées qu'à moitié." [1]

Goslinga himself was amongst these "meilleures têtes". He has often been mentioned in this chapter, and would have here received more particular notice, were it not that within a year of Slingelandt's accession to power he was sent as plenipotentiary to the congress of Soissons, and died shortly after his return. It is not intended to treat at this point of ambassadors.

His very intimate friend was Vegelin van Claerbergen, who sat as a deputy of Friesland in the States General. He was a well informed man of business, and in this, like a few others in the assembly, who did not represent Holland. None of them requires special notice. [2]

It was with these men that Slingelandt had to deal as Grand Pensionary. His own characteristics, and the nature of his office have already been reviewed.

The personal part of this introduction is therefore complete, and we may pass to its more material part, the examination, namely, of the state of European politics in general before and at the moment of Slingelandt's accession to power and of the place of the Republic in them, in particular.

---

[1] 23 July 1726. F. G.

[2] The particulars as to these personalities are drawn chiefly from Fénelon's *Mémoire Instructif*, his Mémoires quoted on p. 28, that of 12 May 1732 (A. E. Hl. 388), and the letter of Louis XIV. to him of 9 Jan. 1727 (ibid: 367).

CHAPTER II.

THE REPUBLIC AND EUROPEAN POLITICS FROM THE PEACE OF
UTRECHT UNTIL THE PRELIMINARIES OF PARIS.
1713—1727.

When Slingelandt was chosen Grand Pensionary, on 17 July
1727, there had recently been considerable changes in Europe.
For two years a general war had been threatening, but at last
there was a prospect of peace, as the result of the preliminaries
signed at Paris on the last day of May 1727 and at Vienna thirteen days afterwards. They constitute a fixed point in the intricate history of eighteenth century diplomacy; and since they nearly coincided with Slingelandt's accession to power, they shall be
our starting point. But first the events which led to them must be
examined, the previous course of European politics with especial reference to the Republic.

A. BRIEF SURVEY OF EUROPEAN POLITICS FROM THE PEACE OF UTRECHT UNTIL THE TREATIES OF VIENNA.
1713—1725.

On the eve of his death, William III had rallied round him a
considerable number of princes, to combat the imperialistic tendencies of Louis XIV. This Grand Alliance, of which the Emperor, England and the Republic were the principal members, kept
firmly together for years, but its final dissolution was rapid, and
was caused by two important events, the fall of the Whig cabinet in 1710, and the accession of Charles of Austria to the imperial throne in the next year. England betrayed alike, the Emperor
and the Republic, by a secret negotiation with the common enemy, and so prepared the peace of Utrecht. The Republic gave way,
however unwillingly, but not so the Emperor, who continued the
war by himself. It is true that a year later he concluded peace, for
himself and for the Empire, with France; but not with Spain. The

war of the Spanish Succession is generally said to have ended in 1713 and 1714, but it should be remembered that the two rivals who contested the succession, Charles of Austria and Philip of Anjou, were avowed enemies, down to as late as 1725. They were not fighting throughout that period, but neither submitted to the stipulations of Utrecht. On the contrary from the date of the conclusion of that peace, each of them planned its modification, in his own favour.

To attain his end, the Emperor desired to resume his old friendship with the Maritime Powers; and when a German prince, brought up under the system of William III, ascended the English throne, he was for a while in good hopes of success. It might have been supposed that Philip V., who had the same object in view, would have been led by it to continue his friendship with France. But he broke away from that power, after the death of Louis XIV; and the efforts of the Duke of Orleans, Regent for the young king, to retain his alliance were vain. For despite all his solemn renunciations, Philip still hankered after the French throne, and would have no dealings with one who, like the Duke, would claim it in the event of the death of the delicate little king. Therefore Philip like the Emperor applied to the Maritime Powers, and Orleans, when thus abandoned by him, followed his example.

The Maritime Powers, were thus solicited from three quarters. The outcome of manifold negotiations, was that George I., and Orleans were brought together, each of them being actuated by personal motives; for as the latter desired to defend his claims to the succession, so did the former wish to defend against the Stuarts, the throne he had acquired. The States were admitted into their agreement, and in 1717 the Triple Alliance between France, England and the Republic was formed. Its main aim was the mutual guarantee by its members of the rights and possessions obtained by the Treaty of Utrecht. It was of a peaceful character, whereas an alliance with the Emperor or with Spain would sooner or later have led to war.

This is indisputable as regards Spain for her policy at this time was most aggressive. Philip's second wife, Elizabeth Farnese, dreamt only of winning Italy for her offspring, and the Prime Minister Alberoni, devised many schemes for the attainment of her object within the shortest possible time. Schemes, in the summer of 1717, became deeds. Spanish troops were landed at Cagliari, and occupied Sardinia; whereupon the Emperor, to whom this island had been allotted, appealed to England who had guaranteed it to him. England and the other members of the Triple Alliance were equally disinclined for war, for they considered peace most necessary to the recovery of their damaged finances, and unsatisfactory economic condition. Neither had they any desire to incur the displeasure of Philip V., France wishing for peace for political reasons; since a war with Spain would have been most unpopular, and the Maritime Powers desiring it on commercial grounds. England, supported by France, and the Republic was expected to agree with them, adopted conciliatory tactics. A proposal [1]) was made that the Emperor should renounce his claims to Spain, and in return receive Sicily in exchange for Sardinia; and that Philip should recognise the right of Orleans to succeed to the French throne; while Don Carlos, his first born son by Elizabeth, should be suffered to succeed to the Duchies of Parma, Piacenza and Tuscany. Not without trouble, the Emperor was brought to accept these conditions, and there ensued in 1718 the so-called Quadruple Alliance, which had a peaceful aim, that of preventing a war which might easily become general. But for the moment this was defeated by Spain, who rejected the proposed arrangement and attacked Sicily, and it became necessary to enforce the stipulations of the alliance. For the maintenance of the objects of the alliance only, England and France went to war on the Emperor's behalf. Charles VI. however, wished to make his own profit of the conduct of Spain, and attempted to deprive Don Carlos of his expectations with regard to the Italian Duchies. In this he had no support from England and France, in whose view he had gained sufficient power by the Quadruple Alliance, and the treaty of Passarovitz, which at much the same time considerably increased his territory in the south east. Therefore they preferred that the Duchies should be given to Don Carlos, whom moreover they could not disown without incurring the enmity of Elizabeth. And this was far from their intention, as is proved by their invariable treatment of her with all possible consideration. She had at last to give way: Alberoni

[1]) It had been in course of preparation before the invasion of Sardinia.

was dismissed, and Spain acquiesced in the Quadruple Alliance.

Throughout these negotiations England and France took the lead. The third power of the Triple Alliance, the Republic, played the part of the knight of the rueful countenance: she desired to participate in great affairs, but did not act accordingly; she lacked both decision and constancy, and her weaknesses were well illustrated by the negotiations which preceded and followed on the Quadruple Alliance. For although it was called quadruple, the Republic, regarded as its fourth member, never entered it: for months she put off her intended adherence. [1]) In the following years international affairs were often managed without her knowledge, and at the Congress of Cambrai, she did not occupy her usual place amongst the European powers.

The session of this Congress had been determined when Philip V. had acquiesced in the Quadruple Alliance, and its object was the settlement, by the mediation of England and France, of the remaining differences between Spain and the Emperor. The task did not promise to be easy, for both the powers at variance had accepted the alliance unwillingly, and hoped to profit by the Congress, to withdraw their concessions, in so far as was possible, and to obtain new advantages. The main difficulty concerned the establishment of Don Carlos. The Emperor was in no mind to grant him investiture of Parma, Piacenza and Tuscany; but the Spanish sovereigns, in their desire to make their son's future as sure as possible, aimed at stationing Spanish garrisons in these Duchies, and at freeing them as vassal states of the Empire. There were many other differences of less importance. In the circumstances, England and France did not expedite the meeting of the two rivals, each of whom was ominously tenacious of his claims, but put it off as long as possible. Their predilection was undoubtedly given to Spain, for they favoured Philip exactly as they had done before his entry into the Quadruple Alliance; Orleans wished to restore the old intimate friendship between the related courts of Versailles and Madrid, and England strove to regain the commercial privileges she had lost by the war. Philip was disposed for a reconciliation with France; for at this time his desire to succeed Louis XV. was surpassed by his desire to abdicate in order to devote his life wholly to the service of God; but on account of Gib-

[1]) cf. p. 41.

raltar, he was averse to an alliance with England. It was a thorn
in the flesh of the proud Spaniards that that small corner of their
country, was still held by another nation; and they exacted that
to obtain an alliance, England should restore Gibraltar. At the
request of Philip V., Orleans tried to persuade the English to
this step: their government set little store by Gibraltar, yet from
fear of Parliament, shrank from yielding. In the eagerness of desire
for a renewal of the commercial treaties George I. however finally
wrote to the King of Spain, promising to lay the restitution of
Gibraltar before Parliament at a proper time. Philip contented
himself with this engagement, and thus the way was cleared for
the Anglo-Franco-Spanish alliance which was secretly concluded
in June 1721. Shortly afterwards, the reconciliation between France and Spain was sanctioned by the proclamation of two marriages: Louis XV. was to marry the Infanta of Spain, and the
Crown Prince of Spain, a daughter of Orleans. Orleans was still
further engaged to the interests of Don Carlos, by the betrothal of
another of his daughters to that young prince. By the alliance,
Spain evidently hoped to win back Gibraltar, and to secure beyond danger the succession of Don Carlos.

She was disappointed. The new allies had promised to support
the Spanish claims at the Congress in whatever did not run counter to the Quadruple Alliance, possibly even to deviate from its
terms. To some extent they were true to their word, for they forced
Austria to a more tractable attitude; but they were unwilling
to yield entirely to the desires of Spain. Their delays retarded the
opening of the Congress until January 1724. At once, as had been
foretold, the claims of Spain and Austria were seen to be in sharp
opposition. When the Emperor utterly refused to make the least
concession, Philip called on the allies for justice; but vainly, for
the French court wished for peace beyond all things, and would
help only by diplomacy; and George I. took up a like attitude. He
had not, moreover, in the course of three years, found a "proper
time" in which to lay the question of the cession of Gibraltar before Parliament. Elizabeth felt herself to be the dupe of her allies,
and was convinced once more, that from that quarter no effective
help was to be expected. Turning from them she entered into
direct negotiations with the Emperor, and these, hastened by the
sending back of the Infanta from the Court of France, soon led to

a remarkable conclusion, namely, the Vienna treaties of 1725. By their provisions the old rivals, Charles VI. and Philip V., not only ended twenty five years of hostility, but also entered into a close alliance between themselves.

The astonishment and alarm, caused by this sudden change, account for another alliance, that of Hanover, concluded in September 1725 between England, France and Prussia. Thus Europe was divided into two camps, each of which strove to gain friends. The allies of Hanover were able to secure the Dutch Republic, whose adherence according to a well-known writer of political history "seemed to give to the alliance an irresistible preponderance."[1] This appears strange, in view of the loss of consequence suffered by the Republic, who had seemed to sink from her great position at the conclusion of the peace of Utrecht. The matter must be explained before the subject of the Vienna-Hanover conflict is resumed.

B. The Republic and foreign politics after the Peace of Utrecht.
1713—1725.

I.

"There was a time when the balance of Europe's power was not adjusted by her princes, but that the Dutch maiden, who sat side by side with them at the tribunal, with them cast her sword or her olive branch into the scales, which sometimes she turned."

Thus opens an essay of one of the greatest Dutch authors[2], in which he presents to his compatriots the glory of their golden age. It is a marvellous picture which he has drawn in his strong and rich language, of the greatness of his country in the seventeenth century; of her warriors and statesmen, sailors and merchants, scholars and poets, and, above all, her painters. She was great indeed. When she had shaken off the Spanish yoke, she kept the balance of power in the Baltic, by defending northern Europe against Swedish imperialism, and, an even greater achievement, she saved Europe from serfdom, and, Protestantism from utter ruin, by taking the lead in the struggle against the supremacy of

---

[1] J. G. Droysen, *Friedrich Wilhelm I*, I. 427.
[2] E. J. Potgieter, *Het Rijksmuseum*.

France. Nor was her sphere confined to Europe, for her trade extended over the whole world; she laid the foundations of her still considerable empire in the East Indies; she colonised in America; explored the Arctic regions, and discovered Australia. Dutch science and art compelled the admiration of contemporaries, and was disseminated, even as was her merchandise: Sweden owes to her much of her culture; she taught Russia shipbuilding; and she brought Japan into contact with Western civilization.

"There was a time", but in the period with which we have to deal it was already past. In the seventeenth century there were everywhere life and action, in the eighteenth, stagnation and decay. National interest has consequently been fixed on the former and has neglected the latter period, which had, as all agreed, been a dull and colourless time; and the more that was known of it, the more cause for shame there would be.

Since the war of the Spanish Succession represented the last great national effort, the peace of Utrecht has been regarded as the term of the country's existence as a European power. Such has even been the Dutch view. "Has the Republic erred in standing aloof from foreign policy after the peace of Utrecht?" is the title of a treatise of 1843, in which the standing aloof itself is taken for granted. [1]) In a contemporary address, she is represented as having fallen at that very moment, from one extreme into the other, as having devoted too much attention to foreign affairs during the reign of William III. and the war of the Spanish Succession; and neglected them utterly after the peace of Utrecht?" [2]) Some decades later the same thought was expressed by Jorissen: "In the history of the Dutch nation, the 12th of April 1713 is a remarkable day. Early in the morning, a couple of field guns had been placed before the town-hall at Utrecht: they were shot off punctually at ten o'clock. It was the sign that peace had been concluded; the peace which put an end to the War of the Spanish Succession and enriched the Republic with the barrier in the Austrian Netherlands. That 12th of April was the last day on which the Republic was numbered among the great powers of Eu-

[1]) Hugo Beyerman, *Vaderlandsche Letteroefeningen* (1843), II, 205—230.
[2]) J. C. de Jonge, *Over de Staatkunde hier te lande na den Utrechtschen vrede; een waarschuwend voorbeeld voor onzen tijd. Verslag van de Openbare Vergadering van de 2de klasse van het Instituut* (1840), 45—62.

rope." [1]) This is dramatic indeed, but not equally true. Thanks to a more profound study of this period, the idea of so sudden a change in the position of the Republic is now losing ground within the country [2]), although it still exists.

Abroad, it still prevails. Some scholars indeed, among them, Huisman, Pribram and Srbik, are better informed, but as a general rule, the Republic, after the peace of Utrecht, is left out of count. After the peace, leave is taken of her with some generalities which every author borrows from one of his predecessors. Constantly she is said to have fallen to a place of absolute dependence on England; she is called England's "satellite", or, according to a saying of Frederick the Great, generally applied to this period, although it referred to a much later one, "the shallop following the man of war" which takes her "in tow". [3])

These general conceptions have always something of truth in them, but never deserve full confidence; for complete truth cannot be comprehended by a terse formula. They must be submitted to serious enquiry, before the reliance due to them can be measured, and such an enquiry will now be undertaken with reference to this case.

II.

The meaning of the peace of Utrecht to the Republic cannot be understood without a knowledge of the character of the war of the Spanish Succession. Its title has "such a monarchical ring" [4]) that we are inclined to believe, the succession to the Spanish throne to have been its only concern. This is indeed the case, as regards three of the powers engaged in it, Spain, Austria and France, and historians have said the same of the Maritime Powers. These have been stated to have taken part in the war, while they

---

[1]) *De Republiek in de eerste helft der 18de eeuw*, Historische Bladen II³, 45; cf. De Bosch Kemper, *Geschiedenis tot 1830*, 185—186; Thorbecke, *Historische Schetsen*, 69.

[2]) G. Blok, *op. cit.* 2nd. ed., III, 345 et seq.

[3]) Wiesener, *Le Regent* etc. I, 138; Malet, *Histoire Diplomatique de l'Europe au 17e et 18e siècle*, I, 451; Bourgeois, *Manuel* I., 200, 248, 555; Weber, *Quadrupelalllianz*, 11; Arneth, *Eugen von Savoyen*, III, 183; Droysen, *Friedrich Wilhelm I*, II, 119; Bourgeois (*loc. cit.* 248) says: "En 1713.... la Hollande, satisfaite d'avoir humilié la France et l'Empereur à la fois, heureuse de ses conquêtes aux Pays-Bas, se laissa entraîner comme une chaloupe à la suite des vaisseaux anglais qui sillonnaient les mers triomphalement." We suppose Bourgeois was the very first to think the Republic was "satisfaite" and "heureuse" in 1713.

[4]) Seeley, *The Expansion of England* (Tauchnitz edition), 141.

did not themselves aim at securing any portion of the inheritance, in order to maintain the balance of power in Europe and to maintain the Protestant religion, which interests William III. had so well taught them to have at heart, that they continued his policy for a considerable period after his death. This theory is in itself unlikely, and it has been refuted by facts to such a degree that Seeley opined the war of the Spanish Succession to have been "the most businesslike of all English wars." [1]) We dare affirm, that in so far as it was a Dutch war, it held the same relation to the others in which that nation has engaged. To the Maritime Powers, material considerations were uppermost, or at least, they far outweighed such as were ideal.

To explain how material considerations affected the Maritime Powers in connection with the Spanish Succession, it is necessary to take into account their relation, in particular that of the Republic, to Spain, in the second half of the seventeenth century. The Republic was then no longer in opposition to Spain, but had combined with her against France. On behalf of Spain, she defended the Southern Netherlands against conquest by Louis XIV.; and for this she naturally expected payment. She got it, in the shape of a grant by Spain of important commercial advantages, of which the benefit was later extended to England. Especially in the Southern Netherlands, the Maritime Powers, more particularly the Dutch, acquired a privileged position; for to gratify them Spain reduced the import duties, leaving them free to raise their own. She also suffered the Dutch to garrison some Belgian fortresses.

This privileged position threatened to become precarious when the grandson of Louis XIV. mounted the Spanish throne: there was a danger that the French would then command the whole of the lucrative trade with Spain and her colonies, and that the Southern Netherlands would fall to France or at least be rescued from their economic dependence. William III. saw clearly the dangers of the union of the French and Spanish crowns in one house. The Dutch and English nations, however, were above all afraid that by a war, they would lose their considerable privileges, and it was not without difficulty that they were finally persuaded to join the Emperor. When they committed themselves, their privileges naturally became their especial care. Those enjoyed by

---

[1]) Seeley, *The Expansion of England* (Tauchnitz edition), 142.

them in a part of the Spanish monarchy, were confirmed by the treaty of the Hague of 1701, otherwise the Grand Alliance; which provided that countries and cities to be occupied in the Spanish Indies should remain theirs; and that the Southern Netherlands should be conquered, to serve as a barrier to the Republic (*"ut sint obex et repagulum, vulgo barriere"*). [1]

It was not without regret, that the Emperor acceded to these conditions, which to a large extent placed the Belgians politically and economically at the mercy of the Dutch, and therefore the Dutch felt no security that he would fulfil his promises, when the time came for performance. They desired also to gain more than they could rightfully claim, and to this end, the help of England was indispensable to them. England made her profit of their need and ambition. In 1709 the pride of Louis XIV. had been brought low by several serious defeats, and by the misery of his subjects, and he offered most reasonable terms of peace, which would most certainly have been accepted by the States had they not listened to the lures of England. The Whig Cabinet was now well disposed to a treaty which promised to the States all desired support with regard to the Southern Netherlands, and this complaisance induced the Dutch to decline the offers of Louis XIV., and to sign in 1709 the proposed treaty, the first barrier treaty.

Their confidence in England was to prove fatal to them; for the Tories shortly afterwards succeeded to power, and by private negotiations with France ended the war at the expense of their ally. They secured for themselves important advantages, but left the Dutch in the lurch. They obtained Gibraltar, which had been conquered by the combined English and Dutch fleets, Port Mahon and a considerable increase of territory in North America; and also from Spain separate privileges, the rights of importing negro slaves into her American colonies and of sending annually to Panama a ship of 600 tons, laden with goods for the Spanish colonies. But the Dutch had to be content with the confirmation of their old trading privileges in France and Spain, and a far less advantageous barrier treaty than that of four years earlier.

They were again disappointed, as regarded the Emperor, for he was unwilling to fulfil the promises of the Grand Alliance or to submit to the later barrier treaty of 1713; and the necessary new

---

[1] The Grand Alliance is more amply dealt with in the Appendix.

negotiations made clear, that the Dutch had not gained by the change. The faineant Kings of Spain had been replaced by a young Emperor, jealous of his power, filled with pride, and more careful than they of his subjects' interests. The Dutch were soon involved in serious difficulties, and the prize of victory, the Southern Netherlands, became an apple of discord.

England concluded peace at the expense of the Dutch, Austria disputed their claims, even such of them as were just; and a third power, the young Prussian Kingdom, obtained a considerable advantage, on which they had set their hopes. One of the aims of the Republic in the war had been the more effective fortification of her frontiers. To that end, she had sought an increase of territory, and a barrier, not only to the south but also to the southeast. Spanish Upper Guelders suited her purpose well, and had she been able also to acquire the right of placing garrisons in Bonn, Liège and Huy, she would have had a continuous barrier from the North Sea to the Rhine. By the barrier treaty of 1709, which has been mentioned, England guaranteed her in this possession and this right; but by the peace of Utrecht a large part of Upper Guelders was, to her great mortification, allotted to the King of Prussia, and only a small part to her, while her expectations with regard to Bonn, Liège and Huy proved entirely deceptive. Instead of a fortified position in this quarter, she found on her frontier a troublesome neighbour eager for a further expansion of power.[1]

This was the position in which the Republic was left by the peace of Utrecht. Her future place amongst the powers of Europe was to be largely decided by domestic affairs.

First of these were the conditions of her machinery of government. The constitution of the Republic had never been favourable to prompt action. Unanimity was too often required, and secrecy was difficult, seeing that so many persons and bodies were involved. Now, as has been said, defects were more manifest than ever before. The almost total lack of harmony, could not fail to have a bearing on foreign affairs, for dissension brought irresolution. The delays of the States became proverbial in Europe: their resolutions had sometimes become superfluous, when they were at

---

[1] R. Dollot, *Les origines de la neutralité de la Belgique,* 367; G. J. Rive, *Schets der Staatkundige Betrekkingen tusschen de Republiek en Pruisen 1701—1767,* 36—8, 52.

last passed, and at other times were so timorous and empty, that they had no decisive effect. There were times also, when despite all delays, no resolution was obtained. The history of the Quadruple Alliance is typical. Since the Republic had not become a party to it before it was concluded, an opportunity of doing so was subsequently given to her. No less than a year and a half were lost in discussions and negotiations, and finally the object of the Alliance, the bringing of Spain to reason, was attained before the States had come to a decision. Even then they were unable to reach one: six of the seven provinces, and seventeen of the nineteen votes of the seventh, were indeed in favour of adherence to the Alliance, but two vetoes, and one would have sufficed, prevented the necessary resolution, so that the Republic never joined the Quadruple Alliance. [1]) On this and on other occasions foreign powers attempted to influence her; both officially and privately. Not seldom they entered into relations with members of the States and attempted to win them, sometimes, though less frequently than has been believed, by means of hard cash. [2]) The attainment of a decision was thus rendered the more difficult.

None of these circumstances however were peculiar to this period. The defects of the constitution had always existed; they were only more apparent than ever before.

Much more attention should be paid to the lack of money. It was the natural consequence of overstrain: the Republic had for some decades played a part beyond her powers; she had fitted out big armies and fleets, and provided her allies with large subsidies. Her expenditure had far exceeded her revenue, especially as she had no good system of taxation; and one loan had followed another, debts had been piled upon debts. Most unfortunately the Grand Pensionary Heinsius was no financier. He contented himself with the supplying of immediate wants, and had not the courage to reveal the real state of affairs, and so effective meas-

---

[1]) Wagenaar, *Vaderlandsche Historie*, XVIII, 214—5; Bussemaker, Introduction to Fénelon, *Memoire Instructif*, 100; Srbik, *Oesterreichische Staatsverträge. Niederlande*. I, 597—8. We want to emphasise that the Republic never acceded to the Quadruple Alliance although said to have done so, by nearly all authors treating of this period e. g. Weber, *Quadrupelalliantz* 103; Pribram, *Oesterreichische Staatsverträge. England* I, 359, 407—8; Leadam, *History of England* 1702—60, 280.

[2]) Bussemaker mentions a French pensioner in 1715 (*Nijhoff's Bijdragen* IVde reeks I, 288); an English one in the first years of Slingelandt's administration was W. van Ittersum, who was paid £ 600 a year for his services, as is proved by his correspondence with Townshend (R. O. Hl. 296; cf. *Hist. Mss. Com. Rep.* X, 248—9).

ures of reform were not taken. Sometimes it was even impossible to
carry on the business of the state: in 1715 the pay office was, as
has been said, closed for nine months, which was tantamount to
national bankruptcy. [1]

This lack of money was serious because it affected every department controlled by the government, and, most important of all,
the army and navy.

Of the 130,000 men who had been in the service of the States
during the war of the Spanish Succession, only 34,000 had been
theoretically retained. Their real number did not exceed 30,000,
and of these 12,000 occupied the barrier towns, while the others,
who were very scattered, were quite inadequate for the defence of
the old and true frontiers of the Republic. Moreover the most
necessary repairs of important fortresses were neglected and
insufficient stores were provided. [2]

The navy was perhaps in an even worse state. It was managed
by the Boards of Admiralty, who derived their revenues from the
import and export duties. These had been abated by the decline
of trade, and even more by the frauds practised in raising them,
and their improvement was strenuously resisted by the merchants who were interested in the frauds. In time of war they
were absolutely insufficient for their purpose, and the States
therefore granted to the Boards subsidies, of which the burden
was distributed among the provinces. But the inland provinces,
who considered that the navy was of little regard to them, were
not always willing to pay their share and excused themselves on
the score of the fraudulent profits of the inhabitants of Holland
and Zealand. Then the boards had to take refuge in loans; and
finally involved themselves in obligations to pay so large a sum in
interest that the remainder did not suffice to maintain the navy
in good order, still less to build new ships. Extraordinary efforts,
not always possible, were required before a small squadron could
be equipped. "The Republic had no other title but courtesy to the
name of a maritime power", said Chesterfield in reference to a
later period, [3] and his words are almost equally true of this time.

The weakness of army and navy was most felt in foreign rela-

[1] Fénelon, op. cit. 97—98, 107—110; Bussemaker, Gids 1899, III, 44—7; Wiesener
op. cit. I, 135—136.
[2] Fénelon, op. cit. 110—11, 140—2.
[3] Letters (ed. Bradshaw) II, 624.

tions, for defencelessness rendered the country a less desirable friend and less terrible enemy. The Republic, instead of supporting or intimidating others, stood in need of their help or in awe of their anger, and consequently began to shrink from any undertaking which might involve her in difficulties. So she incurred slights and injuries, especially from the Dey of Algiers, who treated her most shamefully.

She had dealings with him in the matter of piracy, for Dutch trade in the Levant and the coast of Italy suffered sorely from the pirates of Barbary. Other seas as well as the Mediterranean were unsafe, so that merchant ships had imperatively to be convoyed by men-of-war. But these were not sufficiently numerous for the adequate protection of the large commercial fleet of the country; and many a ship fell into the pirates' hands, to the loss and annoyance of merchants. In the Baltic, where the United Provinces had once dictated the law, they now incurred much loss from Swedish privateers, from annoyance inflicted by the Danes, to whom they owed old debts; and from the new masters of the Eastern shores, the Russians. [1]) Other causes contributed to the decline of their trade, especially English competition, which will presently be noticed; but Fénelon is undoubtedly right in ascribing it largely to the incompetence of the Republic to protect her interests adequately.[2])

This incompetence had more lasting results than the occasional loss of a ship. Those who had been interested in commercial enterprise preferred to invest their money more safely; and since plenty of opportunities were offered by the loans contracted by several governments, they sank their money in public funds, especially in England. In 1728 it was estimated that of Dutch money, one hundred millions of Dutch guilders were in English public funds, and other large sums had been invested in the English East India Company and the South Sea Company. There is no need to explain how strongly the Dutch nation were thus bound to England. That such an extraordinary amount of Dutch money was involved in English funds, public and private, was a powerful motive to the Republic not to sever her connection with England, but closely to maintain it. [3])

---

[1]) Bussemaker, *Nijhoff's Bijdragen*, IVde reeks I, 284, 285; Wagenaar *op. cit.* XVIII, 101—4, 123—5.

[2]) Fénelon, *op. cit.* 121—2, cf. p. 97—8.

[3]) Fénelon, *op. cit.* 98—9, 136—8; Wiesener, *op. cit.* I, 146.

These weakening agents at work at home, were combined with others abroad. "The precedence taken by the Republic during a large part of the seventeenth century amongst the states of Europe was due not only to her boldness, her spirit of enterprise and the freedom of her inhabitants, but also to the backwardness of her neighbours. As soon as the causes of that precedence ceased, she could not retain it, on account of her small territory and her limited population." [1]) When several nations who had been in the background in the seventeenth century had become prominent, nations who much outnumbered the Dutch, and whose territorial base was larger, the decline of the United Provinces was inevitable. Had all the defects and abuses from which they suffered been removed, had it been granted to Slingelandt to realize all his wise and salutary projects, they would still have lost ground.

With regard to the significance to the Republic of the peace of Utrecht and subsequent treaties, we have emphasized that the dispositions made of the Southern Netherlands soon proved unfavourable to her. In those provinces Spain had been supplanted by the Emperor, who became much more powerful than any of his predecessors in the seventeenth century had been. The Austrian dominions, enlarged by acquisitions in virtue of the treaties which have been mentioned, of the Quadruple Alliance, and of the Peace of Passarovitz, reached the widest limits to which they have ever extended. Austria's rival, Spain, had lost her Italian states and the Netherlands, but thrown back on herself she renewed her energies, and she took a place superior to any she had occupied since the Peace of Westphalia. At the opposite side of the continent, in the north-east, a new power had appeared, Russia, who held the other Baltic powers in awe and inspired Europe with respect. In the Empire the Elector of Brandenburg had raised himself to be King of Prussia; and the second king of Prussia, strengthened by new acquisitions of territory and provided with a large army and a filled treasury, was considerable enough to be treated with respect by the Emperor, and taken into account by the other powers, not least by the Republic, in whose immediate neighbourhood he had established himself. Another King-Elector was still more important to her, George of Hanover, who on the death of Queen Anne had succeeded to the English throne, and who

[1]) Bussemaker, *Gids* 1899, III p. 47.

thence exerted himself on behalf of his German state, often no less to the disadvantage of his kingdom than to that of the Republic.

His kingdom had advanced considerably ever since the "Glorious Revolution." In the seventeenth century England had been engrossed by the great national struggle for parliamentary government, saving for one short interval, the time of Cromwell, in which she took a prominent position in Europe and withstood the supremacy of Dutch trade. She recurred to this double attitude when the dispute between king and nation had been settled. The political preponderance of England was distinctly manifest after the peace of Utrecht, when she acted singly, without dependence on other powers; and this is proved by the forming of the Triple and Quadruple Alliances. Dutch commerce felt her competition not less than in the days of the Protectorate; everywhere it met with English rivalry. In the Baltic Sea, where formerly trade had been almost exclusively in the hands of the Dutch, the number of their ships was equalled by those of the English. The commander of Gibraltar, with the knowledge of his government, even countenanced and helped the Algerians who aimed at capturing Dutch vessels. [1])

Jealousy was suffered not only from England; there was a general movement in Europe towards partaking in the trade of the world, for the wonderful prosperity of the United Provinces had awakened in other nations the desire to acquire riches by the means they had employed. The Dutch found, that these other nations had, as a stimulus to energy, raised tariffs to exclude foreigners, and had established trading companies. Companies shot up everywhere, and although many of them were very short lived, others succeeded, and the tendency itself boded no good to those who for long had been, in the words of Chesterfield, "the general sea-carriers of Europe", [2]) whose flag had been seen throughout the world.

Weakened by these factors, both external and internal, by the government's want of decision, the decay of the army and navy, the decline of trade, the rise of other powers and foreign competition, all of which were mutually connected and co-opera-

[1]) Fénelon op. cit. 118—119; Eng. Hist. Review XV, 275.
[2]) Letters (ed. Bradshaw) II, 624.

tive, the Republic seems to have lost importance almost entirely; and if she played a part at all, it was only one which was passive. In her existing state several members of the government believed it best that she should remain quiescent and abstain from interference in foreign politics. By taking part in them too largely she had brought about her miserable disorder, and it seemed that she must find relief in the opposite course. [1])

Among these members was the Frisian statesman Goslinga, who always kept up a correspondence with Slingelandt. In his letters he spoke his mind freely, as for example on the matter of the participation of the States in the Quadruple Alliance. He could account for the eagerness of some for this step, only by the long dependence on England's advice in which the people had grown to maturity. But he protested against the influence of fear; he considered that submission to rivals in trade could only, as the past had taught, prove disadvantageous, that the weakness of the Republic would expose her to all manner of losses, while she would receive no compensating share of profits. Therefore he advised the least possible interference with the affairs of crowned heads, and resort to arms only in defence of the country, and of trade. He desired that the States should not depend on the help of other powers, but first improve their domestic condition; for their finance and trade required rest; and some sacrifice of brilliancy would in the long run be justified by the increased respect of neighbouring and other European powers.

The arguments which Slingelandt opposed to his friend's ideas, are worthy of note. He did not deny that the situation of the Republic was alarming, and that she required rest above all things else, for more than anyone he was convinced of this. But in his view the welfare of the Republic depended not only on herself, but also on general conditions, which on the other hand she could affect. This opinion is most evident from his answer, for he advocated participation in the Quadruple Alliance on the grounds that it was high time to confirm the treaties of Utrecht, on which the rest and safety of all Europe, especially of the Republic, depended; and to settle definitely the separation of the French and Spanish monarchies. He favoured this policy all the more because it involved the support, against the true interests of France, of

---

[1]) Fénelon *op. cit.* 122.

a prince [1]) who would be in need of allies if the French throne should fall vacant. If however the Regent at any time failed the allied powers, their friendship would then be all the more necessary to the Republic, because she would have to be on her guard against France. Like his friend, Slingelandt wished to encumber the Republic as little as possible, and he agreed that she would be better off if she could enjoy the profits of the treaties without exposing herself to their ill effects; but he held the contingency to be inconceivable. What, he asked, would be the result, if the Opposition in the English parliament were to avail themselves of the conduct of the Republic to force the King in the next session to abandon the measures which had been taken, and so to desert the Regent and the Emperor?

Goslinga's biographer reproves Slingelandt sharply for what he calls a halting between two opinions: he accuses him of wishing, at the same time, to reform internal affairs, and to maintain his country's old influence abroad; of continuing, when aware of the weaknesses from which she suffered and her inability to enforce her demands, to interfere overmuch in foreign politics. [2]) We consider this reproof unjust.

III.

As appears from his answer Slingelandt believed that the conduct of the Republic could affect the course of general affairs, and therefore that her decision was by no means immaterial, and in this most of his contemporaries agreed with him.

For, although perhaps strange, it is yet undeniable that the Republic was much courted from various sides, in the years which followed the peace of Utrecht. Immediately after it, Louis XIV. sent to the country, to inspire the members of the government with favourable sentiments to France, a skilled diplomat, the Marquis de Châteauneuf; and the more to gain them, brought about a peace between the Republic and Spain. He would fain have concluded an alliance with her for his own country, and so would Orleans after him. She had but to choose: on the one hand was France, on the other England, who desired her co-oper-

---

[1]) The Duke of Orleans.
[2]) Slothouwer, *Sicco van Goslinga*, 137—149.

ation in the renewal of ties with Austria. For months the two earnestly contested for her alliance, and when at last they separately came to an agreement with each other, they still set so much value on her concurrence, that they deferred making their treaty public until they had admitted her to it on favourable terms. This Triple Alliance was indeed very profitable to her, for it secured to her the help of two powerful kingdoms; the Franco-British friendship opened up to her a prospect of peace; and she secured a considerable advantage for her trade with France.

A third power which paid her much attention was Spain. This was the case before the Triple Alliance, [1]) but still more so, when the Republic had been requested to render the so-called Quadruple Alliance true to its name. Beretti-Landi, the Spanish ambassador, left no stone unturned to prevent this consummation. [2]) When the States continued their hesitation, he had a medal struck, which represented the "Quadruple" Alliance as a car falling down for lack of a fourth wheel, [3]) and bore the motto *foedus quadruplex imperfectum, republica batava cunctante*. This, others as well as Spain believed to be true, for both sides endeavoured to secure the Republic by offering her considerable advantages and largely conforming to her demands. [4])

In these years the Hague witnessed many negotiations. There the Triple Alliance was concluded, and there the declaration by which Spain finally entered into the Quadruple Alliance was signed. In 1723 an Italian politician called the town "il centro di quasi tutti gli affari," [5]) and this conclusion from his observation has been reached through study by an English historian who states that "the Hague was still the diplomatic, as the neighbouring Amsterdam was the banking centre of Europe." [6]) Its position may have been partly due to its situation, on the con-

---

[1]) Baudrillart, *Philippe V et la Cour de France*, II, 223; cf. Weber, *Quadrupelallianz*, 14; Bussemaker, *Nijhoff's Bijdragen*, 4de reeks II, 261.

[2]) Baudrillart, *op. cit.* II, 304; Weber, *op. cit.* passim.

[3]) Bourgeois, *Le secret de Dubois*, 71—2.

[4]) Weber, *op. cit.*, 88—9; Wagenaar *op. cit.* XVIII, 182—7. In August 1719 Alberoni requested the Republic to act as mediator (Weber *op. cit.*, 98; Bourgeois, *Secret de Dubois*, 71)

[5]) Blok, *op. cit.* VI, 92; the same in Ranke, *Zwölf Bücher Preuszischer Geschichte*, III—IV, 23:.... "nach dem Haag, wo noch immer alle Fäden der Politik ineinander griffen"; cf. also the titlepage of Lamberty's *Mémoires du 18ième siecle*:.... "la Haye, qui a toujours été comme le centre de toutes les negociations."

[6]) A. W. Ward, *Great Britain and Hanover*, 107—8.

tinent and yet near England, but it testified also to the fact that the principal powers still appreciated the friendship of the Republic.

This may be partly accounted for by tradition, for tradition often counts for more than actuality. The terrible weakness of the Republic was not at once realized, so strong an impression had her rise and her greatness made on the world. To have humbled her, was extolled as the most glorious deed of the reign of Louis XIV. The fact is forced upon the mind of whoever beholds the triumphal arches in Paris, and the ceiling paintings at Versailles, which bear witness to the glory of that mighty King of France. The Republic had evinced such power in the war which had just ended; again and again she had procured troops, ships and subsidies; her resources had seemed inexhaustible. In 1709 and 1710 that king, who once penetrated to a point within some hours' distance of Amsterdam and the Hague, and who had had mass read in the Cathedral in Utrecht, had himself been humiliated, for at the Hague and Geertruidenberg his plenipotentiaries had been compelled to acquiesce in nearly all the hard conditions set by the allies. It is true that since the fatal day on which the States had rejected the offers of France, everything had gone against them, so that the Abbé de Polignac who had attended the conferences at Geertruidenberg, had the satisfaction of speaking afterwards at Utrecht the much quoted words: "nous traiterons de vous, chez vous, sans vous." But we must beware of ascribing to his famous phrase a larger bearing than really belongs to it, for it was no more than a retaliation for the scorn of Geertruidenberg and in no sense signifies that from this time France looked upon the Republic as a negligible quantity. Louis XIV., as has been said, sent Châteauneuf to the Hague immediately after the peace, that he might work upon the regents; and did all in his power to counteract the influence of that warlike party which he firmly believed to exist among them; and even twelve years later, the French government regarded the power of the Republic as much on a par with that of England. [1] Nor do the words of De Polignac mean that he had foreseen the decline of the Republic,

---

[1] "deux nations qui toutes deux presqu' également puissantes ont un interèt essentiel à ne point prendre l'une contre l'autre des engagements de guerre" (A. E. Hl. 356, Instruction de Fénelon, January 10, 1725).

for at Utrecht he said repeatedly to those in his confidence: "les millions d'hommes et les millions d'or ne reduiront jamais les Hollandais; cette république ne peut être abattue qu'en coupant les branches de son commerce." [1])

Contemporaries perceived the relapse but did not know whether it would be lasting. They knew how, after the terrible disasters of 1672, the Republic had raised herself as never before. Her finances were in a deplorable condition, but other powers also were exhausted by the war, and no nation was as rich as the Dutch, for most curiously, while the state sank under its burden, the nation was wealthy, so that there was a sharp contrast between the commonwealth and individuals. This contrast suggested to a Frenchman the right comparison, that the Republic was like Tantalus, for no other European power possessed such riches in gold, silver and credit as she; yet she did not dare to touch them. [2]) She had not a good fiscal system and her people were not properly taxed, so that she only profited by their wealth in that she was able to raise loans at the very lowest rate of interest. [3]) But there was always the chance that Tantalus, in a case of pressing danger, might dare to lay his hand on the riches so near at hand. Heinsius was no financier but Slingelandt was, and if the latter became Grand Pensionary he might introduce a new system of levying taxes, and do away with the crying financial abuses. The task would certainly be most difficult owing to the defects of the governing machinery, but Slingelandt was striving with might and main to remedy these. They might moreover be counterbalanced, in the future as in the past, or perhaps more effectively, by a Stadtholder. Formerly there had always been two Stadtholders, but the extinction of the line of William the Silent left only one, who therefore might simultaneously be Stadtholder of all the provinces.

These were doubtless possibilities and no more, but they were in harmony with the past; and the fact that they were reckoned within the sphere of practical politics, is proved by the efforts made by French diplomacy in 1720, as well as in 1727 to prevent the elevation of Slingelandt to the office of Pensionary, and to

[1]) Archives Nationales (Paris), K. 1373. No. 36.
[2]) Quoted in Fénelon, *op. cit.* 99.
[3]) ibid. 132—5.

frustrate those who wished to raise the young William of Nassau, Stadtholder of Friesland, to the same dignity in the other provinces.

But the Republic received attention not only because of a possible future, but also for reasons of the present. It was especially on account of the dependence on her of England that she remained a considerable factor in the politics of Europe.

For, strange though it may seem, England depended on the Republic in various respects. The first was due to England's deficiency in land forces, for the nation disliked standing armies, and therefore maintained in time of peace no more troops than sufficed for immediate needs. Since new levies required the approval of parliament, foreign help was most welcome in case of a sudden danger, and the nearest and best friends were the Dutch. Therefore an alliance with them was regarded by the large majority of the nation as almost indispensable to their safety. [1] The Jacobites however were of a far different opinion, for they regarded the Dutch as the surest supporters of the Protestant succession. The Dutch were indeed alone in that position in 1715, when peril was at its highest, and when the British ministers feared that they would consider the failure of England to perform the succession and barrier treaty of 1709, to have absolved them from obligation to maintain the House of Hanover. But they falsified these alarms, and declared themselves willing to fulfil all their promises, to the great joy of the Whigs who extolled the Republic as the *salvator* of the kingdoms. King and ministers were at a loss to praise her conduct as it deserved, and to profess their thankfulness. The Princess of Wales, afterwards Queen Caroline, told Duivenvoorde, one of the ambassadors who had come to compliment the new King on his accession, that in the diary she kept for her son, she had set down in strong terms the obligation the King and his house had to the Republic for the friendship shewn on this occasion, and had recommended the young Prince always to cultivate the friendship of the Republic as the strongest supporter of the crown. [2] In 1719, when Spain made an attempt on behalf of the Pretender, Dutch troops were again sent to England, and

---

[1] Bussemaker, *Nijhoff's Bijdragen* IVde reeks, I. 308.
[2] ibid: 317—318.

they would have crossed the sea for a third time in 1722 had Bishop Atterbury's plot not proved abortive. [1]

Not only in the matter of the Protestant succession, but also in almost every other point of her policy, England needed Dutch help. It was of vital interest to her, that the Southern Netherlands should not pass under French rule, and in general that no continental state, whether France or Austria, should become so considerable as to endanger the balance of power in Europe. But poor as she was in land forces she could not exert much influence in this direction unless she were supported by some power on the continent. With regard to the Southern Netherlands, she naturally depended first upon the Emperor, who had the greatest body of troops there, but even he was less concerned than was the Republic, that the Southern Netherlands should be independent of France. In the matter of the balance of power in Europe, the Republic and England were also interested in common. Austria and France strove each of them to obtain all they could; Prussia might be of service as a makeweight, but at this time was ruled by an unsteady and wavering king; England could place reliance only on the Republic, who was moreover her neighbour.

A good understanding with her was no less requisite for commercial, than for political interests. For while her exports to England amounted only to £ 550,000 a year, those of England to her shores were of the annual value of £ 2,000,000. [2] In other words, according to the estimate of Sir Charles Davenant, one third part of the whole exports of the country went by way of the Republic. [3] But, most strangely, the strongest motive why England sought the friendship of the Dutch was founded not on trade relations but on trading rivalry. For although Dutch trade was losing ground, it still was very considerable, and as yet by no means second to that of England. [4] Therefore the English desired in all their acts of importance, to have the co-operation of the Dutch, who thus would be prevented from taking a part of their trade, while they themselves were engaged in war, and would

---

[1] Wagenaar, op. cit. XVIII, 203—4, 242.

[2] O. Pringsheim, Beiträge zur wirtschaftlichen Entwickelungsgeschichte der vereinigten Niederlande, 16 (Staats-und socialwissenschaftliche Forschungen X, 3).

[3] quoted ibid: p. 11.

[4] Pringsheim (op. cit. 11) seems to be mistaken when he dates the beginning of the decline of Dutch trade as late as 1730, cf. Fenelon op. cit. 118—22. This subject urgently needs further enquiry.

share the disadvantages consequent on war, rendering easy a return to the former respective positions of the countries. If the Dutch did not so co-operate, the powerful business class of England would at once raise a clamour against the war, and it would become impossible to obtain from parliament the necessary credit. This consideration arose regularly, whenever parliament contemplated an undertaking which might bring difficulties. It was an important factor in politics, and inevitably gave the Republic a valuable hold on England. [1]

The position was definite to such a point that other powers would not have feared England had she gone to war alone. This appears in a note, sent to Horace Walpole by the Sicilian Abbots, two well-known contemporary politicians, who were closely acquainted with general affairs. It has reference to the year 1735, when England seemed inclined to interfere, by means of force, in the war of the Polish Succession. "The French," it states, "do not fear the effects of England, even though she should come into a war, for they take for granted that if the Dutch being neutral England enters into a war, they shall take their trade with Spain away and raise disturbances at home, by giving it out that the interest of the House of Hanover has caused a war which ruins the trade of the nation, whilst Holland who is the most exposed, has neither known this war to be just or necessary." [2]

The interest of the House of Hanover in this connection, appears then to have been particular.

The first Georges felt themselves to be not kings of England, but still Electors of Hanover. On the death of Queen Anne, the Earl of Albemarle hurried to Hanover to render homage to his new sovereign, and was courteously received by George I. who mentioned to him, a Dutchman by birth, his friendly sentiments towards the Republic. "The friendship which I have for the Republic, I will cultivate more and more, for in the future, the States will have to give me passage through their country that I may go *from England into mine.*" [3] The Republic was moreover so near

---

[1] cf. Bussemaker, *Gids* 1899 III, 58; *Nijhoff's Bijdragen* IVde reeks, I, 334—5; *Tijdschrift voor Geschiedenis* XVI, 66, 204; Weber, *Quadrupelallianz*, 49, 88—9, 91; Charles Wager to Townshend, 1 January 1726/7 (Townshend Mss, *Hist. Mss. Com. Rep.* XI., Part IV); Ranke, *Englische Geschichte* VIII, 85.

[2] inclosed in Horace Walpole to Harrington, 24 August 1735 (R. O. Hl. 346).

[3] *Nijhoff's Bijdragen* IVde reeks, I, 265—6.

to his electorate as to be able to send troops for its protection, whenever they were required. As will be seen she actually did do so in 1729. She also exerted some influence in the Empire. The Protestant princes, especially the more petty of them, looked to her to support their cause; and the Catholic princes on the Rhine, such as the Elector Palatine and the Elector of Cologne, esteemed her friendship. It was therefore important to George I., where his relations with other German princes were concerned, to have on his side the Republic. But apart from these considerations he set much value on her. As appears from his words, his country was and continued to be Hanover, in whose interest he would fain have used his authority in England. Ministers to forward this aim were to be found, but Parliament had attempted to provide against this contingency by the Act of Settlement, and were on their guard against it. Therefore he attempted to get the better of Parliament by winning Dutch concurrence for his schemes, and therefore he brought pressure to bear on the Dutch, as when he attempted, again and again to induce them to join England in warlike measures against Sweden, although the true interests of both Maritime Powers would have been to interfere in favour of Sweden rather than against her. He knew that a Dutch squadron could be of very little value, but he was none the less eager, for if the Dutch acted with him, Parliament might be convinced that commercial interests were at stake and might be prevailed upon to fall in with his Hanoverian policy in the Baltic. [1])

Dutch co-operation was required by the personal interests of the King, and no less by the party interests of the Whigs. The Whigs were at this time in power, but the nation was by no means Whig. Only, according to Lecky, their "accidental passions" were so; "their settled habits of thinking" were Tory. The Whigs therefore found welcome support in the Dutch alliance, which was desired by the nation as well as by themselves, and which was favourable to their relations with the King.

Thus on his accession they were by no means certain that he would not choose his ministers from both parties, Tory and Whig, and therefore they attempted to influence him by means of their Dutch friends. Slingelandt had letters from Townshend and Halifax: the latter stated that the advice of the Dutch would have

---

[1]) cf the essays of Bussemaker.

more effect than anything that could be said by himself and his
fellows, who would be suspected of partiality. The English Whigs
received in truth some help, as they desired; although the extent
to which the recommendation of their Dutch friends, especially
Heinsius, Fagel and Slingelandt, influenced the King's decision
cannot be ascertained. It is known that he consulted these statesmen, and that before leaving the Hague, he appointed some of the
ministers, among them Townshend. [1])

For all the reasons which have been set forth it was of primary
importance to the English government to have the support of
the Republic, and that less for the Republic herself, than with
reference to their own people. No other power possessed such means
as she for the thwarting of an English king with whom she was
dissatisfied, and for the inciting against him of his subjects.[2]) A modern English historian has called Austria, France and Spain, the three
principal powers with which England had to deal during Walpole's
administration. [3]) He overlooked one which, as regards importance
for England, was second to none of these, viz.: the Republic[4]).

But she was not overlooked by contemporaries. Other powers,
knowing England stood in want of her alliance, tried to avail
themselves of her position.

This is true of Spain in the days of Alberoni, who constantly
tried to secure the Dutch, hoping at one time through them to
acquire the support of England, at another by detaching them
from England to checkmate her.

This is true in particular of France, but that power was wise
enough not to attempt to sever the connection of the Dutch with
England knowing the enterprise to be hopeless. Fénélon strongly
advised his successor to prevent the suspicion that it was contemplated, [5]) for he considered that nothing could be more calculated to cement the alliance of the Dutch with England, and

---

[1]) Bussemaker, *Nijhoff's Bijdragen* IVde reeks, 1, 266—9; Mahon, *History of England,* 1713—83, I, 109—10.

[2]) "Le gouvernement Anglais, de son coté, a un interêt capital de ne pas se détacher de
cet Etat, nulle autre Puissance n'ayant autant de moyens que la Republique de traver-
ser un Roi d'Angleterre dont elle ne serait pas contente et de lui susciter sa propre nation", Fénelon, *op. cit.* 139—9.

[3]) *English Historical Review* XV, 265.

[4]) cf. Horace to Robert Walpole, October 28, 1736 (Coxe, R. W. III, 426—8)

[5]) cf. Fénelon, *op. cit* 140.

their distrust of France. Moreover the Republic would, if separated from England, be of no use to the court at Versailles; she could serve France only, while she was bound to England, but bound in a manner which did not involve slavish and unfailing submission to her ally, but rather gave her the power to lead where the other must follow. [1])

That France sometimes succeeded in this policy is due to the fact that the Republic did not depend on England to the same degree as England did on her, and that moreover the Republic had earnestly to reckon with France.

There is no need to explain that she had almost as much interest as England herself in the preservation of the Hanoverian dynasty. The restoration of the Stuarts would have been dangerous to her from political and religious, and also from financial points of view. It has been said that large sums of Dutch money were invested in English public funds. This money had been borrowed in the reign of William III. or afterwards under the administration of the Whigs, and there would probably be very slight security for the payment of interest on it, if the Stuarts were restored. A strong motive for Dutch support of the Whig government, was thus naturally supplied, since the Tories were suspected of Jacobitism; and the consideration greatly affected Anglo-Dutch relations, less, however, than would have been the case, if the English government had not depended on the Republic, in so many respects.

It depended on her, as has been explained, in the matter of trade, and wished for constant Dutch co-operation, with a view to a possible war. But the situation of the Republic compelled her to avoid war, and therefore this dependence was not mutual. As regards the trade between the two countries, Dutch exports were not equal to a third of those of England, and Dutch commercial relations, did not on the whole require the Englis halliance, but the Republic being weaker, were rather harmed by it.

For this reason several Dutch merchants were well disposed towards France. She had by the Peace of Utrecht granted them some commercial advantages, and had it in her power to grant others,

---

[1]) cf. Dureng, *Le Duc de Bourbon et l'Angleterre* (Paris 1911), 337: "les Provinces-Unies, fort intimes avec l'Angleterre, pouvaient devenir comme le régulateur de la politique anglaise, inconstante et changeante au gré du Parlement" (taken from one of Pecquet's memorials).

and it was her interest, as it was that of the Dutch, to resist English supremacy on the sea.

Another consideration made the French desirable friends. The Dutch had disbanded by far the larger part of their militia, and were unable to protect themselves adequately. England, who was deficient in land forces, could not help them; their relations with Austria became increasingly unfriendly; and Prussia would have desired to encroach on their territory had she found an occasion. It was therefore advisable to be on amicable terms with France. This circumstance had most weight with the inland provinces, which in time of war would be more exposed, than those near the sea.

In the relations of the States with England and France, much importance attached to the question as to the revival of the Stadtholdership, in those provinces in which, after the death of William III. the office had remained vacant. The English court sided with its supporters, in the hope that it would render the Republic a stronger and more profitable ally, and all the more surely an ally if the Stadtholder were in some way connected with the House of Hanover. Townshend for a time even wished that the King himself would stand for the office, and it has been said that he would also have recommended the King's brother, the Bishop of Osnabrück, as a candidate, on the supposition that the latter would marry the mother of the Prince of Nassau. [1]) At all events the English Court soon decided to take up the cause of the young Prince himself, who alone could ever meet with success, and to give him as wife an Hanoverian Princess. [2]) The very reasons which determined the Court of St. James's to promote the revival of the Stadtholdership induced that of Versailles to thwart it. If the Republic were more closely and firmly united to England, she might resume that part which she had played in the reign of William III. and the war of the Spanish Succession, and no longer be of use to France; and therefore France preferred to see her weak state continue, together with her need of French friendship. [3])

Such being the condition of affairs, the provinces which were opposed to the promotion of the young Prince, among them the

[1]) Wiesener op. cit. I, 144; Wagenaar, op. cit. XVIII, 128—9.

[2]) Little is known as yet of the steps taken on his behalf. An important document would appear to be the "Relation sur l'état present des affaires en Hollande", R. O. Hl. 274 fol. 235 et seq. (about 1721).

[3]) Fénelon, op. cit., 164.

powerful province of Holland, had an interest in preventing English influence from becoming decisive; while those, such as Guelders, which favoured the Stadtholder, were, by their inland situation, more dependent than the others, on France. If what has been said of the necessity for England to ally herself with the Republic be taken into account, the reason is clear for the long delay before William of Nassau was proclaimed hereditary Stadtholder in all the provinces; for to recommend him strongly or to act openly in his favour meant losing the confidence of Holland and Zealand, and to drive the Republic into the arms of France. There can be no stronger proof of the relative nature of English influence on the Republic than the fact that the English court had to wait for decades, until as late as 1747, before the Frisian Prince, who in 1734 had married the Princess Royal of England, attained his end, no less eagerly desired by himself than by his father-in-law. This is what some authors call the absolute dependence of the Republic on England.

It was never so absolute as it has been represented to be, not even in those first years after the peace of Utrecht, when the Republic relapsed so deplorably from her proud position. Thus, in spite of the pressure applied by George I. she refused to act offensively against the Swedes; she would enter into a triple alliance with the Emperor, only on condition that a similar one be at the same time concluded with France, and she refrained from entering the Quadruple Alliance. Her attitude was on the whole rather passive than submissive. Her ally sometimes dealt unreasonably and unjustly with her [1]), but she did not always dare to give utterance to her discontent. As a rule she followed England, with whom she renewed in 1716, all the old treaties and conventions which existed between the two nations. Her compliance was largely due to distrust of France, which drove her nearer to the other country.

This distrust was still very strong in the first years after the war. Châteauneuf was sent to the United Provinces to weaken it,

---

[1]) Unreasonably as when the English government, though partaking in the profits of the barrier-treaty, utterly refused to bear a share in its charges (Bussemaker, *Nijhoff's Bijdragen* IVde reeks, I, 310); unjustly e. g. with regard to the arrears England owed to the Republic for the 13 regiments which had followed William III to Ireland. Though acknowledging the debt the government would not do justice, notwithstanding the claims which the Dutch put forward strongly (Wiesener, *op. cit.* II. 7).

but his professions that France had given up all idea of expansion, found little credence. Men feared that she was peaceable for a time only, that when she had regained her old strength she would resume her old courses. A fair number of the regents, including those of Amsterdam, were more favourably disposed towards France; but even they were not convinced that the Southern Netherlands, which had so long been the objective of Louis XIV, had suddenly lost all attraction for his country. Fénelon thought it necessary to admonish his successor not to give the least reason for the revival of these old suspicions. [1]

But it was the general weakness of the Republic, more than her distrust of France, which prevented her from making the most of her advantageous position, that of being wanted by England on the one hand, and solicited by France on the other. She turned it to good account sometimes. Both in 1715 and in 1718, England was obliged to support her in her dealings with the Emperor; and she obtained some profit by the Triple Alliance. Her gains would, however, have been far greater had she shewn firmness and held to her point in the negotiations of 1716; and, again, considerable advantages were promised to her in 1718 and 1719, but she was too slow in the matter of adherence to the Quadruple Alliance, and suffered the opportunity to escape her. Heinsius, broken by the unhappy issue of the war of the Spanish Succession, was very timid in his last years, and his successor Hoornbeek was too peaceable to act vigorously, while others, like Goslinga, advised withdrawal from foreign politics.

Such counsel was most imprudent. The Republic had so many interests, political, financial and commercial, which brought her into relations with England, France, Spain, Austria, Prussia and the Empire in general, Turkey, Russia, and Denmark, that she had no choice as to whether or not she should meddle in foreign affairs. "Il n'y a que les montagnards et les insulaires," wrote Slingelandt, "qui peuvent, et encore avec beaucoup de peine, songer à la neutralité dans les troubles générales"; [2] and he showed by his words his understanding of the Republic's position. There was hardly a public event in Europe which had not its bearing on her fortunes. Had she stood aside she would have surrendered

[1] Fénelon, op. cit. 144.
[2] to C. Hop, 6. Nov. 1728 (R. A. Hl. 2974).

herself absolutely to England, and would have received from other powers even more wrongs than those which actually fell to her. "Qui se fait brebis, le loup le mange", Fagel once replied to Goslinga. [1])

Yet Goslinga was right in the stress he laid on the necessity of improvement at home, for, as Fagel said, it was useless to expect help from friends before there had been resort to self-help. [2]) He erred however, in the opposition he set up between the policies of domestic reform, and of intervention in foreign affairs; for not the one or the other of these was requisite, but both of them. Slinge-landt did not "halt between two opinions", but was convinced that action in both spheres was necessary, and that to neglect either, was to do nothing. To withdraw from foreign politics must be harmful to national trade and welfare, [3]) and neither would it prevent foreign influence, for France especially would do her utmost to hinder domestic reform.

Slingelandt saw clearly what was needful, but unhappily his influence on foreign affairs was, until 1727, only indirect. He was destined however to use the Republic's position to the best possible advantage from the moment when he was chosen Grand Pensionary. She was in his time anything but a "satellite" of England, a "shallop following the man of war". Baudrillart in the introduction to the third volume of his excellent work on Philip V. and the French court speaks of England, Austria, France and Spain as being chiefly responsible for all diplomatic combinations. The hand, however, is as complete without the little finger, as Europe without the Republic after the peace of Utrecht, at least in the years of the administration of Simon van Slingelandt.

It has been seen that from the date of the peace, until about 1720, the Republic made little use of her position. She made still less in the following years, or rather her position was then less advantageous; for it had been largely founded on the differences between France and England, on the opposition of their interests as to the Hanoverian succession, in the fate of the Southern Netherlands, in

---

[1]) Slothouwer, *Sicco van Goslinga,* 143.
[2]) Fagel to Goslinga, 17 Nov. 1725, F. G.
[3]) e. g. if the Republic had joined England and France in the Quadruple Alliance, she would probably have been admitted to the treaty of 1721 by which Spain granted to England important commercial advantages.

the general affairs of Europe, and in trade. The English court had, however, become allied to France, and had even acquired a certain ascendancy in France, and English interests were therefore in no danger from that country. Since England was also on good terms with Spain, the possibility of a war, which could injure her trade, and necessitate the support of the States, was almost excluded. Such condition greatly lessened the value to her of friendship with the Republic, and had it continued, Slingelandt would have found it far more difficult than he did, to play a part of consequence. Before his accession to power however the aspect of general affairs had greatly changed. And the Republic had awakened from her lethargy, for she had been hit in her dearest part, her trade, and she nerved herself to avert, if possible, the impending danger.

IV.

For the sake of convenience we have omitted for a time to notice Austria. Although the conduct of the Republic was chiefly determined by her relation to England and France, her relation to Austria was by no means immaterial to her, especially since the peace of Utrecht had allotted the Southern Netherlands to the Emperor.

At the time of the peace these provinces were still ruled by the provisional Anglo-Dutch government which had obtained since their occupation in 1706. It was understood that they should be transferred to the Emperor when he had concluded peace with France, as he did at Rastadt in 1714. The conditions of the transfer had, however, to be settled before it took place; and, as has been related, arrangements as to these conditions, had been made without the Emperor's knowledge. The States had in 1709 concluded with England a barrier treaty which in 1713 was superseded by another, but the Emperor would accept those stipulations of the peace which regarded the Southern Netherlands, no more than the others. New negotiations were therefore necessary. They opened with an offer by the Emperor to the States of the right of garrisoning three fortresses, which, since they had enjoyed as much under the Spanish administration, cruelly disappointed them, and provoked from them a series of counter-claims. Baron Heems, the Austrian ambassador at the Hague, thereupon protested in much indignation that the Emperor would never suffer laws to be prescribed to him, in countries which were his; he admitted that former negotiations had been on a basis proposed by the States, but affirmed that times had changed, since, contrary to expectations, his master had not obtained the whole of the Spanish monarchy. [1])

Negotiations had hardly begun when they were brought to a standstill by the opposition of two irreconcilable views: that of the States who, justifying themselves by the terms of the Grand Alliance, held that the Emperor should not possess the Southern Netherlands as an ordinary sovereign, but should keep and defend them on their behalf; [2]) and that of the Emperor who pointed to altered conditions, and would suffer hardly any limitation of his authority.

A solution was difficult, and a year and a half were spent in negotiations. The Emperor threatened a forcible occupation of his new territory, and the States were tenacious of their claims. Finally when, menaced by the Pretender, England took the affairs of the Republic more to heart, an agreement was reached by the barrier treaty of 1715. [3])

This provided that the Southern Netherlands should be rendered the sole, indivisible and inalienable domain of the Emperor, inseparable from his German States. They were to be defended by an army of from 30,000 to 35,000 men, of whom three fifths should be maintained by the Emperor, and two fifths by the States, who also received the exclusive right of garrisoning the fortresses of Namur, Tournay, Menin, Furnes, Warneton, Ypres and Knocke; while Dendermonde was to have a garrison half Dutch and half Austrian. A considerable part of Flanders and a small part of the present Dutch province of Limburg were ceded to the States in full sovereignty. They were to receive annually from the Emperor, a grant towards the maintenance of their troops, of 1,250,000 Dutch guilders, to be paid out of the surest revenues of the country; and he acknowledged the debts of the Spanish Government, and the loans contracted under the provisory administration of the Maritime Powers. The famous article XXVI, dealt

---

[1]) Bussemaker, *Gids* 1899, III, 82; cf Srbik, *op. cit.* I, 440—1.
[2]) cf. Secr. Res. Hl. VIII, 153.
[3]) An account of the negotiations is in Bussemaker, *Nijhoff's Bijdragen* IVde reeks, I, 289—326, and in Srbik, *op. cit*, I, 432—70.

with commercial affairs. It enacted that the import and export
duties of the Southern Netherlands, should continue on the footing they had occupied after the barrier treaty, with the proviso,
that a new treaty should be settled as soon as possible by the
Emperor, in conjunction with the King of England and the States.
For the rest between the Dutch and the Belgians, trade was to remain on the basis established by the treaty of Munster.

This agreement was not however destined to be final, for the
negotiations were shortly afterwards reopened. The Emperor,
influenced by his European policy, might perhaps himself have
acquiesced in the barrier treaty. He was eager to conclude if not
an offensive, at least a defensive alliance with the Maritime Powers. The Belgians however were by no means inclined to agree to
a disposition of themselves, made without their knowledge, and as
the news was spread abroad, there arose a storm of indignation.
They felt that they had been sacrificed to the Dutch, and to procure an alteration of this treaty, so injurious to their interests,
they applied to the Emperor. He found himself in something of a
dilemma, for on the one hand he did not wish to distrust the Dutch,
and on the other he desired to give some satisfaction to his ag-
grieved subjects. After long hesitation, and against the opinion of
Eugene of Savoy, the Conference [1]) advised in favour of resuming
the negotiations. In these the States took part, although they understood that to negotiate anew was to grant new concessions.
Since they did not agree to all the Emperor's claims, matters were
not brought to a close until 1718, when he wished to have their
concurrence in the Quadruple Alliance. A treaty, altered somewhat importantly in favour of the Southern Netherlands, was then
brought about: the Flemish territory to be ceded to the Republic
was reduced to one fifth of its former extent, and new arrangements were made as to the revenues from which the subsidy
granted to the Dutch troops, and the interest on the loans, were
payable. On the whole however the barrier treaty was maintained
as it had been determined three years earlier. [2])

By its terms the Emperor had incurred several obligations towards the Republic, but that power had at the same time become

---

[1]) A body consisting of the principal counsellors of the Emperor.
[2]) Gachard, *Histoire de la Belgique au commencement du 18ième siècle*, Chap. XX, XXI;.
Huisman, *op. cit.*, 124—5; Srbik, *op. cit.* I, 532—53.

dependent on him in various respects. She was so politically, in that the safety of the Southern Netherlands, which concerned her, even more nearly than their sovereign himself, had been mainly entrusted to imperial troops; financially in virtue of the subsidy and the interest which the Emperor was bound to pay her annually; and commercially in respect of considerable advantages which she could not easily relinquish. For all these reasons, the Emperor believed that the Republic was in his power, and that in case of a war with France, she would be obliged to join him because the French would certainly invade the Southern Netherlands. Had he been prudent he would have learnt a lesson from the events of the end of 1715, when the Duke of Orleans had proposed to the States, that the Southern Netherlands should be proclaimed neutral.

At this time it was the aim of the Emperor to revive the Grand Alliance. Conditions had altered in his favour, when in 1714 George I. had mounted the English throne; but since the latter was neither willing, nor able, as yet to reopen the war, he confined himself for the moment to an endeavour to procure a defensive alliance. The necessity for the participation in such a combination, of the Republic was no more apparent to the Emperor and George I., than to the Duke of Orleans. It was naturally the Duke's aim, to prevent the revival of the alliance, and to this end he pursued the course which has been indicated. Fear of the French desire to expand, had always been the chief motive of Dutch enmity to her, and this fear had to be overcome. Hence the proposal to declare the Southern Netherlands neutral, which however aimed not only at removing the distrust of France, but also at rendering the Republic independent of the Emperor. [1])

There is no need to explain why the Emperor would not hear of it. [2]) It was a principal reason for his interest in the Southern Netherlands that he wished by their means, to secure the help of the Republic in his European policy; and as soon as they were declared neutral he would lose his hold on the neighbouring country. This was out of the question for the time, because the States understood the proposal as not meant seriously, and therefore rejected it. Several regents however received it well, and given different conditions, it might have been generally approved, a

[1]) Bussemaker, *Nijhoff's Bijdragen* IVde reeks, II, 189—198.
[2]) ibid. 217.

lesson which the Emperor could have learnt from the episode. [1])

He was however confident that the Republic would follow his lead, if not on account of the Southern Netherlands, then at least in the train of England. His ambassador in London, Count Volkra, tried to persuade the British ministers to conclude the alliance without delay, alleging that the States would certainly follow such an example. [2]) The issue proved how mistaken the Court of Vienna was. For the Emperor, in endeavouring to secure the Republic by means of England, failed not only to gain her, but also to retain even England. French diplomacy shewed its superiority over that of the Austrians: it took an opposite course, applying first to the Republic, or at least applying to her in the same degree as to England, and it succeeded.

The Emperor's procedure was indeed anything but fitted to engage the Dutch, as is instanced by these very negotiations. Baron Heems, his minister at the Hague, was instructed to acquaint the States with his master's desire to conclude a defensive alliance with them and the King of England. When, however, the Emperor was informed that there was question of a similar alliance with France, on the basis of the Peace of Utrecht, he declared that he could never approve of the articles of that treaty, which had been made against his interest, and without his consent; that he would consider as prejudicial to himself, any alliance with France on that basis; and that if the States persisted in their intention to negotiate with France, befcre or after the conclusion of a treaty with himself, he would not ask them to join him in an alliance. [3])

This haughty attitude is at first sight inconsistent with the Emperor's vacillations in the barrier negotations. But the conduct of England must be taken into consideration. The concessions he made in the affair of the barrier were induced by the English government, who in 1715, and again in 1718, had strong reasons for not disobliging the Dutch. Where however the combination of that people with the Emperor in a triple alliance was concerned,

---

[1]) Dollot has taken this proposal to have been serious and imputes its want of success to the unwillingness of the States (*Neutralité de la Belgique*, 412—17). Bussemaker however thinks it was no more than a manoeuvre (*op. cit.*) which, considering the lately concluded barrier-treaty is very probable; cf. p. 78—9.

[2]) Bussemaker, *op. cit.*, 200.

[3]) Wiesener, *Le Regent etc*, I. 232—3. This was in June 1716, the month in which the treaty of Westminster between England and the Emperor (25 May o.s. 1716) was concluded.

England then sided with him. If ever he shewed goodwill to the Republic, it was solely on account of England.

The effect on the Republic was necessarily evil. At first, immediately after the Peace of Utrecht, when the Tories were still in power, she maintained a close alliance with the Emperor, notwithstanding the alluring offers of England. [1]) In 1715, during the troublesome negotiations about the barrier, the States General still called the friendship of the Emperor and Great Britain indispensable, and based on it some advice to the provinces to adopt towards the Emperor a less positive attitude.[2]) Distrust of France was still very strong, especially among the leaders, and therefore there was an approximation to Austria, which, as a land power, could help the Dutch against France, better than England. This distrust however gradually weakened, and concurrently relations with the Emperor became less cordial.

Ill feeling towards him had in 1724 become so strong, that many regents believed it would be advantageous that Spain, rather than he, should possess the Southern Netherlands; and probably the States would have remained neutral, had a war then broken out between the Emperor and France, even if the latter power attacked the Southern Netherlands. [3]) This change in national sentiment cannot all be ascribed to the barrier negotiations, which, although they had not improved relations, still lacked importance to produce more than a transitory estrangement. They had been concerned chiefly with the cession of land, and with financial arrangements; they had left trade disregarded or in the background. It was trade which the Dutch had most at heart, and it was a difference of opinion about trade which gave rise to a serious conflict.

V.

To acquire wealth by commerce and navigation was the general desire of the time, and it was nowhere so strong as among the Belgians. Largely by such means they had attained the wonderful prosperity which they had enjoyed in the middle ages and the

---

[1]) Bussemaker, *Gids* 1899, III, 69—76.
[2]) Bussemaker, *Nijhoff's Bijdragen* IVde reeks, I, 312.
[3]) Srbik, *op. cit.* I, 598.

16th century, and largely to their extinction they had owed their subsequent misery. The Spanish Government, far from listening to the supplications of their Belgian subjects, had debarred them from all trade with the Spanish colonies; had even given other nations a preference over them, with regard to trade with Spain herself; and had suffered the Dutch to close the Scheldt and to exclude them from the East Indies. When however the Emperor became their sovereign they again took courage. They did not even wait until the government had been transferred to him, but in the spring of 1715 their first ships sailed for China and the country which is now British India. These ships came back in the next year laden with rich cargoes; and the people were encouraged by success to continue in their course.

They had met however not only with success but also with the bitter opposition of the Dutch who tried to stifle the effort at its very inception. The newcomers suffered all manner of violence from the Dutch East and West India Companies, of whom the latter traded also on the West coast of Africa; and from the first the monopolists were supported by their government. In 1717 the States issued a severe edict prohibiting their subjects, even under penalty of dealth, from signing on in Belgian ships.

The Belgians found their government less loyal to them. Had the Marquis de Prié, who as plenipotentiary to the Governor, stood at the head of affairs, had his way, all maritime enterprise would have been delayed until better times, more particularly until the accomplishment of the barrier treaty. [1] The Governor, Prince Eugene of Savoy, was less extreme: he advised against the establishment of a company, but favoured the granting of new patents to private persons; and since the Emperor concurred in his opinion, this course was decided on. Thus in these years several ships sailed to the Far East, and since on the whole they were very prosperous the jealousy of the Dutch was more and more aroused: they redoubled their acts of violence; they went so far as to capture a Belgian ship. This last act could not be overlooked, and from Brussels and Vienna remonstrances and claims for satisfaction were sent to the Hague, but the States justified the company in question by a reference to the Treaty of Munster. [2] Soon afterwards another

---

[1] Huisman, *op. cit.* 102.
[2] Ibid; 126—31.

ship was taken, and this time the Belgians retaliated by taking
a Dutch ship. This seizure provoked a storm in the Republic. The
States hotly protested against it as an act of violence, and to ex
culpate their own subjects referred again to the Treaty of Munster. When these representations were unsuccessful, they had re
course to other methods: they applied to the English government. [1])

This date, the year 1720, was not the beginning of English
concern with the burning question of the Ostend trade, to give it
its usual name derived from the harbour whence it was carried on.
For in this matter the English East India Company had acted in
concert with the Dutch companies and had, like them, committed
acts of violence, and done their uttermost to check the new enterprises from the outset. [2]) But the English company had not to
the same extent as theDutch, found government support,although
some attempt had been made to satisfy their desires. At the company's request, the government of England had made a remonstrance as to the granting of Belgian patents to British merchants,
and the engagement of English captains for Belgian vessels. [3])
Later on, in February 1718, St. Saphorin, the English ambassador at Vienna, had delivered a note, advocating the complete
suspension of the issue of patents. But in contrast to the acts of
the States this note was neither hostile nor reclamatory, but rather conveyed friendly advice given by a good ally, and it represented the limit to which George I. was prepared to go. It fell to
the Dutch to take the initiative, if they considered vigorous action necessary. The East India Company seems to have foreseen
this attitude of their government, for at the end of 1718, they sent
Sir Matthew Decker, one of their Directors, to the Hague in order to determine with the Dutch East India Company a line of
conduct, to be pursued with reference to the Ostend trade. [4])

Not improbably it was a result of the deliberations between
these commercial organizations, that the Dutch, when satisfaction as to the seizure of their ship had been denied them, applied
to the English government. The application, made by the States,
at the instigation of the East and West India Companies of their

---

[1]) Huisman, *op. cit.* 131—5.
[2]) Ibid: 92, 102.
[3]) Ibid: 118 (cf. ibid: 103).
[4]) Ibid: 121—4.

people, received support at least from India House. The proposal was made that the Maritime Powers should take combined action against the trade of the ships of Ostend.

Prié feared a combination of the governments, and deemed it best to give as much satisfaction as possible to the English court. He had followed this policy before on the occasion of the remonstrance which has been mentioned; [1]) and now once more he endeavoured to content the English, convinced that without them the Dutch would not risk any undertaking. India House was dissatisfied with his offers, and was able to frustrate an attempt to conclude an Anglo-Belgian commercial treaty: yet Prié succeeded in preventing the combination of the two governments. [2]) ·

Their methods were evidently and notably different, for while from the beginning the States adopted as their own the cause of their companies, English rulers extended to India House, only that measure of complaisance which was forced upon them. [3]) The difference was to the profit of the Belgians, for it stood in the way of a combination of the Maritime Powers. The Court of Vienna proceeded to establish the Ostend Company.

This last event came about at the end of 1722. From the beginning of the rise of the Ostend trade, there had been question of uniting the various separate enterprises and substituting a monopoly for the system of granting patents to private persons. Such a course had been suggested, as early as 1716, by the merchants Ray and De Potter; but Prié had advised against it, in view of the still outstanding negotiations with the Dutch, [4]) and Eugene of Savoy had feared that it might arouse English animosity. [5]) The scheme was brought forward again at the end of 1719.

The Dutch negotiations had been closed and the Court of Vienna judged that there was no longer reason to delay the proposed incorporation on account of that nation. The Dutch had indeed hampered the Ostend ships to the extent of their ability, and they had shewn no counterbalancing complaisance, where the general affairs of Europe were concerned. Instead of concluding an alli-

---

[1]) Huisman, *op. cit.* 119—20.
[2]) Ibid: 135—8.
[3]) Of this difference we treat more fully in the Appendix.
[4]) Huisman, *op. cit.* 102—3.
[5]) Ibid: 159.

ance with the Emperor, they had become parties to an alliance
with France; and, notwithstanding his concessions in the affair
of the barrier, they had, to his grave disadvantage, put off again
and again their entrance into the Quadruple Alliance. He had
made the concessions chiefly under pressure of England, directed
to produce moderation; [1]) but the English government did not
support the Dutch in their attitude to the Ostend trade. Therefore he listened more than before to the requests of the Belgians,
in the belief that if he supported them effectively, an end would
soon come to the opposition of the Dutch, whose general condition was depressed, and who in various respects depended on him.
To Prince Eugene, Dutch opposition was the motive of his es-
pousal of the cause of the Ostend trade, and of his advocacy of
the establishment of a company [2]), but the Emperor was otherwise
impelled; by sympathy with the cause itself. He was deeply convinced of the importance of commerce and navigation to the welfare of a country, and eagerly desirous of bestowing those bless-
ings on his subjects; and the powerful position he had reached,
by the treaties of 1718, made efforts in this direction more possible to him than ever before. He had no longer any reasons for
considering the Dutch.

Consideration of them certainly did not account for the delay
of three years before the company came into being. At length in
November 1722 the charter of the Imperial and Royal Company
established in the Austrian Netherlands, usually called the Ostend Company, was drawn up and approved by the Emperor.

This charter, however had not yet been published, and the
Dutch tried as far as possible to prevent this. At the request of
their companies, the States ordered their representatives at Brussels and Vienna to hand in remonstrances, containing juridical
arguments against the establishment of the Company, together
with arguments as to its undesirability.

The former constituted an attack on the legality of the Ostend
trade, which the other side persistently rebutted. This controversy
between the Dutch and the Belgian lawyers, was dealt with some
years ago by Michael Huisman in a work admirable in many respects, *"La Belgique Commerciale sous l'Empereur Charles VI. La*

---

[1]) Pribram, *op. cit.* I. 385.
[2]) Huisman, *op. cit.* 158—9.

Compagnie d'Ostende." In this book, the Belgian author severely condemns the Dutch, who seem to him to have been influenced by sheer greed and hate; by mean motives only. The grounds for disagreeing with his opinion, cannot here be set forth but save for a short review of the other aspect of the question, will be relegated to an appendix.

Let it be granted that the Dutch treatment of the Belgians in this period deserves reproof in several respects. The conduct of the Dutch was certainly not that becoming a sister nation, and their arguments as to the Ostend trade, contained much unsound reasoning. Yet some of this was sound enough: an important part of Huisman's refutation, has been built up on a clause in the barrier treaty, which he has misread, but which in truth is decidedly creditable to the Dutch.

Another more general fault in Huisman's work, is that he has dealt with this subject, rather as a juridical controversy than as an episode in history. He has thus largely neglected the subject of the Grand Alliance, which is necessarily relevant to any just estimate of the conduct of the Dutch towards the Belgians in the 18th century.

It was, as has been said, by the Grand Alliance that the Republic attempted to complete and confirm the system imposed upon the Belgians in the 17th century. This involved the service of the North by the South as a buffer, politically and no less economically, against France. The Dutch helped Spain to defend the Southern Netherlands against France, and received in return, commercial advantages and the right to garrison some fortresses. Thus Belgium was the object of a transaction between her sovereign and the Dutch. After the death of the last Spanish Habsburg, his Austrian relatives claimed the right to succeed him, and in their turn wanted help from the Dutch, who however, no more than the English, to whom the Emperor also applied, desired to go to war. They feared that by a rupture with Spain, they would lose their trade, and hesitated; and finally they refused unless the privileges they already enjoyed were secured to them, and others granted as reward for help rendered. The Emperor submitted to these conditions, and thereby there was foreshadowed the continuation of the system of the second half of the 17th century, in the 18th.

The cruel manner in which Dutch expectations so raised were disappointed has been told. In spite of the extraordinary exertions of that nation, in the war of the Spanish Succession, on behalf of the House of Austria, they were at last obliged to accept a barrier treaty, which fell far short of their reasonable expectations. It was modified some years later still more, to their disadvantage. And then, to crown all, the Emperor who was so much indebted to the Republic founded a company which, it was feared, would in the long run certainly ruin her fortunes.

It is true that the company was calculated to benefit the Belgians themselves to whom their dependence on the Dutch was on the whole most injurious. From their own point of view, therefore, they were right in trying to break loose from the system. But it would be unreasonable to blame the Dutch for adhering to it: they had borne and they still bore its burdens, and they were entitled to keep its profits. However much they may have wronged the Belgians, their conduct towards the Emperor was justifiable. It was only most rarely that he found resolution to defend the Ostend trade, and after some years he abandoned it, in spite of its remarkable prosperity.

But this is to anticipate. The Emperor was very positive when the States requested him not to publish the charter. He would not, he said, deny to his subjects the sea, which was open to all men. And he pointed out that it was to the interest of the Republic, that the revenues of the Southern Netherlands should increase, for these provinces were financially self-dependent and could not, unless their trade flourished, support the large body of troops quartered on them, or pay the heavy debts and the subsidies which they owed to the Republic. [1]

Perhaps in fear of the insufficiency of their unaided representations, the States sought the support of other powers. They applied first to the English government, in the beginning, with slight success, for England adhered to her former policy, and would promise only good offices. As before however, her rulers were compelled to a more active course by the East India Company, who demanded satisfaction for the loss they had suffered by the competition of the Ostend trade to China. Parliament passed a string-

---

[1] Huisman, *op. cit.* 228—9.

ent Act which forbade any participation in the enterprise of the Ostend Company, and St. Saphorin was instructed to ask for the repeal of the Company's charter. [1]) When he obeyed, Eugene of Savoy asked him again and again why his master had not before declared his intention of opposing the Ostend trade. The time for going back was past. [2])

On this occasion the Dutch also made application to their second ally in the Triple Alliance, France. This power seemed more amenable than England, for she hoped to advance her anti-Austrian policy. Dubois saw in compliance, the way to nearer connection with the Maritime Powers; and while on the one hand he caused representations to be made at Brussels and Vienna, he attempted on the other, to rouse the English. "Il faut prendre interêt aux avantages des Hollandais, et exciter les alarmes de la cour de Londres" he wrote, defining his policy; [3]) but his lack of vigour, in espousing the Dutch cause, is proved by the representations "aussi faibles qu' équivoques", which he inspired. [4])

It was not likely that this faint pressure from France would turn the Emperor from a decision which he would not abandon for England's sake. The charter was published in July 1723. There ensued a new application from the States, who requested France to declare formally that in case of hostilities with Austria she would support them by force of arms. Orleans followed in the steps of Dubois, whom he had succeeded as prime minister, and would by no means go so far as he was asked to do. To give some satisfaction, he issued an edict similar to the English Act, forbidding all manner of participation in the activities of the Ostend Company, but at the same time he instructed the ambassadors abroad, to declare the desire in general of Louis XV. to contribute to the maintenance of the peace of Europe. [5]) He ordered remonstrances to be again made, at Vienna and Brussels; but when C. Hop, the Dutch ambassador at the Court of Versailles, asked for a declared guarantee against the Ostend trade, he replied that France, by the Triple Alliance, had guaranteed the Republic in her

---

[1]) Ibid: 229—31.
[2]) Pribram, *op. cit.* I, 446 note.
[3]) Dubois to Destouches, April 16, 1723 (quoted Bourgeois, *Le Secret de Dubois*, 375, 2nd footnote).
[4]) Huisman, *op. cit.* 235.
[5]) Ibid: 246—7.

possessions within, but not without Europe; a subterfuge said to have been suggested to the foreign secretary Morville, by one of the Austrian plenipotentiaries at Cambrai. [1])

The English Court was in a no more improved frame of mind than the French. Immediately after the issue of the charter, the States sent Pesters, their resident at Brussels, to George I. at Hanover, with a commission to arrange with the English statesmen, the steps necessary to the final and utter extinction of the Ostend trade. He was received somewhat coolly: the King refused to give a written declaration, so long as the States, who were more concerned in the trade than he, had not submitted their plan to him, and declared the form which an appeal to his guarantee would take. [2]) Obviously, he was unprepared to take strong measures, and still further to take the initiative. It took Pesters two months to draw from Townshend the admission that George I. considered this affair to be a *casus foederis* (2 October 1723). [3])

The Court at Vienna felt at ease and took courage. "I believe Prince Eugene and some of the first ministers here will be very reasonable about this commerce", wrote an informant of the English Court in May 1723; [4]) but in the beginning of 1724, the Conference unamimously resolved to maintain the Company, and even to consider the barrier treaty annulled *ipso facto*, if it were not recognized by neighbouring powers. [5])

Some weeks after this resolution had been passed, on the 26th of January 1724, the Congress of Cambrai was formally opened. It had, as has been said, to settle several outstanding differences between Spain and Austria. The Republic also wished her differences with Austria to be dealt with, but could not bring them forward herself, as she did not take part in the Congress. The task must therefore be entrusted to a participating power; but neither France nor England had, as yet, her interests at heart. Spain, how-

---

[1]) Huisman, *op. cit.* 315.

[2]) Ibid: 246.

[3]) Ibid: 314; from this page of Huisman Bourgeois (*Secret de Dubois*, 375, note 5) quotes the following words "Il est vrai, que si Townshend appuyait energiquement les Hollandais, Walpole refusait de se laisser entraîner à une guerre." Bourgeois has not however, found these words at this page or elsewhere in Huisman's book.

[4]) The sentence continues as follows: "but it is certain the Emperor has it entirely at heart as much as is possible to imagine," Pribram *op. cit.* I, 446 note.

[5]) Huisman, *op. cit.* 316.

ever, was herself much incensed against Austria, and her help would be the more valuable, because she had been the other contracting party in that Treaty of Munster to which the Republic had time and time again referred in her dispute with the Emperor. Therefore she applied to Spain, and was heard favourably. Spain drew from the Treaty of Munster, a deduction very consonant with the Dutch interpretation. In accordance with an agreement with the Dutch, the Spanish ambassador in London, Pozzo-Bueno, represented to the English Court that the Ostend Company must be supressed, since the Company subverted the arrangement between Spain and the Republic, as to the trade of the world, and might prove as detrimental to Spanish trade in the West Indies, as to Dutch trade in the East Indies. Pozzo-Bueno pointed out further, that the easiest way to end the Company would be to force Austria at the Congress to rescind it. [1])

This time the English Court shewed more interest in the Ostend affair. The language of Stanhope, the ambassador at Madrid, was most vigorous; and the English plenipotentiaries at Cambrai recommended to the French ministers, that the matter should be brought forward at the Congress. [2]) The Austrians grew uneasy. They were already considering the advisability of offering some concessions to the Maritime Powers when all their fears were dissipated. It appeared that the King of England had not after all sanctioned a demand for the suppression to be made at the Congress without the concurrence of the French Court. And the French Court pursued its former line of conduct: Morville, the Secretary of State, desired above all things, to maintain peace. He wished to reserve this affair of the Company, as a means of influencing the Emperor, until such time as his consent was needed to the conclusions of the Congress, and he dissuaded Spain from interference in a new dispute foreign to the affairs of the Congress. In compliance with his wishes she promised to act in the matter, only in concert with the Court of France. [3])

For the third time, the Republic had failed to reach her aim of making the Ostend affair the common business of the parties to the Triple Alliance. On the first and second occasions she had

---

[1]) Huisman, *op. cit.* 318—20.
[2]) Baudrillart. *op. cit.* III, 75.
[3]) Huisman, *op. cit.* 320—21.

applied directly to her allies, on the third indirectly, by way of Spain. Her two earlier failures were due to the complete agreement between France and England, which, as has been shewn,[1] exempted both from the necessity of considering her. The explanation of the third is less easy, and involves a review of the general course of European politics.

It has been said[2], that France and England concluded a secret treaty with Spain in the year after her entrance into the Quadruple Alliance, and by its terms they were bound to support her at the Congress of Cambrai. They foresaw however, that the mutually unfriendly relations of Austria and Spain might cause the Congress to result in war, and therefore again and again they put it off, so that it was not opened until 1724. That year found Spain and Austria no better disposed to each other. Each of them voiced her claims, largely concerned with Italian affairs, and these proved to be entirely irreconcilable. When the Emperor refused absolutely to make the least concession, Spain intimated to England and France, the mediating powers, that henceforth she would look upon them as having guaranteed her the justice to which she was entitled. Since nothing could be won from the Emperor peaceably, there remained, she declared, only the weapon of war. [3]

England and France were alike in their lack of warlike intentions, but not in their selection of an alternative course. These two powers were less firmly united than formerly, for by the death of the Duke of Orleans, in 1723, they had lost the bond supplied by the mutual interests of the Houses of Hanover and Orleans. The Duke of Bourbon, who succeeded as Prime Minister of France, did not immediately sever the existing alliance, yet he felt no sympathy with England, and strove rather for a closer union with Spain. [4] But the English also were eagerly desirous of maintaining friendly relations with Spain, on account of the attendant commercial advantages. It became their policy, with reference to this nation, to outbid the French, and at the same time to use the French as their scapegoat, if their promises should not realised. [5]

---

[1] p. 60—61.
[2] p. 34.
[3] Baudrillart, *op. cit.* III, 74.
[4] Ibid· 24, 31, 110, 121. of. Syveton, *Une cour et un avanturier*, 48.
[5] Baudrillart, *op. cit.* III, 62—3, 66, 74—5.

They conformed to this general policy, in the particular case of the Ostend affair.

Spain in truth cared not a whit for the interests of the Republic. That power is said to have held out hopes to her, that in the event of a war, she might win back the Southern Netherlands; [1]) and it is certain that the Dutch would then have welcomed the return of those provinces to Spanish rule. This consideration may have had some effect on the attitude of Spain, but she was influenced principally, not by the affairs of Belgium but by those of Italy. It was for the realization of her Italian schemes, that she purposed to reopen the war with the Emperor; and it was in order to embroil the Maritime Powers with the Emperor, and thereby to secure their support for herself, that she brought forward the matter of the Ostend trade at the Congress. [2])

It has been seen that she applied first to England. So far England had moved in the Ostend affair only at the pressing instance of India House; but the language of Stanhope at Madrid, and of the plenipotentiaries at Cambrai, seemed to indicate, that she had at this moment adopted the cause of the Republic. Spain was encouraged to think that by means of the Ostend affair, she could bring about a general conflagration against the Emperor. Her hopes were elusive. Had England been truly interested in the suppression of the Ostend trade, she would have allowed the matter to be introduced unconditionally at the Congress, and thereby, she would indeed, have found herself associated with Spain in a war in which France could not but have joined. But her only aim was, that Spain should believe her to be willing for war. At the moment when her intentions seemed most bellicose, she refused her consent to a demand at the Congress, for the suppression of the

---

[1]) cf. Huisman, *op cit*. 318, 321. This may be true, but what is said at p. 321 seems to us exaggerated. The conduct of the Republic at this point needs further inquiry, for which it will be advisable to make use of the letters of Van der Meer at the Rijksarchief. We remark, that with regard to this point, Huisman principally refers to French sources, which of course in this case are not the most authoritative. Baudrillart who also refers to French sources, ascribes to Van der Meer ideas (*op. cit* III, 75) which would have been quite misplaced in an ambassador of the States, as that, the Republic would be willing to render at a certain moment all the barrier-towns to France. That the Republic offered Philip V., a fleet and troops, as he boasted to Tessé (ibid: 128), we do not believe at all.

[2]) cf. a remarkable passage in a letter from Fagel to Goslinga (7 June 1724, F. G.): "c'est la raison (viz. Spain's object to reconquer the former-Spanish countries in Italy) pourquoi l'Espagne traine le congrès et voudrait que l'Angleterre et l'Etat se brouillassent avec l'Empereur au sujet du commerce d'Ostende, et ce sera peut être dans cette vue qu'ils porteront ce point au congrès."

Ostend Company, unless such were seconded by France. And she knew well that France would never be a party to the movement, and therefore in the conduct of her ally, had an excuse for her backwardness towards Spain.

France, urged to war by Spain, and, apparently by England also, was in a difficult position. She still strove to maintain peace, all the more, because of her distrust of the English, who, Morville feared, might be anxious chiefly or only for the suppression of the Ostend Company, and might, that end secured, leave their ally in the lurch. He feared also that the English might insist that the operations of the war should be confined to Italy, and not encroach on the Southern Netherlands. [1]

His first prognostication, was unfounded, but the latter could not but come true. There was no doubt that the two powers would disagree as to the Southern Netherlands. When in 1714, the exchange of Belgium for Bavaria was discussed, the English opposed it strongly, alleging that they looked "upon the Spanish Low Countries, to be by their situation, the truest and surest pledge of a firm and perpetual friendship between us, the Emperor and the States General." [2] Time had lessened the cordiality of relations with the Emperor, and changed the hostility of France to friendship, but still, England was determined that the French should not enter the Southern Netherlands. This was apparent from the events of 1721, for, when the Triple Alliance with Spain was then discussed, George I. insisted that a clause should be inserted in the treaty, which forbade the contracting powers ever to attack the Catholic Low Countries, for "attacking those provinces was", he said, "attacking England herself." [3] When a similar proposal was made to the States by the Duke of Orleans in 1715, [4] England was as much opposed to it, as the Emperor himself, to whom nothing could have been more repugnant. The difference between Anglo-Austrian relations in 1715 and 1721, cannot be more clearly demonstrated than by the fact that England herself at the latter date, made the proposal, which in 1715 she had utterly rejected. It met with no success, because Dubois refused the clause as dis-

---

[1] Baudrillart, *op. cit.* III 75—6.
[2] Pribram, *op. cit.* 289 note.
[3] Bourgeois, *Le Secret de Dubois*, 274.
[4] cf. p. 64.

honourable to France; [1] imprudently indeed, since thus he closed a way opened by England herself, and perhaps the only way, by which France might have detached her from the Emperor. That "fundamental maxim of the English nation", as Destouches called it, [2] that the Southern Netherlands must be kept from France, was not broken but retained full force; England was left on her guard, lest in case of war with Austria, the French would precipitate themselves into the adjacent imperial provinces.

This consideration is probably also partly accountable for the conduct of England towards the Republic. Only when it was necessary, as during the barrier negotiations of 1715 and 1718, did she help the Republic in her dealings with the Emperor: in the Ostend affair, she left her alone. For with regard to the Southern Netherlands, she depended less on the Republic, than on the Emperor, [3] who had the larger body of troops in them, and was the better able to supply, in case of need, supplementary forces. Huisman ascribes this consideration for the Emperor, to fear of George I. that a war with Austria might involve Hanover. [4]

It may have had yet other motives. The fact is at all events certain, that England was anxious not to be on bad terms with the Emperor. She wished, at the same time to maintain peace and to give to Spain, an impression of readiness to follow where that country led; and for a time the coincidence that France also desired peace made the policy possible. It could however have no permanence. In the case of the Ostend affair, the Republic was compelled to allow herself to be made its dupe, but Spain, its principal dupe, was less submissive. When she perceived that she could not use the Ostend affair to kindle a general war against the Emperor, she dropped it, but she still continued to urge her allies to war. France met her with refusals, and England, with references to the refusals of France. The patience of Elizabeth Farnese was exhausted. Once more she put her allies to the test, and finding England no more willing for war than France, she turned from both of them.

---

[1] Is not this refusal a proof that the neutrality-proposal of 1715 was not sincere? cf. p. 65.
[2] Bourgeois, *Le Secret de Dubois*, 274.
[3] cf. p. 52.
[4] Huisman, *op. cit.* 235, 246.

C. The Vienna—Hanover Conflict.
1725—1727.

I.

It would be difficult to find in history, a second instance of a change of front so bold as that decided upon by the Court of Spain towards the end of 1724. For a quarter of a century Spain had bitterly combatted the House of Austria, either by arms or diplomacy. Quite unexpectedly, although the Emperor had made no sign of friendliness, Spain turned to him for the purpose, not only of concluding peace, but also of cementing a close alliance. Behind such a change must be strong motives.

One of them was certainly keen disappointment. The alliance of 1721, had had for aim, the establishment of Don Carlos; for condition, the restitution of Gibraltar; and it had in both respects fallen short of expectations. The restitution of Gibraltar had not yet been laid before Parliament, and the future of Don Carlos was still uncertain. There was little profit in allies whose diplomatic help availed nothing, and who refused to go to war.

It might have been urged that to turn from them to Austria, was to fall out of the frying pan into the fire, that the position of Don Carlos could not conceivably be bettered by the rejection of English and French help. But such arguments were abundantly defeated by the motherly love and pride of Queen Elizabeth, who led the Spanish court. The Emperor had it in his power to bestow on Don Carlos a gift far greater than any within the reach of her spiritless allies, namely his eldest daughter, the heiress of the Austrian States, to whose husband the crown of the Holy Roman Empire would probably be awarded, after her father's death. The Queen further wished to obtain the second Archduchess for her younger son, Don Philip.

She was willing to make sacrifices for the realization of this splendid project. She offered to the Emperor, the alliance and friendship of Spain, gold to supply his armies, and help for his young trading company at Ostend; and also a favourable interpretation of most points at issue between the countries, and a

[1]) We remark, that little is known, as yet, of Anglo-Austrian relations at this time, and of the influence exercised on them by the various successive administrations, such as that of Stanhope and of Walpole, and by the resignation of Carteret in 1724.

guarantee of the Pragmatic Sanction, by which the Emperor had established his dynasty.

Ripperda, a Dutch country gentleman, who had settled in Spain, was charged to carry these proposals to the Court of Vienna. The imperial ministers to whom he applied, perceived all that was advantageous to them in his mission. Their master was at this time in an isolated position; he was on very unfriendly terms with the Republic; his relations with England and France were less inimical, yet he believed both those countries to have leanings towards Spain; he feared, more than facts justified, that they would join that power to make war against him, and it was obvious that he could expect no help from them in his general policy. In this policy, two points were especially dear to him, the advancement of the fortunes of the Ostend Company, and the obtaining of a guarantee, from the powers of Europe, of the Pragmatic Sanction. Although with much less force than the Dutch, both England and France had yet repeatedly protested against the Company, and they were by no means willing to pledge themselves to the security of his dynasty. It was in these very points that Spain offered satisfaction. To the proposed marriages however, the imperial ministers made many objections, and it was determined to attempt, for the time being, to content Spain with vague promises. A surprise was then provided by the pliancy of Ripperda. In point of fact, he departed from his authorised course, and sacrificed his Queen's interests to his own. He calculated, that if he succeeded in bringing about an alliance with the Emperor, it would greatly enhance his own personal credit, and that he would afterwards be able to move the Emperor to consent to the marriages. For this, he would probably have been disowned by his Court, and punished for exceeding his instructions, had not in due season the French government deeply offended their Catholic Majesties by sending back to them their daughter, the destined bride of Louis XV.

Bourbon, now Prime Minister, bitterly hated Orleans his precursor, and the latter's family. And it was the general belief that Orleans as Regent, had been influenced by motives of family, in promoting the betrothal of the King to the Infanta of Spain, for to delay the time when the King could have a son, was to increase the chances which the line of Orleans had of succeeding to the throne.

6

Such schemes could be defeated by the King's marriage to a princess at the age of puberty, and this Bourbon determined to accomplish at the young Infanta's expense.

Philip and Elizabeth were, as might have been foreseen, beside themselves with anger, and in that condition of mind they ordered Ripperda to conclude the pending negotiations, even if need be without any arrangement as to the proposed marriages.

The arrival of these instructions was soon followed, on April 30th and May 1st 1725 by the conclusion of the Vienna treaties, which provided for peace, alliance and commerce.

They enacted that each of the two powers should recognize the other's possessions, according to the terms of the Quadruple Alliance. In this respect alone, was Spain on an equality with the Emperor, who otherwise had a decided advantage over her. As regarded the Duchies of Parma, Piacenza and Tuscany, Spain yielded those very points on which she had insisted ever since her accession to the Quadruple Alliance: she even suffered the Duchies to be fiefs of the Empire. She guaranteed the Pragmatic Sanction, independently of the proposed marriage. She granted large commercial advantages to the Emperor's subjects. Throughout Spanish territories, saving the West Indies from which Philip V. wished to exclude all foreign enterprise, they obtained all privileges which other nations, particularly the English and the Dutch, enjoyed; and the Ostend Company were rendered as free as were already the Dutch, to import any merchandise which emanated from their own factories. Spain undertook, herself to avenge any insults and losses, which the Ostend ships might incur by attacks on them. The Emperor indeed took upon himself similar obligations, with regard to the Spanish commercial fleet, but he was powerless to perform what he promised. He made an engagement of little more value, in reference to Gibraltar, undertaking not to oppose the amicable restitution of that port and of Port Mahon, to forward it by his good offices as they should be needed, and even by his mediation, if it were required. That he should render help by force was out of the question.

The treaty of alliance of which this engagement was a principal clause, was kept secret but the two others became public. They created a stir in Europe, for they entirely reversed the public situation. An alliance of Spain and Austria had been regarded as impossible ever since the death of Charles II. There were attempts to account for the sudden change; and since the treaties were obviously disadvantageous to Spain, they were believed to be incomplete in their revealed form, and to contain secret articles favourable to that country. An answer to the riddle was provided by the rumour of a marriage between Don Carlos and Maria Theresa. [1] There were prophecies of the union of the Imperial and Spanish crowns in the house of Anjou, probably in the person of Don Carlos.

Certainties and possibilities, seemed alike to menace England and France, and especially England. The alliance was directly contrary to her interests, first and foremost because it transformed her relations with Spain. She had by the treaty of 1721, won back from that power the commercial privileges lost by the war of the Quadruple Alliance, but only after a promise made by George I. that the question of the restitution of Gibraltar should be laid before Parliament. But the English court had been disinclined to fulfil this promise, and had hoped to put an end to the pressure exerted to such end by flattering Elizabeth and driving Spain to Italy. [2] This policy had been followed by England ever since 1721, but was made impossible by the agreement between Spain and the Emperor. It became indubitable that the demand for Gibraltar would be revived, and that its cession would be rendered a condition of the continuance of privileges.

The English considered that these privileges were otherwise threatened, in that the most favoured nation treatment, enjoyed by them in the Spanish colonies, had, as they held, been infringed by the treaty of commerce, [3] especially by its supposed secret articles, which they believed to have given to the Ostend Company the right to send ships to the South Sea. [4] Their supposition affected their policy none the less because it was mistaken.

They made a second error, in ascribing to the Emperor the origin of the new alliance, in supposing that by a promise of giving Maria Theresa to Don Carlos, he had bribed Spain to favour his Ostend Company, at the expense of England. [5] The English Court

---

[1] Syveton, *op. cit.* 121.
[2] Ibid: 22—3.
[3] Leadam, *History of England* 1702—1760, 324.
[4] *Notes of Sir Peter King* (published by Lord Peter King in the 2nd volume of his *Life of John Locke*), 25.
[5] Ibid: 14, 21, 26.

was much incensed against him, and issued to St. Saphorin directions, which caused him to express in violent terms, resentment of the conduct of the Emperor, whom he charged with ingratitude, and to protest that England would never suffer her commercial interests in Spain thus to be injured. [1]) St. Saphorin had his orders from Townshend, who was foreign secretary to the northern department and the most indignant of the indignant. In his anger, he went so far as to conceive the idea of depriving the Emperor of the Southern Netherlands, and dividing them between France, England and the Republic. The scheme was of course too wild for serious consideration, but its existence proved that the Emperor was being regarded as detached from England, who no longer deemed that his Low Countries were a safeguard to her security and liberty.

Every result of the war of the Spanish Succession, seemed to be in danger. The possession of Gibraltar and Port Mahon, was to be disputed, commercial privileges were menaced, and no reliance could any longer be placed on the Southern Netherlands. England was threatened by the dangers of 1701, those contingent on the granting of advantages by Spain, and on the disposal of the Southern Netherlands, contrary to her interest. The difference in the situation was indifferent to England: it lay in the circumstance that Austria had replaced France as the power which stood to profit by the favour of Spain. The parallel can be extended. As in 1701 the union of Spain and France, so at this time that of Spain and Austria, seemed to endanger the balance of power in Europe on which depended the safety of England, and therefore such union could not be suffered. England under William III., had indeed sided with Spain and Austria, but those countries had then been weak, while France was alarmingly powerful. Their combined strength had become such, that in them the menace to Europe was now found. In that earlier time, Spain had seemed to acquiesce in her commercial dependence on England and the Republic, and Austria to have no maritime ambition, but the nations had come together, apparently for the purpose of inflicting a sensible blow on the trade of England, that trade which was most dear to her, and to attack which, as an English minister said to the imperial ambassador, "catching at the eyes of the nation."[2])

---

[1]) Pribram, *op. cit.* I, 448.
[2]) Syveton, *op. cit.* 120.

The Court was from the first firmly determined to withstand such attacks. The Emperor invited the King to accede to the treaties of Vienna, and at the same time, proposed to settle all his differences with Spain, particularly those concerned with Gibraltar and Port Mahon. The King answered that he knew of no differences with Spain, which in view of his friendship with that country, could not be terminated, without the intervention of any other prince. He refused to accede to the treaties, because they had been made without his participation. [1])

The King was in truth still on good terms with Spain, for that power had as yet made no breach in their mutual relations. After the rupture with France, she had declared, that she would still recognize his mediation, if he disassociated himself from France, and Philip himself had professed to Stanhope, a desire for a closer union. [2]) George I. had declined the post of sole mediation, thereby ending the Congress of Cambrai; yet Spain, who still hoped to gain Gibraltar by the help of her new ally, did not proceed against him. England meanwhile supported the efforts of France for a reconciliation with Spain.

This was the first expedient which France adopted, in order to overcome the difficulties caused by the rejection of the Infanta. Louis XV. had moved in such direction before the conclusion of the treaties of Vienna, and he continued on his course. It was a strange policy, first in the most offensive manner, without any step being taken to soften the blow, to send back the Infanta; and immediately afterwards to try and undo the consequences. The French ministers, especially Bourbon and Fleury, were at variance, and wavering and unsteady conduct was the result. Horace Walpole, Robert's brother, who was ambassador at Paris at the time, did his utmost to bring them to vigour and resolution, but he did not succeed, until Spain had answered decisively. [3]) Louis XV. made use of various channels, among others that of Stanhope's influence, in order to gain his ends with their Catholic Majesties; but all was in vain for they set their claim to compensation for the insult they had suffered too high.

The Spanish rulers spoke openly at the same time to England.

---

[1]) King, *Notes*, 14, 21—7, cf. Syveton, *op. cit.* 104 and 154, note.
[2]) Coxe, *R. W.* I, 238.
[3]) Coxe, *H. W.* 98—9.

Since they could no longer hope to gain Gibraltar peaceably, by means of the Emperor's intervention, they applied directly to England, and claimed immediate restitution. Stanhope answered, that as the King was abroad in Hanover, the Houses could not at once meet to discuss the matter, but Elizabeth retorted that the King could return for the purpose of convening Parliament. [1]

Thus provoked George I. ordered Horace Walpole to enquire what steps France would take if England were attacked in her possession. The French Court was at length brought to a resolute attitude. Spain was seen to be indissolubly linked with the Emperor, a union which boded no good for France, and which that country had for two centuries combatted, and had, as she thought, ended for ever by the burdensome war of the Spanish Succession. Its revival was a danger to France, who had become great only after the two countries involved, had been weakened, and whose aims it contravened, in that it excluded her from any influence in Italy; and in that the Spanish guarantee of the Pragmatic Sanction ran counter to her designs with regard to the Austrian Succession. It affected also her commercial interests, for the rupture rendered uncertain the delivery to French subjects of their share in the Spanish expeditions to the West Indies.

No resource was left to her but to accept the friendship of England. Bourbon replied to Horace Walpole, that Louis XV. would if necessary take measures to keep Gibraltar in the hands of England, and to secure the commercial privileges enjoyed by the English in Spain. [2] Thus the policy of France became fixed: she knit more closely her alliance with England, which had been loosened by the death of Orleans, although, owing to the common love of peace, not broken. The two countries had now been thrown back on each other, by the union of Spain and Austria. England had, without a moment's hesitation, at once decided on her course, [3] and she had been successful in gaining France.

She gained the adherence of another power, of Prussia. Frederick William had a scruple against acting in opposition to the head of the Empire, but this was overcome by English diplomacy. His concurrence in the Treaty of Hanover, which was the

[1]) Baudrillart, *op. cit.* III, 192—204; Syveton, *op. cit.* 124—5; King, *Notes*, 14, 21—7.
[2]) Baudrillart, *op. cit.* III. 204.
[3]) *English Historical Review*, XV, 490—1.

result of the negotiations of the three powers, was due to two causes. The first was his desire, henceforth paramount in his policy, to secure on the death of the Elector Palatine and the latter's brothers, the succession to the Duchies of Juliers and Bergh. His claim was disputed by the Prince of Pfalz-Sulzbach, who was supported by the Elector; but now by a secret article in the treaty, he secured the promise of England and France to favour his pretensions and to promote their submission to the arbitration of impartial powers. His second motive was the fear, engendered by the alliance of the Emperor and Spain, and the anticipated marriages, which were its probable consequence, that the Emperor would become too powerful in the Empire, and that Roman Catholicism would be even more arrogant than it had been of late years. [1]) In view of the religious disorders, which had in the preceding year disturbed the town of Thorn in Poland, the King of Prussia insisted that the Treaty of Oliva should be guaranteed to him, [2]) and he also obtained from the contracting powers, a confirmation of the Treaty of Westphalia.

This alliance sealed by the Treaty of Hanover, gives indeed the impression of a particular regard for the interests of the Empire, [3]) and therefore it was deemed Hanoverian, by the Opposition in Parliament. The opinion is refuted by the fact that the Hanoverian ministers of George I. did not favour it. Its anti-imperial character was not due to them, but to Townshend, the father of the alliance, who was, as has been said, greatly incensed against the Emperor. Robert Walpole, it is worthy of note, did not agree with him in this respect, for he considered that commercial privileges were the principal issue, and that the main direction of policy should not have been against Austria. This difference in outlook was later of much consequence. [4])

Although it made no express mention of the Treaty of Vienna, that of Hanover, which was signed on September 3rd 1725, aimed at opposing all its real and suspected designs. The contracting powers guaranteed to each other all their possessions and rights, particularly those which concerned trade. The ostensible motive

---

[1]) Ranke, *Zwölf Bücher Preuszischer Geschichte*, III—IV, 46.
[2]) Förster, *Friedrich Wilhelm I*, II, 58.
[3]) cf. Syveton, *op. cit.* 139.
[4]) Leadam, *op. cit.* 324—5; Mahon, *op. cit.* II, 85—8; Coxe, *R. W.* I 246—50, *Engl. Hist. Review* XV, 673—4; Ward, *Great Britain and Hanover*, 126—7.

of their association, was the maintenance of public security and
the balance of power; and thus a check was given to all project
of conquest, entertained by the allies of Vienna, and to the supposed matrimonial scheme, while commercial rights were vindicat-
ed. It was stipulated also, that none of the parties should separately negotiate or enter into engagements with other powers,
and thus they were excluded from the alliance of Vienna.

The first sequel of the Treaty of Hanover was to strengthen the
bond between Austria and Spain. In April, the Emperor had gone
no further than to promise one of his daugthers in marriage to
one of the Infants, and Ripperda had been momentarily satisfied, although he had remained in Vienna, after the conclusion of
the treaties, in the hope of obtaining more. He had been unsuccessful, for the Emperor scrupled to enter into further engagements, and Elizabeth already began to show herself more reasonably disposed towards England. [1]) Ripperda and Elizabeth then
found a way out of their difficulties, by the Treaty of Hanover;
for after this, the Emperor yielded to persuasion. He declared, that
two of the three Archduchesses should marry Don Carlos and
Don Philip, and Maria Theresa, Don Carlos, in case her father died
before she reached the age of puberty. This was a clear engagement, only in the event of the early death of Charles VI., and even
so, it was subjected to restrictions, which left room for subterfug-
es. The second part of the Convention, dated the fifth of November 1725, was much clearer, for it provided, that the Emperor
and the King of Spain should assist each other whenever occasion might arise, with all their resources, by land and sea. This
was the most clear alliance imaginable; [2]) and there were several
provisions for the case of a war with the allies of Hanover, almost
all of which favoured the Emperor. He was authorised to claim Spanish subsidies, not only if war occurred, but also if war threatened.

Europe was divided into two camps. That party must largely
predominate which was most successful in finding allies.

II.

The Treaty of Hanover contained an express stipulation, that
the Republic should be asked to become a party to it. From the

[1]) King, *Notes.* 23—4.
[2]) Syveton, *op. cit.* 146.

outset this had been the intention of England, and there is no doubt but that Townshend and Broglie, the French ambassador who followed the English Court to Hanover, had discussed the matter with the leaders of the Republic, when during their journey they touched at the Hague. [1] The Dutch had as much cause for alarm, as the English and French; for their commercial privileges in Spain, and their military and economic position in the Southern Netherlands were endangered, and, above all, the Ostend Company threatened to become yet more potent for injury, by virtue of the support and protection of Spain.

To hinder this latter contingency, the East and West India Companies memorialized the States, requesting the suppression of the enterprise of their rival of Ostend, which had in some sort been legalized by the treaties of Vienna. [2] The States did their utmost: they instructed Van der Meer and Hamel Bruynincx, their ambassadors at Madrid and Vienna, to protest and to claim redress of grievances; [3] and they issued an edict most prejudicial to the Belgians, particularly to their salt trade. [4]

To have resort to force unaided, was impossible to them; and therefore it might be supposed that they would immediately accede to the request of the allies of Hanover, and enter into their compact. They, however, made objections, and this Huisman ascribes to the bad condition of the army and navy, and of finance, to the defects of the governing machinery, and finally to a desire to make certain of the profits of the alliance. [5] These factors had in truth some force in the deliberations which took place, as to the wisdom of adhering to it, but they were mainly governed by the desire of the Dutch to secure absolutely the suppression of the Ostend Company.

Huisman has overlooked this circumstance, almost of necessity, as the consequence of his point of view. In his opinion, the Company of Ostend was the initial point, from which the states formed into the two groups of Vienna and Hanover, and it was to be the *casus belli* of the following year. [6] This theory we reject.

---

[1] Syveton, *op. cit.* 123.
[2] Huisman, *op. cit.* 332.
[3] Wagenaar, *op. cit.* XVIII. 314—8.
[4] Huisman (*op. cit.* 334) is mistaken in calling this a notorious infraction of the barrier-treaty. Cf. App.
[5] Huisman, *op. cit.* 333—4.
[6] Ibid: 354.

Too much significance has, we believe, been given to the part played by the Ostend Company in the negotiations of this period. Ward has gone so far as to make the Company responsible for the break-up of the Congress of Cambrai, [1]) a most false allegation, since the matter was never brought forward at the Congress. Undoubtedly it was the main issue to the Belgians and the Dutch, but not to either of the alliances as a whole.

Of the allies of Vienna, Spain cared nothing for the Ostend Company, as will appear, if her conduct of this year be compared with what she had observed a year previously. Then, in a memorial to the English Court, she had sought the destruction of the Company as being illegal; now she recognised and favoured it. She was consistent in an attempt to embroil England and the Emperor, but whilst she opposed the Emperor in 1724, she sided with him in 1725, and her changed attitude resulted. Spain's support of the Ostend trade was indeed a strong inducement, although only one of several, to the Emperor to come to terms with her; but even had it as such been paramount and isolated, the allies of Vienna could not have been said to have been brought together by the Ostend Company, for it would so have influenced only one of them.

There remains the question whether common hatred of the Company impelled to union the allies of Hanover, England, France and Prussia. The supposition is ridiculous in the case of Prussia, and, as has been shown, England and France had hitherto left the Republic to struggle alone. She had applied to them three times, but although they had given her some satisfaction, they had never made her cause theirs, and before the treaties of Vienna, their help had seldom been more than words. That these treaties made of the Company a common stumbling-block, no more objectionable to the Dutch than to the other two powers, was not true in the case of France, nor, as we think, in that of England. For England did not resent the existence of the Company. She feared and complained only of its supersession of herself in the Spanish colonies [2]) and therefore her opposition to it was limited

---

[1]) Ward, *op. cit.* 125.
[2]) King, *Notes* 25; Leadam, *op. cit.* 324; Pribram, *op. cit.* I 448, 449; Ranke, *op. cit.* III—IV, 44, 59; Horace Walpole, "Considérations qui peuvent servir *et. seq.*" in Townshend's letter to Finch, 5 Sep. 1727, R. O. Hl. 294; cf. Huisman, *op. cit.* 357; Dureng, *op. cit.* 287.

to an endeavour to obtain satisfaction on this one point. That such opposition actually continued until the very suppression of the Company, was due to a change in the general political situation, which made the concurrence of the Republic indispensable to her.

It was indispensable in regard to both the allies of Vienna; and to Spain, because, as has been explained, the English could never be persuaded to enter on a war, which might injure their trade, without the Dutch; and to the Emperor, because no reliance could any longer be placed in him where the Southern Netherlands were concerned, and thus, in reference to them, the Republic was in England's estimation raised from secondary to primary importance.

This need of England for the support of the Republic made the latter country more valuable to France. For England was no longer ascendant in the French Court, as she had been in the years of Orleans, when relations between the two powers had been very intimate. They had become loosened, as has been said, after the death of Orleans, [1]) and although the Austro-Spanish union knit them more closely, [2]) the French ministers remained aware of the divergence in the interests of France and of England, and therefore to avoid complete dependence on England they sought the friendship of the Republic.

Solicited by England and solicited by France, the Republic was wise enough not to accede at once to the Treaty of Hanover. She wished first, absolutely to secure the suppression of the Ostend Company, [3]) and taught by many disappointments, she would be content with nothing short of an express engagement. When therefore, the ambassadors of the three allied powers tendered their invitation to the States, these enquired whether the Republic would be guaranteed in her right of exclusive trade with the Indies, in accordance with the Treaty of Munster, and whether difficulties, which might arise from her defence of such monopoly, would be considered a *casus foederis*. The questions were worded with a view to obtaining, in the least offensive manner possible, the suppression of the Ostend Company. [4])

---

[1]) cf. p. 76.
[2]) cf. p. 86.
[3]) Wagenaar, *op. cit.* XVIII, 323; our narrative of her entering into the treaty has been principally drawn from this work and those of Huisman and Rive.
[4]) Fagel to Goslinga, 30 Nov. 1725, F. G.

Fénelon, the French ambassador, soon gave every satisfaction. He formally declared his master's willingness to give a guarantee which would safeguard the Republic's rights according to the Treaty of Munster, and render her secure as to the financial obligations towards her of the Southern Netherlands. At the same time the English ambassador, Finch, gave an assurance that George I. would in every respect support the rights of the States to the India trade. Thus the two powers yielded to the representations of the Republic, and Goslinga who had written with reference to the Ostend affair, shortly after the conclusion of the Vienna alliance, "Je n'y vois point de jour à moins que la France et l'Angleterre ne se brouillent avec l'Empereur" [1]) was justified. That which no pressure from the Republic had been able to effect, was brought about by the needs of England and France for her co-operation. Ripperda had in spite of himself rendered an important service to his native country by the conclusion of the treaties of Vienna, for in order to obtain the adherence of the Republic, England and France professed themselves as being quite willing to destroy the Ostend Company.

It was this willingness which drew her to accede to the Hanover Treaty. Slingelandt was fully entitled to write afterwards: "l'abolition de la navigation d'Ostende aux Indes a été la principale amorce et, l'on peut dire, le principal motif qui a determiné l'Etat à accéder au traité de Hanovre." [2]) Satisfied as she was by England and France, her further delay of some ten months was due to the third power with which she had to deal, Prussia.

The King of Prussia, unlike his allies, would not give a separate declaration against the Ostend Company. He would not thus prefer Dutch interests to those of the Emperor's subjects, but insisted that the States should accept the treaty in the form, so inadequate to their desires, in which it was first offered to them. It included, as has been stated, a confirmation of the Treaty of Oliva, inserted at his instance, and to this the States objected, as also, to the clause concerned with the Peace of Westphalia, by which they feared being involved in many new difficulties. The separate article as to Juliers and Bergh, was kept from them by

---

[1]) Goslinga to Vegelin van Claerbergen, 7 June 1725, F. G.
[2]) Slingelandt to Goslinga, 21 July 1728, R. A. Hl. 2974; cf. Wagenaar *op. cit.* XVIII, 387.

the contracting powers, [1]) with good reason, since the States already demurred at the mutual guarantee clause, not only for possessions, but also for rights, immunities and advantages, in fear that it would secure to Frederick the succession he claimed in those Duchies. The provinces that had William of Nassau-Friesland as Stadtholder, had a special reason for objecting to this clause, as it might imply an acknowledgement of the King's claim to William III's inheritance, as to which he was at variance with that young Prince. [2]) In this matter the Stadtholder had the support of the other provinces however little they might otherwise favour his interests, for it happened that several of the territories and possessions of the House of Orange lay near the frontier of the Republic on either side of it, and that certain of them had already been occupied by Frederick William, in spite of a provisory agreement with the States General who had been appointed executors of the will. [3]) It was his aim to extend as much as possible, the land acquired by Prussia on the Rhine and the Meuse in the 17th century, and by the Peace of Utrecht in the beginning of his reign, and in this district he had already given the Republic some trouble by the erection of new tolls on the Meuse, by advancing several disputable financial claims, and by various devices for extorting money. He had no regard whatever for the Republic, for her army was small and decayed, and his principal care was for armies. His professions of friendship were no more than words [4]) The Republic had naturally no desire that his power on her frontier should increase: and although formerly [5]) she had supported the Protestant Hohenzollern against the Catholic Pfalz-Neuburg, religious considerations were now outweighed by fear; [6]) and her leaders, particularly Fagel, retained so little trust for the King, that they were fearful of the eventuality of a war against the Emperor, which would bring his troops into the Southern Netherlands. [7])

---

[1]) Ranke, *op. cit.* III—IV, 52.
[2]) Slothouwer, *Sicco van Goslinga*, 145—6.
[3]) Rive, *op. cit.* 90.
[4]) Rive, *op. cit.* 86—98.
[5]) In the years 1609—1614.
[6]) Fagel once wrote to Goslinga (F. G., the letter undated): "On ne peut désavouer qu'un tel Roi(with such a splendid army and a well-filled exchequer) ne soit redoutable Je souhaiterais que la République fût en état de ne pas le redouter."
[7]) Fagel to Goslinga, 30 Nov. 1725, F. G.

The Court of Vienna attempted to make profit out of this discord by representing to the Republic the danger of suffering the
Duchies of Juliers and Bergh to fall to Frederick William, and
by tendering thanks at the same time to Frederick William for
his conduct with regard to the Ostend trade. [1] The insinuations
of the Emperor counted for little with the Republic, as compared
with his simultaneous and unsatisfactory proposals with regard
to the Ostend Company, for he was only willing to limit the number of places with which the Company might trade, the kinds of
merchandise they might import from India, and the number of
their ships which might ply thither; but the Republic could be
satisfied with no less than total suppression. Had he subscribed
to this in time, he would probably have obtained a modification
of the barrier treaty, favourable to his financial obligations; [2]
but the success of any of his proposals had been rendered impossible by the cordial declaration of Fénelon, supported by Finch.
That he alternated a conciliatory attitude with menaces, did not
inspire the Republic with confidence in his intentions; and moreover, any good effect which he produced was cancelled by the
vacillating conduct of Ripperda, at this time Prime Minister of
Spain, who at one time by a threatening and peremptory note,
supported the representations of the Austrian envoy at the
Hague, Königsegg-Erps, and at another revealed to Stanhope and
Van der Meer the existence of an offensive alliance between his
master and thie Emperor, by which the latter guaranteed the
restitution of Gbraltar, by force of arms if necessary, and the
former engaged at all cost to maintain the Ostend Company. [3]

The main difficulties were not external, but internal. There was
in addition to the dislike and fear of Prussia, a rather strong discontent with England, whose treason at the end of the war of the
Spanish Succession, was still distinctly present in the mind. [4] In
general, the conduct of England had not been fitted to efface this
impression, and therefore it was hard for the Ministers of the Republic to win over the members of the government to the policy
of acceding to the alliance. "Les ministres travailleraient avec

---

[1] Ranke, *op. cit.* III—IV, 57.
[2] cf. Fenelon, *op. cit.* 142.
[3] Huisman, *op. cit.* 342—50.
[4] Slingelandt to Goslinga, 25 June 1726, F. G.; Slingelandt to Townshend, 18 Feb.
1727, R. O. Hl. 297.

plus de succès auprès de bien des gens, si chez vous on avait un peu plus d'égard aux sollicitations des ministres sur plusieurs articles touchant lesquels tout le monde ici est persuadé que la Grande Bretagne nous traite, je ne dis pas contre l'amitié, dont on fait de temps en temps des protestations si fortes, mais contre la justice et contre le retour que meritent les signalés services que la République a rendus à la Grande Bretagne dans les temps qu'-elle était mieux en état de servir ses alliés." Thus Slingelandt wrote to Townshend. [1] He does not specify the points in which England had disappointed the Republic, but it appears elsewhere that the English Court was unwilling to settle the differences between the States and Denmark [2], and that Algerian and Moroccan piracy, so injurious to Dutch trade in the Mediterranean, was countenanced from Gibraltar and Port Mahon. [3]

If credence is to be given to Fénelon, who however is not always reliable on the subject of Anglo-Dutch relations, this distrust of England gave rise to a good deal of trouble in the province of Holland. He states that the town of Amsterdam was, in virtue of a particular interest in the destruction of the Ostend Company, opposed to any clause which should limit the power of the Dutch companies to injure Belgian ships. The other towns had domestic causes for opposition to Amsterdam, and they also feared an outbreak of a war, not by common consent, but by means of hostilities at sea, secretly concerted between Amsterdam and the English government. They therefore insisted on a clause by which all measures against the Ostend ships must follow deliberations by the allies, and receive their common consent. Amsterdam was obliged to give way, the more so, because several provinces, which owing to their situation were peculiarly exposed to the Emperor's wrath, wished to be certain of French help in case of a rupture. [4]

This dispute is said to have retarded by several months the

---

[1] 18 Apr. 1726. R. O. Hl. 280.

[2] With regard to these differences Fagel wrote in 1723 to Goslinga (22 June, F. G.): "certaines gens agissent comme s'ils aimeraient plutot se noyer que d'être secourus par la Grande Bretagne, tant l'animosité ou la passion parait grande."

[3] The States wanted England and France to take common action with them against that piracy. This was declined (Wagenaar, *op. cit.* XVIII, 358, 388—9) This affair is said to have retarded the accession of the States to the treaty for three months (Chesterfield to Harrington, 1 May 1731, R. O. Hl. 312).

[4] Fénelon, *op. cit.* 128—30.

decision of Holland. That province passed its resolution on February 8th 1726; Zealand, Friesland, and Overijsel in March; and
Guelders in the beginning of April. But the consent of all of them
to an entrance into the alliance was conditional, modified by several additional demands and restrictions. The States desired
that their adherence should depend first on a guarantee of the
India trade and exclusion from the scope of the treaty of debat-
able possessions and rights, if possible on a weakening of the
undertaking, as to the treaties of Oliva and Westphalia, on the
co-operation with themselves of France and England in action
against the Mediterranean pirates, on the mediation of the allies
in general, with reference to Denmark, and on their promise of
immediate support in case the Republic were threatened or attacked. [1]

France and England were inclined to meet the Republic half
way: they held to their declaration as to the India trade, and promised all imaginable assistance in any time of danger for the
Republic; but they withheld their concurrence where Algiers
and Denmark were concerned, alleging that these matters were
foreign to the Treaty of Hanover, and they were unwilling to
disoblige the King of Prussia, by restricting his possessions and
rights, and by omitting the guarantee of the treaties of Oliva and
Westphalia. The Prussian King was himself inflexible; he would
not commit himself beyond the provisions of the treaty, as these
had been communicated to the States.

Negotiations were still dragging out a tedious course when two
important changes in the situation took place. The Prime Ministers of both Spain and France were deprived of office, Ripperda
first and Bourbon shortly afterwards. The consequent uncertainty was unfavourable to a final decision by the Republic; for a fear
arose that since Fleury had replaced Bourbon, who had sent back
the Infanta to her country, Spain and France might be reconciled,
and France thus detached from the alliance of Hanover.

In these circumstances, Goslinga in a letter to Slingelandt advised waiting on the course of events, the more since "our good
friends the English" shewed so little disposition to yield the two
points regarding Algiers and Denmark. [2] Slingelandt's answer

---

[1] Wagenaar. *op. cit.* XVIII, 356—8.
[2] Slothouwer, *Sicco van Goslinga*, 146—7.

was no less clear than strong. "For aught I know, the change of ministers in France and Spain will not entail any alteration of politics. Spain, ruled by the Queen, will hold fast to the Emperor, who will do all the injury in his power to England, the Republic and the Protestants, and will gain ground if we suffer him to have his way, and do not, in as far as we are able, follow the example of France and England. It may be, if Spain break her engagements with the Emperor, that France will be reconciled to her; but for the rest France will follow her own maxims, which clash directly with those of the House of Austria. Without Bourbon, Fleury will be what he was in the time of that statesman's ministry: he then guided the King as he will continue to do. This is a conclusion as apparent and as near to certainty as is possible in the realm of politics, and should therefore, as it seems to me, be acted upon, but always without losing sight of that uncertainty which belongs to things temporal, but which should not prevent us from ranging ourselves definitely with a party. It is more than time for us to take this step if we do not wish to vex our friends, and to make ourselves supremely and universally contemptible. It is useless for us to cling until the winter to the equivocal attitude which we have hitherto maintained. If France leave us against the principles of good policy, we may yet spare ourselves the reproach of having failed to do our utmost to avert such a disaster. At all events we shall have done no harm, if we have drawn closer the bonds of friendship and mutual defence which unite the Republic, Great Britain, and Prussia. We shall at least not err if we place ourselves, in this critical time in which we seem to distrust almost everyone, into a state of defence, and thus avoid the mistake of Pompey, who flattered himself that he had but to stamp his foot in order to raise an army which could oppose Julius Caesar. I know how little we are able for extraordinary expenses, but can they be avoided without staking our all, or by delaying longer our entry into the treaty? It is true, that England treats us ill in several respects; and I am so far from being her apologist that my lord Townshend's discontent with my urgent reproaches, as to the failure of the English cabinet to satisfy either justice or gratitude, does not date only from this winter. Yet, apart from the allowance to be made for exaggeration, it is incontestable that the late behaviour of the Republic to

7

England, all the chicanery made with regard to the treaty of Hanover, the jealous and distrustful talk which can be heard every day, all this is not calculated ardently to interest the English in our affairs. The English are men as we are." [1]

Again, as when their country was asked to enter the Quadruple Alliance, Slingelandt and Goslinga held contrary opinions. This time however, Goslinga did not prevail: otherwise the Republic would not have acceded to the alliance. [2] Circumstances had altered in the six or seven years which had passed: the danger to trade had so gravely increased, that to avert it had become necessary, and for this the friendship of England and France was required.

There were, as has been said, many fears that France would withdraw her proffers, but the event justified Slingelandt's predictions, for Fleury firmly adhered to the Treaty of Hanover. This comforting news at last brought the affair to its consummation. The province of Holland resolved to accept the treaty on the terms to which England and France had agreed; and within some weeks, the other provinces followed Holland's example, not excepting, this time, Groningen. Only Utrecht still hesitated, yet did not prevent the accession of the Republic to the Treaty of Hanover on August 9th 1726.

This entrance into the alliance of one power however, caused the defection of another. The difficulties with Prussia had not been settled, and therefore the Prussian envoy had no authority to subscribe to the arrangement. His master was far from willing to enter into an engagement against the Ostend Company; for although, owing to his fear that the imperial power might increase unduly, he had been persuaded to join in the Treaty of Hanover, he was yet unprepared in any circumstances himself to attack the Emperor. It wounded him deeply that the other allies had aims not communicated to him. He refused the position of a "secondary" or "subaltern" [3]), yet as such he had been treated; and the States which he had so slighted had been preferred to him. He applied to England, who informed him that she could not do without the help of the Republic, which could only

---

[1]) Slingelandt to Goslinga, 25 June 1726, F. G.
[2]) Slothouwer, *Sicco van Goslinga*, 143 *et. seq.*
[3]) L. von Ranke, *Zwölf Bücher Preuszischer Geschichte* III—IV, p. 52. *et seq.*

be obtained by a promise to suppress the Ostend Company. [1]
He objected to this engagement, the more so, because he could
hope for nothing from the Republic in the matter of his dearest
aims, especially his succession to the Duchies of Juliers and Bergh.
He considered that he had been deceived by England and France,
and therefore was easily gained by the Emperor. Although he
did not formally leave his allies, nor accede to the Treaty of Vienna, yet he was lost to the alliance of Hanover.

The Austrian Court won over some other princes of the Empire,
the Elector Palatine, the Electors of Treves, Bavaria and Cologne, and the Duke of Brunswick-Wolfenbuttel. The Elector
Palatine, and the Elector of Bavaria, had also been eagerly solicited by George I., who tried to gain the alliance of several German
princes [2] and succeeded in concluding a treaty of subsidy with
the Landgrave of Hesse-Cassel.

The policies of Austria and England were in conflict not only
within the Empire, but also in northern Europe. It was the constant object of Peter the Great in the last years of his reign to
restore to his son-in-law, Charles Frederick of Holstein-Gottorp,
the Duchy of Schleswig, which that Prince had been deprived of
in favour of Denmark, and to this end he persuaded Sweden into
an alliance. When soon afterwards, he died, the Tsarina, Kathe-
rine I., adopted his aim. She was supported by the Emperor, who
was admitted into the Russo-Swedish alliance; she had a fleet,
fully equipped, with which to attack the Danes. But the English
Court defeated her scheme; for England had guaranteed Schleswig to Denmark, and was forced to maintain Denmark's right
to the province, because the question was "inextricably mixed
up" with that of the cession of Bremen and Verden. [3] Decisive
measures were therefore taken: a squadron was sent to the Baltic, to prevent the Russian ships from sailing, and a sum of
£ 50,000 was judiciously distributed among the Swedish senators.
The Tsarina was incensed against those who had thus thwarted
her, and entered the Vienna alliance on August 6th 1726. Sweden
was however detached from her, and in the following spring joined the Allies of Hanover at much the same time as that at which
Denmark concluded a treaty with England and France.

---

[1] Rive, *op. cit.* 108.

[2] Arneth, *Prinz Eugen*, III, 193; Rosenlehner, *Karl Philipp*, 146, 107—13.

[3] *Engl. Hist. Review.* XV, 680.

III.

In spite of vigorous efforts made by both sides to procure allies, no general war resulted. It was prevented by the varying dispositions which prevailed in either camp.

Of the allies of Vienna, Spain desired war eagerly. Elizabeth had not yet reached the fulfilment of her ambition, the betrothal of Maria Theresa to Don Carlos, and she could exact it from the Emperor, only in time of war, when he would stand in need of her services. Seeing that the very conclusion of the Treaty of Hanover had helped her to the convention of November 5th, it was inevitable that a war would much more advance her purpose. Ripperda concurred in this opinion, and intended to kindle the war as soon as he returned to Spain. When however he did actually return, and moreover reached the position of universal minister of the kingdom, and found Spain anything but prepared for war, he shrank from the enterprise. He endeavoured to gain time, and entered into several negotiations with the object of dividing England and France, and preventing the Republic from becoming a party to the Treaty of Hanover. His irregular conduct however, his boasts, his lies, and above all his confidences to the ambassadors of the Maritime Powers, frustrated all his designs; and in view of the ardent bellicosity of Philip and Elizabeth, war seemed inevitable.

But the Emperor was otherwise disposed, for he saw clearly that he had nothing to gain by a war which would ruin his Ostend Company and force him to give Maria Theresa to Don Carlos. He therefore sought to influence Spain for peace, even by covert hints at a reconciliation with France. He aimed at a diplomatic victory, obtained by gaining the support of so many powers that he could dictate to the others. He spoke of war only in order to extract money from Spain, and this he did successfully, in spite of the delays and obstacles which Ripperda put forward. That minister's fall strengthened rather than weakened the bonds between Spain and Austria; and a similar event which took place some weeks later at the Court of France seemed to give the mastery to the Emperor's policy.

Bourbon was obliged to resign, and his place was taken by Fleury. Since it was Bourbon, who against Fleury's advice, had sent

away the Infanta, the principal objection of Spain to a reconciliation was removed, and the French Court seemed to desire it
eagerly. All Europe expected Fleury to turn from the alliance of
Hanover, to that of Vienna; and there was joy in Spain and Austria, and corresponding fear in England and the Republic.

The Republic at this time, June 1726, had, as has been said,
not yet completed her entry into the treaty. England ran the risk of
finding opposed to her, a triple alliance of France, Spain and Austria, which would undo all she had done. She had been from the
outset the moving spirit of the alliance of Hanover. She had exerted herself not only to gain, as has been related, the support
of the German princes and the Scandinavian powers, but also to
win over Turkey and Poland, and thus to surround the Emperor
with enemies. She had planned moreover to capture the Belgian
ships on their return to Ostend, [1]) and had sent a fleet to the West
Indies to lock up the Spanish galleons in an American harbour.

All her actions proved her absolute readiness for war, but this
remark could not be applied to the Duke of Bourbon. He had
never inclined to warlike measures, and had therefore seconded
only faintly, the efforts of England to unite as many powers as
possible against the Emperor. Sometimes he had even suffered
French diplomacy to thwart these efforts, [2]) and he had objected,
distinctly if timidly, to the action of England in sending her two
squadrons to the West Indies and the Baltic. The English government had however, an easy means of justification in the facts
confided by Ripperda, as to the contents of the Vienna treaties.
Bourbon, who also had begun preparations for war, had seen
that he must adhere to England, but he would have preferred that
Spain should join France in her alliance with England, rather than
that France should combine with England against Spain. He had
suggested this course to the Court at Madrid only some weeks
before his enforced resignation. [3])

Contrary to general expectation, his successor was equally
constant to England. Fleury had indeed great hopes of bringing
about the reconciliation with Spain, but he realized that France
would be at the mercy of the allies of Vienna, if she immediately

---

[1]) Slingelandt to Townshend, 18 April 1726, R. O. Hl. 280.
[2]) *Engl. Hist. Review.* XV, 681 *et. seq.*; cf. Coxe, *H. W.* 113.
[3]) Baudrillart, *op. cit.* III, 247—8.

turned from England to them. Therefore he abode by his engagements with England, yet he was in no mind to follow her, beyond the point to which French interests led. The Dukes of Orleans and Bourbon, had too often consulted their personal likes and dislikes. Bourbon had also lacked resolution: he had hesitated in indecision, and finally followed England, although at a distance. Fleury however wished France to consult her own interests [1]), and to take the lead in public affairs as far as was possible. For this it was necessary to adhere to the alliance of Hanover, but no less necessary to prevent a war which, as Fleury clearly saw, must both profit the Maritime Powers and render impossible the eagerly desired reconciliation with Spain.

Although he openly declared for the Treaty of Hanover, the allies of Vienna did not in the ensuing months omit trying to gain him over, not so much Spain as Austria .The first result of his declaration, was a nearer approach to the Emperor of Philip V., who refused to be reconciled to Louis XV., except through the mediation of the Emperor, and conditionally on the participation of France in the Alliance of Vienna. The Emperor's methods were more engaging: he did not ask France to abandon her allies, but offered to mediate for a reconciliation between her and Spain, and proposed a treaty with himself *de se mutuo non offendendo*. Fleury had wisdom to refuse both offers. He considered the suggestion of reconciliation to be an offensive interference of a stranger between uncle and nephew, and the treaty, a snare to entice him from his engagements. He was equally unbending in the matter of the Ostend trade. When the Dutch had acceded to the alliance, the Emperor saw at last that some concessions would have to be made to them, and he hoped by means of Fleury to bring them to accept a compromise. He shewed willingness to restrict the Ostend Company by reducing the number of their ships or limiting their trade to fixed places, and even offered to submit the dispute to the judgment of a committee. But Fleury stuck to his allies, to the Dutch no less than to the English. [2])

While thus his faithfulness was tried by the Emperor and by the King of Spain, that King was himself tempted to inconstancy,

---

[1]) cf. Bourgeois, *Manuel de Politique Etrangère* I, 467: "Ce fut la première fois depuis 1715 que le royaume ne fut plus gouverné par une faction."

[2]) Baudrillart, *op. cit.* III, 259—60; Huisman, *op. cit.* 406.

by England and by France. The English government itself, as has been said, was in favour of vigorous action, yet would not, and this was particularly the case with Robert Walpole, provoke a war without necessity; and therefore vigour was attended by moderation. Hosier had been despatched to the West Indies, but his instructions stringently forbade him to perform any hostile action; and similarly Stanhope was ordered to persuade the King of Spain into a separate agreement with the allies of Hanover, while at the same time, in August 1726, Jennings was sent to cruise round the Spanish coasts. These measures aimed at convincing the Court at Madrid, that a rupture with the Emperor was desirable and necessary, but they had an entirely different effect. The King of Spain promptly called upon the English Court to reveal its intentions, and he caused Fleury to be asked whether France would support Spain in case of an attack by England. [1]

Fleury had been consulted in the matters of the instructions to Stanhope and the despatch of Jenning's fleet. The fleet had been kept back for some months at his request, and at Madrid, Stanhope had spoken in the name of France also, who had not been officially represented there since the return of the Infanta. Fleury's answer to Philip's question was implied, in a proposal which he made himself. He had seen, and must have been confirmed in the view by Stanhope's ill-success, that for the time all efforts to detach Spain from Austria were vain. Therefore he strove to effect only a personal reconciliation, independent of respective engagements, in the belief that it would be followed by the desired rupture between Spain and the Emperor, and that on the rebound, Spain would inevitably draw near to England. This attempt also failed. Spain, as has been stated, made the reconciliation dependent on the Emperor's mediation, and the entrance of France into the alliance of Vienna. And the estrangement between Spain and England increased. The answer of George I. to the urgent representations of the Spanish Court gave little satisfaction, for it merely expressed astonishment at the form of those representations as entirely unjustifiable, since Jenning's instructions had been peaceable. Immediately after the receipt of this answer, on the 25th of September, Philip was ad-

---

[1] *Eng. Hist. Review* XVI, 74, 78—9; Coxe, *R. W.* I, 260; Baudrillart, *op. cit.* III, 266—269.

vised that Hosier was detaining the galleons, by blockading Porto-Bello. This act was in itself one of hostility, since English men-
of-war were not suffered near the coasts of Spanish America, [1]
and it so angered Philip, that immediately, on the 29th of September, he dismissed from his service all who favoured an approach
to England or France. Thus direct and indirect efforts had alike
completely failed to win him. [2]

Far from having become a friend, he seemed to be aiming at
war with England. La Paz informed Stanhope, that his King
would immediately take measures for the protection of his dominions and his subjects, if the English Court did not without delay procure for him just satisfaction, and Fleury was at the same
time requested to intimate similar intentions. The Cardinal was
in a very difficult position, the English government, on the other
hand, strongly urging him, to declare himself openly in favour
of England, since the English nation distrusted him. His allegiance did not waver, and he justified the acts of the English government to Spain, and let it be understood that he would fulfil
his obligations in case of a war. That war did not seem remote,
for England shewed an inclination, to claim from, rather than to
give, satisfaction to Spain, [3] and Spain in November 1726 gave
the first practical signs of her illwill by taking advantage of a
plague in the Levant, as an excuse for debarring English, French
and Dutch ships from Spanish ports. Soon afterwards, on December the 10th, La Paz handed to Stanhope a note which was tantamount to a declaration of war, and Pozzo-Bueno was instructed to
deliver it to the Government of England, and afterwards, without
waiting for an answer, to leave that country, to which he was accre-
dited. Preparations for a siege of Gibraltar had also been begun. [4]

In face of this provocation the English government was obliged to take up a firm attitude, especially in view of the condition
of the country. The uncertainty of commerce with Spain "which
at that time formed the most extensive branches of the national
trade," [5] exercised the worst effect upon business. "We must

---

[1] Syveton, *Une cour et un avanturier*, 238.
[2] Baudrillart, *op. cit.* III, 260 *et. seq.*, 267 *et. seq.*; *Eng. Hist. Rev. loc. cit.* cf. p. 104.
[3] Memorial of Stanhope to La Paz, 15 November 1726, Rousset *Recueil*, III 358 *et seq.*
[4] *Eng. Hist. Review* and Baudrillart, *op. cit., loc. cit.*
[5] Coxe, *R. W.* I, 260.

lose our trade or engage in a war" was a saying which embodied the common feeling. [1]) Voices rose against the cabinet more and more frequently, and even if it were only on this account, a show of vigour was necessary. It was intended to produce this at the opening of Parliament on the 28th of January 1727.

Thus at the beginning of this year war seemed inevitable. The allies of Hanover had naturally already taken such an eventuality into consideration. In November conferences between the deputies for foreign affairs and the ambassadors of France and England, for the discussion of necessary measures had been opened at the Hague. When the ambassadors pressed for information, as to the sentiments of the States with regard to the European situation in general, and the Ostend Company in particular, the Council of State was consulted, and that body replied with a remarkable piece of preliminary advice, which had proceeded from the pen of Slingelandt.

Since, it ran, it was most desirable that a peaceful settlement should be reached, a final representation should be made to the Court of Vienna, and perhaps also to that of Spain, asking for the revocation of the charter of the Ostend Company, and the redress of other infractions of the treaties. First however, the allies must determine the measures to be taken, in the event of a refusal and must, in particular, provide for the safety of the Republic. When, as was probable, the representation had failed, the Ostend ships must be captured and destroyed, wherever they were found, a matter comparatively easy. It would be a more difficult task to bring the Emperor to repeal the Company's charter, for instead, he would probably stop payment of the subsidy and interest, annually due from him to the Republic. Such a course would have to be considered a *casus foederis*, and thus compel the allies of Hanover to seek satisfaction for her. To do this they could not act against the Emperor in the Southern Netherlands, for these, as he well knew, would always be regarded by the Maritime Powers as their barrier, and returned to him at the conclusion of peace. They were equally debarred from hostility to him in Germany, where it would rouse the Empire against them. They could

---

[1]) Leadam, *op. cit.* 329; cf. Droysen, *Friedrich Wilhelm* I, I, 429.

[2]) cf. Prince Eugene to Walef, 1 January 1727 (Arneth, *Prinz Eugen*, III, 555—6); *Mémoires* de Villars, *sub dato* 1 Jan. 1727 (V. 41, cf. also p. 44); Rosenlehner, *Kurfürst Karl Philipp von der Pfalz*, 257.

therefore contribute to the objects of the allies only by an attack
in Italy, for which it was necessary to gain the King of Sardinia.
Action in Italy would have the further advantage of convincing
Spain that she would be better advised to combat the Emperor
rather than the King of England, for England only held some places,
which she had lost during the last war, as opposed to whole
countries, which had passed over to the Emperor. Probably however, this consideration would not suffice to draw her from her
dependence on the Emperor, on whom she squandered her treasure, and therefore she must be brought to a truer view of her
own interests, by attacks on her by land and by sea, in Europe and
in America, in addition to the action in Italy. [1]

Since at the French Court Slingelandt was considered to be
extremely devoted to England his advice was ascribed to English
influence, probably without foundation. Yet England approved
entirely of his views [2], and had in August acted consistently with
them in attempting to convince Spain of the necessity and desirability of a break with the Emperor, of the necessity, by means
of Jenning's fleet which cruised off Spain, and of the desirability,
by Stanhope's advocacy of Spanish interests in Italy. [3] Yet Spain
remained unconvinced; and since peaceable methods had been of
no avail, it was the opinion of the Maritime Powers that only war
could detach her from the Emperor.

Fleury was here at variance with the allies. His goal was theirs,
but his chosen path to it was that of peace. He desired first, to
bring about the reconciliation of the King with his uncle, and then
gradually, to loosen the bonds which bound Spain and Austria. It
was questionable whether circumstances would allow him to go
his own way; for England already urged him to declare war on
Spain, on the first outbreak of an attack on Gibraltar; and he himself intimated again and again to the Spanish Court, that if war
arose, France would join England. He did his utmost however to
prevent this eventuality. More than once he had already tried to
frustrate, or at least to delay, measures planned by England,[4]
and once again he failed to comply with her wishes. His motives
were strong. The miserable financial and economic condition

[1] Secr. Res. Hl. VII, 718—25.
[2] Villars, *Mémoires* V, 42—3; Townshend to Slingelandt, 10 Jan. 1727, R. O. Hl. 297.
[3] *Eng. Hist. Review*. XVI, 78—9.
[4] Ibid: 72, 78, 80.

of France made peace desirable to her; and moreover as "war with Austria would be without advantage, war with Spain would be against her clearest interests:" [1]) The reconciliation for which king and nation longed so eagerly would be for long rendered impossible by a war, and trade would be sensibly injured. Already the detention of the galleons had caused bankruptcies among the French merchants, whose goods they carried. [2]) Worst of all, while the advantages of war would be felt by France's Allies, its burdens would for the most part fall upon her. Slingelandt's forecast, and England's intentions, both involved France's attacking Spain with her principal forces, [3]) and when therefore the Emperor in consequence opened hostilities against her, she would at once be plunged in a serious war in which she could hope for but little help from the Allies. England would certainly make herself at least partially responsible for attack upon the Spanish monarchy by sea, but even though her fleet might be splendid, her land forces were very poor. As for the Republic, although at last, after much tergiversation, she had resolved on a rather considerable increase of troops, such additional forces were almost all required for the security of the country; and the conferences at the Hague made it clear beyond doubt, that the States intended to rely largely on France and England, in order to obtain their wishes. [4])

Thus France would have to wage a heavy war with little help from those on whose behalf she fought. Fleury could not take upon himself this responsibility. The nation already believed that he was entirely led by the English government. It was said that France was England's cat's-paw, and such views could not be disregarded, for they found supporters even in the King's council.[5]) Therefore, when Horace Walpole required of him a promise that he would join England so soon as Spain had opened the siege of Gibraltar, his position was a very difficult one. He candidly laid his embarrassments before Robinson, secretary to Walpole, who was at the time in London. Yet he undertook to do all that his position

[1]) Bourgeois, *Manuel* I, 475.
[2]) *Eng. Hist. Review.* XVI, 81—2.
[3]) Villars, *Mémoires*, 42—3.
[4]) Huisman, *op. cit.* 407—8.
[5]) So with the Maréchal d'Huxelles (*Eng. Hist. Review*, XVI, 72) and with the Maréchal de Villars, cf. his *Mémoires* in these years (e. g. V, 44).

allowed, for the allies, in spite of the danger to himself. "I might run the risk of being stoned," he said, "if I was thought here to do so much; for you must not imagine that this nation is universally disposed to a war, or will easily be brought to make one upon Spain, and therefore I am at a loss how to answer Mr. Walpole. There is the same reason for me not to disoblige the people of France, as there is with him for satisfying the people of England. But we have one method still to dispose the French to a war, which is by turning wholly upon the Emperor, and making him the chief author of it and sufferer by it." [1]

This was indeed the only alternative left to Fleury, it was also the only thing he desired. Circumstances were such that the only method by which the French might be disposed to a war, was also the only one by which peace might be preserved. Relations between Spain and England becoming increasingly strained, to prevent an explosion between them, would be practically impossible. But if the Emperor could be persuaded into an agreement, it would be easy to impose the conditions of the allies of Hanover on Spain, and thus maintain peace. The experiment was worthy of a trial: the Emperor's willingness would be to the good, and his unwillingness would make it possible to present him as the chief author of the war to the French nation, who then would be ready to follow their government. Thus Fleury had a double motive for turning upon the Emperor, and in doing so followed the best policy possible to him. Needless to say, he hoped for peace, but there would be no peace between the Emperor and the allies of Hanover unless the Ostend affair were taken in hand. The Dutch wished the Company to be suppressed, but Fleury knew that the Emperor would not suffer his honour thus to be trampled upon. He thought it a wiser course, to propose that the Company should be suspended for a fixed time, during which a Congress should examine the questions of the legality of its trade, and the advisability of suppressing it. He had already, some weeks before the conversation with Robinson, apprised the Emperor of his opinion, by means of Papal diplomatic channels. [2]

At this time Charles VI. and his ministers could not conceal

---

[1] Robinson to Horace Walpole, in Coxe, *H. W.* 141—2; cf. Townshend to Slingelandt, 31 Jan, 14. Feb. 1727, R. O. Hl. 297.

[2] Huisman, *op. cit.* 409; Baudrillart, *op. cit.* III, 314.

from themselves, that they were unable to prevent a general war. They had conceived hopes on Fleury's accession to power, that he would leave the Alliance of Hanover, or at least, that he would compel the Republic to be satisfied with certain concessions, in the matter of the Ostend trade; but on these points the negotiations of the autumn, had been completely illuminating.[1]) On the other hand, repeated warnings to Spain, not to provoke the English government, and not to use force against her, had had no effect [2]). When the Alliance of Vienna was concluded, the Emperor had hoped that it would secure peace, and procure for him financial and commercial privileges. It would in fact lead irrevocably to a war, which must be most injurious to him, for he was far from able to defend all the countries of his extensive monarchy, his hereditary dominions, Italy and the Southern Netherlands. One or more of them would inevitably be lost to his rule, although it had always been the aim of his policy to secure the whole in its integrity to Maria Theresa. Still worse, in the time of his need, Spain would oblige him to betroth the Archduchess to Don Carlos; such had been the very object of Elizabeth Farnese in forcing on a war. He stood to lose on every side. His Ostend Company alone could have brought him to fight; but there was little doubt as to the fate of the Company in the event of war, for by sea the allies of Hanover were far more powerful even than they were by land, and they would in a short time reduce to nothing both the Ostend ships and the factories lately founded in India. War suited the Emperor in no respect, but peace could be bought only by important concessions as to the Ostend trade. This price he shewed himself willing to pay because, in the circumstances, it seemed to him better to lose something, than to lose all. [3])

Negotiations went on for half a year, from December 1726, until May 1727; consequent on Fleury's secret overtures, and mainly to determine which concessions should constitute the price. Since the Cardinal had put into practice his method of turning wholly upon the Emperor, the Ostend Company came inevitably to the front. This fact should be understood. Huisman believes the Ostend Company to have been pre-eminently "the apple of

---

[1]) For these negotiations cf. p. 102; the Court of Vienna was quite convinced of the want of success of these efforts, cf. Villars, *Mémoires*, V, 39, 40—1.

[2]) Syveton, *op. cit.* 240.; Baudrillart, *op. cit.* III, 273.

[3]) Huisman, *op. cit.* 410—11.

discord"; and the Anglo-Spanish dispute a mere "accessory point",[1]) but this is going too far. To Spain and France, as has been said, the Ostend Company was indifferent, apart from their engagements. To England the Company counted for little, for far less certainly, than commercial privileges in Spain and the Spanish colonies, and the possession of Gibraltar. The Company was THE apple of discord indeed to the Dutch, and also to the Belgians, but the Belgians had throughout no voice. Their sovereign had come to see that the alliance with Spain was a mistake, and at this point he was listening far more to the advice of Prince Eugene and Stahremberg, who had opposed the alliance, than to its advocates, who had pointed out the advantages it would bring to the Ostend Company.[2]) Far from attaching to it a primary value, the Emperor had already secretly resolved to sacrifice the Company to the interests of his dynasty. Its prominence at this moment, arose not because it was THE apple of discord, but because the condition of affairs had caused peace to depend largely, although, as will be seen, not exclusively, on the degree of the Emperor's indulgence to it.

In the beginning, this was naturally insufficient to satisfy the allies of Hanover; yet the proposals by which the Emperor replied to Fleury's overtures were important. He agreed, that a period should be fixed for the examination of the legality of the Ostend trade; and that during it, the navigation of Ostend should be suspended, saving for the ships which were returning home; and he undertook that if the trade were found illegal he would finally suppress the Company, and that if the question were not decided within the fixed term, either this should be extended or else each party should regain the rights formerly enjoyed. The answer was conveyed through the channel used by Fleury; the proposals were entrusted to the Nuncio at the imperial court, and on December 17th, handed by him to Richelieu and Hamel Bruynincx, the representatives of France and the Republic at Vienna. [3])

In order to bring about peace as he wished, Fleury naturally exerted himself, not only in Austria, but also in the Republic. He represented to that power, that Slingelandt's method of injuring

---

[1]) Huisman, *op. cit.* 409.
[2]) Arneth, *Prinz Eugen*, III. 214—5.
[3]) Huisman, *op. cit.* 409—10; Baudrillart, *op. cit.* III, 314—5.

the Emperor, was fitted rather to strengthen him, since he would like to see an Anglo-Spanish war arise in which he would take part only as an auxiliary, while he still received subsidies from Madrid. It would permit him further to increase his power, already so great, and would render France a less capable ally of the Republic, where opposition to him was concerned, since her principal forces would be directed against Spain. Consequently, Fleury urged that it was to the advantage of the Republic herself, that the Allies turned against the Emperor, her true enemy. Where her commercial interests were concerned, other points were only accessory;[1]) and she could, he assured her, rely absolutely on France to protect her commercial interests, if matters should come to war. Since however Louis XV. preferred to maintain peace, he agreed to a final representation being made, which would however be only so much loss of time, unless a plan of war were first determined upon. For himself he would be willing not only, as bound by the Act of the Republic's entry into the Treaty of Hanover, to supply 12,000 men; but also to support her, if necessary, with all his forces. The States needed to do no more than bring forward a feasible plan of war, a matter which, since only Dutch interests were concerned, would not be expected of France.[2])

But the determination of this plan did not prove easy. The French government found plenty of opportunity to make observations and ask for elucidations, and objected in particular to the tactics by which the States sought to remove the burdens of war on to the allies, and to confine themselves to defensive measures, thereby neglecting all just proportion. Thus Fleury made the Dutch feel, on the one hand their own impotence, and on the other, the power of the Emperor, against whom only France would support them; and consequently he was able at the same time to deter them from war, and to place them under an obligation.

He increased such obligation by means of the Emperor's proposals of 17th December. These had been deemed entirely inadequate by the States, who considered an examination of the legality of the Company useless, and its temporary suspension equivalent to a confirmation of its status, since it would have the effect of a

---

[1]) This does not disagree with what we have said p. 109—10, for it is not what Fleury really thought but what he considered fit to have represented at the Hague.

[2]) Secr. Res. S. G. 27 Nov., 11 Dec. 1726, 2 Jan. 3 Feb., 1727, inserted in the Secr. Res. Hl. VII; Villars, *Memoires* 44—5.

safe conduct for the ships expected from India.[1]) Fénelon declared
that his Court understood perfectly this dissatisfaction with the
imperial proposals; the more so because it had lately been informed that the Court of Vienna intended to demand, as an indispensable condition of the proposed suspension, a guarantee for the
free return of the Spanish ships, the galleons and the flotilla. [2])

In such manner the French ambassador expressed himself at
the Hague, yet it is unlikely that Fleury was unaware of certain
new proposals by the Emperor. These had been drawn up, even
before an answer had been returned to those of December 17th,
and had been conveyed in a letter of February 2nd from the Nuncio at Vienna to his colleague at Paris. They were, that the Ostend
Company should be suspended for two years; that a congress
should be held at Basle, Nancy or Aix-la-Chapelle; that the Emperor should readily accept the mediation of Louis XV. and
Philip V. on the Ostend affair, and in order to make this possible
should first reconcile those princes; that together with Louis XV.
he should mediate on the differences between England and Spain;
that the Ostend ships, the galleons and the flotilla should be suffered to return home unimpeded. [3])

There are indeed several indications that these proposals had
not been made without Fleury's knowledge, [4]) and good reasons
for his acquaintance with them. He could not but recognise that
those of December would avail nothing. The Emperor and the
States still stood too far apart; yet even if they gradually came
together, it remained questionable, whether a general war could
even then be averted. The tidings from Spain were more and more
alarming; no doubt was left but that an attack on Gibraltar had
been planned: and therefore it was most necessary that the
Anglo-Spanish differences should also be drawn into the sphere of
peace negotiations, which consequently must not bear only on
the Ostend affair, but must be general in character. [5])

---

[1]) Wagenaar, *op. cit.* XVIII, 423; Huisman, *op. cit.* 412.

[2]) Secr. Res. S. G. 3 Feb. 1727.

[3]) The Nuncio at Vienna to the Nuncio in France, 2 Feb. 1727, Secr. Res. Hl. VII, 773;
Villars, *Memoires*, V. 76; *Eng. Hist. Review* XVI, 73.

[4]) La Paz to Aldobrandini, 18 May 1727 (Baudrillart. *op. cit.* III, 335 note); Huisman,
op. cit. 413; the two letters of the Nuncio at Vienna (Secr. Res. Hl. VII, 773, 776).

[5]) How they became general is made clear by the proposals of 2nd February. Due notice has not yet been taken of these: they are wanting in Rousset's *Recueil*, Huisman

However this may be, and whatever was Fleury's responsibility for the proposals, they still originated with the Emperor. The circumstance was due to his consideration for Spain. His ambassador at Madrid, Koenigsegg, had communicated the December proposals to Philip V., but had given him to understand that the Emperor himself expected nothing from them, but was on the contrary vigorously preparing for war. Koenigsegg's language was such that the King thought himself authorized by his ally to open the siege of Gibraltar.[1]) The Emperor's anxiety not to lose his ally was apparent, and the new proposals were calculated to make clearer than ever his studiousness, not for his own interests only, but also for those of Spain. He asked for the speedy withdrawal of the English ships from the Spanish seas, and the free return of the galleons and the flotilla, but he committed himself to nothing with regard to the retirement of the Spanish troops, which were before Gibraltar. He left this matter entirely to the King of Spain.

Since the Emperor's proposals had assumed a general character, Fleury wished the allies of Hanover to answer them in common.[2]) Among the allies he had to reckon first with England, whose interests had come to be involved in the negotiation, as deeply as those of the Republic.

Fleury's policy of turning upon the Emperor was most judicious, as has been seen, with regard to the Republic; and it was equally so in reference to England. England could say little against it, for Townshend, her leader in foreign affairs, was much incensed against the Emperor. His anger appeared clearly in the King's Speech, on January 28th at the opening of Parliament, in which the alliance of Vienna was strongly resented; Spain's urgent claim for the restitution of Gibraltar was placed side by side with the Emperor's enjoyment of an unlawful trade, and the allies were stated expressly to have stipulated among themselves for the restoration of the Pretender to the throne of England. "If time should evince that the giving up the trade of this nation to

seems not to have kwonn them, and Baudrillart (*op. cit.* III, 322) has mistaken them for those of 17th December. It is true that they have been mentioned in *Eng. Hist. Review* XVI, 73, but there they have not been placed in the right light. They form in these negotiations the missing link, without which the relation between the proposals of 17th December 1726 and the project of preliminaries of 26th March 1727 remains unexplained.

[1]) Baudrillart, *op. cit.* III, 319—20.
[2]) Memorial of Fénelon, 24 Feb. 1727, Secr. Res. Hl. VII, 783—5.

one power, and Gibraltar and Port Mahon to another, is made the price and reward of imposing upon this nation a Popish Pretender, what indignation must this raise in the breast of every Protestant Briton!" [1])

This speech was directed against both the allies of Vienna, the Emperor as much as Spain, and so different from the measures proposed by the government, and carried by large majorities in Parliament, which were principally directed against Spain, in that they provided for a far greater reinforcement of the navy than of the land forces. Thus England had to depend on the land operations of others. For the protection of Low Germany, she wished Swedish, Danish, Hanoverian, Hessian and Dutch troops to form a line from Pomerania to the Rhine. The Dutch however could send troops into the Empire, only in the event of such an attack by the Emperor on the English King's German dominions, as would leave only a small imperial force in the Southern Netherlands. Moreover the proposed treaties with Sweden and Denmark had not yet been finished. The English government were therefore awkwardly placed; and Townshend frankly owned to Slingelandt, that if these treaties were not concluded, they would be in great perplexity, unless they had aid from France and the Republic.[2])

The situation was most advantageous to France, with a view to both of the Maritime Powers. For if England desired her to go to war, she could pronounce the King's Hanoverian troops and the mercenaries of Hesse-Cassel inadequate, and urge that English troops should be sent to the continent[3]). As for the Republic, she could have gained her object with very little effort, had the Emperor, in accordance with Slingelandt's advice, been occupied in Italy by the King of Sardinia, while the chief attack was directed against Spain. But France, consistently with her disapproval of Slingelandt's plan, refused to co-operate in such an action against Spain; and Victor Amadeus II. asked too high a price for his allegiance[4]); the change was one which bore heavily on the Republic. For since the allies, in fear of arousing the princes of the Empire against themselves, would not attack the Emperor in Germany, he would be free to concentrate his troops in the Southern

---

[1]) Coxe, *R. W.* I. 258.
[2]) See the note p. 116.
[3]) Villars, *Memoires*, V. 40, 57—9.
[4]) cf. also *Eng. Hist. Review* XV, 694—5.

Netherlands; thus it would become most difficult for the Republic to compel him to revoke the charter. She hoped to attain this end, either by the destruction of the port of Ostend, or by the occupation of some places in the Southern Netherlands, which could be retained until he yielded. But the Dutch troops alone were equal to neither of these enterprises; especially in view of the fact that the Republic was herself exposed to an attack from the Emperor. They had indeed lately been increased to 54,000 men, but of these 12,000 were in the barrier towns and only 6,000 or 7,000 could be spared for a campaign in the Southern Netherlands. Thus the Republic was gravely in need of her allies. [1])

Of these France assumed a role of magnanimity. Her true inclination had appeared in her conduct with regard to the determination of a plan of war, yet again and again she strongly protested her desire to help the Republic to the fulfilment of her wishes.

The behaviour of England was in sharp contrast. Far from offering aid to the Republic, England asked it of her: although she contemplated sending no troops to Germany she wished the Republic to do so, in order that the action which that country proposed to take in the Southern Netherlands might be connected with the operations in Germany, where there must be provided, not only a line of troops reaching from Pomerania to the Rhine, but also a French army, between the Rhine and the Moselle, which should keep in touch with them. The Republic was in no way opposed to operations in Germany, but she desired to stand aside from them, to leave them to the deliberation of England, France and the other allies. Her object was the suppression of the Ostend Company, and she wished to decide on the measures necessary to it, in co-operation with England and France only, independently of German interests. The help of England was indispensable in addition to that of France, for although Louis XV. had explicitly declared that he aimed at no extension of his Northern frontiers, yet in the Republic it was considered too risky to leave the occupation of the Southern Netherlands almost exclusively to French troops. There had to be English troops too: a demand to this effect was unreservedly put forward in letters from Slingelandt to Townshend. It met with no success; and Slingelandt complained,

---

[1]) See the next note.

not without bitterness, that although Parliament had given a strong assurance that the Emperor would be forced to repeal the OstendCompany's charter, not a single Englishsoldierhadbeensent to the Southern Netherlands. In his answer Towshend referred to the measures accomplished by Parliament, and Slingelandt replied, that he had never denied them, but that to his mind, the land forces had been too much neglected in favour of the navy. He judged that it would be better for England to have two strings to her bow, to attack Spain by sea, and the Emperor by land. [1]

Thus Fleury's skilfulness not only increased the dependence of England on France, but also weakened her influence with the Republic, who was therefore thrown back upon France. His action ran counter to the designs of the English government, but in the cause of peace; for it was not his object to stand between the English and the satisfaction they desired. On the contrary it was his earnest wish to remain on good terms with them, and he left nothing undone to retain the confidence which he had won by his fidelity in face of the temptations offered by the allies of Vienna.[2] When the English feared that he treated Spain too gently, he informed them that they were in error, for it was not his intention to show as much indulgence to Spain as they supposed, nor to excludewar against her,should the necessity arise, but only to direct the chief attack against theEmperor.[3]He was quite willing to support the claims of the English, when a common answer had to be returned to the proposals of February 2nd, and proposed only one amendment to their project, viz: the suspension of the Ostend Company for seven years instead of indefinitely. [4]

The only thing remaining was that the States should give their consent to the proposed answer, and France had not omitted to again place them under an obligation to her.When the proposals from Vienna had been communicated, Fénélon immediately declared that his Court disapproved of them, and that France could

---

[1] For the schemes of England and the divergence of opinion with the Republic, see the letters of Townshend to Slingelandt, 10, 31 January, 14 Feb. (O. S.) 1727; and those of Slingelandt to Townshend, 28 Jan (herewith enclosed: "Pensées de N.N. au sujet de la formation d'un plan de mesures communes pour obtenir les fins du traité de Hanovre", 25 Jan. 1727), 18, 20 Feb., 4, 7, March (n. s.) 1727 (R. O. Hl. 297).
[2] Townshend to Slingelandt, 3, 10 January, 1727. ibid:
[3] Townshend to Slingelandt, 14 Feb. 1727, ibid:
[4] *Engl. Hist. Review.* XVI, 73—4.

not act as a mediator since she was a party to them. He had
strongly denied an insinuation in the Nuncio's letter, that the
French government had suggested a suspension of the Company
for three years. He had asserted that they would approve only
such a suspension as would be tantamount to a suppression, and he
had asked the States what term they deemed adequate to such an
end. [1]) If the town of Amsterdam had had its way the States
would not have considered any suspension, but would have maintained unimpaired their demand for suppression.[2]) They did not
go to such lengths, yet they were very firm in their desire that the
suspension should be for no less than twenty five years. [3]) This
naturally did not satisfy the French government, for Fonseca,
the Austrian ambassador at Paris, affirmed that to demand a suspension of six or seven years would constitute a "rupture décla-
rée." [4]) The French therefore agreed first, that it should be only
for five years. Then, under the influence of threatening news from
Spain, they increased this period to seven years, but still hoped to
reduce it to five. [5])

The difference between twenty five and seven years, was however too great to be overlooked by the Republic. It was necessary
that she should much abate her claim, and the French government represented to her, that the extinction of the Ostend trade
turned less on the duration of the term of suspension, than on an
exhibition of firmness, when the matter should be discussed in the
Congress. She was assured that whatever happened she could rely
on the permanence of the obligations entered into by Louis XV.,
whether to bring the Court of Vienna to satisfy the States, or to
guarantee to them any satisfaction promised by the Emperor. [6])
The English government made a like declaration: the English
King deemed it most necessary that the allies should mutually
guarantee each other against a revival of the Ostend trade, after
the expiry of the term of suspension. [7])

---

[1]) Memorial of Fénelon to the States General, 24 Feb. 1727, Secr. Res. Hl. VII, 776 *et seq.*
[2]) Fénelon, *op. cit.* 131.
[3]) Secr. Res. S. G. 4 March 1727.
[4]) Villars, *Memoires* V, 47.
[5]) Ibid: 49—51.
[6]) Memorial of Fénelon to the States General, 13 March 1727, Secr. Res. Hl. VII, 786
et seq.
[7]) Memorial of Finch to the States General, 13 March 1727 (Secr. Res. Hl. VII, 788).
A seven years' suspension was also recommended in Townshend's letter to Van Ittersum,
14 March 1727 (R. O. Hl. 296).

It would seem that the States were not entirely set at ease by these assurances, for they qualified their consent to the project by certain observations, particularly by a recommendation that ten years instead of seven should constitute the term of suspension, and a statement that their adherence was given, in the expectation that the assurances they had received would be fulfilled. [1]) In spite of some unwillingness however they were obliged to yield. Both of their allies advocated the suspension for seven years, and they had to reckon especially with France, whom it had become impossible for them to disoblige, by disagreement on this point. The land provinces were entirely opposed to any such stubbornness: they were less interested than the others in the destruction of the Ostend Company, and would in time of war be more exposed to the Emperor's wrath, and consequently more dependent on French help. The sea provinces knew their hands to be tied by the clause which forbade the Republic to take any measures against the Company, before these had been deliberated upon with both her allies. [2])

That George I. recommended suspension for seven years, was probably due to Fleury's readiness to support the demands which were particularly English. On this occasion therefore, Fleury made use of English influence in the Republic, which it was however his constant aim to weaken, as will be seen from what follows.

It has been said that England's chief strength was naval, and not continental. The direction of opposition against the Emperor, had therefore made her most uneasy, and at this point she found an unexpected opportunity of escape from the difficulty. A Prussian officer, Von Polentz, came to London to inform the King of England, that if he gave a declaration that neither he nor his allies would attack the Emperor's German dominions, particularly Silesia and Bohemia, he might well hope to win, through the mediation of the King of Prussia, a like undertaking that his own

---

[1]) Secr. Res. Hl. VII, 792—3; the addition runs as follows: "Moyennant ces remarques L. H. P. se conformeront au Projet de la reponse à donner à la Cour de Vienne, se reposant entièrement sur les assurances données par les Memoires de M. M. le Marquis de Fenelon et de Finch de l'intention de Leurs Majestez T. C. et Br. de confirmer les Articles préliminaires, après qu'ils auront été reglés par une garantie solide et que quand le Congrès sera mené à une heureuse fin, qu'alors les Alliez se garantiront aussi reciproquement tout ce dont on sera convenu par les Traités à faire.

"C'est sur le fondement de cette assurance et de cette attente que L. H. P. sont portées à entrer avec tant de facilité dans ce projet."

[2]) Fénelon, *op. cit.* 131—2.

German dominions would be respected by the Emperor. The intimation was given in the second half of February, and the English government received it with delight. Not being sure of aid from Sweden and Denmark, and foiled in their attempt to secure that of the Republic, they had been apprehensive of a war, in which the King's German dominions would be in serious danger of invasion by the troops of the Emperor and Frederick William. The union of these two princes however, proved not so close as was feared, since Frederick William had thus offered immunity to Hanover. It was little wonder that the English were overjoyed at the proposal, and that it was with recommendations, that they submitted it to the allies before answering it. [1]

The allies however received it differently. France perceived that it would weaken her hold on England, and expose her more than ever before to the Emperor's attacks. Nor did the Republic fail to perceive the dangers it involved. Slingelandt, to whom Townshend had written on the subject, saw in it a trap, which the Emperor[2] had laid, by means of Frederick William: George I. was to be held responsible for his allies, who themselves gained nothing; while the King of Prussia remained free to aid the Emperor in attacking the Republic, where there were several places which he would very much like to acquire. One of the arguments by which Townshend sought to render the proposal acceptable, was that its adoption, would enable the English government to send an increased number of troops into the Southern Netherlands, but even this proved unavailing. The proposal was condemned as too dangerous. [3]

Its advocacy by the English government, could not fail to impress the States unfavourably, and Fleury enjoined Fénelon to seize this opportunity to weaken English influence. [4] Although

---

[1] Droysen, *Friedrich Wilhelm I*, I. 432, 433; Ranke, *Zwölf Bücher Preuszischer Geschichte*, III—IV, 60; Townshend to Slingelandt, 14 Feb. 1727, R. O. Hl. 297. According to Droysen (loc. cit. 438) the King had let Townshend have his way in order that Parliament might grant all possible supplies, but when his German dominions were in danger, Walpole's peaceful views gained the upper hand. However, one needs not to have recourse to the divergence of opinion between Townshend and Walpole to account for the reception the Prussian proposal met with in London, for Townshend was no less uneasy than any other member of the government. cf. p. 114.

[2] The scheme, indeed, originated with him (Droysen, *op. cit.* I. 431).

[3] Villars, *Mémoires*, 48—50; Slingelandt to Townshend, 4 March 1727; Townshend to Slingelandt, 14 Feb. (O. S.) 1727, R. O. Hl. 297.

[4] A. E. Hl. 368, Louis XV to Fénelon, 9 March 1727.

in his own words "the union with England agreed with the moment-
ary interests of France", he liked to see between the two Maritime
Powers a certain dissatisfaction which was favourable to the
achievement of his ends. He had at this moment particular need
of the Republic, for he had just been informed that Spain had
actually embarked on the enterprise for which she had been
preparing for months: on February 22nd, she had opened the
siege of Gibraltar. Fleury expected that within a few days the
English government would urge him to declare war on Spain, but
he was unwilling to do so, and desired the Republic to support
him in his non-compliance. It is clear therefore, why at this very
moment he agreed to the suspension for seven years, and, to
remove the last hesitation on the part of the Republic, gave the
assurances which have been cited. [1]

Events followed the course he had foreseen. When the news
as to Gibraltar was received, England at once required the allies
to declare war. She was herself in the most warlike of moods,
the more so on account of the Emperor's conduct.

It has been said that the speech from the throne was directed,
no less against Spain, than against the Emperor. Both powers
were accused of having entered into engagements with regard to
the restoration of the Pretender, in all good faith, for the English government relied on Ripperda's confidences to Stanhope,
which seemed to have been confirmed from other sources. [2] That
this was a mistake, has been proved recently, and the Emperor
had just cause of offence, which, for the sake of his house, he could
not overlook. He did not confine himself to a protest, but aimed at
nothing short of the overthrow of the cabinet. He was averse to war,
but still indisposed to submit to the allies of Hanover, and to give
up the Ostend Company. He had tried to alienate France from
the Republic, and since that effort had failed, he sought to
estrange her other ally from her. The greatly exaggerated
intelligence which reached him was to the effect that there was
considerable opposition to the cabinet. His representative in
London, Count Palm, entered into negotiations with several
members of the opposition, and even with the Duchess of Kendal,

---

[1] Villars, *Memoires*, V. 50.
[2] Leadam, *op. cit.* 328; the confidences of Ripperda to Stanhope are to be found in
King, *Notes*, 30—4.

the King's principal mistress. The common object was to replace the cabinet by another which would resume the old friendship with Austria. The Emperor however, entirely missed his aim by his imprudence, for he ordered Count Palm to draw up a strong memorial, which utterly repudiated the contents of the King's Speech, and to publish and circulate it "that the whole nation be acquainted, with it." When Palm obeyed, he was immediately, on March 13th, requested to leave the country. [1]

Thus England broke her diplomatic relations with Austria. The rupture with Spain took place a few days earlier when Stanhope left Madrid, on March 11th. War had not yet however been declared. Spain shrank from a declaration which would force the allies of England, and France first of them, to join that power, and she took refuge in the assertion that the siege of Gibraltar and the arrest at Vera Cruz of the "Prince Frederick", a ship of the South Sea Company, were no more than retaliations for the blockade of the galleons. [2] But England rejected this view, considered these actions to be *casus belli* and urged the allies to war. As has been said her war-like spirit was further stimulated by the Count Palm incident, which occurred simultaneously with the arrival of the news as to Gibraltar.

It was not however the bellicose mood of England, but the peaceful dispositions of Fleury, which were to prevail. Slingelandt wrote to Townshend, that he saw no chance that the Republic, and very little chance that France, would immediately declare war as requested, in contravention of the provision in both the Triple Alliance and that of Hanover, that in case of an attack on one of the allies, the others would first for two months seek by good offices to procure satisfaction for the injury done. Even were France brought to the desired resolution, and the Republic dragged along in her train, or set on one side, Slingelandt judged that the allies should still, like Spain, avoid a formal declaration of war. The case would, he said, have been different, if England had herself been menaced by invasion, if Gibraltar had been situated within the British Isles, even if the siege had not been "une entreprise plus digne de Don Quichotte que de gens avisés"; but in existing circumstances, he thought it best to wait for the success

---

[1] Leadam, *op. cit.* 329.
[2] Ibid: 330.

of the allies' proposals to the Emperor. He granted that Palm's memorial had lessened the hopes of an agreement, but he believed that these were not yet shattered; and he reminded the English government that the "grandeur autrichienne" had been wounded, not only by the Speech from the Throne, but also by several writings which were very little pleasing to the Emperor. In an affair of this nature justice should, he said, be rendered to all concerned: private resentment, however just, ought not to prevail, but rather considerations of sane policy and interest. [1]

Thus the Dutch refused to declare war, and reproved the aggressive attitude towards the Emperor which England had adopted. In so far as they were concerned, Fleury's policy had been completely successful. He had hoped further that the Emperor would yield to the proposals of the allies of Hanover, who would, as he alleged in his communication to that sovereign, have demanded the suppression of the Ostend Company, had it not been for the representations of France. He stated that the Dutch, would not accept less than its suspension for seven or eight years, but, as a counterpoise, he encouraged the expectation that the commercial treaty, required by the 26th article of the barrier treaty, would be realized. [2]

And in spite of many difficulties, relations with Spain improved. Spain was still closely united to the Emperor, but that sovereign's offer of proposals as to the Ostend Company had disappointed Elizabeth, and she had made secret advances to Fleury.[3] The Cardinal shewed himself friendly, although he defended the allies and remained true to them. He assured the Queen that the Court of France, was in no way hostile to her, that it was only in spite of themselves that the French would become the enemies of Spain.[4] It is even said, that to reiterated requests not to attack Spain, he invariably answered, with an exhortation to take Gibraltar quickly, lest his country should have to declare war. [5]

Thus as regarded the Republic, the Emperor and Spain, Fleury had good hopes that his policy would secure peace, and the success of the allies of Hanover, and therefore he refused to deviate

---

[1] Slingelandt to Townshend, 18 March 1727, R. O. Hl. 297.
[2] Huisman, *op. cit.* 414—15; Pribram, *op. cit.* I, 453; cf. Baudrillart, *op. cit.* III, 325.
[3] Ibid: III, 315—6.
[4] Ibid: III, 323.
[5] Jobez, *Histoire de France sous Louis XV*, II. 466; cf. Coxe, *H. W.* 144.

from it, the more so because French merchants were complaining more and more of England's action. For this reason he represented to the English government, that since the draft of preliminaries was ready to be sent to Vienna, it would be best to wait for its reception. [1]) If it were rejected France would, he declared, go to war. [2])

Since neither France nor the Republic, was prepared to declare war, George I. also made delays. He also negatived the Prussian proposal; for the English government could not but follow the States in siding with Fleury. [3]) England was well aware that the game was lost. Townshend in complaining of the Dutch refusal to make war, said that people seemed to think the English must have "le mal dans leurs entrailles mêmes" before they could be helped, [4]) and he was no less bitter as to the predominant part played by France, ascribing it, partly to the niggardliness of the Republic, which had rendered her unfit to exact respect, and left her therefore in much fear of the Emperor's power, and more dependent than was desirable on France. [5])

Victory belonged to Fleury: on March 26th the draft of preliminaries was sent to Vienna. The first article demanded, in accordance with the request of the Republic, that the Ostend Company should be suspended for ten years; the second that commercial privileges enjoyed in Europe or the Indies by the English, French, and Dutch nations before 1725, should be restored to them unimpaired; the third that all other rights and possessions should remain as established by the treaties of Utrecht, of Baden and of the Quadruple Alliance. By the last, Gibraltar was confirmed to England, by the second her commercial privileges. In return for these concessions, the Hanover allies agreed to the free return of the Ostend ships and the galleons. [6])

It has been said that the maintenance of peace did not depend exclusively on the degree of the Emperor's tractability as to the

[1]) Villars, *Memoires* V, 54.

[2]) Townshend to Slingelandt, 30 March 1727, R. O. Hl. 297.

[3]) "Tout plia donc pour souscrire aux articles préliminaires et la République ainsy nécessairement entraînée, il ne restoit plus à délibérer à l'Angleterre, à qui il ne convenoit moins dans cette conjoncture que dans toute autre de faire bande à part," Fénelon, *op. cit.* 132.

[4]) Townshend to Slingelandt, 30 March 1727, R. O. Hl. 297.

[5]) Townshend to Van Ittersum, 14 March 1727, R. O. Hl. 296.

[6]) Rousset, *Recueil*, III, 388—90.

Ostend Company. [1]) It was conditional also on the degree of his willingness to abandon the interests of Spain, as was evident from the grounds of the proposals of February 2nd, and as was again evident at this time, when an answer had to be returned to the draft of preliminaries. The demand for the suspension of the Company for seven years, to which term Richelieu had been empowered to reduce that in the draft, would not in itself have been an unsurmountable obstacle, for the Emperor had already given his ministers leave to include the question of suppressing the Company in their deliberations. [2]) If however he agreed to the second and third articles, which excluded from the sphere of the Congress the very points most important to Spain, he risked losing his ally, and so placing himself at the mercy of his enemies. He was the more anxious to maintain his alliance with Spain, because she was again able to provide him with subsidies; for although the galleons were still detained in Portobello, the flotilla had arrived safely in Spanish harbours at the beginning of March. [3])

Apart from these considerations, the Emperor was in no mood to yield Only a few days previously he had been informed of Palm's enforced departure from London, and in his turn, he had ordered the withdrawal of the English and Hanoverian representatives from Vienna and Ratisbon. Moreover in his resentment at the King's Speech, he had taken action of which he could not yet judge the effect: he had not only ordered considerable preparations for war, but had also redoubled his exertions to gain the support of the Princes of the Empire, particularly the King of Prussia, and of the Empire itself. French diplomacy, endeavoured to persuade the Diet to neutrality, by representations that the Ostend affair was of no importance for the Empire, but the Emperor would have the Diet resent the offence given him by George I. and champion the cause of his Belgian subjects. [4])

Prince Eugene and Stahremberg did not expect any results from these measures, and since they foresaw in a war only disadvantage to their master, they advised him to yield. When finally they consented to a delay, strongly advocated by Sinzendorff, it was

---

[1]) p. 110.
[2]) Arneth, *op cit*, III, 225 (cf the notes ibid. 557).
[3]) Baudrillart *op. cit.* III, 327; Villars, *Memoires* V. 54.
[4]) Droysen, *Friedrich Wilhelm* I, I. 434—5; Huisman, *op. cit.* 417—8.

partly in deference to the Emperor's wishes, and partly in the confident expectation that their opinion would be confirmed by the news from Germany and Spain, which was to decide the Emperor's further conduct. The counter-project, which was accordingly put forward, on the 13th of April, in order to gain time, referred to the first and second articles, which concerned the suspension of the Company and the commercial privileges, to the deliberation of the Congress, and weakened the third article. [1]

The despatch of the project of March 26th, which this one answered, was a triumph for Fleury. The objections made to its contents by the Republic, and to its despatch by England, had alike been overcome. But Fleury understood that this complaisance of the allies gave them the more right to expect him to remain true to them. In the King's Council therefore, on March 30th, he highly praised their reasonable attitude to France, which, he said, entitled them to a reciprocal steady friendliness: and he sent two squadrons to the Mediterranean. [2] When the counter project, which naturally brought discontent to the allies, arrived he was again zealous for them. He did not indeed yield to the representations of Horace Walpole, in defiance of renewed protests from the French merchants, [3] and declare war, but still he displayed much vigour. He knew himself suspected by the allies of weakness, and seized the opportunity to improve his reputation. A new project which he prepared, met the Emperor's wishes in some points, as in reducing the suspensory term from ten years to seven, but maintained on the whole the demands of March 26th; and this, which was issued on May 2nd, he declared to be an ultimatum. If within a month it had not been answered definitely, he intimated that the allies of Hanover would take silence for a rupture of negotiations. He proved himself otherwise in earnest; for he ordered considerable preparations for war, and promised the King of England to make war on Spain as soon as he did.

The English King would have preferred adherence to the earlier project [5], yet suffered Fleury to have his way, a compliance

[1] Pribram, *op. cit.* I, 453—4; Huisman, *p. cit.* 416—7, 420; Rousset, *Recueil*, III, 390—3.
[2] Baillon, *Lord Walpole à la Cour de France* (Paris, 1867) Chapter IX; Coxe, *H. W.* 146—8.
[3] Baillon, *op. cit. loc. cit.*
[4] Baudrillart, *op. cit.* III, 327—8, 331—3; Fleury to George I, 9 May 1727, R.O. Hl. 293.
[5] Townshend to Finch, 21 April, 1727; the deputies for foreign affairs expressed the same opinion, cf. Finch to Townshend, 6 May 1727, R. O. Hl. 293.

which aimed at further securing French support in case the project met with a refusal. At the same time, the King endeavoured to remove a cause of offence, of which France, and even more the Republic, had complained, the failure of England to send troops to the Continent. This had undoubtedly contributed, not a little to the ill-success of English politics in March. The conclusion of the treaties with Sweden and Denmark had however placed the English King in a better position with regard to France; and he had the wisdom to give to the States a promise that he would send a body of 12,000 English men to the Southern Netherlands. An excellent impression was made: [1]) the States who, in spite of their dissatisfaction with the Court of Vienna, had had little inclination for war, were infused with new spirit and vigour by this well-timed promise of George I.[2]) They saw that they could attain their end only in one way, and therefore made several provisions in the event of a war, among them the raising of a sum of 500,000 guilders for first necessities. The harmony which obtained between the two Maritime Powers is worthy of note. The attempts of Spain to prevent the States from participating in the war, which in the years of the Quadruple Alliance had been successful, were this time fruitless. [3]) In his despatches to Townshend, Finch again highly commended the conduct of the States, whose wishes were very kindly heard in the English Court. One of their principal concerns was to prevent the Belgian ships, which were returning home, from entering the port of Ostend; another was to blockade this port. For both they asked the help of some English ships, which was at once promised to them. For their further gratification, the English government assembled the troops assigned to the Southern Netherlands, in the neighbourhood of Harwich, in order that they might embark rapidly directly they were wanted. [4])

This negotiation had reference only to a part of the action against the allies of Vienna, of which the general plan was being settled in Paris. [5]) England sent Armstrong to Paris, and the Republic

---

[1]) Finch to Townshend, 29 April 1727, R. O. Hl. 293.
[2]) Id. to id. 6, 9, 16, 23, 27 May 1727, ibid.; Van Ittersum to Townshend, 14 April 1727, R. O. Hl. 296.
[3]) Wagenaar, op. cit. XVIII, 415—6.
[4]) See the correspondence of Finch and Townshend, May 1727, R. O. Hl. 293; besides the "Verbaal" of H. Hop, dato May 30 1727, R. A. Legatie 837.
[5]) The conferences at the Hague about the settling of a plan of war (cf. p. 105) had at

Pesters, her resident at Brussels, and Grovestins; and these men held several conferences in the second half of May, with the representatives of the French government, which however came to a rapid conclusion owing to the course of events.

For on this occasion the Court of Vienna decided to surrender. To hold out longer would entail a war to which no circumstances were favourable. The expected subsidies from Spain failed to arrive, and the siege of Gibraltar did not prosper. War was equally undesirable with a view to the Empire; for although the land forces of the allies of Vienna were as a whole superior to those of the opposite camp, yet within the Empire, they were inferior to them.[1]) In the Diet the advocates of the neutrality of the Empire, had become predominant; and several Princes who had entered into relations with the Court of Vienna, such as the Elector Palatine, the Elector of Bavaria and the King of Prussia, were uncertain in their allegiance. [2]) French diplomacy, seconded by that of the Dutch, was at work at Ratisbon, and several courts, and Frederick William was doing his utmost to preserve peace and had better relations with the English Court than were agreeable to the Emperor. The Emperor had been no more fortunate in Northern Europe; in March and April, the two Scandanavian powers had entered into engagements with his enemies; and his surest friend, the Tsarina Catherine I., was at this moment on the point of death. [3])

Everything made surrender advisable, but inevitably the nature of the Viennese statesmen caused them to make difficulties. The vigorous and yet conciliatory attitude of Richelieu convinced them however of the uselessness of their exertions. The only concession they obtained from the French ambassador was merely formal: he allowed them to draw up a new project, that of May 21st, substantially identical in every respect to that of Fleury. In this form Fonseca, the imperial ambassador at Paris, was em-

---

last resulted in a project (inserted Secr. Res. Hl. VII, p. 763—5) which then became a point of discussion between the French and English governments. Of the further lot of this project we do not know anything, but that the English government approved of it (Townshend to Van Ittersum, March 14, 1727, R. O. Hl. 296).

[1]) *Eng. Hist. Review XV*, p. 696—8.

[2]) Ibid. 690; Droysen, *Friedrich Wilhelm I*, I. 436, 439. As it seems to us, both Droysen and Ranke (*Preuszische Geschichte*, III—IV, 61) have much overrated the influence Frederick William exerted at this juncture

[3]) Arneth, *op. cit.* III, 224—5; Pribram *op. cit.* I, 454; Huisman, *op. cit.* 421—2.

powered to sign the preliminaries. Since neither Fleury nor the representatives of the Maritime Powers advanced objections, they were signed on May 31st 1727, in the name of four powers, Austria, France, England ànd the Republic.

The conferences at Vienna had in part been attended by Bournonville, the Spanish ambassador. Needless to say, he had raised several objections to the ultimatum, particularly to the exclusion of the questions of Gibraltar and English trade with Spanish America, from the scope of the Congress; and he had refused Fonseca permission to sign in the name of Spain too. [1] When however the preliminaries had been signed at Paris, he completed that work, although not without some new difficulties, by adding the signature on behalf of Spain. This was at Vienna on the 13th of June. [2]

IV.

Four days afterwards Isaac van Hoornbeek, Grand Pensionary of Holland, died. He had been ailing for six months, and had been seriously ill since the middle of May, therefore his death was not unexpected, and several men were being named as fitted to succeed him. Among these Slingelandt stood first. Many indeed disliked his character, and others, dishonourable though the fact be to the Dutch regents of the time, thought him too skilful, for their own influence was in inverse ratio to the ability of the Grand Pensionary. [3] The uncertain condition of foreign affairs was however favourable to his candidature. The preliminaries were in existence, but they had yet to become a definite peace; the rival company had been suspended but not yet suppressed. [4] It was doubtful whether the allies would procure for the Republic the full satisfaction she desired. England had not been very tractable at the beginning of the year, and even in May, there were various indications of the aversion of France to war. [5] The Republic had more than ever before need of "a capacité éprouvée" [6] and none had a better right to such a title than Slingelandt.

---

[1] Hamel Bruynincx to Fagel, 19 May 1727, R. A., S. G. 7191.
[2] Baudrillart, *op. cit*. III, 335—8.
[3] Finch to Townshend, 30 May 1727, R. O. Hl. 293.
[4] Fénelon, *op. cit*. 166.
[5] Finch to Townshend, 3 June 1727, R. O. Hl. 293.
[6] Fénelon to his Court, 20 May 1727, A. E. Hl. 369.

The fact was perhaps even better realized by the Court of France than by his fellow-countrymen. The desire of the French to frustrate his election was so much the greater, for they consider- ed him to be entirely devoted to England and capable of restor- ing the Stadtholdership. As early as January the French Court had enjoined Fénelon to work against Slingelandt's selection and had informed him of the means successfully employed to that end after the death of Heinsius. Such, however, was the superiority of Slinge- landt's party from the outset that Fénelon did not think fit to in any way oppose him, and his Court forbade him strongly to take any action while the situation was unchanged. In the begin- ning he was on the watch for any attempt on the part of Koenigs- egg-Erps, the Imperial envoy, to place obstacles in Slingelandt's path, but he soon became convinced that his election would be far from disagreeable to the Court of Vienna. And since England also favoured it, there was no possibility of preventing it by the use of foreign influence. [1])

There remained the chance that those who had the office at their disposal, the States of Holland, might be manipulated, and Fénelon was keenly on the alert. Slingelandt's friends however were very active. It is impossible here to dwell on the internal aspect of the election, on the obstacles which had to be overcome and the promises which had to be given, before an able and merit- orious man was raised to the position of Pensionary. Only two incidents will be particularized, and these for their bearing on foreign affairs. Among the members of the States of Holland was a regent of Gorkum, Abraham van Hoey, a man of limited capa- bilities, but unbounded ambition, who by intrigues had secured several petty towns so that he had their votes in the assembly of the States at his disposal. When the Pensionary's office was last void, Slingelandt's friends had paid him little attention, but, taught by experience, they now tried to gain his support. He was willing to give it in return for the vacant place of ambassador to France; and although he was quite new to foreign affairs, Slingelandt, in spite of a marked personal dislike to him, had no choice but to promise to support his application. Slingelandt gained other

---

[1]) cf. the despatches of Fénelon to his Court (A. E. Hl. 367—370), besides the "Mémoire sur le choix d'un pensionnaire en Hollande," 14 Dec. 1726, and a similar memorial of December 1731 (ibid: 366).

supporters by declaring, at their request, that he would do nothing to bring about a change in the constitution, a promise which
meant that he would not promote the revival of the Stadtholdership. [1]) Only Amsterdam attempted to defeat his election, but
with so little success that this town at last joined his supporters,
and on July 17th. he was unanimously appointed.

At last, at the age of sixty-three, Slingelandt had obtained
the office to which his rare abilities fully entitled him. It placed
him, as has been said, at the head of the foreign affairs of the Republic. With foreign affairs he had always been concerned, but
his influence on them had only been indirect, exercised by means
of either his conversations with Fagel or his correspondence with
Townshend. The late Pensionary, Hoornbeek, had not been guided by him: rather had there been jealousy between Hoornbeek
and himself. [2]) Now Slingelandt became himself the official and
recognized leader of foreign affairs. To this dignity, in the circumstances in which he received it, there belonged the particular duty
of extricating the Republic from the difficulties in which she had
been involved by her conflict with the Emperor. Slingelandt was
not to fail to discharge this trust. He was to go beyond it, to
strive for no less an aim than European peace.

----

[1]) Fénelon, *op. cit.* 162.
[2]) Van Ittersum to Townshend, 14 Jan., 11 Feb. 1727 (R. O. Hl. 296); Townshend to
Finch, 16 Ap. and Finch to Townshend, 29 Ap. 1727 (R. O. Hl. 293).

CHAPTER III.

The Preservation of Peace.

June 1727—March 1728.

I.

The Preliminaries had been concluded in spite of Elizabeth
Farnese. She would have preferred war, as then only could she
impose on the Emperor the formal betrothal of her first-born son
to his eldest daughter. Now, however, there was not only peace,
but no chance of war in conjunction with him, as by the Preliminaries he had abandoned the Ostend Company, the only raison
d'être for his alliance with her. Though not acknowledging it
to herself, she nevertheless felt that he was breaking away
from her, and henceforth the Court of Spain would no longer
deliver herself unconditionally over to that of Vienna. This
view was advocated by the Minister of Finance and Marine,
Patiño, a highly gifted man whose influence was increasing daily.
As he was no longer inclined to send further subsidies to Vienna,
the Austrians stopped at nothing in their efforts to get him removed, but he was retained in his position by the Queen.[1]

Spain now began to think better of the Vienna Alliance, as did
France with regard to that of Hanover. The latter's reason for
being in it was not from choice but from necessity. In 1725 the interests of the country at the moment were served by joining the
Insular Monarchy, but the two years which had passed had made
it very clear to France that this union was quite incompatible
with her real interests. England's naval strength, displayed in
1726 when she simultaneously equipped three fleets, did not fail
to make a deep impression upon France, whose leading states-

---

[1] Baudrillart, *op. cit.* III 339—41; Syveton, *op. cit.* 247—9; Arneth, *op. cit.* III, 227
—32.

men became more and more suspicious of England's designs and grew jealous of her power. [1])

Thus it came about that when, after the conclusion of the Preliminaries, England wished to strengthen the Hanover Alliance still further, and thus continued to urge the accession of the Landgrave of Hesse-Cassel, she did not meet with the support of France. According to a letter written to Fénelon, this power thought the scheme no longer suitable now that people began to contemplate tacitly doing away with the Treaties of Vienna and Hanover "pour donner une nouvelle face à la situation de l'Europe." [2])

From what followed we shall see that the Preliminaries did indeed open a new epoch. In 1725 European politics were all at sixes and sevens, but now a beginning was being made to put things in proper order and to return to normal relations. When the Emperor forsook the Ostend Company he gave up not only the bond which bound him to Spain, but also what had separated him from the Maritime Powers; the way was now opened for him to rejoin them and this he could not fail to do as soon as the unnatural Anglo-French union was dissolved. Thus did the Preliminaries usher in a new era, which first occupied itself with the breaking up of the Vienna Alliance, and then with the separation of France and England and the re-union of the Maritime Powers and Austria; the first of these acts was accomplished by the Treaty of Seville in 1729, the latter by that of Vienna in 1731.

The Preliminaries really constitute one of the outstanding points in the political history of the 18th century, but we must not lose sight of the fact that it was only in principle that these Preliminaries destroyed the work of 1725. At the moment this seemed to be unshaken and both Alliances continued in full force. Elizabeth was very far from turning all at once from the Emperor, and he for his part did all he possibly could to retain his hold over her. In the opinion of Prince Eugene the Preliminaries ought not to make any difference in the relations with the Spanish Court; on the contrary the two Courts ought to draw still closer together. [3])

---

[1]) *Eng. Hist Review* XVI, 83; Villars, *Mémoires* V, 80.
[2]) Morville to Fénelon, 10 July 1727, A. E. Hl. 370.
[3]) Arneth, *op. cit.* III, 226.

As to the Hanover Alliance, France had not the least intention of immediately withdrawing from it. This was very obvious on the death of George I., which took place suddenly only three weeks after the conclusion of the Preliminaries (June 22nd. 1727). This might have caused an important change in England's foreign policy. We are not thinking now of the Pretender, for at this time his chances of being restored were almost lost, but of the cabinet which it was generally thought would be dismissed. As Prince of Wales, the new King had thrown in his lot with the Opposition in Parliament and opposed his father, thus it was thought that he would certainly take his ministers from the ranks of the Opposition. However, as a matter of fact he did not do so, but kept his father's ministers. This was in a great measure due to Fleury, who gave him to understand that the retention of the cabinet would be agreeable to France. [1]) The Cardinal apparently feared that a new cabinet might be inclined to restore the Alliance with the Emperor and thus leave France isolated, while, acting as he did, he would bind the English government still closer to him. It was not long before George II. would declare that he was fully determined to continue the existing union with France. [2])

For the present France could not do without England, but at heart she was weary of her. This however was not her feeling towards the Republic, with whom she really wished to remain closely allied, with a view both to England and to the Emperor. The former, in the event of a rupture, would be far less formidable so long as the Republic sided with France. Nor was she likely to throw in her lot again with the Emperor so long as the Republic held him at a distance. In this respect France was somewhat uneasy. The attitude of the States on the East Frisian affair, of which we shall have to treat more fully, was a bad sign for her, as well as the prospect of the election of Slingelandt, who was considered in Paris as quite capable of reviving the Grand Alliance. [3]) Thus she considered it best to give the strongest assurances of her good feelings. Fénelon represented the Preliminaries as a strong proof that the alliance with France was the most certain way in which the inter-

---

[1]) Coxe, *R. W.* I, 287—8, *H. W.* 151 et seq.
[2]) Horace Walpole to Fleury, 3 July 1727 (Baillon, *Lord Walpole à la Cour de France* 298—9).
[3]) Morville to Fénelon, 26 June 1727, A. E. Hl. 369.

ests of the Republic could be definitely served, while he further
gave the assurance that, at the Congress, Louis XV. would take great
care that the work begun should be brought to completion. Not
content with confining himself to generalities he went further by
making it understood that his Royal Master was intended absolutely to insist upon the withdrawal of the Ostend Company's
charter. [1]) Nothing was more calculated to hold the Republic
aloof from the Emperor who could hardly be expected to agree
to this.

These assurances were never meant seriously, for the French
did not object to any equivalent for the suppression of the Company. They were, however, afraid of the Republic's acquiescing in
the equivalent of leaving to the Emperor some barrier-towns with
the corresponding part of the annual subsidy due to her; this did
not suit them, as they would much rather see Dutch troops garrisoning the barrier-towns than Austrian, and by no means
wished to see the Emperor's power in the Southern Netherlands strengthened. In order to prevent this, they pretended to
object to any equivalent whatever. This was also done with the
intention that the Republic, with regard to the suppression of the
Company, might be less dependent on her own moderation than
on her alliance with France. [2])

There was another object why these assurances were given, viz:
to prevent a new engagement. As will be remembered, the States
had not agreed to the proposals of March the 26th., but on the understanding that when once the Preliminaries had been concluded, they should be confirmed by the mutual guarantee of the
Hanover Allies. They wished to be secured by a new Act against
any re-opening of the Ostend trade, either before or after the
expiry of the period of suspension. Goslinga lost no time in
writing to the Maréchal d'Huxelles on this subject, but the
reply which he received was couched in very vague terms.[3]) And
when, after the Preliminaries had been concluded, Fénelon was approached on the subject of the promised guarantee, he tried to
avoid a direct reply by making the above-mentioned assurances

---

[1]) Two despatches of 12 June 1727 from Morville to Fénelon and subsequent
despatches from Fénelon to his Court, A. E. Hl. 369.

[2]) ibidem.

[3]) Goslinga to d'Huxelles, 26 March 1727; Fénelon to Morville, 18 April 1727; A. E.
Hl. 368.

in a firm manner and to as many people as possible. Now that the Congress — so reads a letter written to Fénelon — is so near at hand, nothing must be done which might offend the Court of Vienna, whose actions on the last occasion were very moderate. [1])

This of course refers to the negotiations preceding the Preliminaries. It was with the help of the Court of Vienna that France had been successful. This success however was only temporary, as, up till now, no well established peace had been concluded. In order to attain this the Emperor might perhaps be useful too. Hence it might be very profitable to keep him in the right mood. With this object the Cardinal impressed upon England the necessity of repairing the broken relations with him and of sending an envoy to Vienna [2]), while he himself continued to hold out hopes that the States might give a substantial equivalent for the suppression of the Company. [3]) By acting in this way, Fleury only made the Emperor more obstinate upon this point. In his dealings with the States he was, of course, wise enough to preserve the most absolute silence concerning this, while to them he insisted upon their standing out for unconditional suppression: in this way he tried to inspire the States with confidence in his intentions.

France therefore left no stone unturned in her efforts to maintain her alliance with the Republic, as also did England. The professions of friendship made on the accession of the new King left nothing to be desired. Finch was commanded to give the assurance that His Majesty, "looking upon the interests of the two nations to be so blended together, that their happiness and security depend upon the mutual good understanding between them, is fully resolved, not only to stand by the present alliances and the measures that have been taken in pursuance of them, but also to do everything in his power for supporting their State in the enjoyment of all their rights and privileges and for promoting the joint interests of both nations, as becomes an affectionate and

---

[1]) Morville to Fénelon, 12 June 1727. A. E. Hl. 369.
[2]) cf. the first instructions to Lord Waldegrave (26 May 1727, R. O. Germany 62), given by George I. shortly before his death. This exhortation of Fleury's is not in disagreement with what we have said his aim was, viz: to keep England from entering into an alliance with the Emperor. He had very much regretted the rupture of March, and in the interests of peace wished to heal it.
[3]) Huisman, *op. cit.* 423 note.

faithful friend and ally, intending to live with them upon a foot of the most perfect harmony and intimate union" [1]) These professions were repeated in a more terse form: the States might rely on George II. as on "their firm, true and inseparable friend and ally." [2])

The States on their part replied in the same way." It is impossible" — wrote Finch — "for any men to express greater zeal and inclination to H.M's person and government than the people of Holland do." [3])

The King considered the election of Slingelandt as a strong proof of the truth of these professions. Townshend assured Slingelandt that the King received the intelligence with the greatest joy, as he was convinced of his friendship for H.M. and his House as also of his zeal for the joint interests of the two countries, and that he looked upon it as a matter of congratulation to both himself and the Republic. [4])

In reply to this the new Pensionary requested Towshend to assure His Majesty on his part "que l'on ne peut être plus pénétré que je le suis que de la prospérité de son règne et de la stabilité de son throne dependent *vita salusque* de cette République." [5])

There is no doubt that in Slingelandt's opinion the prosperity of the reign of George II. and the stability of his throne depended on the continuation in power of the Whig administration. He was very much rejoiced at the retention of office by the ministers, especially so by that of Townshend, with whom he had been on terms of friendship for about twenty years; "un des plus facheux contretemps" — he wrote to him — "qui eût pu arriver dans mon nouveau ministère, eût été de vous voir déplacer du vôtre". [6]) There is no evidence that either he or any other man of importance in the Republic tried to prevent this "contretemps". In so far as the retention of office of the cabinet was influenced by foreign affairs, the intervention of Fleury must be mentioned in the first place, although it is by no means unlikely that, in addition to this,

---

[1]) Newcastle to Finch, 16 June 1727, R. O. Hl. 294.
[2]) Townshend to Finch, 30 June 1727, R. O. Hl. 294.
[3]) Finch to Townshend, 8 July 1727 R. O. Hl. 294.
[4]) Townshend to Slingelandt, 11 July 1727, R. O. Hl. 297.
[5]) Slingelandt to Townshend, 25 July 1727, R. O. Hl. 280.
[6]) Slingelandt to Townshend, 12 August 1727, in Vreede, *Voorouderlijke Wijsheid* 100—101.

Slingelandt's close relations with Townshend had some influence on the King's decision. [1]) In any case His Majesty set great hopes on co-operation with him.

In this he was quite right, although he would have been mistaken in thinking that, led by Slingelandt, the Republic would follow him in everything. France was as much her ally as England. Slingelandt, it is true, sided with the larger part of the regents who were of opinion that the alliance with England was the one which should be kept in the first place, [2]) though at the same time he set great store on being on good terms with France. In some respects Dutch interests were even better served by the alliance with France than with England, for instance, in regard to the superiority which the latter aimed at acquiring over Spain's commerce. The detention of the galleons and flotilla, though forwarding the objects of the Hanover Alliance, had caused a good deal of discontent, not only in France, but also in the Republic, while the joy, to which the safe arrival of the flotilla gave rise, was just as keenly felt in Amsterdam as in Spain [3]). It was also very well known that the Preliminaries were due in the first place to France and not to England. In the Republic the Cardinal was held in very high esteem, not only by those who feared war but also by the regents of Amsterdam who had strongly opposed a mere suspension of the Ostend Company instead of its total suppression. These latter were pleased that something had been achieved, while it was not difficult to set their minds at rest as regards the intentions of France. Fénelon's assurances contributed to this, as also the report delivered by Grovestins, who had been in Paris for the purpose of attending the conferences for settling a plan of campaign in the event of war. So there was now no longer any talk of a new guarantee. [4])

Slingelandt, however, understood perfectly well that all these protestations of France could not be taken with absolute seriousness. How strongly had she not asserted her intention of going to

---

[1]) The less so, if it be borne in mind that Townshend's elevation on the late King's accession, was in some measure due to the recommendation by the leaders of the Republic.

[2]) cf. the descriptions of the principal regents in Fénelon, *op. cit.* 165—191: at p. 188 he speaks of the "système de ceux qui supposent l'union avec l'Angleterre absolument nécessaire à la République, et *il faut avouer que c'est un système fort général*."

[3]) Wagenaar, *op. cit.* XVIII, 448—9.

[4]) ibidem 438—9; Fénelon to Morville, 9 June, 2, 17, July '27, A. E. Hl. 369, 370; Slingelandt to Goslinga, 5 July '27, F. G.

war should the proposals of May 2nd. meet with a refusal!
But owing to the curious ideas expressed and the motions moved
by the French members at the above-mentioned conferences (e. g.
that of attacking the Prussian fortress of Wesel and thus forcing
Frederick William into open enmity[1]), Slingelandt was very doubtful whether France really would have drawn the sword. But after
all, thanks were due to her for the suspension of the Ostend Company, and it was only with her aid that there was any hope of
having that suspension converted into suppression. So before
Goslinga left the Hague for his country home in Friesland, Slingelandt and Fagel discussed with him the policy which the Republic
should pursue, and the conclusion they came to was that she
could not do better than to closely maintain the alliance with
France. [2]

In accordance with this view the Pensionary acted from
the very first. Returning a visit to Fénelon who had called
to congratulate him on his election, Slingelandt said he
would be pleased if affairs could be treated "en toute ouverture et
confiance." To convince the French Ambassador the more of the
desirability of this method, he mentioned that Dubois had once
consulted him as to the best means of being successful with the
Republic, to which Slingelandt had answered that if France had
good intentions towards the Republic she could not do better
than send men who would deal openly and not be afraid of speaking their mind to the ministers; if, however, she wished to embroil
the Republic the case would be different and it would not be
necessary for him to give any advice at all. [3]

In this way Slingelandt tried to gain the confidence of France.
England wished to use the Republic as an auxiliary, and did not
wish to see her on too intimate a footing with the common Ally.
But Slingelandt was to maintain his independence and to go his
own way, as will be seen, to begin with, by his behaviour during
the difficulties which had arisen in the meantime.

II.

These difficulties came from the side of Spain. This power had

---

[1] Grovestins and Pesters to Fagel, 28 May 1727, R. A., S. G. 7317; Villars, *Mémoires* V, 66—70; Finch to Townshend, 3 June 1727, R. O. Hl. 293.

[2] Fagel to Goslinga, 30 Sept. 1727, F. G.

[3] Fénelon to Morville, 30 July 1727, A. E. Hl. 370.

been compelled to acquiesce in the Preliminaries, but had the intention to go back upon the concessions which she had made on the first opportunity. The death of George I. appeared to offer this. The King had issued mandates ordering Admirals Wager and Hosier to withdraw their fleets from the coast of Spain and from the coasts of Spanish America while he further commanded the Governor of Gibraltar to cease hostilities. Van der Meer, the Dutch Ambassador at Madrid, however, who was also entrusted with British interests at this time, was instructed not to forward these orders until Philip V. sent similar orders to his Generals and Admirals, which absolutely guaranteed to the English the return of all the Spaniards had seized, and in particular to the South Sea Company their ship the "Prince Frederick" with all her cargo. [1] Being disinclined to give any such orders, the King of Spain, on hearing of the death of the King of England, became even more so. He demanded the withdrawal of the English fleets but at the same time refused to raise the siege of Gibraltar. As to the yielding up of ships, he contended that the clause in the 5th article of the Preliminaries where this was stipulated only referred to the ships of the Ostend Company, and therefore in no wise to the "Prince Frederick". [2] In a letter which reached Fleury through Papal diplomatic channels, the decision as to Gibraltar was left to the French King, but the "Prince Frederick" and other ships won from the English were claimed by Spain on the plea that Hosier's squadron had done her so much damage. [3]

The English government was very indignant at this attitude. Newcastle wrote to Horace Walpole, that if things were going to continue in this way, the King would have to consider the necessity of sending reinforcements to his squadron off the Spanish coasts and to the fleet in the Indies. For the moment, however, he did not go so far as this, but Horace Walpole induced Fleury to write an answer which was to be forwarded through the Nuncio Massei, in which the English claims were set forth and fully justified and the Spanish Court urged to comply with them. [4]

---

[1] Horace Walpole to Van der Meer, 22 June 1727, R. A. S. G. 7358.
[2] Van der Meer to Horace Walpole, 8 July '27 with en cls., copy, R. A., S. G. 7358.
[3] La Paz to Aldobrandini, 5 Juny '27, cf. Horace Walpole to Van der Meer, 26 July '27, and other papers enclosed with Van der Meer's to Fagel, 1 Sept. '27, R. A. S. G. 7358.
[4] Newcastle to Horace Walpole, 13 July '27, Fleury to Massei, 25 July '27, ibidem.

England applied not only to France but also to the Republic. Townshend urged that Van der Meer should be instructed to declare that the parties to the Hanover Alliance insisted on the prompt and exact fulfilment of the Preliminaries. This request found favour with Slingelandt, who was greatly concerned about the attitude of Spain and expressed the opinion that if the Allies allowed themselves to be so played with before the Congress, they might be certain of meeting with little better treatment in it; in his opinion, the States would not object to giving the instructions now asked for. [1])

It is probable that he was less doubtful on this point, as just at this time the States were themselves discussing the sending of instructions to Van der Meer on a grievance of their own. The States had just learned from their ambassador that Patiño intended to make those persons who were interested in the "effects" (i. e. the cargoes) of the flotilla pay the piaster at the rate of nine and a half reals de plata instead of eight. This would mean a serious loss to the merchants concerned, and thus also to the Dutch traders. [2]) To prevent this Van der Meer was ordered by the States to make representations to the Spanish Court, while Hamel Bruynincx was instructed to do the same at Vienna (July 29th 1727). [3])

This resolution was communicated to Finch and Fénelon. The latter was not at all pleased with it, thinking that it had been drawn up secretly in concert with England in order to implicate the Republic. The difficulty made by the Republic was in his opinion intended to strengthen England with regard to the difficulties raised as to the releasing of the "Prince Frederick". For this purpose he wrote to Slingelandt that with regard to all their interests the Allies would have to act in concert, and that therefore it would be far better that the affair should be submitted first to the deliberations in Paris, between the Cardinal, Horace Walpole and Pesters, the Dutch envoy at Brussels, who on the death of the ambassador in Paris was now temporarily employed there. The Pensionary replied that he felt the force of these reflections and accordingly worked to get the resolution modified. As a result of

---

[1]) Townshend to Finch, 11 July '27, Finch to Townshend, 25 July '27, R. O. Hl. 294.
[2]) Secr. Res. S. G. 11 July '27.
[3]) Res. S. G. 29 July '27.

this Pesters was ordered to consult with Fleury and Horace Walpole and to withhold the instructions from Van der Meer and Bruyninx should the two former raise objections (July 30th.). [1]

This was indeed what they did. The Cardinal did not wish to compromise the success of his negotiations with Spain by any further difficulty, and in this, Horace Walpole and the English Government supported him. For Fénelon was mistaken in ascribing the resolution of the 29th. of July to their influence, they being wise enough not to run counter to their own interests. [2]

The origin of the resolution was not England but in all probability the province of Holland. Although Slingelandt was inclined to facilitate matters as far as possible, he would not have been able to prevent it alone. Fénelon's uneasiness, however, now provided him with a good reason for referring the matter to Paris where it certainly would be thrown out.

Fénelon, although mistaken, was not very far from the mark, for England had, as a matter of fact, attempted to bring influence to bear on the Republic. Neither was his action against her without effect. The effect, however, was indirect. The direct effect was that the instructions prepared for Van der Meer were never sent, but now those prepared for him at the request of England were not sent either. On the one hand the States could hardly be expected to instruct Van der Meer to make representations with regard to English grievances, while they were not allowed to send him orders with regard to their own. On the other hand from Fénelon's conduct Slingelandt could not but infer that France would take any representations from the Republic in bad part. He therefore apologized to Finch for not sending the instructions to Van der Meer by saying that the latter's representations could only add very little force to those of Fleury who appeared to be bent upon taking the lead in the negotiations. [3]

Thus far, Slingelandt had no reason to regret Fénelon's action. It had enabled him in the first place to render useless the resolution about the effects of the flotilla, and in the second place to excuse

---

[1] Fénelon to Morville, 30 July '27, A. E. Hl. 370; Res. S. G. 30 July '27; Wagenaar, op. cit. XVIII, 453—5.

[2] Louis XV. to Fénelon, 14 August '27, A. E. Hl. 370; Secr. Res. S. G. 19 August '27.

[3] Finch to Townshend, 12 Aug. '27, R. O. Hl. 294.

the Republic from assisting England, which, it seems, he had considered unnecessary, knowing that France was looking after the interests of England very well. This he had learned from Fleury's letter to Massei, which, however, had only been read to him and Fagel. Nobody else knew of it, and as they might mistake Fénelon's action and suspect France of being biassed in favour of Spain, Slingelandt asked Fénelon to let him have a copy to show to some of the principal men and thus to prevent the suspicion from taking root. He brought forth several arguments to prevail upon him. People would not believe him, he said, if he told them he had not a copy, and would consequently from the very beginning of his term of office as Grand Pensionary look upon him as a man who wanted to conduct affairs despotically. There was another argument which counted more than the personal one; some weeks previous to the Preliminaries a small squadron had been sent out under Rear-Admiral Spieringh to cruise in the Channel. Should war have broken out it would have co-operated with the English fleet in preventing any Belgian ships which might try to enter or leave the harbour of Ostend from doing so. At present however it was lying in English ports. Slingelandt told Fénelon that at the Assembly of Holland which would be held in a few days the question of the return of this squadron and its disarmament would be raised. It would, however, be very difficult for him to procure such an order unless he could go with some of the leading men into the details of the Cardinal's letter, and of the hopes which it revealed of the removal of the difficulties. [1]

It would undoubtedly have been to the interests of France had Slingelandt had a copy of this letter. The squadron was small and would only throw very little weight into the scales, yet the fact of its staying in an English port or not, was of no little importance. Things might come to such a pass that England would urge the co-operation of the Dutch navy. It would not so much matter to her that this consisted of only a few ships, or even of only one ship: it was for her merely a question of showing that there was co-operation. Slingelandt who foresaw this, wanted to make it impossible

---

[1] Fénelon to Morville, 5 Aug. '27, A. E. Hl. 370.

for the squadron to join the English fleet, and Fénelon ought to have supported him in his object. But instead he declined to give him a copy of the letter. Fénelon considered Slingelandt to be entirely devoted to England, and thus the Pensionary was compelled to combat the intentions of England without receiving any help from France.

III

These intentions were to draw the Republic with her into any measures which she might think necessary to take. To that end she showed herself most zealous on behalf of Dutch interests. As we have seen, the resolution of July 29th. was not to her liking and together with France she rendered it of no effect. Yet Townshend wrote to Finch that Horace Walpole had had orders to support it. [1]) Shortly before he had received intelligence that at Ostend, despite the suspension, two ships were being equipped for a voyage to Bengal, and although he had no confirmation of this he asked Finch to tell Slingelandt and at the same time to give him the assurance that should it prove true, the King would be willing to co-operate with the States in taking the necessary steps to prevent these ships from sailing. [2]) A few weeks later he even went so far as to urge that a strong protest should be made to the Emperor in the joint names of the Republic and England. [3])

He wished that this protest should be made, not only because it would not be easy to move the Republic to support England in her differences with Spain, unless her own interests should also appear to be at stake; but Townshend was also aroused to action against the Emperor by a further motive i. e. his bitterness against him. In Townshend's opinion the Emperor not only had been, but continued to be, the great enemy of England. [4]) He had attributed to him the authorship of the Vienna Alliance and now he imputed to him the difficulties made by Spain, this being in the Secretary's opinion his means of getting a share of the rich cargo of the "Prince Frederick." [5]) As a consequence of this

---

[1]) Townshend to Finch, 25 July '27, R. O. Hl. 294.
[2]) Townshend to Finch, 14 July '27, R. O. Hl. 294.
[3]) Hop to Slingelandt, 12 Aug. '27, R. A. Hl. 2978; Secr. Res. S. G. 19 Aug. '27.
[4]) Hop to Slingelandt, 9 Sept. '27, R. A. Hl. 2978; cf. Rosenlehner, op. cit. 331, 335.
[5]) Townshend to Finch, 25 July '27, R. O. Hl. 294; memorial inclosed in Horace Walpole's private despatch of 21 & 22 Aug. o. s. '27, R. O. France 186.

view of Townshend, Waldegrave, who had been sent out to Vienna to resume the broken relations, was now detained in Paris. It was only after much persuasion on the part of the Cardinal, that the late King had assented to the sending of this representative. [1]) The new King was hardly any better disposed towards the Emperor. He inveighed sharply against the actions of the Court of Vienna with the Prussian ambassador who had been sent to compliment him on his accession to the throne, saying that he had no intention of yielding to her or of allowing the despotism she exercised within the Empire to extend still further. [2])

On the whole the opinion of the Court of Vienna formed by the English was wrong. To be sure, she remained prepared for war [3]), but this could not be laid to her charge [4]). While as to her relations with Spain, she only supported her Ally in so far that she approved the latter's reading of the 5th. article of the Preliminaries, but then the Dutch envoy at Vienna, Hamel Bruynincx, also gave the same reading to this article, [5]) while a modern English historian has also agreed that the wording is by no means clear. [6]) As a matter of fact the Emperor had not as yet given any real cause for complaint to the Hanover Allies. On the contrary, the Preliminaries concluded with him in Paris on May 31st. were there ratified on July 29th.

Hence there was no reason why the Republic should flare up all at once on receipt of news from Townshend, for the truth of which he was in no way able to vouch. It was, of course, very well understood that the Belgians would not leave any means untried to evade the suspension. For this reason the Dutch were very much on the alert. On the conclusion of the Preliminaries the Ostend-Bruges canal was being deepened and dredged in order to attract thither the public sales of the Ostend Company. [7]) As to this Slingelandt instituted an inquiry to find out if

---

[1]) Coxe, R. W. I, 349. Instructions to Waldegrave, 26 May '27, R. O. Germany 62.

[2]) Droysen, Friedrich Wilhelm I, I, 442; of. the exaggerated information of De Broglie in Villars, Mémoires V, 77.

[3]) Droysen, op. cit. I, 443.

[4]) As was done by St. Saphorin, who believed that she continued tob e warlike, Pribram, op. cit. I, 456 note.

[5]) Hamel Bruynincx to Fagel, 9 Aug. '27, R. A., S. G. 7191.

[6]) Eng. Hist. Rev. XVI, 310.

[7]) cf. Huisman, op. cit. 424.

this work was being continued, and as a result of this inquiry learned that such was the case, and that no less than 2500
men were employed on the work. [1]

On receipt of the information about the two ships the Pensionary also had inquiries made at once, but the intelligence he
received was contradictory. [2] Certainty being desired, he instructed Pesters who, now that Spain's answer was pending, and that consequently affairs in Paris were at a standstill, had returned to
Brussels, to have a thorough investigation made and to spare neither expense nor trouble on it. [3] Now it happened that Pesters was
acquainted with a man who knew one of the Directors of the Ostend
Company personally, and this man was willing, for a reward, to go
to Ostend and Antwerp as a spy. His instructions were drawn up
by Slingelandt himself, and contained no less than thirteen questions embracing not only the Company's present action, but
also what its intentions were with regard to the suspension. [4]

Thus we see that Slingelandt was continually on the qui vive
as to whether the Ostend Company was in any way violating
the Preliminaries; his means to this end, however, were all carried on in secret. As to his public actions, he avoided giving offence
to the Court of Vienna as far as possible. The East Frisian affair
was an especial reason for this cautiousness.

Some years previously, violent quarrels arose between the Prince
and the States of that country, but to understand these properly,
and how the Republic was concerned in them, we must go
back for a while to the close of the 16th. century. As early as
the time we are now speaking of, the Count, afterwards Prince,
of East Frisia, was at variance with his subjects and particularly with the powerful town of Embden. Their discord
became mixed up with the struggle between the Dutch and
the Spaniards, the Count taking the side of the latter, while

---

[1] cf. Cronstrom to Slingelandt, 7 Aug. '27 and another letter, both enclosed in
Finch to Townshend, 19 Aug. '27, R. O. Hl. 294.

[2] Finch to Townshend, 1, 12, Aug. '27, R. O. Hl. 294.

[3] Finch to Townshend 19 Aug. '27, R. O. Hl. 294.; Pesters to Slingelandt 25 Aug. '27,
R. A. Hl. 2981.

[4] "Articulen om te dienen voor instructie van N. N.", enclosed in Pesters to Slingelandt, 26 Oct. '27; the questions are answered in the same paper; the spy's second depos-
ition is enclosed in the letter of 13 Nov. '27 from Pesters to Slingelandt, R. A. Hl.
2981. As to Slingelandt's thought cf. his letter to Pesters, burgomaster of Maastricht,
7 Oct. '27, about a certain De Rougemont of Liege. who pretended that he had an important secret to divulge, R. A. Hl. 2994 k.

10

the town of Embden applied to the States General for support. [1]
As it was a matter of great moment to the States General that
the town of Embden should not be compelled to side with Spain,
they garrisoned the town themselves. At first, this was only a
temporary measure, but it soon became one of a lasting nature,
and when, in 1611, they succeeded in concluding peace, the peace
of Osterhusen, between the Count and the States of East Frisia,
they obtained the right to garrison Embden and also the castle
of Leerort. [2] In this way the Republic occupied two strong
positions which served her as a cover on the Lower German side
and in Slingelandt's opinion these were just as important to her
as were the barrier-towns on the French side. [3]

East Frisia became, as time went on, more dependent on the
States General, as the States of this country repeatedly contracted loans with Dutch subjects, giving as security a first charge on
some part of the public revenues, this being guaranteed by the
States General. This the East Frisian States did in one instance
close upon the period of which we are treating, viz: in 1720 and
1721, for the purpose of repairing the dykes of their country,
which had been swept away by violent floods.

The military and economical position occupied by the States
General in East Frisia was accompanied by great political influence. The numerous "accords" between the Prince and the States
of this country, on the whole favourable to the latter, were concluded through their mediation and were guaranteed by them,
while should any dispute arise the States General had the right
of decision and explanation. Their influence was so great that
East Frisia was often called the eighth province of the Republic.

In the last quarter of the 17th. century however this influence
began to decrease. When, in 1681, the East Frisian States were
again at variance with their Prince, they did not apply, as was
usual with them, to the Hague, but to Vienna, and the Emperor
then entrusted their protection to the Elector of Brandenburg.
Taking advantage of this commission the Grand Elector put a
garrison into Embden beside that of the Dutch. There was all
the more reason for this garrison's remaining there, as in 1694 the

---

[1] Blok, *op. cit.* III, 334, 429, 462, 472, 472, 502.
[2] Blok, *op. cit.* IV, 65—6.
[3] Slingelandt to Townshend, 11 July '26, R. O. Hl. 280.

reversion of East Frisia was bestowed upon his son. The Republic was very indignant at Brandenburg's interference and at the cause which had given rise to it: i. e. the application to the Emperor, but at that time circumstances did not allow of her taking any action against it and asserting her rights.

But the time was yet to come when the East Frisian States would regret having turned aside from the Republic. The latter was very deeply concerned in the maintenance of the "accords", which conferred such a large share of authority upon the States of East Frisia, and gave only a very small one to the Prince. But the Emperor was not concerned in it; on the contrary, as it was just on these accords that the position of the Republic in East Frisia was founded, he could not when he thought of his own interests, be other than hostile to them. It is no more than natural that the Head of the Empire should try to put an end to the ambiguous position that East Frisia had occupied ever since the 14th. century, between the Empire on the one hand, and the Netherlands on the other. [1]) Hence it is no wonder that when Prince George Albert (1708—'34) aimed at extending his sphere of authority in spite of the "accords", he met with the support of Vienna.

It must be admitted that the East Frisian States themselves gave an incentive to his taking action. They allowed serious abuses and irregularities to creep into the administration of the finances, and denied to the Prince the right of supervision which he claimed. When, in 1720 and '21, he applied to the Emperor, he was justified by an Imperial decree. The States, however, declined to recognise that right, asserting that the constitution of the country was not in accordance with the law of the Empire, but according to the "accords," not "reichsconstitutionsmäszig", but "accordenmäszig".

This was not merely a theoretical dispute. When the Prince was denied the exercise of his right of supervision conferred by the Emperor, he forbade his subjects to pay taxes any longer to the Board of Administration at Embden. The Board, however, did not scruple to use force in the collection of the taxes and this gave rise to many collisions, and when the Prince convened a meeting of the States at Aurich, which town he had fortified, the Board

---

[1]) cf. F. Wachter, *Ostfriesland unter dem Einflusz der Nachbarländer*, Aurich 1904; H. Reimers, *Die Bedeutung des Hauses Cirksena für Ostfriesland*, Aurich 1905.

summoned the States to meet simultaneously at another place. Those which went to Aurich, were called the new, while those which went to the other place were called the old, States.

George Albert cared little for this opposition, as he considered himself sure of the support of the Emperor, who repeatedly issued decrees in his favour, and who, in 1723, commissioned August II. as Elector of Saxony, and the Duke of Brunswick-Wolfen- büttel with the carrying of these decrees into execution and the examining into and settling of these disputes between the Prince and the States. The "sub-delegates" sent by these Princes to East Frisia acted entirely in accordance with the wishes of George Albert. They summoned a new Diet, from which the partisans of the old States, who were now called the "Renitents", were excluded. All the old members of the Board of Administra- tion were dismissed by this Diet and others were appointed who were to sit at Aurich instead of at Embden (1724). The original Board, however, continued to meet at Embden, and hence there were two Boards for the same purpose, and as both of these Boards let out the excise duties on leases and as each tried to take possession of the offices set apart for this purpose, often by the use of violence on both sides, many fights ensued from time to time.

The Prince would have nothing whatever to do with an amic- able arrangement. The States had frequently expressed their will- ingness to come to some such arrangement, but all their efforts were in vain owing to the Prince's demand that they should sub- mit unconditionally to the Imperial decrees, it might perhaps ra- ther be said owing to the repugnance of his Chancellor Brenn- eisen to such a course. The latter was a stern, imperious man who absolutely ruled the Prince. Once, in 1725, they offered submission with scarcely any limitations, but at the behest of this man their submission was declined.

The most pressing representations of other powers were not of any use either, the States having more than once applied to the two powers who on former occasions had taken their inter- ests very much to heart and who still had garrisons in the coun- try, viz: the States General and the Elector of Brandenburg, who had now become King of Prussia.

It would by no means have been a matter for surprise if the latter had joined them, for neither the Prince nor the Emperor

liked the position which he occupied in East Frisia. The Prince
had repeatedly pressed upon the States the withdrawal of the
Prussian troops, and upon representations from him the Emperor
had enjoined the King to withdraw them himself. The latter was
just as little inclined to withdraw them, as the States were to send
them away, but did not support the States in any way. He advised
them to be reasonable in their dealings with the Prince and offered to act as mediator: in this way he remained quite neutral. [1]
Nevertheless the Emperor forbade him to interfere in any way
with the affairs of East Frisia and passed him over when the
above-mentioned commission was appointed. The princes who
should have been appointed were the Directors of the Westphalian
circle, as it was to this circle that the country belonged, but as the
King of Prussia, in his capacity of Duke of Cleves belonged to
their number, the Emperor with intent chose the commissioners
from outside the circle. This attitude of the Emperor's was not by
any means exceptional, he was unceasingly occupied with
schemes for the extension of his authority within the Empire: to
this end the Aulic Council was an instrument in his hands. So it
was that the King of Prussia came continually into collision
with this body, his power in particular always being a thorn
in the Emperor's side. [2]

Just as to Berlin, the East Frisian States also appealed to the
Hague, with equal lack of success. The States General continued
to repeatedly reinforce their garrison at Embden but not, however,
with a view to supporting them, but only for the purpose of
protecting the town from attack and to lend force to their ad-
monitions. They observed a strict neutrality; it is true that in the
beginning when there were disturbances they requested the Prince
to allow taxes to be collected by the Embden Board, as had been
the custom, but that the interests of their own subjects were their
only concern, was evidenced by the fact that when there were
two Boards they recognised the one just as much as the other.

This conduct was anything but to the liking of the States,
they wanted the States General to give them military support
in their struggle for the lease offices, and not only this,

---

[1] cf. Droysen, *Friedrich Wilhelm* I, I, 367.
[2] R. Koser, *Brandenburg-Preuszen in dem Kampfe zwischen Imperialismus and reichs-
ständischer Libertät*, Hist. Zeitschrift 96, 212—20; cf. Droysen, *op. cit.* I, passim.

bnt according to them the States General ought to maintain the "accords" and also their right to adjudicate in case of disputes. The latter, however, were very unwilling to do this: as often as they were urged in this direction, they remonstrated with the States of East Frisia upon their conduct in 1681, and later, when instead of appealing to them, as usual, they had applied to the Emperor, thus giving them clearly to understand that having brought about the present state of affairs on their own responsibility, nothing was now to be hoped for on the part of the Republic. Had the States indeed continued in their appeal to her, the Emperor could not have taken offence had she again acted the part played by her before, but having now taken action himself he would allow no foreign power to resume that part. Had the States General pretended to do so they would at once have been at loggerheads with him; so being fully aware of this they persisted in an attitude of neutrality.

Although they were neutral, they were not passive observers of the state of affairs. Again and again they exhorted the people of Embden to abstain from hostilities and respect the rights of the Prince while on the other hand they advised the latter to be reasonable and not to be too insistent upon an unlimited submission. In April 1726 they even went so far as to send a delegate to him, in the person of Lewe van Aduard, offering to act as mediators. Neither his efforts nor any other official offers were of the least avail with the Prince, even as a private effort on the part of Slingelandt. This latter at about this time took upon himself the trouble of drawing up a project which he thought might lead to a settlement. Really this was very advantageous to the Prince, but on its being communicated to the Chancellor it was considered by him as not being favourable enough, it being his aim, as Slingelandt observed, by the favour of the Court of Vienna to make his Master absolute and under him, to become the actual ruler himself. [1]

The States General applied also to the Court of Vienna, Hamel Bruynincx being repeatedly enjoined to make representations similar to those which were made to the Prince. The object of the

---

[1] Slingelandt to C. Hop, 21 Aug. '28; the project "Onvervankelijk projet van accommodement der verschillen in Oostfriesland" was an addition to this letter, R. A. Legatie 84.

States General, not only here, but also at any other Court wherever there was the least chance of their representations bearing fruit, was to work on behalf of an arrangement in the affairs of East Frisia which should avert the occupation of the country by military forces.

They worked very energetically indeed, for although they were not willing to take upon themselves again the maintenance of the "accords", still they had no intention of giving up "le pied" they had had "depuis un temps immémorial dans ce pays-là"; it was their desire to retain their garrisons not only as a means of safety on that side, but also as a means of securing the capital which had been invested in the East Frisian States and which would otherwise be in rather a bad way. [1]) While they became more and more aware that if the Prince should achieve his aim he would do away with their troops no less than with those of the Prussian King; striving as he was after absolutism, he would not allow these upholders of the liberty of the States, who had always been looked upon with envious eyes by his predecessors and himself, to remain any longer in the country. The Emperor was no better disposed towards the Republic either, and had all through approved the implacable attitude of the Prince. He also regarded the East Frisian affair as a very good means of exerting pressure upon the Republic in other matters. With regard to the Republic, as well as with reference to Prussia, the Emperor's conduct in this affair was inspired by his general policy, so much so that Slingelandt even got the impression: "c'est autant ou plus pour chagriner la République que pour gratifier le Prince, que l'Empereur sous l'apparence de justice use de force et contraint les Etats et les pauvres habitants du pays à s'opposer à l'introduction d'un despotisme qui anéantit tous leurs droits et privilèges et rend le Prince absolu de très borné qu'il a été jusqu'à cette heure." [2])

This petty monarch who constantly declined any amicable arrangement with the States of his country, whether director through the mediation of some outside power, caused the situation in East Frisia to go from bad to worse. From 1726 onwards there had been complete civil war. In that year the Renitents had been

---

[1]) Slingelandt to Townshend, 11 July '26, R. O. Hl. 280.
[2]) ibidem.

most prosperous; this fact, however, did not make the Prince any more amenable, but rather caused him to urge upon the Court of Denmark, with which he was related, the necessity of sending troops to his aid, and first with his own troops only and then with the aid of those sent him from Denmark he defeated the Renitents again and again in April and May.

Things looked very black for them, the more so as just at this very time (April 23rd. 1727) the Emperor had entrusted the coercion of the country to the Directors of the Westphalian circle, and more particularly to the King of Prussia. This latter proceeding may at first sight appear very strange, he having previously been ordered to withdraw his troops and to abstain from interference in any way with East Frisia [1]), and yet he was now entrusted with such a commission. It is, however, very easily accounted for as a consequence of what had happened in the meantime. As has already been said, the Emperor wanted to wean the King from his allegiance to the Hanover Alliance and had tried to win him over; in October 1726 he had succeeded in doing so, and by the Treaty of Wusterhausen promised him that he would try to bring about an arrangement with the Prince of Pfalz-Sulzbach as to the succession of Juliers and Bergh within six months. As this period had expired in April 1727 without the arrangement having been accomplished, the Emperor was compelled to ask for an extension of time, for a further three months. In order the better to retain his hold over him under the circumstances he now entrusted him with this commission.

This turn in affairs caused great uneasiness among the Renitents. For more than forty years Prussia had been one of the protectors of the States of East Frisia, and although Frederick William had remained neutral with regard to the difficulties, his garrison had all the same been a guarantee for the safety of Embden; now, however, it looked as though he were about to join their adversaries. The Emperor had already turned his back upon them, and now Prussia did the same thing. Hence they now began to repent of ever having forsaken their first love, and

---

[1]) Even as late as June 1726 the Emperor had conferred an "auxiliatorium" upon the Elector Palatine and on the Elector of Cologne, both of them Directors of the Westphalian circle, but not on the third director Frederick William, while he also conferred the same honour on George I. (Wiarda, *Ostfriesische Geschichte*, VII, 305—6).

again applied still more urgently to their first and oldest protectors, the States General. Two deputations went to the Hague
to lodge a request for the maintenance of the "accords" and of
the Embden Board and to ask that representations should be
made for the withdrawal from their country of the Danish troops.

Their reception was not of the most encouraging. Fagel reminded them that in 1681 they had applied to the Emperor; so far as
Embden was concerned, he added, the States General would look
after that town; he told them, however, that they need not expect
that the States General would make their own the cause of people
who had brought all this misfortune upon themselves by their own
acts. The States General, however, did not leave them to their
fate; these reproaches arose from the uneasiness of the moment.
The Prince's success, and the arrival of troops from Denmark had
made them apprehensive of the fate of their own garrisons,
and they thought that the position had been made worse by the
commission entrusted to Frederick William. [1]) As long as this
Prince had been on bad terms with the Emperor, it had not been
very dangerous for the Republic, their interests in East Frisia
then assuming something like conformity. [2]) Now however the
tables were turned, for it was feared that His Majesty of Prussia,
who had proved such a troublesome neighbour at other places,
would now acquire a much stronger position in East Frisia, and
that, at the expense of the Republic.

At this juncture little was to be hoped for from her Allies. When
the Danish troops had arrived in East Frisia in the preceding year
the Republic had preferred a request to both France and England
asking them, by virtue of the existing treaties, to support her
in maintaining her rights in the event of Embden's being attacked;
France, however, had declined to recognise this as a *casus
foederis*. [3]) England who was under special obligation on this
point, did not refuse, nor on the other hand did she evince
any interest in the affairs of the Republic. [4]) It was not that
the affairs of East Frisia were immaterial to the King-Elector for

---

[1]) Res. S. G. 15 May '27; Finch to Townshend, 20 May '27, R. O. Hl. 293; cf. Fénelon,
op. cit. 156—7.

[2]) cf. Wiarda, *op. cit.* VII, 186; Rousset, *op. cit.* IV, 456.

[3]) Chauvelin to La Baune, 18 Apr. '28, A. E. Hl. 374; Mémoire de Pecquet sur l'affaire d'Ostfrise, ibidem 375 f. 73—5.

[4]) Fénelon to Morville, 9 June '27, A. E. Hl. 369.

he was just as much a pretender to the succession to that prin-
cipality as the King of Prussia. But as long as the latter King
was more or less bound to the States, it was only natural, that he
should side with the Prince and support him, and it is a fact that
when he had interfered in the affairs of East Frisia it had always
been in favour of the Prince. It is very probably out of regard
for Frederick William, whom for other reasons he did not wish
to disoblige, that his interference had been so rare. At all
events, he was 'not by any means inclined to run contrary to the
Prince's views; thus the Republic's application met with but
scant success.

There seemed to be very little chance of relief, from whichever
side they looked, when suddenly the Court of Vienna extended
the helping hand. She held out hopes that provided the Renitents
submitted unconditionally the differences should be settled according to equity, and that the Renitents who had, under the letter of the decrees, forfeited all they were possessed of, should be
treated with clemency. In this state of affairs the States General
thought they could not do better than take the proffered hand
thus extended to them. This they did all the more readily as it
was just at this time (in May), a few days before the conclusion of
the Preliminaries, that the general trend of affairs was towards a
pacific solution. They therefore recommended the Renitents to
submit unconditionally, at the same time promising that they
would make representations that in the meantime the coercion of
their country should be adjourned. This they did without delay. [1]
The Renitents then lodged their submission without attaching
any conditions; this was on June 16th. 1727.

It is evident that the States General, by relying thus so much
upon the Emperor, had to some extent made themselves
dependent upon him. Hence the Court of France, which as we
have seen desired that there should always be some cause for fric-
tion between the Emperor and the Republic, on being informed
of what had been done at the Hague, immediately instructed
Fénelon to exhort the States General, in their relations with
the Emperor, not to lose sight of the fact that they were
the guarantors of the East Frisian "accords". It was not neces-

---

[1] Res. S. G. 15, 16, 20, 23, May '27.

sary that they should declare their opposition to any right
of pronouncing upon East Frisian affairs which the Emperor as
Head of the Empire might possess, but still they ought to let
him know that as there existed between the Prince and the
States of that country "accords" of which they were the guarantors, and on which the Imperial decrees encroached at several
points, they could not recommend the States of East Frisia to
submit, at least not until such time as they were authorised by
him to assure them of amnesty for what had passed, and to
guarantee that Justice should be done with regard to their rights,
by instituting an amicable examination into those Imperial
decrees, against which equitable objections were raised. On
receipt of these orders the resolutions of the States General had
already been passed, so Fénelon was not able to carry them out;
he therefore simply communicated them to Fagel and Goslinga.
These two statesmen expressed their regret that the resolution
had been arrived at so hastily. [1] Thus the States General could do
nothing more, they having in this respect thrown themselves
upon the Emperor. [2]

That the Republic had to be very careful in her dealings with
the Emperor would further appear from her conduct towards
other members of the Empire. In the spring of the year, disquieted
by the Treaty of Wusterhausen and by rumours to the effect that
in the event of war the German Princes and Circles would march
their troops into the Southern Netherlands, she had taken part
in an action favouring the neutrality of the Empire. With
this object in view, she had sent Keppel to the King of Prussia,
and Isselmuiden to the Electors and Princes along the Rhine,
as also to the Elector of Bavaria. [3] The second of these envoys
had been ordered, among other things, to deliver remonstrances to
the deputies of the five circles who had assembled at Frankfort,
but now after the conclusion of the Preliminaries, these remon-

---

[1]) Fénelon to Morville, 2, 9, June '27, A. E. Hl. 369. Fagel said it had been taken in
spite of him. From this it would appear that Slingelandt, who was not yet Pensionary, was
also against it, while expressions of opinion of his both in '26 and '28 regarding the Emper-
or's conduct as to East Frisia would agree very well with this.

[2]) This aperçu about East Frisian affairs has been built upon Wiarda, *Ostfriesische
Geschichte*, VII, Book XXX—XXXII; Fénelon, *op. cit.* 147—57; Rive, *op. cit.* 110—116;
Wagenaar *op. cit.* XVIII 282 et seq., 511 et seq.

[3]) Rosenlehner, *op. cit.* 307—8.

strances were countermanded without delay. [1]) Just at their
conclusion Isselmuiden was working for the accession of the
Landgrave of Hesse-Cassel, but the States gave him his instructions indicating that his work should now .be more the giving to the Princes of the Empire the assurance of the Republic's
friendship, than all this talk of the Hanover Alliance. [2]) As has
been seen, France did not promote this accession either, but, unlike France, the Republic had not tired of the Hanover Alliance.
To her it was not so much a question for the Alliance at that
time of seeking expansion as the retention of the power it
held. This is evidenced by what Slingelandt did on behalf of that
same Landgrave. The latter was very much afraid that England
would cease to pay the subsidy in return for which he kept 12,000
men on foot for her; not being able to provide for them himself, he
would fall an easy prey to the vengeance of the Court of Vienna
The Pensionary now advised Townshend against any such
course. [3])

With regard to the affair of Juliers and Bergh too, the Dutch
Government had to proceed very cautiously. We have already
mentioned that with regard to this they had not the least desire of
countenancing Prussia. This frame of mind had been one of the
reasons prompting them in their objection to theHanoverAlliance,
and why, once they had joined, Prussia broke away from it.

The Elector Palatine who had at first tried to prevent the Republic from joining, was much rejoiced at this turn in the state
of affairs, and when after the Treaty of Wusterhausen he became very uneasy lest the Emperor should oblige him to cede
Bergh to Prussia, he also applied to the Hague. His representative
there, Schmidmann, sounded all the principal men, including
Slingelandt, who, although they did not commit themselves to any
definite declaration, nevertheless expressed themselves as being
in favour of the Prince of Pfalz-Sulzbach, assuring him of their ap-
preciation of this and the Elector's constancy in not entering
into any agreement with the King of Prussia. [4]) This constancy could

---

[1]) Secr. Res. S. G. 5 June '27.
[2]) Secr. Res. S. G. 12 June '27.
[3]) Finch to Townshend, 8 Aug. '27, R. O. Hl. 294; H. Hop to Slingelandt, 12 Aug.
'27, R. A. Hl. 2978; by Townshend's influence only 1200 of the Landgrave's soldiers
were disbanded.
[4]) Rosenlehner, *op. cit.* 221—4.

not possibly be sustained, the Emperor brought great pressure to bear on the Prince and he had to send a plenipotentiary to Vienna, but then without any delay the comforting news was sent to the Hague, that not a single part of the succession would be ceded. [1])

The Court of Mannheim was really not in earnest about an agreement with the Berlin Court, and as soon as peace appeared to be assured her only concern was that the matter should be brought before the Congress and be decided there in her favour. In the final treaty an article should be inserted that the House of Pfalz-Sulzbach was to succeed to Juliers, Bergh, Ravenstein and Winnenthal while the House of Brandenburgh should remain in possession of Cleves, Mark and Ravensbergh, until such time as the dispute might be settled in a legal manner. This, however, was not possible except with the help of one or more of the parties to the Congress i. e. those who had settled the Preliminaries. The Elector applied to the Vienna Allies for this object, but seeing that the Emperor was trying to get a general authority in the name of the Princes of the Empire to act for them at the Congress, little was to be hoped for from that quarter; he therefore placed his hopes upon the Hanover Allies, and of these he applied to France and the Republic. [2])

The men at the Hague were very careful what they did. However much inclined they were to favour the Palatine scheme, they nevertheless took great care not to incur the displeasure of the Court of Vienna. Towards her they observed the strictest neutrality. In answer to dispatches written by Hamel Bruynincx in which he stated he was being asked on all sides the opinion of the States, he was instructed to reply that they took no part in the dispute, it being an affair belonging to the Empire, which it was better to leave to the competent judge. On account, however, of the proximity of the Duchies a friendly settlement was the one which would most appeal to them, either at, or outside of, the Congress. [3]) Somewhat more favourable instructions were sent to Isselmuiden although these, too, were vague. [4]) Even if the leading men praised the article in their conversations with Schmidmann, they too went no further than generalities, and repeatedly advised great caution.

---

[1]) ib. 255—6, 308.
[2]) ib. 272—310.
[3]) Secr. Res. S. G. 7, 28, July '27.
[4]) Secr. Res. S. G. 30 June '27; if he really did allude to an alliance, as Rosenlehner says (*op. cit.* 310—'11), he went beyond his instructions.

At the same time they showed a friendly disposition: Slingelandt took it upon himself to advocate the interests of the Palatinate with Townshend, who was to call at the Hague on his way
to Hanover. [1] Not only did he do this, but he sent him later a
copy of the article in order that he (Slingelandt) might learn the
opinion of the English Court upon it. It will not be out of place here
to remark that the relations between the English and Mannheim
Courts were by no means cordial, the former having taken offence
at the Elector's having joined the Emperor in the previous year in
spite of all her efforts; the English Court also complained at his
conduct with regard to several affairs of the Empire. [2] The
Dutch now tried to restore the former good understanding, and
to this end Isselmuiden advised the Elector to avail himself of the
opportunity presented by the accession of the new King to the
throne, to fill the vacant position of representative at London,
unfilled for some time on account of the rupture in the relations.[3]
Slingelandt, as we have seen, also used his influence with Townshend for the same purpose. Townshend did not consider the
article as being unsuitable, if only the legal way were excluded,
as then the affair would come up at the Aulic Council, and in
this way to the disposal of the Emperor. He however did not
think that the Elector Palatine and his family had deserved anything like that from the Hanover Allies. The King of Prussia
would also be very much annoyed by it, the very proposing of
such a thing would have the effect of bringing him more on to the
side of the Emperor. It would be very foolish indeed, to estrange
the one, when it was not even sure that an advantage would be
obtained from the other, but should the Electors of the Bavarian
and Palatine houses be willing "to act a right part in relation to
the Empire and to the Public" and to co-operate to that end with
the Hanover Allies, it would not be a bad thing to encourage
them and to insinuate that an article of that nature would probably not be disapproved of. [4]

By this acting a right part Townshend meant: opposition to

[1] Rosenlehner, *op. cit.* 311.
[2] Rosenlehner, *op. cit.* 113, 222, 312—4, 323—4; Fénelon to Chauvelin, 27 Feby.
'28, A. E. Hl. 373.
[3] Rosenlehner, *op. cit.* 342.
[4] Townshend to Finch, 15 Aug. '27, R. O. Hl. 294; cf. the conduct of Horace Walpole
towards Grevenbroch, the representative of the Elector Palatine at Paris, Rosenlehner,
op. cit. 314, '18, '23—'24 & '25.

the Court of Vienna. This is what he was constantly aiming at, as for instance when he proposed a union with the Protestant Princes to support the religious and political liberties of the Empire. Slingelandt, however, at once remarked that this could only lead to a counter. union of the Catholic Princes. [1]) The difference between them was not that religion came first with England and not with Slingelandt; for this was not the case with England either. At this very time Waldegrave was given instructions that he should on arrival at Vienna bring home to the representatives of all the Princes of the Empire, without distinction as to religion, the dangerous consequences which might result from the general authorization which the Emperor sought to obtain, and advise them that, far from giving such authorization, they should take advantage of the opportunity offered bij the Congress in order to obtain redress for their grievances and a guarantee against any further encroachments on their rights and privileges. [2]) The difference between England and the Republic was that the former was decidedly hostile to the Emperor, while the latter wanted to spare him and was at least as anti-Prussian as anti-Austrian. Isselmuiden also had instructions to warn the Princes against the Emperor's scheme, but in these instructions quite a different note was struck, namely that they, the Princes, must not lose sight of the fact that the Emperor's interests might be quite other than theirs. [3]) The Dutch did not neglect their own affairs, but their hostility towards the Emperor was so small that they even went so far as to try to improve the relations between him and England. When Slingelandt heard that the Court of Vienna feared the return of St. Saphorin, he immediately applied to Townshend in order to prevent it. [4]) This rumour proved to be erroneous, Waldegrave being already in Paris, where, as we saw, he was detained as a result of the difficulties which had arisen with Spain. This caused Slingelandt to apply a second time to Townshend to allow him nevertheless to go to his post. [5])

This was one of the ways in which Slingelandt worked for the

[1]) Townshend to Van Ittersum, 18 Aug. '27, Van Ittersum to Townshend, 9 Sept. '27, R. O. Hl. 296.
[2]) Townshend to Waldegrave, 7 Aug. '27, R. O. Germany 62.
[3]) Secr. Res. S. G. 1 Sept. '27; Fénelon to Chauvelin, 19 Sept '27, A. E. Hl. 371.
[4]) Hop to Slingelandt, 12 Aug. '27, R. A. Hl. 2978.
[5]) Hop to Slingelandt, 9 Sept. '27, R. A. Hl. 2978.

preservation of peace, but he also worked in another way. Spieringh's squadron had been ordered to return home and to disarm. No sooner was Townshend informed of this than he pressed for a delay in the carrying out of this order; before this request reached the Hague however, the resolution had already been passed. [1])

Slingelandt was obliged to bring this about alone, Fénelon having refused him the assistance asked for, though this consisted merely in his being furnished with a copy of Fleury's letter to Massei. This request, which had been for a time dropped, was again made when England tried to make sure of the Republic by asking her what her intentions would be should England be denied the satisfaction she required from Spain. Then the Pensionary again had recourse to France. [2])

In doing this it was not Slingelandt's aim that England should fail to obtain this satisfaction; this is evident from his expression of opinion regarding a suggestion of Buys. The Preliminaries of Paris which had been concluded with the Emperor had also been ratified, as we have seen, but on account of the difficulties raised by Spain, the Hanover Allies had delayed ratifying the Preliminaries concluded with this power at Vienna. In a conversation with Fénelon, Buys now expressed the fear that this delay might cause the Congress to be postponed too; he therefore suggested that this should be opened with the Emperor alone. Slingelandt, however, rejected this idea: the difficulties must first be removed and then the Congress should be opened with the two Vienna Allies. In his opinion England would not come if there were no representative from Spain, and what was there to be done without England? [3])

Although in this respect he supported the interests of England, he still at the same time gave Fénelon clearly to understand that he was by no means so entirely devoted to this power. Speaking of Gibraltar, he said that the conduct of Spain had made it impossible for England to fulfil the promise of George I., made in his letter to Philip V. "assez formellement", for as to

---

[1]) Hop to Slingelandt, 12 Aug. '27, R. A. Hl. 2978; Res. Hl. 8 Aug. '27; Res. S. G. 12 Aug. '27.
[2]) Fénelon to Chauvelin, 27 Aug. '27, A. E. Hl. 370.
[3]) Fénelon to Morville, 30 July '27, Fénelon to Chauvelin 27 Aug. '27, A. E. Hl. 370.

the consent of Parliament "ce n'a point été une promesse d'enfant faite à l'Espagne et quand le feu Roi d'Angleterre a promis, il a du savoir les moyens de faire consentir son parlement"; and with reference to the commercial privileges which England enjoyed, Slingelandt regretted that the deference one owes to one's allies did not often allow of the taking advantage of favourable opportunities when they presented themselves. These privileges, he added, had been acquired by England to the disadvantage of the Republic. The latter had first considered these a violation against which she was entitled to complain, yet which she had later guaranteed to England, not in ignorance but of necessity. [1]

These observations were made by Slingelandt in order to induce France to support the Republic in counteracting England's schemes. And how could France do this? By removing everything that caused confidence in her to decrease; for the more trust the Republic placed in France the less likely was she to follow England. Circumstances had recently arisen which caused confidence in France to fall from the place it had occupied immediately after the Preliminaries. The reconciliation between the two Courts of Spain and France took place in August 1727. This was accompanied by the dismissal of Morville, who was disliked by their Catholic Majesties on account of the share he had had in the sending away of the Infanta, but who on the other hand passed as a friend of the Hanover Alliance. Thus it was feared that France was entering into too close relations with Spain and also with the Emperor. The origin of this fear was very trifling. It was that it had been rumoured that the Congress which, it had been settled, should meet at Aix-la-Chapelle, would now meet at Cambrai. As a matter of fact this alteration was made, the better to suit the convenience of the Cardinal, but in the Republic it was attributed to a desire to gratify the Emperor, and the fact that the States had not been informed of this change's having been made, appeared to give some colour to this suspicion. [2]

Slingelandt did not harbour either this or any other such sus-

---

[1] Fénelon to Chauvelin, 27 Aug. '27, A. E. Hl. 370.
[2] Van Ittersum to Townshend, 12, 22, Aug., 9, 16, Sept. '27, R. O. Hl. 296; Finch to Townshend, 26 Aug. '27, R. O. Hl. 294; Fénelon to Morville, 20 Aug. '27, A. E. Hl. 370; Fénelon to Fleury, 12 Sept. '27, A. E. Hl. 366; Hop to Slingelandt, 29 Aug. '27, R. A. Hl. 2978.

picion. He acknowledged that the fact that the Republic had not
been informed was owing to nothing more than an omission. He
was not opposed to the reconciliation either. It is true, that in his
opinion it was not a matter for the Republic to promote, so that
when Van der Meer was of opinion that it was his duty to exert
himself to this end, he received a hint from the Hague not to do
so .[1]) Slingelandt nevertheless considered that the reconciliation
might be in the interests of the Hanover Allies, France then being
the better able to influence Spain if the friendship and diplomatic relations were resumed. [2]) It was, however, not enough that
he should think so, others must also be brought to this way of
thinking; to this end he took the opportunity of letting Fénelon see
what had given rise to the suspicion. The ambassador admitted
that in this the Pensionary acted as one who desired that suspicions should be removed, not as one who would strengthen them
and profit by them in order to alter the established confidence.
Fénelon, however, did not trust him, and again declined to give
Slingelandt a copy of Fleury's letter, which better than anything
else would have enabled him to strengthen confidence in the good
intentions of France. [3])

It should be mentioned that Fénelon's conduct was not altogether in accordance with the wishes of his government. When
Slingelandt made his first request the government had approved their ambassador's refusal, but at the same time they instructed him to yield to the request, should it be made a second
time. [4]) Chauvelin, Morville's successor, wished that this permission had been made use of; not that he believed in Slingelandt's
intentions, for he considered the Pensionary's conversations
with Fénelon had all the appearance of being false confidences,
but in his opinion Fénelon was not to let it be seen that these
confidences were received with distrust; he must avoid the
snare that was set for him, without appearing to see it. [5]) The
Cardinal for his part too was no less desirous of inspiring the Republic with confidence in France: he himself sent an apology for the

[1]) Baudrillart, *op. cit.* III, 342—3; Van der Meer to Fagel, 30 June '27, R. A., S. G.
7358; Van Ittersum to Townshend, Finch to Townshend, 25 July '27, R. O. Hl. 296, 294.
[2]) Finch to Townshend, 12 Sept. '27, R. O. Hl. 294.
[3]) Fénelon to Morville, 20 Aug. '27, idem to Chauvelin, 27 Aug. '27, A. E. Hl. 370.
[4]) Louis XV to Fénelon, 14 Aug. '27, A. E. Hl. 370.
[5]) Chauvelin to Fénelon, 4 Sept. '25, ibidem.

omission which had occurred. Fénelon read it to the Pensionary, and the latter persuaded him, notwithstanding the lateness of the official announcement, still to inform the States of the change of place for the holding of the Congress. [1]) In this and similar ways Slingelandt was continually trying to allay all speculations which might in any way impair the good understanding with France, but owing to Fénelon's conduct he did not meet with that measure of success which it was so desirable to achieve with a view to England.

This power became more and more uneasy; the answer to Fleury's letter to the Nuncio Massei was not yet to hand; the Court of Spain was in no hurry. First they had an excuse in the fact of the Queen's confinement and secondly in the state of the King's health so that the reply which ought to have been, and could very well have been, in Paris in the middle of the month of August had not arrived at the beginning of September. [2]) The English government now began to fear more and more that, abiding by her interpretation of Article 5 of the preliminaries, Spain would not give up the Prince Frederick. Townshend was furious: the article, he asserted to Hop, was perfectly clear, it had no more reference to the Ostend ships than it had to those in the Indies and therefore under that article the Prince Frederick must be given up absolutely. As long as matters stood so, there could be no exchange of ratifications with Spain, neither would Waldegrave be instructed to proceed on his journey from Paris to Vienna. [3])

This latter measure had reference to the Emperor, for according to England he was the mentor of Spain, and therefore action had also to be directed against him. England had naval strength enough to enforce Spain to return the Prince Frederick, but supposing there were a collision with the Emperor she would have to greatly rely upon her Allies for landforces. [4]) Therefore her policy was to incite these Allies against him, a policy which, however, had very little effect, France showing hard-

[1]) Fleury to Fénelon, 23 Aug. '27, R. A. Hl. 2981; Fénelon to Fleury, 2 Sept. '27, idem to Chauvelin, 5 Sept. '27, A. E. Hl. 366, 370; Res. S. G. 4 Sept. '27.
[2]) Van der Meer to Horace Walpole, 30 Aug. '27, R. A., S. G. 7358.
[3]) Hop to Fagel, 29 Aug. '27, R. A., S. G. 7348.
[4]) cf. Hop to Slingelandt, 12 Aug. '27, R. A. Hl. 2978.

ly any disposition to second England's strenuous policy [1]), while
Slingelandt preferred to pursue a serious inquiry before embark-
ing upon it. Now, according to the last news received from Pesters the story of the equipment of the two ships at Ostend was
without foundation. [2]) Hop was instructed by Slingelandt to
inform Townshend of this, but the latter would not admit that
his information on this point had been somewhat hastily delivered [3]); he was not desirous of losing the only thing by which he
thought he might be able to induce the Republic to take part
in activities against the Emperor.

At this juncture he did not by any means regret the appearance of a matter which seemed to justify his distrust of the Court
of Vienna, the list affair. As to the suspension of the Ostend Company, it had been stipulated that those ships which had set out
before the Preliminaries, should be allowed to return freely. In
order, however, to prevent any evasion, a list of these should be
drawn up and be delivered by the Emperor. This list had been
long delayed, but on August 30th. it was at last handed to
the States.

This list, however, did not meet with their approval, as it included
some ships which had left Ostend only after the Preliminaries. What
gave more cause for dissatisfaction however, was the note added
to the nomenclature of the ships, in which the Directors of the Ostend Company stated that before the establishment of the Company the late Marquis De Prié had occasionally given a blank
passport to Hume who was the Director-General of the factory
at Bengal, to be made use of should an opportunity arise of
buying ships in India and sending these home to Europe. The
directors explained that this was only added *pro memoria*,
it might ensue that Hume had now done the same thing in the
name of the Company. [4]) The intention was very obvious: in
this way more ships than were allowed by the Preliminaries —
nobody could say how many — might be chartered for Ostend.
At the Hague it was thought that instead of the twelve
mentioned on the list perhaps fifty might come; this appeared

[1]) *Eng. Hist. Rev.* XVI, 313.
[2]) Pesters to Slingelandt, 21, 25 Aug. '27, R. A. Hl. 2981.
[3]) Hop to Slingelandt, 29 Aug. '27, R. A. Hl. 2978.
[4]) Rousset, *op. cit.* III, 412—4; cf. Huisman, *op. cit.* 249.

rather to consolidate the Ostend Company than to suspend it. [1])

This incident was not calculated to make people think well of the Court of Vienna, and this being connected with the many difficulties raised by Spain, the same tendencies were perceived in both. As a matter of course all this caused the above-mentioned suspicions to gain ground. [2]) This was not favourable to France, she, however, could do nothing to allay the uneasiness caused by the lodging of the list, for any such measures which she might adopt, would have been attributed to partiality for the Emperor. Fénelon was as a consequence enjoined to avoid any and everything which might either tend to allay or increase the excitement of the Dutch. [3]) This contretemps however, suited England very well indeed. The news about the two ships having failed in its effect, new hopes were now awakened that the list would rouse the Republic against the Emperor and also simultaneously against Spain, with whom he appeared to be so very intimately allied. This would be of so much the more consequence to England now that Spain's answer had at last arrived.

IV.

This answer was rightly characterised by the Duke de Villars as "très obscure sur les raisons, mais claire sur la résolution" [4]). A very confused document, it did not, however, leave any doubt as to the great point i. e. the releasing of the Prince Frederick. This was again declined, the matter having still to be discussed at the Congress. What use would the holding of this meeting be if the points at issue were already settled by the articles of the Preliminaries? In that case, these would not be preliminary but definite points. [5])

It was expressly said that these views were approved of by the Emperor, and it was this that caused Philip V. on the one hand to persevere in his conduct; on the other it was the expectation that his nephew, the King of France, would so soon after the reconciliation do nothing in the support of his adversary.

---

[1]) Van Ittersum to Townshend, 9 Sept. '27, R. O. Hl. 296.
[2]) Fénelon to Chauvelin, 5, 11 Sept. '27, A. E. Hl. 371.
[3]) Chauvelin to Fénelon, 10 Sept. '27, ibidem.
[4]) *Mémoires* V, 94.
[5]) La Paz to Aldobrandini, 28 Aug. '27, translation, R. A. S. G. 7358.

This expectation, however, was not realised. Rottembourg who was to go to Madrid as ambassador, was ordered (Sept. 18th.) to urge the release of the Prince Frederick, and in every way by his actions and words to show that France was true to her Allies. [1] This time action on the part of France was not confined to Spain; she also made representations to the Court of Vienna. Richelieu had to complain of her conduct and not to conceal the fact that his government attributed Spain's answer in a great measure to her. [2] In answer to Fonseca's solicitations, that the Hanover Allies should send the ratifications of the Preliminaries concluded at Vienna thither, that they might be exchanged for those of Spain, Fleury told him very plainly that Spain should previously have acted up to the Preliminaries. [3]

Although, as we have seen, France went a long way in supporting Englands' interests, yet she did not go far enough according to Horace Walpole. On the arrival of the answer from Spain he was furious, and though not altogether excluding diplomatic measures, he was none the less vehement in his desire that from that moment vigorous measures should be taken in concert. This was not to the liking of the French Ministers, but it is very doubtful if they could have resisted his pressure, had he been assisted by Pesters; the latter, however, did not support him, but on the contrary spoke with great moderation. Spain must be compelled to give up the Prince Frederick, but on the other hand war must be avoided too, while peace must be preserved by all means. [4] So, unsupported by Pesters, Horace Walpole's vigorous measures met with no measure of success.

He was quite well aware to whom this was due, and a reproach to Pesters was implied in his observation to him that he had been too careless about the list. [5] For the English government had calculated that the Republic would join the affair of the list to that of the Prince Frederick and support them on the latter point, in return for their support on the former. [6] The position

---

[1] Baudrillart, *op. cit.* III, 348—'9.
[2] Louis XV. to Richelieu, copy, R. A. Hl. 2981.
[3] Pesters to Fagel, 20 Sept. '27, R. A. S. G. 7317.
[4] Chauvelin to Fénelon, 18 Sept. '27, A. E. Hl. 371.
[5] Pesters to Slingelandt, 21 Sept. '27, R. A. Hl. 2981.
[6] cf. Townshend to Finch, 5 Sept. '27, R. O. Hl. 294. No sooner were they informed of the objections to be made to the list than they consulted the Directors of the East Ind. Co. about it (Hop to Fagel, 12 Sept. '27, R. A. S. G. 7348).

had changed since July, for they were now in favour of adding to the English grievance a Dutch one. This calculation, however, was not fated to meet with success; the result of the deliberations in Paris fell far short of expectations. Rottembourg's instructions, it is true, were "as right and hearty as could be desired", [1] but the Allies ought to have gone further than "simple offices". At this juncture vigour had to be shown. What George I. said on this subject to Broglie, was by no means equivocal, and suiting the action to the word, he gave Wager orders to prevent the sailing of the Spanish squadrons, which were then lying in the port of Cadix. [2] Further, not being disposed to content himself with what had been decided at Paris, he enjoined Horace Walpole to propose the making of a joint declaration to Fonseca that the Hanover Allies should not be obliged to allow the Ostend ships to return freely, unless the Emperor procured from Spain the complete execution of the Preliminaries and acted up to them himself. The ambassador also had instructions to press for a naval expedition to Ostend. [3]

It is worthy of notice that most of these measures were directed, not against Spain, but against the Emperor. The reasons for this were twofold: in the first place, the English attributed Spain's conduct to the advice and encouragement which she got from Vienna; and secondly with a view to the States General, who were especially interested in the Ostend affair. Knowing as they did that little was to be expected from France, the English were very keen on winning the States. Pesters' conduct did not cause them to desist in their efforts to thus win the States, as his action had been only provisory, his masters having not yet been informed of Spain's answer; now, however, both that and the instructions given to Rottembourg and Richelieu would be made known to them. It was of the greatest importance to England that they should take a vigorous resolution this time; in order to promote this, taking up the same position followed with regard to the list affair, England desired that all grievances should be set side by side, not only the English but also and in no less degree the Dutch, and particularly those which had reference to the Ostend affair. To

---

[1] Townshend to Finch, 15 Sept. '27, R. O. Hl. 294.
[2] Villars, *Mémoires* V, 96.
[3] Pesters to Slingelandt, 20, 21 Sept. '27, R. A. Hl. 2981.

further this end, Townshend was not at all sorry that he could again bring forward the news of the two ships being equipped at Ostend, concerning which he received confirmation in these very days from various reliable and trustworthy sources. So much zeal for the interests of the Republic would be sure to bear fruit, and induce her to join issues with England, and if this were so then France would be obliged to follow suit. [1]

As yet France was of a contrary mind, her ministers being opposed to the use of vigour. Unlike the other members of the King's Council, who were very uneasy at hearing of England's warlike disposition and preparations, [2] these were not without hope that it would still be possible to preserve peace. This hope had the Republic for its foundation. Pesters' conduct appeared to be a good sign of her being well disposed, and Fénelon wrote from the Hague that the anger about the list was abating and that people there were in a mood to avoid flaring up at such things as might delay the opening of the Congress. The ministers relied so much upon the Republic, that in their secret instructions to Rottembourg they mooted the idea that the Prince Frederick should be delivered to her; still, however, they were not by any means sure of her. [3] Chauvelin thought it was not beyond the regions of possibility that what were taken to be signs of her good disposition were only signs intended for no other purpose than that of indirectly sounding the real intentions of France. It was a difficult matter for him to believe that the Republic, ruled by Slingelandt, should differ so widely from England. If this really were the case, and if before going to war it were the desire to exhaust all means of persuasion and in any case to open the Congress with the Emperor, then quite another scheme ought to be framed. Instead of working alone in order to stop England, France would then be able to make the Dutch contribute a share towards this end; and perhaps, especially as the Emperor was urging for a speedy opening of the Congress, she could manage affairs, so that the demerit of entering into negotiations from which his Ally would be excluded as long as the difficulties concerning the Prince Frederick were still unsettled,

---

[1] cf. Townshend to Finch, 5, 15 Sept. '27, R. O. Hl. 294; Hop to Slingelandt, 19 Sept. '27, R. A. Hl. 2978.

[2] Villars, *Mémoires* V, 96.

[3] Baudrillart, *op. cit.* III, 349.

would fall upon him. It was really worth the trouble, to clear this matter up. So Fénelon was now instructed to institute an investigation to find out whether the Dutch would be ready to go to war, merely over the giving back of this ship or whether they would be inclined to contemplate expedients for getting it away from the hands of the Spaniards, without its being for the present handed over to England. [1])

In order the better to secure chances of success, the French ministers tried to make the zeal, shown by England for the Republic, look suspicious; and at the same time to prove that it was France who really had the interests of the Republic at heart. Fleury addressed himself in this strain to Pesters. [2]) While Fénelon received instructions to add to the communication of the above-mentioned documents, the answer of Spain and the instructions to Rottembourg and Richelieu, that it was for the purpose of saving time that his Royal Master deliberated with Horace Walpole and Pesters, but that his measures were in the common interests, and should the States have any matter which they desired to see accomplished, they were expressly invited to make it known. Fénelon was also instructed to add another matter to this communication, viz: the firm assurance that the King of France would not sacrifice his Allies' interests and his good faith to the resumption of friendship with Spain. [3]) In this way the Court of France hoped to remove the suspicion that she was in too close relations with Spain. Fénelon was further enjoined most earnestly to avoid above all things, in the negotiations he was to open on handing over the documents, the raising of any mistrust. [4]) Without, however, being conscious of it himself, he was to fail to observe this very wise precept.

No sooner had he received the documents (Sept. 24th.) than he went to Slingelandt and Fagel; [5]) these were most satisfied with

---

[1]) Chauvelin to Fénelon, 18 Sept. '27, A. E. Hl. 371.

[2]) He told him, we have to be vigilant "sur ce que nous pourrions désirer et demander pour les interêts de notre commerce au lieu que l'Angleterre cherche de nous mettre en jeu par l'affaire d'Ostende qui nous regarde principalement, nous accusant d'etre trop mols et trop timides," Pesters to Slingelandt, 25 Sept. '27, R. A. Hl. 2981.

[3]) Secr. Res. S. G. 27 Sept. '27.

[4]) Chauvelin to Fénelon, 18 Sept. '27, A. E. Hl. 371.

[5]) The account of the negotiations at the Hague from 24 Sept. till 3 Oct. '27, is founded principally upon the dispatches from Fénelon to his court (30 Sept., 1, 2, 3 Oct. '27 A. E. Hl. 371) and the resolutions of the States General (the secret ones of 27, 30 Sept. and 3 Oct. and the ordinary one of 30 Sept.)

them. A few days previously, the Pensionary had expressed the opinion that France would be acting more to the purpose, if she strongly insisted upon Spain's giving satisfaction than if she continued to argue on this point. [1]) This was a very precise description of what France had been doing. Slingelandt was just as little in favour of vigorous neasures being taken now, as he had been ever since the Preliminaries. The affair of the list had not caused him to change his mind; he considered it as harmless, for he understood that the Emperor would not stick to the Directors' note. [2]) This was the reason why he had prescribed Pesters' course of conduct, and why at the Cardinal's request he had postponed the passing of a resolution about the list, until the answer to Spain should have been settled. [3]) The policy which France pursued was exactly as he would have had it, and it would not be his fault, if it were not fully agreed to by the Republic. In order the better to be able to promote this he asked that he might be provided with copies.

So too did the deputies for foreign affairs, when Fénelon communicated these same documents to them (first conference on Sept. 26th.), this being the formal way of making anything known to the States General. The copies, they said, would be of great service to the people in the provinces, who would have to deliberate upon affairs, should Spain persist in her present obstinacy. Fénelon asked if this was so at the moment, and declined the request. That he refused them to the deputies was not wrong, as these would have had to submit them to the States General, but with regard to the Pensionary, he ought not to have declined his request, he not being under any such obligation, and he would have used them to allay the suspicions which many harboured against France. [4]) Fénelon committed another imprudence in the question which he put to the deputies, since this could be construed as implying too great a confidence in Spain's intentions.

Slingelandt and Fagel were very concerned in trying to remedy the ill effects which Fénelon's conduct might produce. Now it was the latter's task to draw up the report of the conference

---

[1]) Finch to Townshend, 23 Sept. '27, R. O. Hl. 294
[2]) Fénelon to Chauvelin, 16 Sept. '27, A. E. Hl. 371.
[3]) Finch to Townshend, 16 Sept. '27, R. O. Hl. 294.
[4]) Finch to Townshend, 26 Sept. '27, R. O. Hl. 294; cf. Slingelandt to Pesters, 25 Sept. '27, copy, A. E. Hl. 371.

which was to be presented and read next day at the assembly of the States; he went to Fénelon beforehand and showed him the draft report, in which he represented the French ambassador as insinuating that it would be well to think from this moment of steps being taken in the event of Spain's protracting the difficulties. When Fénelon saw this he expressed himself as greatly surprised; Fagel admitted having added these words himself, saying, however, that he had done so with the best intent. The members of the States were most inclined "à mettre la tête sur le chevet", and would thus be put on their guard against thinking that there was plenty of time. Further, England urged that the States should assent to a joint declaration being made to the Courts of Vienna and Spain. Fénelon asked, "What kind of declaration?" "A l'Anglaise", was the reply, which Fénelon construed as being a rather vigorous one. When he proceeded with his questioning, Fagel said that he considered such a declaration premature until the effect of the new representations to be made by Louis XV. was known; if, however, these should fail, then a decision would have to be come to, it being unreasonable to adhere to Preliminaries which were not being observed. On hearing Fagel argue thus, Fénelon thought it was his and the Pensionary's object to embroil the Republic against her true interests in the vehemence of England, and since it did not suit him to be helpful in this, he objected to the period in question, even if, as Fagel suggested in the second place, it did not voice his own personal opinion, but the general opinion in the conference. If it were to remain, he said, it would have to become part of the resolution to be passed upon the report, and would thus express the opinion of the States, but this he understood would not coincide with the Greffier's intention.

There was indeed no such period in the report, nor in the resolution of Sept. 27th., as had been read to Fénelon in the second conference (Sept. 29th.). Thus he was under the impression that he had gained his point. However, not being satisfied with this, Fénelon felt himself called upon to complete at this second conference what he had said at the first, by expressly stating that there was no reason up till now to despair of success in the negotiations with Spain, and he pointed to the reconciliation as a ground for this hope. In his own opinion he thought he had acted prudently, and had absolutely no idea how far he was in error.

As to Slingelandt and Fagel, in the first place; in inserting the period in the report they had no other object than the convincing of the States of the sincerity of France in her intentions with regard to supporting her Allies, should need be by force of arms; and at the same time the dispensing with the giving of an express assent to the making of such a declaration as was urged upon them by England, for the resolution which was to be submitted was to contain nothing but a profession of thanks to the French Court. Fénelon was also under a misapprehension when he thought that, by acting as he did, he was favouring the national interests of the Dutch; he overlooked the fact that the proposed declaration had reference principally to the Ostend affair. It was certainly moved by the hope of prepossessing the Republic in her favour that England wanted it to be joined to the matter of the Prince Frederick, but Amsterdam wanted this too, though from a different standpoint, the city fathers here being afraid that the Prince Frederick affair would cause the matter of the Ostend ships to be placed in the background. [1]) In all probability they would have acquiesced in a resolution comprising merely a profession of thanks if the report had contained such a period as that suggested by Fagel, but this having been declined, it was not the latter's fault that the States gave in addition their consent to the making of the declaration as proposed by England. By the latter half of this resolution Pesters was instructed, the French ministers and Horace Walpole agreeing, to represent to Fonseca, that the Court of Vienna should exert influence upon Spain and should rid herself of the suspicion of strengthening Spain in her actions; and to further show what would be the consequence should matters remain in their present state: the Preliminaries would lose their force and the ships returning to Ostend might be molested.

Thus the States struck a menacing note, and combined the issue of the Ostend affair with that of the Prince Frederick. England appeared to have gained her point, and the Pensionary to have failed. He, however, did not lose courage, and just as before was not disinclined to counter the designs of England. Now, as we have seen, the latter part of the resolution resulted far less from regard for Eng-

---

[1]) Van Ittersum to Townshend, 30 Sept. '27, R. O. Hl. 296.

land than from deference to the desires of Amsterdam, and in general of those who were afraid that national interests would be neglected. Slingelandt was keen enough to avail himself of this circumstance; if only those who thought so could be brought to see that France was taking Dutch interests well to heart, things might even now be managed in such a way that the latter part of the resolution might never be carried into full effect.

To this end Fénelon would have to contribute, and for this purpose the latter part of the resolution was kept from his knowledge. He would be sure to mistake it, and would thus so much the more have crossed the Pensionary's aims, even at the very time when the latter gave him another opportunity of restoring confidence in France. For it was at this same conference (the second) that Slingelandt informed both Fénelon and Finch that they would be invited to another on the affair of the list, upon which, so far, no resolution had yet been passed. Now, nothing could have a better effect than the promise from Fénelon that France would render effectual assistance on this point; such a promise was thought to be all the more likely since Fénelon had invited the States to formulate their wishes, should they have any. But Fénelon was not in the mood for giving promises. He was greatly surprised, for when he had at the first conference asked after the list, Slingelandt had answered that he and Finch need not be invited to a conference; it would be sufficient if Fagel gave them copies of the resolution to be passed. He accounted for this change of front in a very erroneous manner: now that the period had been struck out, as he surmised, the list would be taken advantage of to induce the States to make common cause with England.

An occurrence at the close of the conference might have opened his eyes as to his error, for it was then that Slingelandt asked for information from Finch concerning the two ships said to be equipping at Ostend for India. Pesters' information about these did not agree with the information received from the English Government. According to the former only one ship was being equipped while one was on the stocks and as to the destination of both nothing was known. If, however, Finch could produce conclusive proof as to this, then representations could be made on this point as well, and at the same time as those about the list, but the Republic must have some ground for complaint. Finch's reply was that in England they were sure that ships were being equipped. This however, Slingelandt replied, was not conclusive evidence, as the destination of a ship could only be judged when it was known what kind of a crew had been signed on, what was the quantity of provisions shipped, and the nature of the cargo; such particulars were necessary. To this Finch did not know how to answer, and according to Fénelon he was not able to impress the conference. But not even this could make Fénelon change his mind. With any other Pensionary, he wrote, he would have considered this an attempt to put the Republic on her guard against the strenuousness of the English, but concerning Slingelandt, he had so many reasons for diffidence, that he even suspected this had been done on purpose, the better to cover his secret understanding with them. Being desirous as he was of knowing whether his suspicion were correct, he looked forward eagerly to the conference in which the resolution as to the list was to be communicated to him.

This was passed on September 30th.: After a full statement as to the defects of the list, the deputies were ordered to consult with Fénelon and Finch as to the making of a joint representation to the Emperor, in which redress should be claimed for those defects, while it was also declared that the Allies would not allow any of the Ostend ships other than the nine which were entitled to it to return freely, and in addition two others, on condition that they really were, as was said, advice-yachts without cargo. The deputies were also authorised to submit to the two ambassadors the giving of notice to the Emperor that a rumour was afloat about the two ships said to be equipping at Ostend, so that he might make provision against any such design; and further, whether the time had not yet come for the carrying into effect of the resolution of July 29th. with reference to the delivery of the effects of the flotilla in the customary way.

At the third conference, held on October 1st., at which Fenelon was made acquainted with the resolution, he was also informed of a note which had that very day been lodged by Finch with the States. In this the English ambassador, in accordance with his orders, informed the States that the King his Master hoped that they would not allow themselves to be misled any longer as to the equipping of the two or three ships at Ostend destined for India, and that they should instruct Hamel Bruynincx and Pesters, the latter in conjunction with Horace Walpole and the French min- isters, to make representations respectively to the Court of Vien- na or to Fonseca on this point, and at the same time to press for the release of the Prince Frederick and the delivery of the South Sea effects, both of which affairs might have been settled long before had it not been for the action of the Court of Vienna.

There was a very great difference between these two docu- ments. The resolution was exclusively on Dutch matters; the note, although it put a Dutch grievance in the forefront, had two English grievances added to it. The note was rather strong, urging representations as to the two ships without adducing any proof of same, while the resolution was confined to simply giving notice of the rumours about this; there was, it is true, a sort of menace in it too, with regard to the Ostend ships, but this had reference only to those which were not entitled to a safe return, a restriction which England had not made. The note also required that the States should send orders immediately to both Vienna and Paris, whereas the resolution provided for preliminary deliberations with Fénelon and Finch.

How ever much these two documents might differ, there was still at first sight some uniformity in them, inasmuch as they both contained references to representations, to the equipment of ships and to the delivery of effects. Thus it was that Fénelon, who from the first had suspected Slingelandt of connivance with England, at once came to the conclusion that the two documents were connected one with the other. In his opinion the note of Oc- tober 1st had already been complied with in the resolution of September 30th, which he thought could only be a consequence of previous arrangement between Slingelandt and Finch, and this had led to the addition of the English to the Dutch points. The Dutch were responsible for the objections made to the list, the rest having been suggested by England! He came all the sooner to this conclusion, since he had also ascribed the resolution of July 29th. to English influence. As he had already foreseen, there was no other object than to mix up the Republic, against her own interests, in the schemes of England. He, however, would protect her against her mischievous leaders. He therefore resolved to stop this movement in time, and for this purpose he would deliver a note to the States.

This he did on the next day at the fourth conference on October 2nd. This note was a most disagreeable document; the only thing attractive in it was the reference to the objections to the list, to which the Court of France entirely agreed. For the rest it contained objections to the making of representations either upon this point or upon the questions of the equipment and the effects. Such representations would be now entirely out of season. The difficulties standing in the way of the opening of the Congress, viz.: the raising of the siege of Gibraltar and the release of the Prince Frederick, must first be removed, and so long as the effect of the representations, which Rottembourg and Richelieu had been charged to make, remained unknown, no other representations could, or ought to be set on foot.

Before delivering this document, Fénelon called upon Slingelandt and showed it to him. The Pensionary did all he possibly could to prevent him from delivering it. Uneasiness would be aroused, he said, if it were seen that all France's energies were being displayed in favour of England, whereas she made so many remarks on what concerned the Republic in particular; this manner of acting did not leave any room for the idea whether the Congress could not, at all events, be opened with the Emperor (to which idea, owing, we think, to the course of events, Slingelandt was now by no means so unfavourable as he had been at first [1]), it being as little to the interests of France as of the Republic that the English kept Gibraltar, as well as the superiority given to them by the Treaty of Asiento. Fénelon considered the artfulness of this insinuation as being too evident, after what he had recently seen, to allow himself to be led astray by it. It was his prepossession for England, he thought which made the Pensionary apprehensive of the effect of such an anti-English document as his, but instead of keeping him from delivering it, it was an incentive the more for doing so. In his opinion it was certain to open people's eyes to Slingelandt's machinations in conjunction with Finch.

The effect, however, was quite otherwise, for it aroused strong ex-

---

[1] cf. Finch to Townshend, 9 Sept. '27, R. O. Hl. 294.

citement. The few words of approval given to the resolution were entirely undone by the many others of disapproval. Moreover, by separating the Dutch points so sharply from the English and by emphasising so strongly that these must be settled first, it called up the idea that France was just as unready to favour the Republic's interests as she proved to be ready to favour those of England, while from some expressions it was inferred that France intended to reserve the Dutch grievances till the opening of the Congress. [1]) The Amsterdam deputies revealed their uneasiness to Fénelon himself; one of them, De la Bassecour, told him that even if Spain should desist from her points of variance with England, the ratifications of the Vienna Preliminaries ought not to be exchanged before the effects had been delivered and the list revised. But not even this declaration could make Fénelon realise that he was at fault; he continued to think that he was promoting Dutch interests and endeavoured to convince De la Bassecour and his fellow-townsmen, that his note could not have replied in a more satisfactory manner to the resolution. The excitement to which it gave rise did not lead him to any conclusion other than that the Dutch, fearing their interests would be neglected, would agree to a congress if the list were revised and the effects delivered, even if the English, with reference to the Prince Frederick, had to be satisfied with expedients. Should this be so, then Slingelandt would see himself compelled to turn towards the side of Dutch interests, and to justify himself towards England by asserting that he had made a last effort on her behalf.

Even now Fénelon could not see that he had been guilty of a blunder. He was glad that he had revived the jealousy of the Dutch with reference to the English trade, as he had indeed done, but not, as was his impression, to the advantage of France; this was really very much to her disadvantage, she appearing in this to side with England contrary to the interests of the Republic. Bent as he was on crossing England's intentions, Fénelon had in reality run counter to the interests of his own Government. In spite of solemn warnings by Chauvelin, he had caused the suspicions against France to increase still further; this he had done by every one of his measures taken since he had received

---

[1]) Finch to Townshend, 3 Oct. '27, R. O. Hl. 294.

the documents from Paris. His last measure, all the worse as he then expressed his opinion not orally but in writing, even exceeded his previous ones in grossness.

What he ought to have done was to have availed himself of the opportunity to make these good, and to have returned a favourable answer, not to a small part of the resolution of September 30th., but to the whole of it. Had he done so, Slingelandt, whose continual efforts had been towards the restoring of confidence in France, would certainly not have hastened to refer this resolution to the deliberations to be held in Paris. Now, however, it became imperative to withdraw the negotiations out of Fénelon's hands without any further delay, as the latter was continually causing doubts and jealousies to arise which gave the Pensionary a great deal of annoyance.[1]) Hence, as early as the following day (Oct. 3rd.), the States passed a resolution ordering Pesters to consult the French ministers and Horace Walpole about the resolution of Sept. 30th., and to join them in any representations which might be made to Fonseca. Should other representations be made either at Vienna or Madrid, then the Dutch ministers in those places were to act according to instructions which they would receive from Pesters.

With this resolution, Slingelandt sent a letter to the last named in which he complained of Fénelon, who by his scrupulousness with regard to everything except the matter of Gibraltar and the Prince Frederick, caused an increase in the suspicions of those who "suivant leurs vieux principes" had not a good opinion of France. As it seemed to him, the time had now come for the juxtaposition of all contraventions against the Preliminaries and for demanding the redress of them all at the same time. If this were not done the Dutch were very much afraid that they would come off badly, fearing that the Emperor and the King of Spain might then think that, provided Spain yielded on those two points, the Allies would not insist with so much vigour on the others. Should there be any foundation for such fears, Slingelandt hoped that the French ministers would then cause them to cease, by taking measures in consultation with Pesters. [2])

Pesters, however, did not at first meet with a friendly reception.

---

[1]) cf. Finch to Townshend, 3 Oct. '27, R. O. Hl. 294.
[2]) Slingelandt to Pesters, 3 Oct. '27, extract in A. E. Hl. 371.

When, together with Horace Walpole, he proceeded to carry out his orders contained in the resolutions of Sept. 27th and 30th., he was met at almost every point with a refusal, first of all with regard to the joint declaration as to the return of the Ostend ships. [1]) The French ministers were prejudiced against any and every thing which Pesters might say or do, owing to Fénelon's letters, which were very full of Slingelandt's supposed manoeuvres. As a result of these they were "extrêmement blessés", the more so as they had at first put some trust in his intentions. However, to combat these they pursued a better policy than that of Fénelon's; they tried to set the Dutch at ease as to their own interests, and in this way to prevent them from going all the way with their warlike Pensionary. Fénelon was therefore instructed to inform the States that his Master was taking both the affair of the list and that of the effects of the flotilla very much to heart; but in the meantime it had been settled in conjunction with Horace Walpole and Pesters, that as long as the matter of the Prince Frederick was not settled, so long should the other matters also be held in abeyance, thus Louis XV. could not insist just as strongly on these either. In due time, however, he would not fail to give them all the support they desired. In addition to making this known to the States, Fénelon had, in conversations with the leading men in the Republic, to leave no doubt at all as to the Dutch interests being no less dear to his Royal Master than those of England. In this way the French Government met the "English intrigue".[2])

The French Government was not the only one to be mistaken in what had happened at the Hague, for at the beginning the English Government was also mistaken. With the resolution of September 27th. they were very pleased, [3]) but that of September 30th. was not at all to their liking. It did not escape Townshend that it was a juxtaposition of Dutch points only, no mention being made in it either of the release of the Prince Frederick or of the South Sea effects. That was not what he had desired, thus it did not

---

[1]) Pesters to Slingelandt, 10,12 Oct. '27, R. A. Hl. 2981; idem to Fagel on same dates, R. A. S. G. 7317.

[2]) Louis XV. to Fénelon, and Chauvelin to Fénelon, 13 Oct. '27, A. E. Hl. 371; cf. Secr. Res. S. G. 18 Oct. '27.

[3]) Hop to Fagel, 7 Oct. '27, R. A. S. G. 7348.

matter to him that Fénelon had written a note against it, the best proof indeed of the latter's wrong view of things! Townshend wrote that it would have been better if he had not delivered it, it was, however, in accordance with what Fleury had wished all along, viz.: not to raise too many points at one time and not to mix up new matters with the questions as to the Prince Frederick and Gibraltar. But, taking matters as they were, Townshend still tried to get the English affairs joined to those of the Dutch. Finch was therefore instructed to ask Slingelandt that Pesters and Hamel Bruynincx might be instructed on these points also. [1])

In doing this, however, Finch did not meet with success, for, just as he had done after the incident of July 29/30, the Pensionary now again turned Fénelon's conduct to good account. The Republic, said he, took it much to heart that George II. and his subjects should be given full satisfaction, but the Court of France had so dominated the negotiations, and had shown herself to be so jealous at interference by any one else, that Fénelon had not even been allowed to give him copies of the documents he had received. It was, therefore, very difficult to know what France would take amiss and what she would not take amiss. The King, however, might rest assured that, so soon as the result of Rottembourg's negotiations was known, the Republic would act entirely in concert with him. [2])

In this way the juxtaposition of the points as desired by England was declined, as was the naval expedition to Ostend, about which Finch had received orders only after the termination of the negotiations with Fénelon. The idea of this scheme was to waylay the ships returning to Ostend in October and to hold them until the Courts of Vienna and Spain should have given full satisfaction. [3]) But the time had come when Slingelandt could take advantage of the precaution he had taken at the beginning of August, so he replied by informing Finch that the Republic had no ships ready, and that those which had been out in the Summer had now been dismantled and disarmed, so that it would be impossible

[1]) Townshend to Finch, 29 Sept. '27, R. O. Hl. 294.
[2]) Finch to Townshend, 14 Oct. '27, R. O. Hl. 294.
[3]) Townshend to Finch, 19 Sept. '27, R. O. Hl. 294.
[4]) Finch to Townshend, 7 Oct. '27, R. O. Hl. 294.

to equip them in time. [4]) Upon hearing this Townshend wrote that it would suffice if only one or two ships were sent, no matter how small they were or how slightly equipped, the King having enough men-of-war at his disposal, and it was only a question of the States showing their co-operation! [1]) When Finch acquainted Slingelandt of this, the latter remarked that even for the slightest assistance a resolution was required, and how could this be kept secret, when it came to be submitted to the provinces? while it was also very possible that some of these would oppose it out of fear of arousing the jealousy of France. [2])

If the English had not yet come to a right understanding of the negotiations at the Hague, they had certainly now at last come to it, and meanwhile the French came to the right understanding too. After the first indignation had passed away, the ministers could not but acknowledge that Pesters behaved with much moderation. Nor did his representations as to the riskiness of such a document as Fénelon's fail in its effect; what he said about the old principles still clung to by some of the regents greatly struck the Cardinal; and while at first they had agreed that Fénelon had been perfectly right, now both he and Chauvelin admitted that he would have done better had he expressed himself verbally rather than in writing. [3])

It was not only Pesters who kept quiet, Horace Walpole also preserved silence; this he would not have done had the result of the negotiations at the Hague been what he had desired. He thought in the beginning that this was so, and was at that time very pleased at the orders which Pesters had received; but no sooner did he become aware of what these really were than he pressed forward the idea of making representations, not to Fonseca, but to the latter's colleague at the Hague, Koenigsegg-Erps. [4]) Seeing that now the Republic was not going to insist on the English points equally with the Dutch, he evidently preferred to leave these without any connection with the chief matters to be dealt with in Paris.

---

[1]) Townshend to Finch, 3 Oct. '27, ibidem.
[2]) Finch to Townshend, 21 Oct. '27, ibidem.
[3]) Pesters to Slingelandt, 12, 16 Oct. '27, R. A. Hl. 2981; Chauvelin to Fénelon, 5 Oct. '27, A. E. Hl. 371.
[4]) Pesters to Slingelandt, 5, 10, 12 Oct. '27, R. A. Hl. 2981.

The French ministers approved of this, but deferred from one
day to the other taking a decision upon it. After a while, however,
they no longer minded concealing the reason for this procrastination: they expected within a few days the Emperor's answer to the representations made by Richelieu. [1] They very much
preferred making new representations apropos of this reply rather
than at the solicitation of the Republic, which they believed
had been inspired by England. [2]

Neither Pesters nor Horace Walpole raised any objection to
this delay, [3] while their conduct proved to be exactly in accordance with the dispositions of their Governments. As regards the
States, they replied to the matters which Fénelon had, at the
instance of Chauvelin, submitted to them, saying that they had
not been informed that any such agreement had been arrived
at, as was said to be the case, in Paris, as neither Pesters nor
Fénelon had made mention of it. On the contrary, the latter had
invited them, to make known any wishes they might have,
and it was this which had given rise to the resolution of September 30th. Thus they did not see that they could have acted with
greater prudence, they not having taken any decision, but having
left everything to the deliberations to be held in Paris. They
did not object to the delay in the satisfaction due to them,
as they reposed the very fullest confidence in the King of
France, that on this account it would not become weaker. [4]
Chauvelin read this resolution with much pleasure, as probably
also the information given by Slingelandt to Fénelon, that the
Republic had no men-of-war at sea. [5] It will not have escaped
him either that it was this fact which induced England to
give up the idea of a naval expedition to Ostend. All this caused
him to think better of the negotiations at the Hague, and he began
to look with disfavour on Fénelon's continual reports of the distrust evinced by the Republic towards France. There had, he wrote
to him, to be no more complaints as to the intrigues of Slingelandt,
and for the future he must avoid expressing himself on such

---

[1] idem to idem, 12, 13, 16 Oct. '27, ibidem.
[2] cf. Chauvelin to Fénelon, 19 Oct. '27, Louis XV. to Fénelon, 22 Oct. '27, A.E.Hl. 371.
[3] Pesters to Fagel, 16 Oct. '27, R. A., S. G. 7317.
[4] Secr. Res. S. G. 20 Oct. '27.
[5] Pesters to Fagel, 26 Oct. '27, R. A. S. G. 7317; Fénelon to Chauvelin, 14 Oct. '27,
A. E. Hl. 371.

subjects; he had carried his suspicions too far; should there again be any reason for complaints he had better keep them to himself. [1]

This reproof was what Fénelon really deserved, for he might have spoiled the whole business; that it was not so spoiled was owing to Slingelandt's skilful management of affairs. He, in spite of great obstacles, including Fénelon's continued opposition and the suspicions which he aroused among those with whom the Pensionary had to do, had succeeded in frustrating the English designs, viz.: the taking of vigorous measures by the Hanover Allies jointly.

V.

Affairs in Paris were not at a standstill for a long time. The affair of the list had been delayed, pending the arrival of the reply to Richelieu's representations, and this arrived as early as October 23rd. In this the Emperor expressed himself as being very eager that the Congress should be opened; he regretted that Waldegrave had not yet arrived, that the Vienna Preliminaries had not yet been ratified and that the term for the meeting of the Congress had elapsed without the fixing of a new one; he trusted however, that the Court of France would find a means of settling the difficulties. As for himself he had never opposed the release of the Prince Frederick; at the commencement he had certainly not disapproved of the conduct of Spain, considering La Paz's arguments as being very strong, but after he had seen how the Hanover Allies took matters, he had used his influence with the King of Spain, exhorting him in the interests of peace to sacrifice the ship. France could be further assured that Rottembourg would be supported by his Ambassador. [2]

The Cardinal built the most sanguine hopes on this reply: with the help of Koenigsegg, Rottembourg was shortly to bring the negotiations to a happy conclusion. He felt so sure of this that he immediately sent him a very private letter, advising him not to be too stiff and not to have too great a regard for England, [3] while on the other hand he requested England not to delay the

---

[1]) Chauvelin to Fénelon, 27 Oct. '27, A. E. Hl. 371.
[2]) cf. Pesters to Slingelandt, 26 Oct.' 27, R. A. Hl. 2981 (enclosures).
[3]) Baudrillart, op. cit. III, 361—'2.

departure of Waldegrave any longer, who on going to Vienna was to take with him the ratifications by the Hanover Allies, which were to be exchanged as soon as the pending difficulties should have been removed. [1])

Whatever else Fleury did, he did not now open the matter of the list [2]); it is likely that he did not think it wise to trouble the Emperor (who showed himself to be so well disposed) with a further representation, making sure that the Republic would wait a while longer for satisfaction regarding this point. He now put so much trust in the Republic that he for the second time broached the matter of the delivery of the Prince Frederick to the Dutch, in the above-mentioned letter to Rottembourg. It was, however, questionable whether the Dutch would agree to this. Fénelon had been instructed to inquire into this, but up till now he had been so engrossed with the supposed manoeuvres of Slingelandt that he had paid very little attention to it. Apropos of the Emperor's answer, the order to Fénelon was now repeated. [3])

It was repeated a second time apropos of Spain's answer. At one of the first audiences which Elizabeth gave to Rottembourg she proposed that the Prince Frederick should be put into the hands of the King of France (1st. proposal, October 15th.). [4]) Fleury would have liked to accept this; in his letter to Rottembourg he had himself suggested delivering it to either the French or the Dutch, but now on second thoughts, he realised that it would arouse an extraordinary jealousy with England. So, instead of advocating the proposal, he preferred to gratify this power by declaring that Louis XV. would never accept. However, what England would not allow to France, she might perhaps allow to the Republic. So Fénelon was again instructed to inquire into the question very cautiously, as to whether the ministers were absolutely opposed to the Republic's being made the depositary of the ship. [5])

He, however, did not succeed in coming to any definite opinion

---

[1]) Pesters to Slingelandt, 26 Oct. '27, R. A. Hl. 2981.
[2]) "différons donc cet article "in the draft from Chauvelin to Fénelon, 2 Nov. '27, A. E. Hl. 371.
[3]) Chauvelin to Fénelon, 27 Oct. '27, ibidem.
[4]) Baudrillart, op. cit. III, 360; for further particulars cf. Horace Walpole to Newcastle, 31 Oct. '27, enclosed in Townshend to Finch, 27 Oct. '27, R. O. Hl. 294.
[5]) Chauvelin to Fénelon, 2 Nov. '27, A. E. Hl. 371.

on this point; not that the expedient to which he more than once alluded was not present in Slingelandt's mind: the latter once spoke of it jocosely, but avoided giving his opinion on it. He could not agree, as he did not know how England would take it, and on the other hand, disapproval might have been misconstrued by France. He did not, however, conceal all his mind from Fénelon. He said the best solution of the matter would be that Spain should be given the assurance that the Congress should decide whether any smuggling had been going on. Speaking generally, he said that any expedient with which England did not comply was not an expedient; and at another time, the Hanover Allies must not, by relaxing with regard to the execution of the Preliminaries, give the Emperor any cause to think that he was to be the master of the Congress; there were circumstances in which it was of primary importance that one must not allow oneself to be put in the wrong. [1])

The Pensionary's question put to Fénelon on this point is worthy of note; with regard to the Emperor's reply, he asked Fénelon if a new term had not been fixed for the opening of the Congress, as it was very desirable, should it be necessary again to take vigorous measures, to be fully acquainted with the intentions of the Court of Vienna before the end of the Winter. Fénelon replied to this that Spain's answer to the new instructions, which Rottembourg was to have, would have to be waited for. Slingelandt agreed to this, and added that the Court of Vienna must have time to exert influence on the Court of Spain. [2]) It is evident that at the time he expressed his inclination for an expedient he was also pressing upon France the necessity of acting with firmness. This is not in any way inconsistent in him. Circumstances had changed: the danger of an outbreak of war had passed, but now in Slingelandt's mind another danger arose, namely, that France would not act with the necessary vigour. In the midst of all, however, his object remained the same, viz.: to confirm the peace so that the Congress might soon be opened.

In order the better to attain this end, he entirely ignored the Dutch points, even that of the list, as Fénelon remarked

---

[1]) Fénelon to Chauvelin, 31 Oct. '27, 7, 11 Nov. '27, A. E. Hl. 371, 372.
[2]) Fénelon to Chauvelin, 31 Oct., 7, 18 Nov. '27, ibidem.

to his great astonishment. [1]) The latter did not render such a course easy for Slingelandt; notwithstanding Chauvelin's reproof, his conduct continued to be of the most disagreeable kind, [2]) but inasmuch as the suspicions against France had not been removed by what he had been instructed to communicate, these were now removed by her conduct in reference to Spain's proposal, which excluded any thought of a secret understanding being made with this power. And now since more trust and confidence were being put in France, impatience became less with regard to seeking satisfaction concerning the list. [3])

The declaration of Koenigsegg-Erps on November 6th was another matter which helped towards this. [4]) As we have already seen, no representation had as yet been made to the Court of Vienna with regard to the resolution of September 30th., but of this Slingelandt had privately informed the Austrian envoy. [5]) The latter was now authorised by the Archduchess Regent of the Southern Netherlands to inform the States, that the Ostend Company was entirely forbidden to trade with India for a period of seven years, and was forbidden in particular to send out the two ships — and now it would appear that the English information really was correct — that were actually being equipped for the Far East. Koenigsegg-Erps added to this that he was shortly expecting instructions from Vienna upon this point and also upon the list. [6])

This declaration could be taken as a sign of the Emperor's good will. The answer given to Richelieu had not been looked upon as such; Slingelandt and Fagel had their doubts as to whether Koenigsegg would indeed support Rottembourg; but such firm assurances were given to Hamel Bruynincx that they at last put faith in them. [7])

In England they refused to put any faith whatever in anything coming from the Emperor. They were annoyed that he put

---

[1]) Fénelon to Chauvelin, 28 Oct. '27, A. E. Hl. 371.
[2]) Van Ittersum to Townshend, 28 Oct. '27, R. O. Hl. 296; Finch to Townshend, 4 Nov. '27, ib. 294; Fenelon to Chauvelin, 4 Nov. '27, A. E. Hl. 372.
[3]) Van Ittersum to Townshend, 25 Nov. '27, R. O. Hl. 296.
[4]) Van Ittersum to Townshend, 25 Nov. '27, R. O. Hl. 296.
[5]) Fénelon to Chauvelin, 8 Dec. '27, A. E. Hl. 372.
[6]) Res. S. G. 6 Nov. '27.
[7]) Finch to Townshend, 31 Oct. 11, 14 Nov. '27. R. O. Hl. 294; Van Ittersum to Townshend, 28 Oct '27, ib. 296.

the blame for the non-opening of the Congress on to George II. and his Allies, whereas this was to be attributed to him and his Ally, who threw all kinds of difficulties in the way and so retarded its being opened. [1]) Nevertheless Waldegrave was ordered to proceed to Vienna. This, however, was only done to gratify France, in whom the English Government now reposed the fullest confidence, her attitude with reference to the Spanish proposal being entirely to their liking. Not only had France rejected it from the beginning, but she had also fully approved of what England would return as an answer to Madrid. This power suggested the very expedient which, quite independently, Slingelandt had also hit upon, viz.: to leave to the decision of the Congress, whether the Prince Frederick and the other prizes on either side had committed any illegal acts. A declaration to this effect was made to the Count de Broglie, the French Ambassador in London, and written by him in a letter to his Court; afterwards orders based upon this were sent to Rottembourg (November 10). [2])

Perfect harmony now reigned among the Allies of Hanover, and they would very probably have overcome the resistance of Spain had not Fleury run into the danger which Slingelandt had feared.

The letter he wrote to Rottembourg on the arrival of the Emperor's reply was very imprudent indeed. No sooner had the Ambassador received it than, without waiting for the answer to the proposal of October 15th., he re-opened negotiations with the Court of Spain. The upshot of this was that a new proposal was sent (2nd. proposal, Nov. 14th.), according to which all Spain's pretensions should be left to the Congress, including the question of Gibraltar, and that the Prince Frederick would have to make up for the losses sustained by the blockade of Porto-Bello. France

---

[1]) Newcastle to H. Walpole, 26 Oct. '27, enclosed by Townshend to Finch, 27 Oct. '27, R. O. Hl. 294. It is worthy of attention that it was not Spain who refused to ratify the Vienna preliminaries, as Pribram (*Staatsverträge, England* I, 446) and Huisman (*op. cit.* 435) think. On the contrary Spain was as ready to do this as the Emperor, and just as the latter's ministers Bournonville also complained to Hamel Bruynincx of the non-ratification by the Hanover allies (Hamel Bruynincx to Fagel, 17 Sept. '27, R. A. S. G. 7191). But it was the allies of Hanover, in particular England, who refused to ratify preliminaries about the execution of which opinions differed so much, cf. the speech from the throne, 27 Jan. '28 (Cobbett, *Parl. Hist.* VIII, 634).

[2]) Baudrillart, *op. cit.* III, 379—'80; Townshend to Finch, 7 Nov. '27, R. O. H. 294; the above-quoted letter from Newcastle to H. Walpole.

and the Emperor should further guarantee to Spain the punctual
carrying out by England of all matters settled at the Congress.
This went far towards separating France from her Allies. Of these no
mention at all was made of the Republic, but her interests were menaced very particularly by the Article that, once the Anglo-Spanish difficulties should be settled, under no pretext whatever
would the opening of the Congress be any longer retarded, as in
this way the matter of the list was written off. [1])

This proposal, though resulting from Fleury's letter, went
much farther towards gratifying Spain than had been his
intention; on seeing this he very soon realised that it had no
chance of success. Horace Walpole opposed vehemently, while
it was very evident from Pesters' conduct and also from the way
in which Slingelandt had spoken with Fénelon, that the Republic
was no more likely to agree with it than England. It was to be
feared that she would now join England in enforcing vigorous
measures upon France. To prevent this France left nothing
undone, Chauvelin immediately wrote to Fénelon that time
had not yet allowed of having a copy made of the new proposal, but that he had seen with great astonishment that among
the points which were said to retard the holding of the Congress
the list had been omitted, and that in the wording of some of
the Articles it would seem that the Republic was excluded from
her engagements with France; the Republic, however, could be
sure that nothing would be decided contrary to the common deliberations. [2]) We now notice that the affair of the list was receiving attention. For almost two months France had ignored it,
but now she appeared to think fit to delay it no longer. Besides displaying zeal for the interests of the Dutch, France also
tried to inspire them with fear on this head, for Fénelon was instructed to impress upon the Dutch merchants that they would
suffer from the detention of the effects of the flotilla not only
directly, but also indirectly, as the losses falling on the French
merchants would bring in their train losses for them. [3])

These representations had not very much effect: what had hap-

---

[1]) La Paz to Rottembourg, 14 Nov. 27, copy and Dutch translation in Van der Meer
to Fagel, 15 Nov. '27, R. A. S. G. 7358.

[2]) Chauvelin to Fénelon, 26 Nov. 27, A. E. Hl. 372; cf. Secr. Res. S. G. 2 Dec. '27.

[3]) Chauvelin to Fénelon, 4 Dec. '27, A. E. Hl. 372; cf. Pesters to Slingelandt, 5 Dec.
'27, R. A. Hl. 2981.

pened in Spain roused the greatest uneasiness. It was feared that there had been a secret and cunningly devised scheme between France and Spain, and now the pretended good will of the Court of Vienna was no longer believed in. It was Slingelandt's opinion that no time should be lost by the Hanover Allies in putting their heads together for the taking of measures which would prevent them from becoming the dupes of their enemies, and on his initiative an extraordinary equipment of twelve men-of-war was moved for in the Assembly of Holland. It is characteristic of the feeling that the States of this province were unanimously in favour of this and at once gave their deputies to the States General orders to introduce it there. [1])

The Pensionary took no trouble to conceal his opinion from Fénelon either; it was not clear to him, he said, how Rottembourg could have taken upon himself such a proposal, "le plus étrange assemblage qui pût partir d'une tête espagnole", and even, as he had done towards his fellow-ambassadors, expressed his satisfaction with it. According to it, matters came back to what Spain had desired all along, viz.: the submitting of affairs to arbitration, but this was what England would never agree to, and neither, he added dryly, would the Republic. In his opinion the Allies ought to declare that they declined to allow the Congress to act as a tribunal, and that they would stand to the letter of the Preliminaries. A third point upon which they should express themselves was that the Companies interested should be at liberty to take such of the Ostend ships as had not been named on the list. On this point he complained of the action of the Court of Vienna, as the explanations announced in the declaration of November 6th. were still delayed. His tone being somewhat passionate, Fénelon became afraid that he was contemplating some vigorous resolution, and, rather than have his silence taken for consent, he contradicted him; this caused Slingelandt to lose his temper altogether, and he railed against Rottembourg afresh. Fénelon pointed out to him the assurances which his Court had given; to this Slingelandt replied that he was quite conscious of them; but this was merely in the manner of a compliment. At least, the next moment he said that France was taking things so quietly

---

[1]) Fénelon to Chauvelin, 4, 8 Dec. '27, A. E. Hl. 372; Finch to Townshend, 2 Dec. '27, R. O. Hl. 294; Res. Hl. 2 Dec. '27; Res. S. G. 5 Dec. '27.

because she had not to suffer so much as England and the Republic. Fénelon then pointed out the effects of the flotilla; the calmness of France on that point was absolutely incomprehensible, replied Slingelandt with "une émotion visant à l'aigre", as he had during the whole conversation.

Chauvelin's impression on reading the account of Fénelon's experiences, was, that instead of English, Dutch interests seemed to be at stake. [2]) The Republic now really seemed to be siding entirely with England. Yet this was by no means the case. Slingelandt, who had declaimed so vehemently against Rottembourg to Fénelon, was quite calm in discussing him with Finch: he considered his conduct strange, but would withhold judgment till he heard what the Court of France said of it; [3]) while, contrary to Fénelon's fears, no resolution was taken, but the answer which would be drawn up in Paris was being waited for.

In the settling of this answer Pesters was very calm. Horace Walpole was not; at first he was against any answer other than instructing Rottembourg to ask for a plain yes or no, and, in the event of the latter answer, to leave immediately. [4]) However, while with regard to the strict carrying out of the Preliminaries he met with the strong support of Pesters, owing most likely to the absence of such support, Rottembourg was ordered to depart after a week or ten days only, and even then his departure was not imperative. Orders were simultaneously sent to Richelieu: he had to make known the disappointment of his Court at the proposal of November 14th., which had been so much the greater, hopes having been entertained of the assistance which Koenigsegg would give; he had also to press upon the Emperor the giving of satisfaction to the States with regard to the list (December 2nd.). [5])

The French ministers were rather hasty about these orders, and not without reason. They had to be sent off before Horace Walpole should receive his, which would no doubt be very strong. And so indeed they proved to be. If the unconditional carrying out of the Preliminaries should be refused or delayed, then the three ministers of the Hanover Allies ought all to leave Madrid

---

[1]) Fénelon to Chauvelin, 8 Dec. '27, A. E. Hl. 372.
[2]) Chauvelin to Fénelon, 18 Dec. '27, ibidem.
[3]) Finch to Townshend, 9 Dec. '27, R. O. Hl. 294.
[4]) Chauvelin to Fénelon, 4 Dec. '27, A. E. Hl. 372.
[5]) Pesters to Slingelandt, 5 Dec. '27, R. A. Hl. 2981.

on a fixed day, while a declaration should be delivered to the Emperor that none of the Ostend ships, not even excepting those which had been excluded by Slingelandt, should in that event be allowed a safe return. [1])

Though the King of England did not withhold his assent from what had been settled at Paris previous to his instructions having arrived there, still he tried to assert his will, and in this he wanted the Republic to help him. For this purpose Pesters ought to be ordered to press, in conjunction with Horace Walpole, for the making of a declaration to Fonseca with reference to the return of the Ostend ships; and Van der Meer, to consider the answer to be given to Rottembourg as returned to the three powers, and, in the event of this being in the negative, to leave Madrid as well. [2]) As a matter of course England herself sent orders in this strain to Keene, and if only the Republic could be prevailed upon to do the same with regard to Van der Meer, then in spite of France the ministers of the Allies at the Court of Spain would have to adopt exactly the same line of conduct.

Finch had to speak with the Dutch ministers about the issuing of such orders. It would appear, however, that he did not do so during the few days that intervened between his receiving his instructions and December 16th., when intelligence reached the Hague that the negotiations had passed to a new stage, for a third proposal had arrived in Paris from Madrid.

Here the success of the second proposal was not waited for, just as, before making this, they had not waited for the answer to the first proposal of October 15th. When this answer arrived, Rottembourg perceived that the proposal of November 14th. was sure of not being agreed to. [3]) But he did not perceive that it would be utterly rejected, otherwise he would not have accepted a convention which differed very little from it. This came about in the following manner. In order to put matters right before the answer to the proposal of November 14th. arrived, he held a conference with La Paz and Koenigsegg; at this it was agreed to bring matters to a close by an exchange of letters: Rottem-

[1]) Newcastle to Finch, 21 Nov. '27, R. O. Hl. 294.
[2]) Newcastle to Finch, 28 Nov. '27, R. O. Hl. 294.
[3]) Van der Meer to Fagel, 3 Dec. '27, R. A. S. G. 7358.

bourg was to deliver one to La Paz containing the conditions
offered by George II. to Broglie, and upon this La Paz should
return one to him, in which these conditions were to be inserted
and the King of Spain declared to accept them. In his answer to
Rottembourg, however, La Paz made some very material alterations in the words used by George II., which were to the effect
that, taken altogether, Spain stood by the proposal of November
14th.; this answer was nevertheless accepted by Rottembourg
(convention or third proposal of December 3rd.). [1]

In Madrid it was generally thought that things had come to
a happy conclusion; Van der Meer and Keene even went so far
as to give a kind of approval to it. The latter might have had his
doubts, as, to a certain extent, he had been let into the negotiations, but Van der Meer had been altogether excluded, and so
could not think otherwise than that Rottembourg had an authorization unknown to him for what he had done. [2]

In Paris too, it was thought that matters had now come to an
end, but Horace Walpole soon disillusioned them. He drew to
Fleury's notice and made him clearly perceive that the upshot
of La Paz's alterations had already been rejected by France in
the reply to the proposal of November 14th. The Cardinal was
then greatly embarrassed: he was desirous of satisfying his obligations towards England, but was at the same time afraid that
a disavowal of Rottembourg would be equivalent to breaking
off the negotiations. Chauvelin did his utmost to prevent this
extreme, and his draft of an answer to Rottembourg went a long
way in justifying him. Owing, however, to the vigorous protests
of Horace Walpole, who met with strong support from Pesters
and Van Hoey, the new Dutch Ambassador in France, who had
recently arrived, and owing, too, to the consideration of the "ex-
cès de vivacité" evinced by Slingelandt in his last conversation

---

[1] Baudrillart, *op. cit.* III, 380—'1.
[2] Keene to Newcastle, 15 Dec. '27, B. M. Add. 32753: Van der Meer to Fagel, 3, 8,
15 Dec '27, 12 Jan. '28, R. A. S. G. 7358. Baudrillart (*op. cit.* III, 379—'80) has ascribed
too great a share in the negotiations to Van der Meer and Keene, in any case to the
former. He was not consulted at all, and was not present at the conference of Dec. 1st, as
Baudrillart says he was. Nor was Keene. It was however not without the latter's knowledge that Rottembourg agreed to the alterations made by La Paz, and he ought to have
inquired for his authority before allowing it. Unexperienced as he was, he reposed too
much confidence in Rottembourg, for this he was severely reprimanded (*Eng. Hist.
Rev.* XVI, 315).

with Fénelon, Chauvelin was obliged to send him orders by which La Paz's alterations were declined, and Rottembourg was tied down to what had been sent to him in answer to the proposal of November 14th. (December 19th.). [1])

It stands to reason that Horace Walpole informed his Government of the convention immediately upon its arrival from Madrid. They considered it "still more astonishing and unaccountable than the proposal of November 14th.", "perfect madness", "a monstrous affair", at which the King felt "highly offended." [2]) These expressions testify to an extraordinary excitement. This sprang from fear of Parliament, which was to meet within a few weeks. In those days the English Cabinet was not, as it is to-day, an executive committee of the majority in the Parliament, but they were a set of men who enjoyed the confidence of the King, and against whom Parliament was always filled with a certain distrust, and which had thus in every matter to be convinced that the ministers were taking good care of national interests. They had to be able to justify their actions, and therefore the nearer the meeting of Parliament approached, so much the more impatient did they become of results.[3]) This time there were so far no results. For two years enormous expenses had been incurred, but nothing achieved. Ministers were becoming nervous. [4]) Matters must come to an end somehow. Horace Walpole was instructed to urge the complete disavowal of Rottembourg and the giving of a short time limit to the King of Spain, after which not only the French Ambassador, but also Keene and Van der Meer should leave. [5])

Just as the previous time when the English orders arrived in Paris, those to Rottembourg had already been sent off some days. This time, however, simultaneously with the arrival of the courier from England came one from Spain. Horace Walpole now insisted on the latter's being sent back with a declaration to be made by Rottembourg in the terms of the orders just received from his Court. He urged the necessity of this by pointing out that

---

[1]) cf. the letters of Pesters and Van Hoey to Slingelandt (R. A. Hl. 2981, 2979) and Fagel (R. A. S. G., 7317), 14 Dec. '27 and following dates.

[2]) Newcastle to Finch, 8 Dec. '27, R. O. Hl. 294.

[3]) cf. Michael, "Walpole als Premierminister", Hist. Zeitschrift, Band 104 (1910), 504 et seq, especially 521.

[4]) Villars, Mémoires V, 112—3,116—7; Pesters to Slingelandt, 19 Dec. '27, R.A.Hl. 2981.

[5]) Newcastle to Finch, 8 Dec. '27, R. O. Hl. 294; Chauvelin to Fénelon, 26 Dec. '27, A. E. Hl. 372.

Parliament was about to meet; however, he urged this in vain. Except for one single point, the orders of December 24th. were only a repetition of those of the 19th. [1])

That the English Ambassador met with so little success this time, was in a great measure due to the conduct of the Dutch representatives. At the negotiations which resulted in the orders of December 19th. they were sufficiently well up in the intentions of their Government to support the English Ambassador, but with reference to what was now demanded they had no instructions whatever. True, Pesters did not altogether forsake him, but on the other hand Van Hoey did, he being eager to ingratiate himself with the Court of France, and therefore having no intention of speaking in a disagreeable tone unless at the express command of his masters. [2])

It was not this want of success which induced the English Government to apply to the Republic, as before hearing of it they had already sent orders to Finch. In order to retain the unity of the Hanover Allies the co-operation of the States was now absolutely necessary. The King would rather begin a war than allow himself to be so shamefully treated and thus forced to a congress under such unjust and ignominious conditions. According to Horace Walpole, the Cardinal himself entirely agreed with England, but meeting as he did with great opposition at the Court, he could not act so strongly as he would have wished; the joint representations, however, of the King and the States would very probably turn the balance. Thus the States ought now to take such resolutions as the great crisis required. With their aid a short time-limit was to be put to both the King of Spain and the Emperor, after which all negotiations with Spain should be broken off, while unless the Emperor should prove willing to become friends separately with the Hanover Allies, measures should be taken to capture the Ostend ships. [3])

The English Government again paid especial attention to these ships, and when two of them happened to touch at Plymouth on their

---

[1]) Pesters and Van Hoey to Fagel, 26 Dec. '27, R. A., S. G. 7317; Chauvelin to Fénelon, 26 Dec. '27, A. E. Hl. 372.

[2]) Pesters to Fagel, 22 Dec. '27, R. A. S. G. 7317; Van Hoey to Slingelandt, 26 Dec. '27, R. A. Hl. 2979.

[3]) Townshend to Finch, 12 Dec. '27, R. O. Hl. 294; cf. Pesters to Slingelandt, 29. Dec. '27, R. A. Hl. 2981.

homeward bound voyage, orders were immediately sent to delay them under some pretext or other. [1]) They also informed the Dutch ministers in London that the two ships which were being equipped at Ostend, and about which they had so often sent information, were now ready to sail. [2]) This they did not only to show the States how zealous they were for their interests, but also to make them uneasy about those interests.

The French, however, on this point tried to set the States at rest: they should not be uneasy about the list, strong orders having already been sent to Richelieu, and they might rest assured that should these fail in their effect, the King of France would not fail to do what the States required of him. This difference between the two powers is very easily accounted for: the English wanted the Dutch to fall in with their plans, while the French tried to dispose them against these To this end, the latter omitted nothing. The meeting of Parliament, so Pesters and Van Hoey were very plainly told in Paris, as were also Slingelandt, Fagel and the other leading men at the Hague, was not a reason why the method hitherto followed by the Allies should be altered, this being sure to lead to war, while for war there was not sufficient reason: what must still be done was only that some words should be revised. Moreover, France had no funds for war, for since a war with Spain would be very unpopular it would be practically impossible to raise the necessary resources from the nation. Further, the issue was by no means secure, the less so as it would appear that the Emperor had concluded a treaty with the King of Sardinia, and very probably by going to war the Hanover Allies would only be playing into his hands, for then he could again claim subsidies from Spain. [3])

It was not without reason that France went to all this trouble to scare the Republic from going to war: affairs in Europe had reached a crisis. Spain proved to be disinclined to do what the Hanover Allies desired. On receiving the reply to the proposal of November 14th. (December 12th.) Rottembourg saw that he had gone too far in admitting the alterations made by La Paz,

---

[1]) It was in vain; the ships had already left port: Vreede, *Voorouderlijke Wijsheid*, 102—'4.

[2]) Van Welderen, Sylvius and Hop to Fagel, 19, 23 Dec. '27, R. A., S. G. 7348.

[3]) Chauvelin to Fénelon, 26 Dec. 27, A. E. Hl. 372; Pesters' and Van Hoey's letters during the last days of Dec. '27 and 1 Jan. '28.

and he then applied to Elizabeth asking for them to be recalled, but to this application she replied that she would rather go to war. In this she was fully in earnest, and to get the necessary supplies she claimed an unusally heavy "indulto" upon all the foreign effects of the flotilla. [1]

The situation in which France found herself was a very difficult one indeed; there seemed to be no way between the two extremes, war with Spain, which would be contrary to both the commercial interests and the feelings of the nation at large, and breaking loose from England, which would be altogether too risky. In this state of affairs she set her hopes on the Republic. England also did the same thing. For once the time returned when the decision as to peace and war would appear to rest with the Republic. What would it be, a sword or an olive-branch, which she would throw into the scales?

VI.

Through congratulations from Van der Meer the States received the first intelligence of the convention of December 3rd. Though surprised at the sudden facility of England, they did not doubt the matter, being caught as they were with the notion of its being good. Even Slingelandt was inclined to believe in it, yet he had his doubts and considered it wiser to be reserved in his conversation with Fénelon. The Republic, at all events, he said to the latter, had no cause to be satisfied, no mention having been made of the list. [2] Upon being fully informed a few days afterwards of what had passed, he disapproved entirely of Rottembourg's conduct; in his opinion nothing remained than to disavow him. Hence the orders of December 19th. implying a disavowal were to his liking; yet he was not altogether content with these. Should they have effect, he said to Fénelon, à la bonne heure! but the time had now come to decide what should be done should these orders fail in effect. This was necessary with a view to the opening of Parliament. If it had been Koenigsegg's object by persuading Rottembourg into this convention to get the English

---

[1] Baudrillart op. cit. III, 383; Van der Meer to Fagel, 15, 20 Dec., R. A , S G. 7358.
[2] Fénelon to Chauvelin, 19 Dec. '27., A. E. Hl. 372; Finch to Townshend, 19, 23 Dec. '27, R. O. Hl. 294.

Government into grievous trouble, and to rouse distrust among the Hanover Allies, he could not have done a better thing. War would not suit the Republic, but in this way she would certainly be brought into one. If France continued to redress mildly the wrong done, matters would never come to an end. Interrupting the Pensionary, Fénelon remarked that the orders which France had sent had always been drawn up in consultation with the English and Dutch ministers in Paris; Slingelandt retorted that the conduct of France and that of Rottembourg were two different things; the Cardinal acted satisfactorily and with the utmost frankness, but Rottembourg he could not understand, he passing as both an honest and a capable man. Neither had Fénelon any more success on pointing to Van der Meer's approval. He had been absolutely excluded from the conferences, was the reply. [1])

The States were very discontented at this exclusion, and they were all the more ready to accept a resolution in accordance with the intentions of Slingelandt. Pesters and Van Hoey were instructed to thank the French ministers for the orders of December 19th.; at the same time, however, they had to submit to them the putting of a time-limit to the King of Spain, and in conjunction with Horace Walpole they had to ask what France was going to do, and what measures the Hanover Allies ought to take should either Philip V. or the Emperor, or both, refuse to yield (December 25th.).

Fénelon tried, but in vain, to put a spoke in the wheel just before this resolution was passed, and on being informed of it in a conference he did not take any pains to conceal his dissatisfaction. He observed that the States, while pretending to be pleased with the orders of December 19th., nevertheless appeared to desire something more, and he plainly insinuated that this had been suggested by England. His observation was correct; his insinuation, however, was not, for if that part of the resolution had originated with England, it would have contained an order to Van der Meer to return together with Rottembourg and Keene. The resolution lacked such an order: not that it was an omission, for it was left out purposely. The King of England had mentioned

---

[1]) Fénelon to Chauvelin, 23, 25 Dec. '27, A. E. Hl. 372.

the matter to the Dutch ministers in London, and their letter was
read at the same session as that at which the resolution was passed.
Two other points discussed with them by the King were attended to,
but not the recalling of Van der Meer. This could all the better be
put on one side as it was not urged by Finch; he could very well
have done so, by virtue of his previous orders; he, however, waited
for new ones. His silence suited Slingelandt very well, it being far
easier to avoid the giving of a special order, once a resolution had
been passed, than to refuse to insert it on urgent requests
being made by Finch. Indeed, two days afterwards Van der
Meer's return came under discussion, but was of course not decided upon, the States resolving to consider the matter further. [1]

Neither did Finch meet with any success, when about this time,
after having received fresh orders, he applied to Slingelandt. The
latter remarked that whatever the Maritime Powers might do,
France would never be a party to Spain's being so restricted as
England desired that she should be, and even should the Allies
push Spain very hard she would still, in order to give herself airs,
add something to their answer; should the Ambassadors then have
to leave, war would be the immediate result, and considering the
strong opposition the Cardinal was meeting with at the Court of
France, Slingelandt feared that England and the Republic would
be very much concerned to see that France had the same consideration for Spain upon this occasion as she had had in the negotiations. It was not his opinion that the King of England should
accept even the smallest addition made by Rottembourg, but if
Spain should come near to what the King had agreed to, acceptance would be preferable to a breach in which the Maritime Powers would be supported only half-heartedly by France. The immin-
ence of such a breach would make the States most cautious as
to the sending of the desired orders to Van der Meer. It would
be considered as a certain precursor of war; further, if it were done
at all, a good deal of time would first be taken up, as the provinces would have to be consulted upon it. [2]

In this way Slingelandt averted the solicitations of England.
The part he took at this critical juncture, however, was not merely

[1] Fénelon to Chauvelin, 25, 26 Dec. '27, A. E. Hl. 372; Secr. Res. S. G. 25, 27 Dec. '27;
Van Welderen, Sylvius and Hop to Fagel, 19 Dec. '27, R. A. S. G. 7348.
[2] Finch to Townshend, 30 Dec. '27, 2 Jan. '28, R. O. Hl. 294, 299.

negative, for it must have been on his orders that Pesters asked
Chauvelin if some expedient could not be found to induce their
Catholic Majesties, without their being brought to extremes, to
suppress Rottembourg's fatal letter. For this purpose he suggested that France should give an assurance that everything that
Spain was entitled to claim from England, pursuant to the Preliminaries and expecially under Article 8, should be carefully
gone into at the Congress. Chauvelin did not reject this, but
proposed another i. e., to induce England, with regard to the due
carrying out of the Preliminaries, to rely implicitly on France and
the Republic. What he meant by this he did not say; probably
he meant the releasing of the Prince Frederick into the hands of
the Dutch; he, however, was not reticent on the question as to by
what channel this expedient would be made agreeable to England, for he considered that there was nobody more suitable for
this than the Pensionary. [1])

The latter did not follow this suggestion; but before being
informed of it, he had already tried to exert some influence in
that direction. He had written a private letter to Townshend in
which he stated that in his opinion "il faut sortir d'affaire le
moins mal que nous pourrons et, pourvu que conjointement nous
mettions à couvert l'honneur du Roi votre maître et celui de ses
ministres, ne pas trop nous mettre en peine des gros mots du Marquis De La Paz touchant la réparation des dommages soufferts
et la décision par des Puissances indifférentes, et semblables idées
espagnoles, lesquelles par la nature même des choses ne peuvent
avoir d'effet". [2])

Townshend's answer shows the greatest uneasiness. Slingelandt made nothing of those "gros mots" of the Spaniards, but
in his opinion these might entail "suites fatales". For, should the
English Government now agree to such conditions as were proposed by Spain, they had on the one hand this power claiming at
the Congress not merely indemnification for damages suffered,
but also equivalents, such as for example the restitution of Gibraltar; while on the other hand, a storm was sure to arise in Parliament against the King and those who served him. Instead of
"sortir d'affaire" the situation would become more and more crit-

---

[1]) Pesters to Slingelandt, 26 Dec. '27, R. A. Hl. 2981.
[2]) Slingelandt to Townshend, 26 Dec. '27, in Vreede, *Voorouderlijke Wijsheid* 101—'2.

ical, not only to England and the Republic, whose union would
run the risk of being entirely upset, but even to Protestantism
as well. That this union was still in full force was his only conso-
latory argument: "notre salut et celui de notre sainte Religion
tient uniquement, dans cette crise, à la ferme et inébranlable
union entre S. M. et votre République, et si Elles parlent le même
langage, et agissent dans le meme esprit d'une manière bien sou-
tenue, Elles attireront de plus en plus les regards de la France et
se feront respecter même par l'Empereur. J'avoue que nous nous
trouvons dans un état très-violent et exposé à de grands dangers,
mais voilà à mon avis le seul moyen qui nous reste pour nous en
tirer avec honneur et sûreté". [1]

Despite Townshend's wishes the Republic did not speak quite
the same language. Slingelandt pointed out this difference when
in a conversation with Fénelon he thus justified the resolution of
December 25th.: it only strengthened Rottembourg's order by
a "coup d'épron de plus", the Republic did not, like England, go "à
bride abattue", but rather kept the mean between her and France. [2]

The French ministers were quite cognisant of this. They considered the resolution rather strong, yet manifesting great deference to France. Owing in some measure to the disposition of the
Republic, they did not agree to everything that England desired.
A menacing declaration to the Emperor about the Ostend
ships was not made. As regards Spain, it has been said that "the
inconceivable folly of Spain in further estranging France rendered any consideration for her impossible", [3] but this is not right,
for though the heavy "indulto" of which that folly consisted
caused Chauvelin to lodge a strong protest, France none the
less prevailed upon England to make a further concession to
Spain, viz.: that she might make an inventory of the contents
of the Prince Frederick. Notwithstanding Horace Walpole's vehemence, and it often came to high words between him and Chauvelin, England was not successful in the most important point,
the simultaneous return of the three ministers stationed at the
Court of Spain. It is true, orders were sent in which there could be

---

[1] Townshend to Slingelandt, 22 Dec. '27, ib. 102—'4.
[2] Fénelon to Chauvelin, 1 Jan. '28, A. E. Hl. 373. In this same letter Fénelon records
Slingelandt as having repeatedly expressed his fear lest Rottembourg after being disavowed would keep too scrupulously to the letter of Broglie.
[3] *Eng. Hist. Rev.* XVI, 315.

no question of ambiguity: Rottembourg was to finish matters on the basis of Broglie's letter, and should no satisfactory answer be forthcoming, to leave within two days. But this order had only reference to himself and not to Van der Meer and Keene, his instructions being to consult them in everything with the exception of his return (January 8th., 1728). [1])

By making this reservation, France kept the way open for the Republic to work in her turn for the adjustment of the difficulties, should Spain not yet be inclined to give way. It was possible that England might perhaps accept an expedient from her. Fénelon soon got instructions to prepare her for playing this part; he was ordered to inform Slingelandt that should Rottembourg have to leave Spain, his master neither would, nor could, propose an expedient; in that event he could only encourage his Allies, who desired the preservation of peace, to a new effort, or support the States in any vigorous measures which they might deem it necessary to take against the Emperor and Spain. It was, however, taken for granted in France that when the Republic did not respond to the desires of England or acted in any way contrary to them, this was done in opposition to the wishes of the Pensionary. Therefore Fénelon ought no longer to confine the negotiations to him and his brother-in law, but to look for "resources dans l'intérieur de la République". Without Slingelandt's being aware of what he was doing, Fénelon had to persuade the leading men in such a way that the Pensionary would be obliged to propose an expedient. [2])

Just as the French, the English Government also tried to influence the Republic. They did not fail to notice that the comparatively little success which they had had in the latest negotiations, was owing in a great measure to want of support on the part of the Republic; this they attributed, not to the Dutch Government, but to Van Hoey, who, they said, continually leaned towards Chauvelin's "method of expedience at His Majesty's expense". Fearing that, on the arrival of Spain's answer, he would again play a wrong part, they requested Slingelandt not only to reprimand him, but also to allow Pesters, who, now that the new Ambassador

---

[1]) Baudrillart, op. cit. III, 382—'4; Chauvelin to Fénelon, 8, 19 Jan. '28, A. E. Hl. 372, '3; cf. Mémoires de Villars V, 118.

[2]) Chauvelin to Fénelon, 19 Jan. '28, A. E. Hl. 373.

had arrived, would soon be leaving, to remain for a while longer
at the Court of France. Finch was further ordered to represent
that the States should send these ministers strong resolutions in
the event of Spain's answer implying a refusal. [1]

Both Finch and Fénelon made their representations to Slingelandt. What was the latter's opinion of the situation, and what
was his attitude towards them? Though more so than England,
he was not pleased with the orders of January 8th. either; he considered them too mild and not in any way suitable for such a
Court as that of Spain. In these it was admitted that the King
of Spain had consented to all that was essential, but it was
thought that he ought now also to yield to what was formal, for
the purpose of facilitating the task of the English ministers in the
new Parliament. Slingelandt feared that this argument would
have the opposite effect on the Court of Spain, it being something
of a temptation to her to procure another delay in the hope of
being able to perplex and embarrass affairs in England. [2] Being
of this opinion, he had no objection to reprimanding Van Hoey,
who he also considered had gone too far, [3] while Pesters was not
yet recalled. Nor did he conceal his opinion from Fénelon: "il
était fort sombre sur notre condescendance dans les dernières
dépêches", so wrote the latter to Chauvelin. Probably, not to encourage the French ministers in this disposition, Slingelandt gave
no answer whatever to what Fénelon represented to him: he remained pensive and did not utter a single word. [4] At least his
silence did not arise from any desire to support England's policy
unreservedly, for he took advantage of the orders of January 8th.
in exonerating the Republic to Finch for her not taking a resolution
with regard to the recalling of Van der Meer, this being, in his opinion, out of place now. Further, he again pointed out to him the
strong fear there was in the Republic of a breach, to which France
was so much averse. [5] He reserved to himself in relation to both parties full scope of action in the coming crisis; for he did not entertain
much hope of Spain's answer being favourable either. In his

---

[1] Townshend to Finch, 17 Dec. '27, 2, 9, 19 Jan. '28, R. O. Hl. 294, 299; Van Hoey
to Slingelandt, 23 Jan. '28, R. A. Hl. 2979.
[2] Finch to Townshend, 16 Jan. '28, R. O. Hl. 299; cf. Baudrillart, op. cit. III, 382.
[3] The same to the same, 2, 20 Jan. '28, ib.
[4] Fénelon to Chauvelin, 16, 27 Jan. '28, A. E. Hl. 373.
[5] Finch to Townshend, 20, 27 Jan. '28, R. O. Hl. 299.

opinion the heavy "indulto" levied forboded little good. [1])

In this state of uncertainty, in which Fénelon and Finch were equally eager to secure the Republic, they were both glad they could just now support her in her own private affairs. At last an answer had arrived about the list. This had already been promised by the declaration of November 6th., which also gave information of the embargo passed on the two ships which were being equipped for India. Several weeks afterwards Koenigsegg-Erps had made overtures to Slingelandt to still permit these ships to sail, in return for the deleting of the note which had been added to the list, but the latter had prevailed upon him not to mention the matter to the States. [2]) The Austrian envoy, making sure that his Court would not stick to this proposal, positively denied the statement asserted by England that those ships were to set sail for India. [3]) However, in spite of his opinion, and despite the representations made by Richelieu in consequence of his orders of December 2nd. which were of course seconded by Hamel Bruynincx, the Court of Vienna stood by her proposal and gave Koenigsegg-Erps instructions to deliver a memorial on the subject to the States. This memorial of January 14th. did not meet with any success. In Slingelandt's opinion the note clashed with the Preliminaries, and consequently the expedient in return for which the Court of Vienna would give it up, fell through. The States readily agreed to this; no resolution however was passed before consulting the Allies' Ambassadors. These Ambassadors had no instructions on this point, but considered it wholly unnecessary to wait for such, and fully approved of the proposed reply. Both of them were desirous of obliging the States; Fénelon had another reason for this: as, once their own desires had been satisfied, it would be all the more difficult for Slingelandt to move them into taking vigorous resolutions. [4])

In this way the difficulties with the Emperor came to an end He might still have stood by the note, the possibility of which the Pensionary recognized, but he did not do so. At this junc-

---

[1]) Fénelon to Chauvelin, 16 Jan. '28, A. E. Hl. 373.

[2]) Fénelon to Chauvelin, 13 Jan. '28, ib.

[3]) Secr. Res. S. G. 25 Dec. '27; Res S. G. 3 Jan. '28.

[4]) Res. S. G. 15, 17, 24, 27 Jan. 28; Finch to Townshend, 16, 27 Jan. '28, R. O. Hl. 299; Fénelon to Chauvelin, A. E. Hl. 373. We have looked in vain for confirmation of what Huisman says (*op. cit.* 430): les Hollandais reclamèrent même que les navires fussent *désemparés et dématés.*

ture of affairs he did not think it advisable to complicate matters in any way. He had himself tried to evade the Preliminaries, on behalf of the Ostend Company, and further had in some measure stiffened Spain in her obstinacy, but not with the intention that war should result. Just as in the previous year, his interests required peace. At this very time he was not sure of Prussia, who was negotiating with Saxony. [1]) And only a few weeks ago George II. had succeeded in dealing a serious blow to him, by concluding a treaty with the Duke of Brunswick-Wolfenbüttel (December 6th.) by which, in the event of war in Germany, a great advantage would be gained for the Hanover Allies. [2])

The Emperor not only yielded himself, but he also exerted his influence over Spain in this direction: Koenigsegg was instructed to countenance the measures of the Hanover Allies. In quite another way the Emperor also helped to bring Elizabeth to a more reasonable state of mind, as she had become aware that he was counteracting the interests of Don Carlos in Italy. What contributed also to making her more reasonable was the serious illness of her husband. On the latter's death, which appeared to be imminent, her step-son Ferdinand would succeed to the throne, and her position and that of her sons would then become very precarious. All these circumstances caused her to lend a more ready ear to Rottembourg, who offered her the declaration which Horace Walpole had tried in vain to carry through, and which he had then sent to Keene. It is a proof of the pitiful situation in which the Queen found herself that she accepted it with only two not very material modifications. On January 13th., before Rottembourg could have received his orders of the 8th., this 4th. proposal was sent from Spain and on the 26th. quite unexpectedly arrived in Paris. [3])

The French ministers at once perceived that by this Spain demanded less than she had already been granted by the orders of January 8th.; they therefore considered the difficulties as settled. Slingelandt was also of the same opinion, for he said to Fénelon

---

[1]) Droysen, *Friedrich Wilhelm I*, II, 8 et seq.

[2]) Coxe *R. W.* I, 301—'2.

[3]) Baudrillart, *op. cit.* III, 385 et seq. This author ascribes the 4th proposal to Rottembourg (p. 399), but it is proved to have originated with Horace Walpole from Chauvelin's letter to Fénelon, 26 Jan. '27, A. E. Hl. 373; cf. Slingelandt to Townshend, 3 Feby. '28 R. O. Hl. 297, and Townshend to Slingelandt, 30 Jan. '28, R. A. Hl. 2994.

that he thought they could now congratulate each other, and when the latter drew his attention to the two modifications, he replied: "il fallait bien que les Anglais s'en contentassent". If this were to be so, was of course the most important question. In order to promote this, France tried to make use of the Republic. Fénelon urged the States into expressing themselves immediately, not merely thus to prevent their waiting for England's decision, but also that this decision might be influenced by theirs. This intention of Fénelon's was evident to Finch also; when, at a conference, Slingelandt inquired of him as to what his Court thought of matters now, he said that he would probably receive this opinion in the course of one or two days, thus giving a hint that they should wait so long. Slingelandt, Fagel and several deputies said that they would do so, otherwise a resolution would be passed such as he would be satisfied with. [1])

There was no waiting, however. The matter was taken in hand at once, owing to Fénelon's strong representations to several of the leading men, and not, it would appear, in the face of Slingelandt. He too desired that the Republic should exert influence on England, but he did not desire that France should know anything of it; so the resolution was drawn up with particular care. In the first part, containing the instructions for Van Hoey and Pesters and for Van der Meer, the States were very reserved: they expressed the hope that the King of England would not make any objection. In the second part, intended for the Dutch ministers in London, they were more positive: these were exhorted to press the English government to agree to the proposal, should they not have done so already, pointing out that according to the Court of France, and also to the States, the modifications were not disadvantageous to England or at least not greatly so; while if there were any disadvantage, it was not in any way to be compared with the possible consequences of the rejection. [2])

---

[1]) Van Hoey and Pesters to Fagel, 27 Jan. '28, R. A., S. G. 7317; Chauvelin to Fénelon, 26 Jan. '28; Fénelon to Chauvelin, 2 Feb. '28, A. E. Hl. 373; Finch to Townshend, 3 Feb. '28, R. O. Hl. 299.

[2]) Finch to Townshend, 3, 20 Feb. '28, R. O. Hl. 299; Secr. Res. S. G. 2 Feb. '28. In spite of Slingelandt's precautions the resolution was read in its entirety at a conference where Fénelon was present. Finch complained to Slingelandt, and as a result Fénelon was denied a copy of the resolution. Some difficulties with the latter concerning the giving of resolutions to foreign Ambassadors ensued, which, however, soon came to an end, Fénelon not daring to maintain his point too strongly.

In a private letter to Townshend, Slingelandt dwelt more in detail on the arguments for acceptance, and told him that one of the principal reasons why he had advised giving the Dutch ministers in London such instructions, had been that in case any difference might arise as to acceptance or refusal, he, Townshend, as far as he knew his sentiments, would not be angry if he could point to the opinion of the Republic as well as to that of France. [1])

Both this letter and the resolution are worthy of remark as affording an insight into Slingelandt's intentions, but they did not influence the decision. Before these arrived the resolution had already been passed. Discussion had of course only been on the modifications. The second of these: "que toutes les prétentions respectives de part et d'autre soient produites, débattues et décidées au même Congrès", in particular passed under review. The question was, whether in these indefinite words the pretension to Gibraltar was included. This being on several grounds answered in the negative, no objection to acceptance remained. On the other hand there were a number of arguments in favour of it. France ardently wished it. In the crisis of December, Slingelandt had already worked towards making things easier. Parliament was to meet in the course of a few days, so that, even if only on that account, a decision had to be come to. Hence the proposal was agreed to, except that an amendment was made in order to render the engagements of George II. and Philip V. reciprocal. A few days later, in the speech from the throne, the settlement of the difficulties was announced (February 7th. n/s). [2])

No obstacle was raised to this amendment: the Court of Spain complied with it. A new convention could thus have been signed about the middle of February had not a new delay arisen in the meantime. Strangely enough this came from England, who had not despatched the necessary authorization to Keene in time. Chauvelin and even Fleury then declaimed violently against England, who had so often accused them of dilatory tactics. An English author says, "The incident, trifling enough in itself, affords an insight into the spirit with which the French ministry were be-

---

[1]) Slingelandt to Townshend, 3 Feb. '28, R. O. Hl. 297.
[2]) King, *Notes* 55—6; Cobbett, *Parl. Hist.* VIII, 634 et seq.; Baudrillart, *op. cit.* III, 401; Townshend to Finch, 21 Jan. '28, R. O. Hl. 299; the same to Slingelandt, 26, 30 Jan. '28, R. A. Hl. 2994.

ginning to regard England". [1]) On the eve of the convention want of harmony between the two powers again manifested itself. It was indeed high time to conclude it. This took place on March 6th. It was named the Convention of the Pardo, after the Castle where the Court of Spain was residing at the time.

This Convention put an end to the negotiations which had been going on since the Preliminaries. The danger of war, sometimes very imminent, had been averted, and peace confirmed. This was undoubtedly a success for the Court of France, which had constantly had this object in view. She had even made the error of allowing this to be too clearly seen [2]) and so at last Spain's yielding was due more to other circumstances, i. e., the attitude of the Emperor and the illness of Philip V., than to the action of France. Rottembourg was so discontented with his mission that he sent in his resignation. [3]) Chauvelin would have liked ,to leave him at Madrid: he even went so far as to request Pesters to procure from the Greffier and the Pensionary their approbation of his being retained in his post there. This, however, they were wise enough not to give. The only answer Slingelandt returned to this was that he was not sufficiently acquainted with affairs at the Court of Madrid to know what would be proper or improper in such a case. [4]) He did not feel called upon to pay a tribute to Rottembourg, upon whose conduct he had so often passed well-grounded censure. The English Government would of course have felt still less inclination to do so. Not that they were unmindful of the praiseworthiness of France as to the preservation of peace. Townshend wrote to Slingelandt, "France has played the part of mediator or rather reconciler, and as matters have turned out after all, we have no reason to be dissatisfied at it." To this acknowledgement, however, he added a complaint: there had been so many things that had an unpleasant aspect; France too had often been so dilatory and spiritless. [5])

---

[1]) *Eng. Hist. Rev.* XVI, 316—7; cf. Van Hoey to Slingelandt, 27 Feb. '28, R. A. Hl. 2979; Townshend to Waldegrave, 15 Feb. '28, R. O. Germany 62.

[2]) Baudrillart, *op. cit.* III, 401, 2nd note.

[3]) Ibidem, 405 and 3rd note. We see no reason to doubt, as Baudrillart does, the sincerity of Chauvelin in the compliments he paid to Rottembourg.

[4]) Finch to Townshend, 20 Feb. '28, R. O. Hl. 299.

[5]) Townshend to Slingelandt, 26 Jan. '28, R. A. Hl. 2994.

More than to France, England ascribed the happy issue to Slingelandt; this is to be seen from what Finch had orders to tell him, "The King was sensible it was much owing to his wise and prudent conduct, and to the weight of that steady concurrence of the States in supporting H. M.'s. demands". [1]) Had the States really deserved this praise? Had they so steadily concurred in supporting the demands of England? Neither in the crisis of September nor in that of December had they responded to her wishes. However, they were so far rightfully praised in that they had constantly insisted on due satisfaction being given to England. Particularly must this be said of Slingelandt, whose conduct had indeed been "wise and prudent". His position had been very difficult: above all things, England wanted satisfaction, while France desired the preservation of peace. The interests of the Republic also required peace, so, no less than the French ministers, Slingelandt, too, had constantly striven with this object. However, he did not allow this to be seen; Goslinga was less scrupulous, he did not conceal from Fénelon his dissatisfaction with the resolution of December 25th., nor in general his preference for France. [2]) If he had had the leading of affairs, then peace might also very possibly have been preserved, but at the expense of a collision between the two Allies and a breach with England, which, in Goslinga's opinion also, would have been fatal. Now, however, owing to Slingelandt, who had more than once prevailed upon France to act more strongly in England's interests than she would otherwise have done, the Hanover Alliance had been maintained. And, while upon several occasions the harmony between England and France had left very much to be desired, the harmony between the former and the Republic had not for a single moment been disturbed. In the end the King of England thanked Slingelandt for his conduct, while the Pensionary, on his part, expressed great joy at the happy course of affairs in Parliament. [3])

If we may believe France, these good relations with England were bought at the expense of his independence. Fénelon considered him so pro-English that he even believed the strong ord-

---

[1]) Townshend to Finch, 23 Jan. '28, R. O. Hl. 299.
[2]) Fénelon to Chauvelin, 9 Jan. '28, Goslinga to Fénelon, 2 Feb. '28, A. E. Hl. 373.
[3]) Finch to Townshend, 20 Feb. '28, R. O. Hl. 299.

ers sent to Horace Walpole concerning the convention of December 3rd. might have been suggested by him [1]), while Chauvelin looked on his temporary indisposition during the deliberations of the States regarding the final proposal of Spain as being a favourable factor. [2]) We have seen the very opposite: in spite of his being in indifferent health he left nothing undone to induce England to accept it. Whatever might be thought in France, Slingelandt was by no means tied to England's apron strings: he had not yielded to her vehemence when, upon several occasions, she had wanted the Republic to take vigorous measures against Spain and the Ostend Company, but, on the contrary, his actions had induced England to be moderate.

Both this power and France had constantly tried to determine the Republic's decision, but Slingelandt had maintained an independent position between the two. Owing to this position he had been able to exercise an influence that may not be overlooked. To him is due more than to either Fleury or Chauvelin the honour of having brought about the Convention of the Pardo, and thus preserving the peace of Europe.

---

[1]) Fénelon to Chauvelin, 30 Dec. '27, A. E. Hl. 372.
[2]) Chauvelin to Fénelon, 5 Feb. '28, A. E. Hl. 373.

CHAPTER IV.

THE CONGRESS OF SOISSONS UP TILL THE TREATY OF SEVILLE: THE SEPARATING OF SPAIN FROM THE EMPEROR.
March 1728—November 1729.

A. BEFORE THE CONGRESS.
March—June 1728.

After the Convention of the Pardo, nothing further stood in the way of the Congress. The ratifications of the Preliminaries concluded with Spain at Vienna were exchanged at the same place on the 1st. of May, and on the 14th. of June the Congress was to meet.

Thus a full year elapsed between the conclusion of the Preliminaries and the meeting of the Congress. During this year the Congress was the constant object of the deliberations of the governments of Europe, the object of their hopes and wishes and of their fears too. As a matter of course each power was intent upon directing affairs according to its own desires. As a consequence of this, negotiations arose which were naturally the more brisk when the danger of a breach of the peace was no longer imminent. From those deliberations, set forth in special notes, from those negotiations, as also from the instructions given to the plenipotentiaries, the disposition of the various powers may be inferred as to the coming Congress.

I.

As to Spain, this power looked forward to it with joy. She expected great things from it, among others the restitution of Gibraltar, and a thorough discussion of the commercial differences with England. Though making a good deal of fuss about these points, they were really immaterial to the leader of Spanish politics, Elizabeth Farnese. She only cared about them in so far as they might be of use in the kindling of a war, in which the Emperor would stand too much in need of her to make hesitation any longer possible in what, with her, continued to be the great and only object, viz: the marriage of Don Carlos and Maria Theresa. Gradually the doubt had grown upon her that unless forced by necessity he would not give his daughter. It was because of this, that towards the end of 1727, she had pressed him to give a definite answer on this point. His reply, however, was that he could not give it before he had ascertained the opinion of France at the Congress. She again gave a proof of her distrust by moving the affair of the succession in the Italian Duchies, which she appeared to have forgotten ever since the conclusion of the Vienna Treaties. At the beginning of 1728, she demanded the Emperor's authorization for the introduction of Spanish garrisons into the Duchies. This point was referred to the Congress, where the Emperor hoped it would be lost owing to the opposition of the Hanover Allies, as being incompatible with the Quadruple Alliance. Queen Elizabeth, however, hoped at this Assembly to carry through both this point and that of the marriage. In these, as well as her demands upon England, she relied upon France to help her. This power had to break with England, join the Vienna Alliance, and force the Emperor to fulfil her desires.[1])

Unlike the Queen, Charles VI. was very uneasy about the Congress; he had nothing to hope from it. The matter which he had most at heart, the Pragmatic Sanction, he was not able to even introduce there. He had to do everything in his power to avoid its being moved, for then he would at once be questioned as to his future son-in-law. However, tied down as he was by his promises, he could not but sound France as to the marriage of Maria Theresa with Don Carlos and as to the introduction of Spanish garrisons. If France agreed to these points, which he thought not unlikely, he would be obliged to open with Elizabeth; then he would either have to grant her demands, which he did not intend doing, or to decline them, which he was not able to do, for if he should lose Spain he would be isolated.

Spain was the only ally he could depend upon. As to the Court of Russia, from the time of the death of Catherine I. this had been engrossed by divisions. Nor was the King of Prussia a sure friend.

---

[1]) Baudrillart, *op. cit.* III, 423—8; Syveton, *op. cit.* 256—'62.

He was not to be relied upon except at the expense of making concessions regarding the succession of Juliers and Bergh. The negotiations, however, which the Emperor had set on foot with the Elector Palatine in consequence of the Treaty of Wusterhausen, and which were continued until November 1727, had come to nothing; nor was the Emperor willing to give the guaranty desired by the King. The latter's confidence in him had, moreover, been seriously shaken when, in the Autumn of 1727, he had heard of the Emperor's treaty concluded in the previous year with the Elector. It was not with him, but with August II., that the King entered into close relations (December 1727, January 1728), which greatly disquieted the Court of Vienna, it being afraid that they would together make a treaty of neutrality. [1])

Relations with the Electors of Southern Germany were even worse; from that quarter real danger menaced the Emperor's interests. The Elector Palatine, supported by the Elector of Bavaria, left nothing undone in order to have the affair of Juliers and Bergh introduced at the Congress, and discussed and settled by foreign powers. This could have no other effect, as was exemplified by the Peace of Westphalia, than to conduce to the reinforcement of the liberty of the Empire and to weaken the authority of the Emperor, which it had been the constant care of Charles VI. to build up. [2])

In his relations with Spain and the Empire, the Congress could only be to his disadvantage. The same applies to his relations with the States, who were to demand the conversion of the Ostend Company's suspension into its suppression. At the best the Emperor could only hope to obtain a suitable compromise, either a limited trade or an equivalent for suppression. But this was not what he most cared about. Naturally his honour must not be impeached, and for his Belgian subjects relief for the loss of the Ostend trade would have to be found, but he was to be reasonable. Since he knew that he could not be successful all along the line, he preferred to give way on this point, rather than on those relating to Spain or the Empire. [3])

Taking the latter points into consideration, he thought it wise

[1]) Droysen, op. cit. I, 446—7, 451—3, II, 6—9, 13—19.
[2]) Rosenlehner, op. cit. 364—5, cf. 331, 362.
[3]) cf Van Hoey to Slingelandt, 12 Mch. '28, R. A. Hl. 2979; Pesters to Slingelandt, 10 June '28, enclosed in Slingelandt to Townshend, 11 June '28, R. O. Hl. 297.

to secure the King of Prussia; his friendship would render a breach with Spain less dangerous, and strengthen his position in the Empire. But, far more important to the Emperor than the friendship of Prussia, who was not to be represented at the Congress, would be that of France. He hoped that this power would help him to get out of his difficulties as well as possible, and first of all out of that of the marriage. With regard to this, he would prefer France to propose a delay of five or six years, in order that he might keep his hold upon Spain for that length of time. For the rest, France should join hands with him in rendering the Congress abortive, not only that the affairs of the Empire should be entirely excluded from it, but that in general as few affairs as possible should be introduced there. A certain term should be fixed, within which it should finish, and in order to accelerate its progress, it should not meet at Cambrai but in Paris. Apart from the Ostend affair, the Congress should have little else to do than to convert the Preliminaries into a formal treaty.

To win France to these views, the Emperor had, as early as January, sent Penterriedter to Paris, designed as plenipotentiary at the Congress. The latter showed all possible deference to the Cardinal. [1])

Not only on the side of the Vienna Allies, but also among those of Hanover, there was a power which wished to set a limit both to the time and to the subject-matter of the Congress, and would like to see the matter settled in Paris, to avoid the intricacies of such an assembly; this power was England. [2])

How is this conformity between England and the Emperor to be accounted for? Not by mutual harmony. After the Convention of the Pardo diplomatic relations had been resumed between them; on receipt of the proposal of November 14th. Waldegrave had again been detained in Paris, but now at last he left for

---

[1]) Baudrillart, *op. cit* III, 428; Townshend to Finch, 6 Feby., 12 Apr. '28, R. O. Hl. 299; Horace Walpole to Newcastle, 20 Mch. '28, enclosed in Townshend to Slingelandt, 15 Mch '28, R. A. Hl. 2994; Fénelon to Chauvelin, 17 Feby., 18 Mch.' 28, R. A. Hl. 373; Mémoires, A. E. Mem. et Doc., France 459 f. 128—'32, 496 f. 53—119, 497 f. 19—20; Villars, *Mémoires* V, 121, 125.

[2]) Townshend to Finch, 6 Feby. '28, R. O. Hl. 299. Referring to the latin text of the Preliminaries (Art. 8), the King of England desired to limit the duration of the Congress to 4 months from the conclusion of the Convention of the Pardo (Townshend to Slingelandt, 15 Mch. '28, R. A. Hl. 2994, cf Fénelon to Chauvelin, 1 Apr. '28, A. E. Hl. 374).

Vienna, and Philip Kinsky was shortly to be sent thence to London. The relations, however, were as yet far from cordial. The very fact of the latter's being sent was evidence that the Emperor by no means promised himself the resumption of the friendship with England, for this Kinsky was a young and inexperienced man, and in his instructions it was expressly said that relations were to be dependent upon the course of events at the Congress. [1])

But to this the English Government, no less than the Emperor, looked forward with uneasiness. Just as he, they had nothing to expect from it other than loss. By the Preliminaries they had already obtained all they wished, so their only desire now was to have confirmed that which they had. It was however very questionable whether these things would be so confirmed. If they had their way, of all the differences with Spain that of the smuggling alone would be allowed discussion at the Congress, but to such a limitation Spain was not likely to agree, while of France they were by no means sure. Recently this power had acted as mediator, more or less, just as all along the Vienna Allies had wanted her to act, and it was feared that at the Congress she would continue to act in a similar capacity. To this England objected very strongly; the Allies ought to act there as allies; they ought to live together in the closest relations, even to constitute one body. This was not only with reference to the form of the Congress, but also to its matter. Before the Congress met, they ought to renew the pledges they were under to each other; they ought further to draw up a scheme as the goal towards which they should strive to direct the negotiations at the Congress, their maxim being that nothing should be undertaken to the detriment of the Triple Alliance, that of Hanover or the Preliminaries. [2])

---

[1]) Pribram, *op. cit.* I, 464—6.

[2]) "Considérations qui peuvent servir à donner quelque idée des mesures préalables que les Alliés devraient concerter entre eux pour régler leur conduite au congrès de Cambrai," memorial of Horace Walpole, R. O. Hl. 294; private instructions of Townshend to Waldegrave, 26 Oct. '27, R. O. Germany 62; Townshend to Finch, 6 Feby. '28, R. O. Hl. 299; Townshend to Slingelandt, 26 Jany., 15 Mch. '28, R. A. Hl. 2994; Coxe, *R. W.* II, 550.

Jorissen, *op. cit.* 63—5, is mistaken in thinking England had much to ask from the Congress, cf Townshend to Chesterfield, 25 June '28, R. O. Hl. 300: "By a fair interpretation of the words of the preliminary treaty all the important interests of the King and the States are already determined, and ought not therefore, strictly speaking, to be brought anymore into debate."

It is hardly necessary to mention that just as Spain and the Emperor tried to win France over to them, so also did England exert herself to retain her. As far back as September Horace Walpole had written a memorial about the Congress, and in March he again made new efforts to move this power in favour of the English method. His government, however, did not feel by any means sure of his success; not that they did not trust the Cardinal, but at the Court of France he was the only one "we have any good hold on, and upon whom we may with safety depend".[1] By wrong advisers he might easily be overborne, and particularly by Chauvelin. Thus to prevent this, there must be unanimity among the Maritime Powers; in other words, the representative of the Republic in France had to be a strong supporter of Horace Walpole. [2] Hence, not being able to promise themselves anything from Van Hoey, the English Government again urged upon the States the continuance of Pesters for some time longer, "the public service", so they wrote to Finch, "requires his remaining there." [3]

How much England stood in need of the Republic, is evident from her readiness to support her in her own private affairs, as well as to spare her sensibilities. Concerning the latter point, the Princess of Nassau-Friesland insisted with George II. on his giving his eldest daughter in marriage to her son. As a preparatory favour, she asked for the Garter for him. The King was well disposed, but would not give such a significant mark of his good grace before consulting the Pensionary and the Greffier. Slingelandt, however, advised him against doing so. The very surmise that the King should countenance the views of the House of Nassau-Friesland, and of a marriage between his daughter and the young Prince of Orange being under treaty, already made the people abate their zeal for England, and should this surmise be

---

The Republic and Sweden had both joined the Hanover alliance, without however entering into any engagement as regards each other. Now to render the union of all members of the alliance as close as possible, Horace Walpole desired that these powers should make the engagements they were each under to England and France mutual between themselves.

[1] Townshend to Waldegrave, 15 Feby. '28, R. O. Germany 62; cf. Townshend to Slingelandt, 26 Jany, R. A. Hl. 2994.

[2] Townshend to Slingelandt, 9 Apr. with enclosure, 21 May '28, R. A. Hl. 2994; Horace Walpole to Newcastle, 19 May '28, B. M. Add. 32755; cf. *Eng. Hist. Rev.* XVI, 311.

[3] Townshend to Finch. 12 Mch. '28, R. O. Hl. 299; cf. King, *Notes* 63.

confirmed, then they might very well throw themselves head-
long into the arms of France. This information was sufficient for
the English Government to hold the matter in abeyance for the
time being. [1])

A matter in which they were glad to support the Republic
was that of the so-called Company of Altona. In order to engage
the funds of the Ostend Company during the suspension of the
latter's trade for the purpose of the Indian Company of Copen-
hagen, which had deteriorated very much, the King of Denmark
just at this time renewed and extended its charter, and granted
it an *entrepot franc* at Altona. [2]) This gave rise to the rumour of
the promotion of a new company. [3]) No sooner did this rumour
reach the Republic (February 1728) than it was connected with
the suspension of the Ostend Company — in this way the Belgians were trying to elude it. [4]) The Dutch at once resolved to nip
the new enterprise in the bud; an application was made to their
East India Company for advice, and in the meantime Slingelandt
asked Townshend's opinion and suggested that the King of
Denmark should be dissuaded from his scheme. Now England had
no more right to protest against it than the Republic, but Townshend told Sölenthal, the Danish minister in London, that if his
master persisted in this scheme, he would not be able to look forward to any support from the Hanover Allies at the Congress, in
particular with regard to the affair of Schleswig, in the place of
which country the Duke of Holstein was wanting the Congress
to give him an equivalent, while on the other hand, if he did
not persist in this course, the Allies would take particular care
of Danish interests; this step was one which greatly pleased
Slingelandt. [5])

Just as in this matter, so also in others was England fully prepared to support the Republic. Finch had instructions from Townshend to give strong assurances on this head. The same day the
lastnamed sent a letter to Slingelandt in which he laid down
England's intentions and insisted on his giving his opinion. This

---

[1]) Jorissen, *op. cit.* 28—31.
[2]) Huisman, *op. cit.* 457—9.
[3]) Secr. Res. Hl. 17 Feby '28.
[4]) Fénelon to Chauvelin, 27 Feby, 12 Mch '28, A. E. Hl. 373.
[5]) Finch to Townshend, 24 Feby., 9 Mch. '28, Townshend to Finch, 20 Feby. '28,
R. O. Hl. 299; Townshend to Slingelandt, 15 Mch '28, R. A. Hl. 2994.

kindness was not disinterested, its object being to predispose the Republic in favour of the English method. [1])

This method, however, proceeded from uneasiness with regard to Gibraltar and the commercial privileges — a feeling which did not trouble the Republic. She had no reason to keep the question of Gibraltar from the Congress à tout prix, neither did she object in the smallest degree to there being an examination made into the abuses committed by the English in their trade with Spanish America, as hers also suffered from them. [2]) The method did not suit her at all. While England had nothing to ask from the Congress, the Republic had a great deal to ask from it. With regard to Spain, this power had to give her redress of commercial grievances. Under the Vienna Treaties Spain had granted several advantages to the subjects of the Emperor which the Dutch did not enjoy and which contravened her treaties with the Republic; further, serious injury had been frequently done by Spanish subjects to Dutch merchants. [3]) As to the Emperor, his Ostend Company had, of course, to be suppressed. Not only that, the Republic desired besides that at the Congress a check should be put upon his "despotism" in the Empire. To this end German affairs had to be brought before it. If that were not done, the Dutch feared that the territory of the King of Prussia, in whose favour the Emperor now applied that "despotism", would soon be to include that of the Republic on all sides. [4]) This fear had reference to the affairs of Juliers and Bergh and East Frisia. It made even greater the uneasiness they were experiencing with regard to the latter.

As has been mentioned before, on the advice of the States General the Renitents had in June delivered their submission. This had been unconditional, except that a request had been added that the accords might be respected and the execution of the decrees mitigated. On account of this addition the Emperor had rejected the submission, and the Renitents had been told that they had to deliver a new submission without any condition whatsoever.

---

[1]) Townshend to Finch, 15 Mch. '28, R. O. Hl. 299, Townshend to Slingelandt, 15 Mch. '28, R. A. Hl. 2994.

[2]) Chesterfield once wrote to Townshend (17 Aug. '28, R. O. Hl. 301), "it is impossible for the Spaniards themselves to be more uneasy at our trade to the West Indies than the Dutch are."

[3]) Secr. Res. S. G. 30 Apr. '28 (instructions for the plenipotentiaries).

[4]) Slingelandt to Hop, 7 July '28, R. A. Hl. 2974; cf. Slingelandt to Townshend, 8 June '28, R. A. Hl. 2994.

In other respects too, they were treated badly. After their submission everything ought to have remained *in statu quo*, but far from this, the Prince, who had now become master of almost the whole country, oppressed them as much as he possibly could. For the support of his Danish auxiliaries, a special Renitent tax was exacted from them; several of them were exiled, while upon others soldiers were billeted. In these and similar oppressions, by which many were more or less ruined, the Prince was joined by the Imperial sub-delegates, who issued hard decrees, containing among others that the partisans of the Prince should be indemnified for losses suffered during the disturbances out of the goods of the Renitents.

Representations by the States General on this unjust treatment were of no effect, though they offered to advise the Renitents to submit, provided the Emperor empowered them to assure these people that the decrees would not be severely carried out, nor that the constitution of their country would be entirely trampled under foot. Not only did their representations fail to find a hearing but even their own interests appeared to be menaced. In the rescript of January 27th. 1728, by which the sub-delegates informed the Magistracy of Embden that the submission was rejected and a new one must be given before March 11th., they at the same time forbade application being made to foreign powers, thus also to the States General. There also occurred in this rescript a period showing the design of depriving the Dutch of their East Frisian garrisons. [1]

The uneasiness which this affair and that of Juliers and Bergh gave rise to, caused them to seek refuge with the Congress. Hence it had an effect quite contrary to that which the uneasiness of the English Government had. The latter, we saw, wished to restrain the Congress as far as possible, and to exclude from it the affairs of the Empire. [2] This was not their intention at the outset, the instructions given to Waldegrave in August of the preceding year having contained a note entirely different in tone; but the interest the King-Elector took in German affairs now receded before the uneasiness with which he looked forward to a Con-

---

[1] Fénelon to Chauvelin, 20 Feby '27, A. E. Hl. 373; Fénelon, *Mémoire* 155; Res. S. G. 22 Aug., 16 Dec. '27, 1 Mch. '28; Wiarda, *op. cit.* VII, XXXIIes Buch, erster Abschnitt.

[2] cf King, *Notes* 62.

gress in which the restitution of Gibraltar and the commercial privileges might come under discussion.

It was thus advisable, with a view to the German interests of the Republic, as also with a view to her other interests, not to follow the English method. It seemed that more might be hoped for from France. This power had in the preceding year brought about the suspension of the Ostend Company, and had largely interested herself in the affair of East Frisia. She would certainly take more interest in that of Juliers and Bergh than England, and would be as little inclined as the Republic to continue England's commercial supremacy.

What attitude did Slingelandt now assume? Did he apply to France for support? To some measure he did. He again spoke to Fénelon about the abuses the English committed with regard to their commercial privileges, and of the jealousy of the Dutch merchants, and gave him to understand that he was not opposed to mediation nor yet in favour of putting a short time-limit to the Congress. [1] For all this the Pensionary had not the separation of the Republic from England for his object. In that case she would have been abandoned to the mercy of France, by which her interests would be as little served, if not less, than if she followed England unreservedly. Slingelandt was the less inclined to follow such a course now that England showed such great zeal for Dutch interests. He rather preferred to return this by showing equal zeal for English interests, as, e.g., in the affair of Dunkirk.

According to the Treaty of Utrecht, the harbour at this place should be filled up, and the locks serving to clean it, demolished. The Dunkirk people tried in every way to evade this enactment. The French Government, however, were inclined to wink at it, but they were obliged to spare England, who had a commissioner in the town. However, on the departure of the commissioner Lascelles in 1725, the locks were worked in such a way, that in 1727 ships drawing 14 to 15 feet of water could enter the harbour. In this year Slingelandt had given information of this to Finch; now he did so again. [2]

His good feelings towards England are also evidenced by the

---

[1] Fénelon to Chauvelin, 17, 27 Feby., 18 Mch., 1 Apr. '28, A. E. Hl. 373, 374.
[2] A. de Saint Léger, *La Flandre maritime et Dunkerque sous la domination française* (Paris-Lille, 1900), 308 et seq, 318—9; Finch to Townshend, 19 Aug. '27 with enclosures, 2 Apr. '28, R. O. Hl. 294, 299.

orders given by the States to Pesters (on March 15th.). Before leaving Paris, he was instructed to inquire as to the feelings both as to the form and matter of the Congress, and further to find out whether certain affairs were fit subjects to be brought up there. These instructions had reference to both of the Allies, Pesters was to interview the French ministers as well as Horace Walpole, but as showing a regard for England, it may be noted that it was he who was entrusted with this task and not Van Hoey, in spite of the facts that he was himself anxious to return, not being on good terms with Chauvelin and Van Hoey, and that the States had already ordered him to do so; hence it was by no means easy for Slingelandt and Fagel to get his stay in France prolonged. [1])

In this way the Pensionary openly showed that he wanted to keep up a close union with England. In doing this however, it was not his intention to follow her in everything, but on the contrary that she might all the more readily give up her own method and fall in with his system.

This he set forth in a memorial dated March 31st., which he sent to Townshend. It opened with a radical criticism of the English method. To settle a plan together before the opening of the Congress seemed very plausible indeed, but it was open to serious objections. This renewal of fresh engagements, would it not rather cause a decrease than an increase of mutual confidence? Would it not, should the Vienna Allies get to hear of it, be made use of to sow jealousy? Or, should there be no fear of this, would not such a manner of acting frighten the two Vienna Allies or at least Spain, thus laying an almost insurmountable obstacle in the way of pacification? Neither the matter of the Congress should be previously settled nor the form, for to begin with, France who on the one hand was of all other powers the least interested in the affairs to be dealt with, and thus the most impartial, and on the other hand the power for which all others had the highest regard, would, whatever way of considering affairs should be settled upon, none the less act as mediator. Besides, it was not on such a method, but on the good faith exhibited and the confidence and the constancy of the Allies, that the success of the Congress depended.

---

[1]) Secr. Res. S. G. 15 Mch. '28; Res. S. G. 12 Feby. '28; Finch to Townshend, 20 Feby. 23 Mch., 9 Apr. '28, R. O. Hl. 299.

So, in contradistinction with England, Slingelandt wanted the scope of action at the Congress to be larger. It might be supposed that he wanted the duration and the subject-matter of the Congress increased as well. Indeed, but not only that : the difference was not one of degree — it was one of principle. To Slingelandt the subject-matter might be looked upon "sous deux faces fort différentes, c'est à dire, ou simplement comme un Congrès destiné pour examiner et terminer les différends, survenus touchant la navigation des Pays-Bas Autrichiens aux Indes, et touchant quelques autres points des articles préliminaires, ou bien comme un Congrès destiné *à concilier les droits et les interêts réciproques des puissances et à établir sur un pied solide une pacification générale*, conformément à l'idée de l'article 6 des préliminaires." If the Congress were only looked upon under the first heading, there was no chance of success. It would not even suffice if the second were combined with the first, for the second had to be regarded as the principal, in other words, on the general pacification the adjustment of the separate points depended. Thus a path towards general pacification had first to be found.

The foundations upon which it had been tried to establish the peace of Europe were generally known; these were laid down in the Treaties of Utrecht, Rastadt and Baden, and in the Quadruple Alliance. These foundations had been shaken, if not altogether upset, by the close union of Spain and the Emperor, and also by the suspicions which were very rightly entertained with reference to the measures taken by these two powers as to the succession to the hereditary dominions of the Emperor, either in their entirety or in part, and with regard to the establishment of Elizabeth's sons, from which the junction of those dominions with Spain might even result. This was just as much to be feared by the rest of Europe as that union, which had been very wisely prevented, between France and Spain.

It was now no use trying to bring about a rupture between Spain and the Emperor, the latter having far more to offer Elizabeth than the Hanover Allies. As to the giving up of Gibraltar and of the commercial advantages, the Court of Spain made a great fuss about them, they being on the one hand popular points, and on the other well-fitted to rouse jealousy among both the French and the Dutch, but in reality they were immaterial to Elizabeth, and consequently the inducing England to become more amenable to reason on this point would not advance matters very much.

But the real and perhaps the only way of coming to a general pacification, and through it to a reasonable settlement of the separate points, would be to examine the precautions and limitations under which the Allies of Hanover might agree with the Emperor and Spain as to the former's succession, should he die without male issue, and with regard to the establishment of Don Carlos and the other sons of Elizabeth. If Slingelandt had his way, the Cardinal would first sound the Emperor and Spain upon this subject in the strictest privacy, and this should then be considered by the Allies.

In a sense this point absorbed the whole of the negotiations and cleared away its principal difficulties. The memorial might thus finish here, had not the Congress, in Slingelandt's opinion, not only to restore the general pacification, but also to remove anything that was likely to disturb this within a shorter or longer period of time. Some other points were therefore touched upon, as for instance the succession of Juliers and Bergh, which might very easily cause similar disturbances, as it had done at the beginning of the 17th. century, and that of EastFrisia, which ought to be brought up at the Congress, in any case with reference to the trouble it might cause should the Republic be disturbed in the possession of her garrisons, or should the Court of Vienna any longer delay the giving of such explanations as would cause the suspicions, to which her conduct had given rise, to cease. There was all the more reason to bring this affair up at the Congress, as the Court of Vienna had evidently made use of it to disquiet the Republic and to exert pressure upon her in general affairs. [1])

According to Townshend this memorial met with a very good reception at the English Court. This would appear to be exaggerated; in any case the English method could now no longer be maintained as it was. The renewal of the engagements was dropped, and it was admitted that France had to be considered as a mediator, and that the success of the Congress depended on the good harmony existing between the Allies. The method, however,

---

[1]) "Mémoire ou considérations au sujet du future Congrès, fait le dernier de Mars 1728" in Jorissen, *op. cit.* 266 et seq.

was persevered in so far, that in order to promote unanimity at the Congress the draft instructions for the plenipotentiaries of the Allies should be drawn up in Paris.

With reference to Slingelandt's system, Townshend agreed that a general pacification was most desirable, but at present it was not possible, thus it would be much better for England and the Republic to be satisfied with the removal of the existing difficulties. Why did Townshend think this better? Because he was afraid that aiming at a general pacification might lead to asking sacrifices of England which she was not prepared to make; he thought that the difficulties that might arise in establishing the peace of Europe upon a sound and lasting basis would be attributed to the King's not gratifying Spain in her demands. [1]) Slingelandt's memorial, however, made no mention at all of any such sacrifice; on the contrary, according to this, the general pacification would make Elizabeth give up these demands. Should this be so, the King would be extremely pleased. Another thing in the memorial was also very much to his liking, viz: the introduction at the Congress of the affairs of the Empire. He would not have touched these of his own accord, but now that the Republic had required his support for some such affairs, he asked in return her support for the investiture of Bremen and Verden and the sequestration of Hadeln, in which he considered he had been wronged by the Emperor. [2]) After all, Slingelandt's memorial gave him sufficient satisfaction to enjoin Townshend to declare that he would not be satisfied with the removal of separate differences, unless it should appear that a general pacification would meet with insurmountable obstacles.

In connection with his intentions George II. was by no means indifferent as to the way employed in bringing about a general pacification; no application should be made to the Emperor, for he believed the latter would not make any concession to the Hanover Allies in return for their agreement to the marriage, whereas if the King should guarantee the Pragmatic Sanction at all, it would only be in return for considerable concessions. But the Queen of Spain had to be given to understand that the Allies were ready to advance her wishes, provided she would procure for

---

[1]) Townshend to Chesterfield, 9 July '28, R. O. Hl. 301.
[2]) cf King, *Notes* 62—6.

them the precautions they asked for as the price of their consent. In the event of her broaching the matter to the Emperor, the latter would either have to refuse, which would put an end to his union with Spain, or to agree, by which to everybody's satisfaction the pacification might become general in a most amiable way. [1]

Slingelandt was acquainted with these sentiments of the English Court in a letter from Townshend, and he was highly pleased with them, he having gained a great point: England had accepted the principle of the general pacification he had laid down. Certainly she had accepted it in a certain form only, but, once having taken this step, he was in hopes she would stick to the principle, even though her method of executing it might miscarry. Slingelandt thought this very probable; still he not only agreed to this method, but to promote its success he drew up, in a short and concise form, what had to be presented to Elizabeth: the brilliant promises of the Emperor could not be depended upon, as long as the Hanover Allies and the German Princes, also those who were most closely united to him, opposed them; the Allies did not ask her to depart from her alliance with him, as far it did not run counter to their rights; they were even ready, if it were only consistent with the balance of power in Europe, to co-operate with him in the establishment of her children; she had only to avail herself of the Congress, of which she had it in her power to take great advantage. [2]

It was the Pensionary's wish that Horace Walpole should propose this scheme to the Cardinal, and that they should together settle it. Before he had disclosed this desire, however, the English Court had given orders to Horace Walpole to advocate to the Cardinal the sending of instructions to this effect to Keene.

So, in an indirect way, Fleury became acquainted with Slingelandt's idea of bringing about a general pacification. Judging from the expressions which the Cardinal used to indicate the goal of the Congress: "une pacification solide et generale," "l'union de l'Europe et la paix générale", [3] it may be supposed that he agreed

---

[1]) Townshend to Slingelandt, 29 Mch. '28, R. A. Hl. 2994.
[2]) Slingelandt to Townshend, 19 Apr. '28, R. A. Hl. 2994; Finch to Townshend, 13, 16 Apr. '28, R. O. Hl. 299.
[3]) Baudrillart, op. cit. III, 410 note.
The following observations concerning the policy of France are built upon a number of

with the Pensionary. This however was not so, for in the latter's opinion a general pacification would only be possible when the question of the marriage was gone into, the very matter to which the Cardinal was opposed. For either refusal or consent on his part would turn out to the disadvantage of France. A refusal would drive Spain and the Emperor closer together, by removing that which had hitherto rendered their alliance precarious, while should consent be given, then two cases presented themselves, either that it was given in concert with the Allies or in opposition to them.

In the first case, France feared that it would be repaid with complaisance on the part of the Emperor towards the Republic, and of Spain towards England, which latter would mean a reinforcing of England's maritime position at the expense of French interests. These interests would be still further prejudiced should this power and the Republic be induced to guarantee the Pragmatic Sanction, which they would certainly not object to, if only their own affairs should be settled to their satisfaction. France would then either become isolated or would be obliged to guarantee the Pragmatic Sanction likewise, but without any return; even should the Emperor be under obligation to the Maritime Powers for it.

As to the second case, there was much that was attractive in leaving the Hanover Alliance and joining that of Vienna. The antagonism between the Houses of Bourbon and Habsburg, which had led to so many wars, would be removed, and the triumph of Catholicism secured; further, commercial interests prompted it — yet it could not be. The union between Spain and the Emperor was most uncertain, its sole foundation being a woman's passion. Should the marriage between Don Carlos and Maria Theresa by any chance fall through, this union would be at an end. France would then have to choose between them. With Spain only, and this had been proved by the war of the Spanish succession, France was too weak. True, a union between England and the Emperor she did not fear, so long as the Republic sided with

---

memorials, A. E. Mem. et Doc. France 459, f. 98—107, 128—132, 162—9; 494, f. 111—121, 122—9, 162—184; 497, f. 19—20, 42—3, 45—9, 62—3, 97—100, 170—177; A. E. Hl.366 f. 263—7; and further upon the secret instructions to the plenipotentiaries, 30 May '28, Mem. et Doc. France 496, f. 53—119, of which Baudrillart has also made use, *op. cit.* III, 408 et seq.

her, [4]) but this was not to be expected. A union with Austria, whether in conjunction with Spain or not, could only take place in the event of France guaranteeing the Pragmatic Sanction, a step which she would not lightly take.

For the Emperor was still regarded as *the* enemy; in order to restrain him, and on his death to profit by the occurrence, relations had been entered into with several of the Princes of the Empire. After the Treaty of Hanover French politics had been directed towards forming a party in South Western Germany that would remain neutral in the event of a war between the Emperor and France. The nucleus of this party had to be formed by a close union of the four Wittelsbach Electors, those of Bavaria, Cologne, the Palatinate and Treves. To bring this about, France tried to influence two of them, viz: Bavaria, who laid claims to the Austrian succession, and the Elector Palatine, who would be glad to see the succession to Juliers and Bergh guaranteed by France to the House of Pfaltz-Sultzbach. These negotiations had not been put an end to by the Preliminaries; the Princes of the Empire must not, so Fleury said to Grevenbroch in August 1727 (this latter was the representative of the Elector Palatine in Paris), allow themselves to be oppressed by the exorbitant power of the Emperor, and in no case allow him to act in their names at the Congress. This proceeding on the part of France was not without success. In November of the same year the Elector of Bavaria had become bound to her by a treaty which renewed and extended the alliance of 1714, which latter ensured him of the support of France in obtaining at the first vacancy the Imperial dignity. Under this treaty the Elector bound himself to found a union with the other three; as a result of his exertions, such a union came into being on April 16th. 1728. [1])

The raising of the questions of the marriage and the Austrian succession — Slingelandt's idea — could, in the opinion of France, only be prejudicial. Did she perhaps prefer to render the Congress abortive, as both the Emperor and England, independently of

---

[1]) This is said expressly in the secret instructions to the plenipotentiaries; so it is erroneous to ascribe to the Cardinal the opinion that "the combination of England and the Emperor would be too strong for France and Spain," as has been done (*Eng. Hist. Rev.* XVI, 318).

[2]) Rosenlehner, *op. cit.* 119, 212 et seq, 226, 256, 314—6, 365—70; Broglie, *Le Cardinal de Fleury et la Pragmatique Sanction, Revue Historique* XX (1882), 257 et seq.

each other advocated, they being both uneasy as to Spain? No, she felt no inclination to help them in this.

As to the Emperor, the longer the Congress would be, the fairer were the chances of his coming into collision with Spain. This power would be urging for the marriage, and in case of a refusal or an evasive answer, would stop the subsidies. A breach might so come about; there was another matter which might also lead to this, that of the garrisons, where France had the advantage of the Emperor by being able to offer instead of neutral, Spanish.

With reference to England, France could not countenance that this power should evade in almost every point the giving of satisfaction to Spain. This was not compatible with her promises to the latter. During the whole of the negotiations France had held out hopes to Spain that she would co-operate with her in order to have a thorough examination made at the Congress of her differences with England. Accordingly, France was willing to promote, as far as possible, Spain's interests as regards both the restitution of Gibraltar and the questions of trade.

In these questions the French were themselves also greatly interested; their trade had suffered, and was still suffering a great deal from the supremacy which England had acquired in the trade with Spanish America, where, according to a contemporary, she had taken the place of even Spain herself. [1]) By the Peace of Utrecht the very lucrative Assiento Treaty had passed from a French company to an English, and afterwards England had greatly consolidated her position, much to the prejudice of France. This power should have guarded against this as much as possible, but during the minority of Louis XV. trade had been neglected, and the emergency of 1725 had again thrown France upon England. The disadvantage of this alliance, however, was becoming more and more felt. The upshot of not a few French memorials relating to the Congress was, that English trade with Spanish America was ruining theirs. Serious complaints were made in these, that too little attention had been given in recent years to matters of trade; this was all the worse because the balance of power was no longer confined to territory; it also included trade; for France this was the main point of the Congress, and she had

---

[1]) Huisman, *op. cit.*, 79; Bourgeois, *Manuel* I, 294.

to avail herself of this assembly to extricate herself from the supremacy of England.

Hence, on account of her own interests and the promises given to Spain, France was not able to fall in with the English method. There were as well other objections. If the Hanover Allies should act so closely in concert and with as little complaisance as this method indicated, they could not do otherwise than drive the Vienna Allies closer together, and the result of this would probably be war. Should this prove to be so, Spain would undoubtedly seize the treasures of the galleons that were expected home and combat France with her own millions. This was what France wanted to prevent at any cost. If war had to come, then it must not come before the delivery of the effects of the galleons. France, however, did not want war, she wanted, on the contrary, a general pacification.

A general pacification — what did she mean by this? Neither joining the Vienna Alliance, for this she was intent upon breaking, nor merely keeping that of Hanover. Still, however, it was not her intention to leave this, for by so doing she would be sure to come to a state of great uncertainty, and not to a general pacification. But what she did mean by it, is evident from an exhortation which Fleury made in the above-mentioned conversation with Grevenbroch. In order to further the general pacification, he said, the Princes of the Empire had to support France in opposing the views of the Emperor. [1] According to Slingelandt, he too had to come under the general pacification, but this was not the view which France took. France meant by it a situation that would give her an overwhelming position in Europe, so that she would be able to keep even the Emperor in a more or less dependent position. [2] This state of affairs had to be brought about by a union of Spain with the Hanover Allies.

This was the task which France set herself. It divided itself naturally into three parts, viz: 1stly., Spain would have to be embroiled with the Emperor, 2ndly., Spain would have to become reconciled with England, 3rdly., the Emperor would have to be kept aloof from the Maritime Powers.

Along these lines France dealt with each of the powers that

---

[1] Rosenlehner, op. cit. 321.
[2] Baudrillart, op. cit. III, 411.

took part in the Congress. Thus she tried to inspire Spain, on the one hand, with envy of the Emperor's dominions in Italy, and on the other, with complaisance towards England. This power had to be used to drive Spain to Italy, and had of course to make considerable concessions to the latter, by which not only the Spaniards, but also the French ought to profit. To keep her away from the Emperor, France tried to dispose her against the Pragmatic Sanction.

France bestowed far greater pains upon the other Maritime Power than upon England. As early as June 1727, Fénelon had been enjoined to promote the appointment of "bons républicains" as plenipotentiaries to the Congress, [1]) and again and again the Cardinal requested Slingelandt to enter into a private correspondence with him. [2]) And no wonder, for the Republic might be of great use to France. It was only too likely that the reconciliation of England and Spain would be very difficult, each being equally tenacious of her claims, but it was not thought to be impossible should the Republic help France in this [3]). Therefore Fénelon had to bring into relief the fact that although there was to be no mediator at the Congress, yet each power would have to act as a reconciler in what was not in her own immediate concern; if England for instance happened to be too positive, the Republic would have to support France in bringing her to moderation. [4]) In connection with this the French ministers were most anxious to know whether the Dutch squadron, that had been resolved upon in the Winter, was indeed, as was said, destined for Algiers, or if it had eventually to serve the intentions of England. [5])

Another object causing the particular attention of France was as to whether the Emperor were making overtures to the Republic. [6]) As long as Townshend remained at the Foreign Office, it would be most difficult for him to arrive at a reunion with the Maritime Powers by way of England, but perhaps he might find the Republic easier. Taking this into consideration, France thought it inadvisable to clear up all the points upon which they

[1]) Morville to Fénelon, 19 June '27, A. E. Hl. 369.
[2]) Chesterfield to Townshend, 20 July '28, R. O. Hl. 301.
[3]) Chauvelin to La Baune, 18 Apr. '28, A. E. Hl. 374.
[4]) Chauvelin to Fénelon, 19 Feby. '28, Fénelon to Chauvelin, 18, 30 Mch. '28, A. E. Hl. 373.
[5]) Chauvelin to La Baune, 20 May. '28, A. E. Hl. 374.
[6]) Chauvelin to La Baune, 25 Apr., 24 June, La Baune to Chauvelin, 10 May '28, A. E. Hl. 374.

were at variance. One of the matters which Pesters was instructed to investigate was as to whether the question of the adjustment of the Republic's frontiers in Flanders, which despite the
Convention of December 22nd. 1718 had not yet taken place, was
a matter upon which the Congress could adjudicate. Fleury advised applying first to the Emperor. [1]) He also continued to encourage the Dutch in their desire for an unconditional suppression. [2]) A third point of difference was the East Frisian affair.
More than any other, this was of a nature to keep the Republic at
a distance from the Emperor. In the preceding year she had trusted his promises, and how misplaced this trust had been! Matters
had turned out exactly as France had foretold they would. Hence
France gained an advantage which she was wise enough to improve upon. So when on receipt of the distressful tidings from
East Frisia, in the early part of 1728, Fénelon was again applied to,
he did not omit to refer to what had happened in 1727. However,
he put aside all bitterness and at once gave assurances of the
support of France, as did also the Cardinal; for the object was
not to embitter, but to profit by the affair of East Frisia as
much as possible. [3]) We suppose the same object underlay the
exhortation which was made again and again in the second half of
1728 and in the course of 1729, that the Republic should establish the rights of the Prince and the States of East Frisia upon
a solid basis. In our opinion this exhortation was for no other
purpose than to know the affairs of East Frisia as thoroughly
as possible, so that France might make use of this knowledge as
circumstances offered. [4])

With regard to Austro-Dutch relations, it was not so much the
purpose of France to keep the Republic aloof from the Emperor.
If she disposed her against him, it was that she would not expect
her satisfaction from a resumption of the Emperor's friendship,
but only from the assistance of France; in other words, that she
would entirely depend on France. It might serve this power's in-

---

[1]) King, *Notes* 58.
[2]) Fénelon or La Baune to Chauvelin, 9 Feby., 30 Apr. '28, Chauvelin to La Baune,
10 June '28, A. E. Hl. 374.
[3]) Fénelon, *Mémoire*, 155—6; Fénelon or La Baune to Chauvelin, 20 Feby., 23, 30
Mch., 30 Apr. '28, Chauvelin to Fénelon or La Baune, 4 Mch., 18 Apr. '28, A. E. Hl. 373,
374.
[4]) Chauvelin to La Baune, 26 Aug., 23 Dec. '28, 3 Feby., 28 Aug. '29 A. E. Hl. 375,
376, 377.

terests to estrange her wholly from the Emperor, but it was also possible that France wanted to hold her in suspense with regard to her differences with him, or even to facilitate an accommodation between them.

To comprehend this well, we must sift to the bottom of France's dispositions towards the Emperor. We have already seen that these were not of a friendly nature. All the same, France was careful to spare him. Chavigny, her representative at Ratisbon, who was strongly anti-Imperial, wanted her to persuade the German Princes to send plenipotentiaries to the Congress, and even to apply to the Diet for a deputation, but this idea was given up so as not to disoblige the Emperor. [1]) France sought to gain his confidence, just as she had already done from before the Preliminaries. This she did by holding out hopes of being able to obtain for him a suitable equivalent for the concessions which he would have to make as to the Ostend trade. [2]) But how could this be? — for on the other hand she encouraged the Dutch in their antipathy to making any equivalent. The intention was no other than that, just as the Dutch were to be kept from entering into direct negotiations with the Emperor, so the Emperor was to be kept from taking a similar course with regard to the Republic. The Emperor had to place so much confidence in France that he would not do everything that was possible to gain the Maritime Powers. Another reason for establishing good relations with the Emperor lay in the Anglo-Spanish differences. Even if the Republic did help France, it might still be very difficult to effect a reconciliation between Spain and England. Should this prove to be so, then the purpose would have to be accomplished in an indirect way: the Emperor had first to be involved in separate negotiations with the Hanover Allies; Spain, upon feeling herself abandoned, would then break away from him, and find herself obliged to approach England.

These reasons for being on a friendly footing with the Emperor both follow from the anti-Imperial system which we have sketched. On the whole, this was the dominating influence in French politics, and the concessions made to the Emperor were, as we shall presently see in fuller detail, most of them unreal, or where

---

[1]) Dureng, *Mission de Chavigny en Allemagne* (Paris, 1911) 54, 58—60; Auerbach, *La France et le Saint-Empire Romain Germanique* (Paris 1912) 294.

[2]) Höfler, *Der Congress von Soissons*, Fontes Rerum Austriacarum, XXXII, 7, 43, 81, 330, XXXVIII, 247.

real, they were simultaneously intended to serve the ends
France had in view. At all events not all the chief men at
the Court of France were filled with ill-will towards the Emperor.
No less considerable a person than the Cardinal was much inclined
towards a union with him; he was, however, too weak to impose
this upon France. On the whole, the traditional anti-Austrian
system was followed, and of this Chauvelin was the soul. Still,
Fleury's influence was strong enough to weaken and disturb this,
time and time again.

There was another factor, of no little consequence, which aided
it: — above all, Fleury wanted to preserve peace. All his actions
went towards avoiding war for the time being, and to this object
even his desire of establishing the peace of Europe upon a lasting
foundation was subjected.

Both his love of peace and his pro-Imperial propensities gave
an irresolute and wavering character to the politics of France.
That she attained hardly anything from 1728 to 1731 must be
attributed to this attitude. In the latter year France stood isolated among the powers of Europe, whereas, in the former, all
courted her.

As we have seen, to gain her support at the Congress the powers out-rivalled each other, but she declined all their blandish-
ments. In order to gain her ends she had to have the confidence
of all. For this reason she avoided giving any offence whatever,
and tried by means of her affable conduct, kind words and friendly
promises to keep each of them in the hope of being supported by
her. But withal she took good care not to enter into any engagement which might hamper her scope of action at the Congress. [1]

So every power failed. Bournonville made vain efforts to gain
her for the Vienna Alliance. [2] Despite the exertions of Penterriedter
she refused to impose a time-limit on the Congress or to
hold it in Paris; she definitely fixed it to be held at Soissons.
Horace Walpole did not meet with any success either; true, upon
his representations (which were prior to Slingelandt's memorial)
Fleury at once relinquished official mediation on the part of
France, which was desired by the Vienna Allies. He also gave all
kinds of assurances and promises. Horace Walpole however was

---

[1] Chauvelin to La Baune, 17 May '28, A. E. Hl. 374.
[2] Baudrillart, *op. cit.* III, 432 et seq, cf. 424 et seq.

not a man to be put off so cheaply, he urged most strongly for
the drawing up of a common plan of action. In order to evade entering into a written engagement, the Cardinal adduced a number of arguments, in a measure the same as had been used by Slingelandt in his memorial. Horace Walpole, however, persisted and
drew up a note to the Court of France. This he did not deliver
personally, but, in order to make it appear that the Republic
were imbued with the same sentiments as England, prevailed
upon Pesters, who was largely under his influence, to do this.
Notwithstanding this, the Court of France returned an unfavourable answer to nearly every point mentioned in this note,
thus showing that she did not approve of the English method. [1]

France also declined Slingelandt's idea, which Horace Walpole
had communicated to Fleury in the form of a draft-instruction to
Keene. According to his orders the ambassador advocated it
with arguments, derived from Slingelandt's memorial, without,
however, mentioning his name. As he wrote, Fleury was very
much of the same way of thinking, but this was not really so.
In the opinion of the Cardinal, Keene had merely to give the
Queen of Spain the assurance that the King of England and his
Allies were by no means opposed to the establishment of her
sons. He ought not of himself to speak of the marriage, but should
the Queen introduce the subject, he had to declare that the Hanover
Allies would not oppose it, provided it could be adjusted without
prejudice to the balance of power in Europe. The English draft
said that they were even willing to contribute towards the marriage, but to this Fleury objected, saying that the German Princes
ought not to be given any offence. Horace Walpole gave way
to this opinion and Keene's instructions were accordingly
altered. [2]

---

[1] Horace Walpole to Newcastle, 20 Mch '28, enclosed in Townshend to Slingelandt,
15 Mch. '28, Townshend to Slingelandt, 9 Apr. '28, R. A. Hl. 2994; King, *Notes*, 56—7,
60—66; Chauvelin to La Baune, 25 Apr. '28, A. E. Hl. 374; Mémoires, A. E. Mem. et
Doc. France 459, f. 98—107, 497 f. 45—9.
That Pesters' memorial was virtually that of Horace Walpole, we infer from two circumstances. The ten points it contained are all of them, except the last, agreeable to
the English method, and not to the resolution of the States of 15 Mch. '28 or to Slingelandt's system. Secondly, it is expressly said that Pesters had drawn it up in collabora-
tion with Horace Walpole (Finch to Townshend, 6 Apr. '28, R. O. Hl. 299; the memorial
is enclosed in this).
[2] Townshend to Slingelandt, 9 Apr. '28, and its enclosures: Horace Walpole to Newcastle, 14 Apr. '28, and the instructions to Keene, R. A. Hl. 2994.

What the upshot of this alteration was, is evident from a conversation they had together some days after the instructions had
been sent off, which was on April 14th. The Cardinal then told
Horace Walpole that he had great doubts as to whether the Queen
would mention the marriage to Keene; nor would she have the
courage to bring it up at the Congress. From this he inferred that
it would be almost impossible to make the marriage the chief
concern of the Congress, for, little as Elizabeth dared, the Emper-
or's wish to bring it up was equally small, it being to his interest
to leave the matter still undecided. He further expressed the fear
that the Emperor would place troops of his own in Tuscany, and
asked Horace Walpole if it would not be better to place Swiss
troops there, according to the Quadruple Alliance, or Spanish. He
immediately answered, "Spanish," for of this, profit could be made
with Elizabeth, and it could serve as a test for the Emperor. [1])

Above all, England wanted to gain the Queen of Spain, and to
accomplish this purpose, preferred embroiling her with the Emperor to discussing the marriage at the Congress. So, in spite
of the promises given to Slingelandt, Horace Walpole readily
endorsed the alteration Fleury made in Keene's instructions,
which amounted to nothing short of eliminating the Pensionary's
idea and making them subservient to the views of France.

II.

After having fulfilled the commission entrusted to him, Pesters
left Paris. His note having met with no success at all, the
Court of France thought his report would be unfavourable, and
would arouse ill-will towards France in the States. The States,
however, were very pleased with it; they were rejoiced at the
Cardinal's exhortation to be firm as to the unconditional suppression, the more so as they were afraid they would have to give
up some barrier-towns. His good words with reference to the East
Frisian affair were no less to their liking. This was written by La
Baune, who had taken Fénelon's place for as long as the latter
might stay in France to attend the Congress in his capacity of
plenipotentiary. In making mention of this satisfaction, La Baune,

---

[1]) Horace Walpole to Newcastle, 19 Apr. 28, in Townshend to Slingelandt, 12 Apr.
'28, R. A. Hl. 2994.

however, added that he did not know what had passed between
Pesters and Slingelandt and Fagel. [1]) But these cannot have
been dissatisfied either. The refusal given to Pesters' note was
not with reference to their ideas but to those of the English, to
which they were just as much opposed as France was. Slingelandt
also counteracted them. Fleury had told Horace Walpole, that the
Spaniards were to claim at the Congress compensation for the
blockade of Porto-Bello. England was not even willing to admit
this claim, but, although Slingelandt thought this unjust and even
extravagant, still he thought that the clause to which England
agreed in February gave Spain the right to put in such a claim.
He therefore represented to Townshend that he should not be too
precise in what Spain would be allowed to bring before the Congress,
for in this way he would give the Emperor a very plausible pretext
for keeping out the matter of Juliers and Bergh and others which
it might suit the Allies to introduce. He even warned him that
such exactitude might lead to misunderstanding among the Allies. [2])

Just as he continued his policy of counteracting the English
method, so he continued working in favour of his own system in
the two months which were to pass between the final settlement
of Keene's instructions and the opening of the Congress. Once
these instructions had beeen settled he did not again revert to
them, except that they gave rise to a remark of his. He had never,
so he wrote to Townshend, imagined that the Queen of Spain,
however much she might be dazzled by the prospect of the whole of
the Emperor's succession coming into her family, would not take
into consideration the possibility of his yet obtaining a male heir,
by his present wife or in a subsequent marriage. She risked marrying
Don Carlos to an archduchess without a dowry, if she had not settled
an apanage for him, which could at all events be reckoned upon
and which would probably consist in Italian countries beyond
those that had been secured to him by the Quadruple Alliance.
As he proved by passages from his memorial, in writing this, the
same thought was in his mind, to which he took the liberty of drawing Townshend's notice, fearing he suspected him of pressing the

---

[1]) Chauvelin to La Baune, 25 Apr. '27, La Baune to Chauvelin, 30 Apr. '28, A. E. Hl.
374.
[2]) Slingelandt to Townshend, 7, 20 May '28, R. A. Hl. 2994.

bringing up of the matter of the succession before the Congress in any way other than with relation to the territories that might be cut from it in favour of a marriage of an archduchess with Don Carlos.[1])

In this way Slingelandt tried to remove the fear of the English Government of being carried too far, should the question of the marriage be brought up. On the other hand, he tried to talk them out of the opinion, which was held by Fleury, that this would be impossible. He, too, considered it as more than probable that the Emperor would carefully avoid the Congress' interfering with his succession and with the marriage of his daugthers. This would not, however, be absolutely dependent upon his will. The Pensionary did not think it impossible that Elizabeth would force him to introduce it himself, at least if she were not blind to her own interests. Otherwise the Hanover Allies might bring the matter up. They had the same reason for opposing the union of Spain with the Austrian dominions, as the Emperor and his former Allies had had for opposing that of Spain and France; while in that they could be sure of the concurrence of the soundest part of Germany, if not from now, then at least, when the case presented itself for opposition to that union.

However, since both ways of bringing up the matter against the will of the Court of Vienna might be missing, would it not be expedient that, before the conclusion of the Congress, the necessary steps for preventing this union be taken by the Allies? And that from its beginning they should make the Vienna Allies feel that this was their intention, rather than allow the Congress to finish without a point of such importance to the tranquility of Europe being settled? This idea was the more plausible, as at all events both the suspension of the Ostend Company and of all hostilities for seven years, and the carrying out of all separate points which might be decided by the Congress, required, in order to have a reasonable certainty, the renewal of the Hanover Alliance and the extension of it, or at least a mutual guarantee of which the guarantees against the union of Spain and Austria might very naturally make an article. In such an alliance the Princes of the Empire would be of great consequence. They ought to be made to understand that there was nothing that so greatly menaced German liberty as such a union. Every opportunity had to be made

---

[1]) Slingelandt to Townshend, 7 May '28, R. A. Hl. 2994.

use of to impress them with the goodwill of the Hanover Allies; one of such opportunities presented itself in the matter of Juliers and Bergh. This offered the chance of gaining not only the Elector Palatine, but also the Electors allied to him. [1]

This exhortation to take German matters more to heart, was not heeded. Townshend thought that the King had done everything to make the Princes of the Empire join the opposition against the union of the Spanish and Austrian monarchies, that could be expected of him. With this object in view, he had entered into a treaty with Hesse-Cassel, a convention with Denmark, and recently a treaty of subsidy with the Duke of Brunswick-Wolfenbüttel. [2] This latter had in his turn entered into a treaty with the Duke of Würtemberg, and these together worked with the object of uniting several Princes of the Empire, both Catholic and Protestant. It was the intention of George II. himself to join also [3] and he recommended the union to the support of the States General. But as regards Juliers and Bergh the conduct of the Elector Palatine and his House had been very strange towards him: they had asked his support without anything further and without offering any return for it, they wanted him to irritate the King of Prussia, while they themselves remained under allegiance to the Emperor. Therefore Slingelandt, who at the Elector's request for support had answered that he would first have to secure the support of France and England, could say further that there was no reason why George II. should advance the matter without some advantage to him or his Allies.

So on this point the King did not follow Slingelandt's ideas, although at this very time Townshend declared that His Majesty agreed with them in every part, and was moreover so very pleased with them, that they should serve for instructions to Horace Walpole.[4] This Ambassador, however, had not to give notice of these instructions to the Cardinal before the States would give similar

---

[1] Slingelandt to Townshend, 20 May '28, R. A. Hl. 2994.

[2] What Rosenlehner (*op. cit.*, 424) tells about this union, is not correct. Wolfenbüttel and Würtemberg were the original parties. Saxe-Gotha and Hesse-Cassel soon joined (Townshend to Dehn, 4 June, in Townshend to Slingelandt, 7 June '28; Townshend to Slingelandt, 18 June '28, R. A. Hl. 2994); much later, as will be seen afterwards, the Kings of England and Sweden in their capacity of Princes of the Empire.

[3] Horace Walpole to Newcastle, 19 Apr. '28, in Townshend to Slingelandt, 12 Apr. '28, R. A. Hl. 2994.

[4] cf. Townshend to Finch, 30 Apr. '28, R. O. Hl. 299.

ones to their plenipotentiaries. [1]) At first sight the meaning of this restriction is not very clear; the instructions, however, appear very strange. How could this be? — Horace Walpole, who had acquiesced in the changing of Keene's instructions, was now ordered to act in conformity with Slingelandt's ideas! Or had the Government disapproved of his complaisance towards the Cardinal? No, they had not, they entirely agreed with the latter's policy with regard to Spain, and would unquestionably have cared very little more for Slingelandt's method, if only they had been sure of France. This power, however, again disappointed them. As we have seen, after Slingelandt's having rejected the English method, they still wanted the instructions of the plenipotentiaries to be settled in Paris. These, of course, had to be as far as possible in conformity with those given to the English plenipotentiaries, which testify to the same fear with regard to the Congress, which we have noticed above: only the necessary things had to be discussed there, even had such of them, as would take up too much time, to be referred to commissaries. [2]) Now, Horace Walpole did not succeed in getting France to agree to these instructions. He did not impute this want of success to Fleury, who as a matter of fact made strong professions, but to his surroundings, particularly to Chauvelin, and to Van Hoey. Horace Walpole made serious complaints against the latter: he was a "flatteur outré" of Chauvelin, he had spoken of Gibraltar and English trade in a manner not becoming a Dutch ambassador, and the support which he did give to him, Horace Walpole, was so weak that France could not but think that the States were only lukewarm as regards England. This could not go on any longer, so he wrote to London and this was sent on from there to Slingelandt; either Van Hoey ought to have precise instructions to change his line of conduct, or the Dutch plenipotentiaries ought to be instructed to look after affairs that had reference to the two countries; unanimity was indispensable; France would certainly agree in everything in which she saw England and the Republic speaking in the same terms. As to the demand for compensation for the blockade of Porto-Bello, Slingelandt

---

[1]) Townshend to Chesterfield, 14 May '28, R. O. Hl. 300.
[2]) Instructions to Stanhope, Walpole and Poyntz, in Townshend to Chesterfield, 14 May, '28, R. O. Hl. 300.

had written that, if Fleury should not succeed in prevailing upon
the Austrian plenipotentiaries to make the Spanish give this up,
then Horace Walpole ought to consider with him, the Cardinal,
what measures the Allies ought to take, and with their decision
the Republic was sure to concur. This, according to Horace Walpole, was putting the cart before the horse; it would be much better that a previous arrangement should be come to between the
English Government and Slingelandt to bring the Cardinal
round to their way of thinking [1]). The reason of England's eagerness for the concurrence of the Republic, Townshend was so guile-
less as to confess to the Pensionary: "si les alliés n'aident pas
le Roi et ses ministres de la manière qui peut plaire au parlement
et au public, nous ne pouvons réussir à conduire la barque ici,
et vous conviendrez que sans cela toutes nos affaires tomberont
par terre." Now, to bring the Republic to pull together in every
thing with England, for that purpose the above-mentioned restriction was added to Horace Walpole's instructions. [2])

The same intention underlay the advice given repeatedly
with regard to the Altona affair. In this the States ought to
apply to the Court of France, which on account of the considerable subsidy she gave annually to Denmark, could exercise great
influence on this power. England was then to support their application in expectation of a suitable return on their part. [3]) She
continued to take this matter to heart. An official request for
support on the part of the States was agreed to, and in the beginning of June a memorial was delivered about it to the Danish
envoy at the Hague, in the joint names of the States General and
the King of England. [4])

This instance of goodwill was returned by the States, by ap-
pointing one of their officers, Cronstrom, to go to Dunkirk to in-
spect the harbour there in company with the English Colonel
Armstrong. [5]) Wherever he could the Pensionary was most ready
to gratify England, but wherever his principles were at stake he

---

[1]) Horace Walpole to Newcastle, 14 Apr. '28, enclosed in the following letter, Townshend to Slingelandt, 12 Apr. '28, R. A. Hl. 2994; Horace Walpole to Newcastle, 19 May
'28, B. M Add. 32755, cf Slingelandt to Townshend, 7 May '28, R. A. Hl. 2994.
[2]) Townshend to Slingelandt, 14 May '28, R. A. Hl. 2994.
[3]) Townshend to Finch, 20 Feby. '28, the same to Chesterfield, 30 Apr. '28, R. O. Hl
299, 300,
[4]) Secr. Res. S. G. 7 May; Res. S. G. 8 May, 1, 5 June '28.
[5]) Secr. Res. S. G. 29 May, 1 June '28; Res. S. G. 23 June '28.

very skilfully declined her urgency. This was so with regard to
the instructions to be given to the Dutch plenipotentiaries. The
instructions of the States could only be general, Slingelandt remarked to Chesterfield, the new English ambassador, but he and
Fagel were to give them instructions in private. [1]) He admitted that Van Hoey went too far in his condescension to Chauvelin,
but he could not help it; he had written to him more than once
very strongly, but without effect. The plenipotentiaries, however,
would have very frank and cordial relations with their English
colleagues, but that there would be limits to this, appears from
what was said in addition. The only matter that might give rise to a
difference of opinion between them, was the Assiento Treaty
and the annual ship. Spain was sure to bring these matters
up, and Dutch trade to the West Indies having been for a great
part lost, he could not prevent anything which might be in the
States' favour being listened to, should it be brought forward by
Spain; he therefore asked Chesterfield to request the King not to
be too precise in this. The Ambassador was very astonished. He
supposed that Slingelandt did not mean that his Royal Master
had to give up the Assiento Treaty and the ship. Upon this the
Pensionary gave way a little; this was not his intention, but
should methods be proposed at the Congress for preventing the
notorious abuses, then he hoped the King would not be too exact-
ing. Chesterfield replied, that if that was all, it would not cause
any difference, as His Majesty did not desire to derive any advantage from unfair trade. [2]) Be this as it may, in this way Slingelandt exhorted England to be reasonable in her differences with
Spain.

Further, he wanted her to work for his ideas with France. Why
did he follow this indirect course? On account of the constitution
of the Republic he could not do otherwise. He could only to a certain extent involve the States in his policy. For this reason the
Dutch plenipotentiaries could not be given such instructions as
England demanded in making the said restriction upon Horace
Walpole's orders. Such a demand, Slingelandt wrote to Townshend, was "gâter le fonds par la forme"; on account of the Dutch
constitution, it would be utterly impracticable for the English

---

[1]) Chesterfield to Townshend, 25 May '28, R. O. Hl. 300.
[2]) Chesterfield to Townshend, 1 June '28, R. O. Hl. 300

and Dutch plenipotentiaries to take every step regarding the French ministers in common. "Il y a des occasions", so he continued, "et celle-ci en est une à mon avis, ou ceux qui sont à la tête d'un parti ou d'une alliance doivent préalablement, comme on dit, sonder la gué, préparer et digérer les matières et les porter ensuite à leurs Alliés pour avoir leur concurrence"; this would be less difficult now that the English plenipotentiaries could consult with such highly esteemed plenipotentiaries as Hop and Goslinga, with whom Slingelandt had conversed very fully, and who knew how to bring to the deliberations of the Republic what, on important and delicate occasions, was being planned in France for the common cause. [1])

An integral part of his system for which the Pensionary wanted England to work unreservedly, was formed by the preservation and confirmation of the political and religious liberties of the Empire. Things looked very black there. At this very time the Dutch representative at Ratisbon, Gallieris, reported to the States that the condition of the Protestants in the Empire was pitiful, especially in countries which had formerly been under a Protestant, and were now under a Catholic prince. The States appealed to England, asking if it would not be expedient to take some measures as to this at the Congress or otherwise. [2])

They certainly took the cause of their co-religionists to heart, but more so the cause of the East Frisian Renitents, with which they were themselves so closely concerned. These people's condition grew worse and worse. All representations on the part of the Republic, to suspend for the time being any action against them, were without effect. [3]) Neither was she given any certainty as to her garrisons. According to a secret piece of information, received by Slingelandt, the Aulic Council in a *votum ad Imperatorem* applied for their being turned out.[4])Things seemed to be tending in this direction. On May 20th. the Embden Seigniories, lying in the

---

[1]) Slingelandt to Townshend, 8 June '28, R. A. Hl. 2994; of Slingelandt to Hop, 21 July '28, R. A. Hl. 2974.

[2]) Secr. Res. S. G. 18, 19 May, 1 June '28; Chesterfield to Townshend, 21 May, Townshend to Chesterfield, 14 May '28, R. O. Hl. 300.

[3]) Such representations had been made lately, in virtue of the resolution of 1 Mch. '28. Instances had also been made with Prussia (Rive, *op. cit.* 116—7).

[4]) Chesterfield to Townshend, 25 May '28, with enclosures, R. O. Hl. 300; Slingelandt to Townshend, 8 June '28, R. O. Hl. 2994. The Aulic Council seems to have done so at the request of the Prince of East Frisia, cf. Res. S. G. 9 July '28, Rousset, *op. cit.* IV, 501.

immediate neighbourhood of the town, were occupied by the
Prince's troops. The town and the Dutch garrison were conse-
quently almost invested and blockaded. No sooner were the States
General informed of this, than they made representations to
Koenigsegg-Erps on it. They further acquainted Chesterfield and
La Baune of it, and asked for their co-operation in preventing
disastrous consequences. [1])

Another matter of the Empire, bearing a great analogy to the
East Frisian affair, came to the forefront just about this time, [2])
viz: the Mecklenburg affair. Just as there, so here the Prince and
the States were at variance with each other, and the Emperor
had interfered. A difference was that in East Frisia the Emperor sided with the Prince, while here he sided with the States.
In 1717 he had conferred a guardianship upon the Elector of
Hanover and the Duke of Brunswick-Wolfenbüttel, who were for
the States. In so doing he had overlooked the King of Prussia, although in his capacity of Duke of Magdeburg he was Director of
the Lower Saxonian circle, to which Mecklenburg belonged. We
have seen the same as to the guardianship over East Frisia, but the
similarity goes even further; in April 1727, in order to keep his
hold over Frederick William, the Emperor issued a decree with
reference to East Frisia, favourable to him; at present it was of
still greater importance to retain him, and as the concessions
which the Emperor offered him would certainly not satisfy him,
the Head of the Empire, on May 11th. 1728, issued a decree
regarding Mecklenburg. By this Duke Charles Leopold was suspended, his brother Christian Louis being appointed administra-
tor of the country, and, last but not least, the King of Prussia
was added to the other guardians. This latter fact and further
the several equivocal stipulations in the decree were well suited
to bring about discord between Prussia and Hanover, which latter had swayed the country, in concert with the nobility of Mecklenburg, almost absolutely, ever since 1719. [3])

Besides gratifying Frederick William, and preventing friendly
advances between him and the King of England, the Emperor's
interference had another object; just as his interference in the

---

[1]) Res. S. G. 25 May '28.
[2]) cf. Wiarda *op. cit.* VII, 83 note.
[3]) Droysen, *op. cit.* I, 213—4, II, 11—13, 26—27; Förster, *Friedrich Wilhelm I*, II, 105.

East Frisian matter had for its aim the influencing of the States General, so this was to influence George II. It had this effect too, but not so as to render the latter more yielding towards the Court of Vienna; on the contrary, to him the decree was a most extraordinary example of Imperial despotism, and the Aulic Council, from which it proceeded, an engine of slavery. He applied immediately to the Republic: Chesterfield was to inform Slingelandt that he was willing to support the States with reference to the Protestant cause in the Empire and also with regard to the East Frisian matter, in return for which he expected their support with reference to Mecklenburg. [1]

Probably quite contrary to his expectations, Chesterfield did not find a friendly hearing with the Pensionary. The Republic, said the latter, could not interfere with Mecklenburg, she not being a guarantor of the Peace of Westphalia. In doing as requested she would only be providing the Emperor with a handle to meddle with her affairs, as he had already done far too much. The conclusion to which the decree led him was not in the King's favour, but in the Republic's: the Emperor was determined to countenance Frederick William in everything, and so no complaisance could be expected on his part in East Frisia, unless the Republic were supported by England and France. [2]

George II. could not understand Slingelandt's coolness. Perhaps, too late, the Republic would regret her carelessness, for "imperial ambition is boundless when backed with the weight and force of an arbitrary sway in the Empire." Should he succeed in Mecklenburg, he would be all the more troublesome in East Frisia. The fact of his countenancing the King of Prussia ought to be no small argument for the Republic to oppose the Emperor's sway in the Empire and to support George II. The latter had thought out a natural method of taking the matter in hand. He wished to invite the Duke of Mecklenburg to lodge his complaints with the Diet. [3] Then as many Princes and other members of the Empire as possible

[1] Townshend to Chesterfield, 17, 21 May '28, R. O. Hl. 300.
[2] Chesterfield to Townshend, 4 June '28, R. O. Hl. 300. A remarkable conversation between Slingelandt and Fénelon with reference to Mecklenburg is related in Fénelon to Chauvelin, 27 Feby. '28, A. E. Hl. 373.
[3] Chesterfield now entered into relations with Sande, the Duke's representative at the Hague. As to their negotiations, cf. R. O. Hl. 300 and subsequent bundles.

were to be exhorted to oppose such an assault on German liberties, and in particular the King of Denmark and other princes of the Lower Saxonian circle, and the King of Sweden. France ought to use her influence with the four Electors, and the States, too, ought to apply their influence in the Empire. If the Emperor did not yield before such opposition, then France and Sweden, as guarantors of the Peace of Westphalia, ought to introduce the matter at the Congress, where of course it would meet with the support of the Hanover Allies. In order to encourage the Republic to agree to this action, it was said that if the German Princes could be brought to act in the proper way in this matter, this would be preparatory to the taking in hand of other affairs of the Empire, particularly the grievances of the Protestants. [1])

The scheme was set up on a large scale; Slingelandt, however, saw that it had very little chance of success. It was not to be expected that all the German Princes should be full of fire for the Hanoverian interests on the matter of Mecklenburg. George II. relied principally upon the Alliance of Wolfenbüttel and Würtemberg, but in the Pensionary's opinion this was not so far advanced that it could be relied upon for such an enterprise. To engage upon such an adventure was not without danger to the Republic, especially now that the enemies appeared to be so powerful and so closely united. Prussia, as we have seen, was on excellent terms with Saxony. This did not concern the Emperor, although the contemporaries were of opinion that he was in compact with them, particularly with Prussia. [2]) Slingelandt shared this opinion too; in what had taken place at the Court of Vienna, the *votum ad Imperatorem* regarding East Frisia and the decree concerning Mecklenburg, he saw protection of Frederick William, and thought that secret measures were being planned to secure to the latter the succession to Juliers and Bergh. From all this he inferred that the Emperor was neither aiming at a sincere reconciliation with England and the Republic nor at making the Congress serve the movement towards a general pacification, or that at least he wished to keep his Allies, particularly the King of Prussia, in order to make a bold stand against the Hanover Allies, and further to make use of him, both in and out of the Empire, against Eng-

---

[1]) Townshend to Chesterfield, 31 May, 4 June '28, R. O. Hl. 300.
[2]) Fénelon to Chauvelin, 27 Feby. '28, A. E. Hl. 373; *Mémoires* de Villars, V, 128, 131.

land and the Republic. At best the extraordinary steps the Emperor was taking tended to make the Allies feel that they could be disquieted by him also indirectly and without matters coming to open hostilities, and by so doing cause them to value all the more a resumption of friendship with him. Time was soon to throw light upon his true intentions, but at all events the Pensionary was confirmed in his conviction of the necessity of making, not the adjustment of the particular points, but the restoration of peace and confidence, which had been entirely upset by the close alliance between the Emperor and Spain, the main object of the Congress. [1])

So Slingelandt looked upon the affairs of the Empire from a European point of view. Any action in it would have to be in relation with general affairs, and of itself be of a general character. To bring this about, the Pensionary more than once had exhorted George II. to enter into relations with the four Electors; until now, however, in vain. Now he took advantage of the King's embarrassment regarding to Mecklenburg. He received the scheme which the King proposed very coolly, on account, it is true, of its uncertainty and of the difficulty of persuading the States to take part in it, but principally for a reason upon which these two were dependent, this action being a special one. George II. ought instead to enter upon a general action. This Slingelandt now again advised him apropos of an application by Gansinot, who had shown him a letter from Bellanger, Secretary of State to the Elector of Cologne.

In this letter, a conversation which the Bavarian minister Von Unertl had had with Sinzendorff was mentioned; the latter was the Emperor's first plenipotentiary, and was on his way to Soissons. Sinzendorff had told Von Unertl, that his Master would in no case allow the affair of Juliers and Bergh to be brought up at the Congress, but he had no objection to the Elector Palatine's trying to obtain a guaranty from France. From this Bellanger inferred that Sinzendorff would distinguish between France and the Maritime Powers, but in the former's opinion their assistance was no less necessary, the Republic in particular being closely concerned in the matter of the succession to the Duchies. The Elector Palatine

---

[1]) Slingelandt to Townshend, 8 June'28, R. A. Hl. 2994; Chesterfield to Townshend, 1, 8 June '28, R. O. Hl. 300.

was to apply again to the Emperor, to bring the matter before the
Congress, and should he decline, he would apply to the Hanover
Allies and address a formal request to the Congress. In this the
four Electors were to act in conjunction.

Slingelandt had no sooner read this letter than he sent a copy of
it to Townshend. He was convinced, so he wrote him, that he would
be able to take advantage of the disposition of the Electors, and
would know how to combine their interests with those of the Princes of the union between Wolfenbüttel and Würtemberg and to
make a common cause of it, which, supported by France and other
foreign powers, might be of great consequence in the Empire,
and keep the Emperor, with August II. and Frederick William, in
check. The Pensionary thought this would meet with less objection as, according to Gansinot, the Electors were already working
to gain other Princes, among them the Duke of Würtemberg. [1]

This proposal met with a good reception. At this juncture, no
regard for Prussia caused George II. to be backward in entering into relations with the Electors. [2] On the contrary, he would
be glad to gain their support on the question of Mecklenburg. He
wanted them to join the Treaty between Wolfenbüttel and Würtemberg, rather than make a new one. Should they do this, George II.
would not delay his joining any longer, as he had done up till
now in order not to retard the joining of some of the other German princes. Once this union had been formed, the matters of
Juliers and Bergh, East Frisia, Mecklenburg and all the other grievances in the Empire, both political and religious, could by joint
action be brought up before the Congress, to be examined and
settled there, under the auspices, and with the support of France,
England and the Republic. To lead things in this direction, the
King thought he could not act better than through Slingelandt;
he therefore requested him to make known these sentiments to
Gansinot. [3]

---

[1] Slingelandt to Townshend, 11 June '28, R. A. Hl. 2994; enclosed with this is an
extract from Bellanger to Gansinot, 4 June '28. As to the conversation between Sinzendorff and Unertl, cf. Rosenlehner, *op. cit.* 378.

Here, at the beginning of the negotiations carried on in 1728—'29 between the Maritime Powers and France and the four Electors, particularly the Elector Palatine,
we must give a warning against Slothouwer's article: "*Un effort pour la formation d'un
Fürstenbund en* 1728." *Rev. d'Hist. Diplomatique* XIII (1899), 188 et seq. It is absolutely unreliable.

[2] cf Rosenlehner, *op. cit.*, 423.

[3] Townshend to Slingelandt, 7 June '28, R. A. Hl. 2994.

In this way he gave up his reluctance to a general action in the Empire. He gave up, in addition, the restriction upon which he had first made contingent the recommending of Slingelandt's ideas to Fleury by Horace Walpole. [1]) Slingelandt seemed to have gained him entirely. Whether this was indeed so, the Congress, which had been opened in the meantime, would soon make clear.

B. THE CONGRESS REACHES A DEADLOCK.

June—August 1728.

On June 14th. 1728 the Congress of Soissons met. Each of the five powers which had signed the Preliminaries sent three plenipotentiaries. Those representing Spain were Bournonville, Santa Cruz and Barrenechea. The first-mentioned was the principal. The Emperor's principal delegate was Sinzendorff; of the other two, Penterriedter died in July, his place being taken by Fonseca, Ambassador at the Court of France. This Court was represented by no less a person than the Cardinal himself; Fénelon was one of his two fellow-plenipotentiaries, but had no influence whatever. England had deputed Horace Walpole, Stanhope, formerly Ambassador at Madrid, and Poyntz. The interests of the Republic were to be looked after by Cornelis Hop, brother of the Dutch Envoy in London, Magistrate of Amsterdam, Goslinga, who, not without difficulty, had yielded before everybody's persuasion, and in particular that of Slingelandt, and by Hurgronje, Burgomaster of Flushing.

The Congress was opened by an address by Sinzendorff, to which the Cardinal replied. In the first weeks several conferences were held, but hardly anything was done at them. Very shortly afterwards the Congress arrived at complete inactivity, from which it did not recover. The *dii minores* among the plenipotentiaries — of the Dutch, Hurgronje, were left at Soissons "to keep the mantles," but the chief ones dealt with affairs elsewhere, either where the Court was or at Paris, with Chauvelin as well as with Fleury, so that virtually no Congress of Soissons was held at all; therefore when such is spoken of, it is in the sense of

---

[1]) Townshend to Slingelandt, 7 June '28, R. A. Hl. 2994.

Slingelandt who said, "Soissons sera pendant le cours de cette négotiation partout où sera le Cardinal et les principaux négotiateurs." [1])

I.

In the days immediately preceding and following the opening of the Congress, the negotiations were of the highest importance. Most important of all was that Bournonville and Sinzendorff proposed to Fleury, under the strictest injunction to secrecy, the marriage of Don Carlos with Maria Theresa. As we have already seen, either a refusal or consent was considered to be prejudicial to France; Fleury therefore did not return a decisive answer. He spoke a few kind words, which could be taken as a sort of approval, but were really rather general. Bournonville and Sinzendorff wanted him to give these words in writing, but this he declined to do, saying that he could not do so without consulting his Allies. Further, in spite of his pledge of secrecy, he acquainted the English plenipotentiaries and Goslinga of what had been proposed to him. [2])

Slingelandt was also very soon acquainted of this, and immediately perceived the importance of the matter. He now took the marriage for granted and considered it as the basis of the Congress. Two points, so he told Chesterfield, were now deserving of attention. Consent, if it should be given, would have to be contingent upon proper precautions as to the balance of power in Europe and to be paid for by the redress of all grievances whatsoever against the Vienna Allies. But would not this consent, if given, disoblige the German Princes and thus make a union of them against the Emperor impracticable? While, should the Allies oppose the marriage, would not this induce so many of them to oppose it likewise as might possibly make it miscarry? It is easy to understand that this latter consideration crossed Slinge-

---

[1]) Slingelandt to Hop, 6 Nov. '28, cf. id. to Goslinga, 7 Aug. '28, R. A. Hl. 2974.

[2]) English Plenipotentiaries to Newcastle, 20 June '28, B. M. Add. 32757; Syveton, *op. cit.* 260—'1.

At first only the English plenipotentiaries were informed of it, Goslinga not. That he was informed of it, is probably due to Chauvelin. At all events the latter advised the Cardinal to so inform him, arguing that if he did not do so himself, Horace Walpole would do so, in spite of his promise of secrecy, in order in this way to gain the Dutch against France (Chauvelin to Fleury, 16 June '28, A. E. Mem. et Doc. France 497, f. 227 et seq).

landt's mind for a moment, just now when there were hopes af forming a great union in the Empire, but it did not prevail. In a letter written one or two days afterwards to Goslinga, he had already decided in favour of bringing the marriage before the Congress.

His opinion, he wrote him, had always been, that to come off well, either Spain would have to be detached from the Emperor, or, in the event of that proving impossible, the Allies would have to agree upon reasonable terms with the Emperor and Spain, or rather with the Queen of Spain, regarding the marriage between Don Carlos and the heiress to the dominions of the Emperor. The first of these alternatives was undoubtedly preferable to the second, as it was more certain to cut off the root of the evil, by preventing the marriage itself, than to prevent its consequences by renunciations, guarantees and other means of this nature, but as the efforts to bring about the first had been useless, the Allies now found themselves forced to have recourse to the second alternative. In order to set the negotiations required by it on foot, Slingelandt suggested that Fleury ought to press Bournonville and Sinzendorff to make the same overtures to the Hanover Allies that had been made to him; before this were done, however, the effect of the Cardinal's answer should be awaited and in particular the effect of the news from Spain, that Philip V. was again about to abdicate, which Slingelandt thought might be of great moment at this juncture. [1])

So he wanted, and this was the upshot of his reasoning, to have the marriage made the basis of the Congress. This was by no means the sentiment of the English Government. They were annoyed that the Emperor and Spain had not made the communication regarding the marriage to George II. also. Elizabeth had further been unwilling, up till now, to grant Keene an audience, that he might acquit himself of the task imposed upon him by the instructions which had been settled upon between Horace Walpole and the Cardinal. For these reasons the English plenipotentiaries were instructed to refrain from even touching upon the marriage; but, quite independently of this, they were to ask Fleury to explain to them in detail what precautions ought, in his opinion, to be demand-

---

[1]) Chesterfield to Townshend, 25 June '28, R. O. Hl. 300; Slingelandt to Goslinga, 26 June '28, R. A. Hl. 2974 (damaged draft of the whole letter) and R. O. Hl. 297 (undamaged but incomplete copy)

ed from the Vienna Allies for the maintenance of the balance of
power in Europe, and for the liberties of the Empire; and what
measures ought to be taken to settle the affairs of George II.
and the States to their satisfaction. The English Government
not only thought the conduct of the adversaries entitled them
to act in this way, but even considered it dangerous to express
themselves upon the marriage so long as the balance of power
should not be restored and the affairs of the Allies still be unsettled. [1])

Slingelandt was perfectly well aware that England might strike
into the wrong path; he, therefore, did his best to keep her in the
right one. There was no objection, thus he wrote to Townshend,
against pressing Fleury to get the same overtures made to the
English and Dutch plenipotentiaries. Should Bournonville and
Sinzendorff be willing to do so and also be inclined to negotiate on
the marriage, they could be made to express themselves regarding
the precautions and other conditions upon which the consent of the Allies depended, "et par une suite naturelle et nullement forcée on serait en état de tirer de la France une explication
nette et précise sur les dites précautions et le reste." This need
not give any uneasiness to the Princes of the Empire, for the
principal precautions and securities concerned them as much as
the Allies, and had even to be settled in conjunction with them.
Should, however, Bournonville and Sinzendorff refuse to enter
into negotiations with reference to the marriage, such refusal
would serve, in the Pensionary's opinion, in a great measure to
determine, from the outset, the conduct of the Allies and of those
German Princes who were not to submit without opposition to the
exorbitant power to which the Emperor, by virtue of this marriage,
would be laying the foundation. In that case the Cardinal himself
ought, on orders from the King of France, to make an official
communication of it to the Allies, in conformity with the Treaty
of Hanover. [2])

It, however, became evident to Slingelandt that Fleury would
not easily be brought to do so. A piece of information which had
reached him from France, suggested something else to him. There
proved to be a remarkable difference between Sinzendorff and

---

[1]) Townshend to Slingelandt, 14 June o. s. 1728, R. A. Hl. 2994.
[2]) Slingelandt to Townshend, 29 June '28, ibid.

Bournonville in their manner of speaking to Fleury. Bournonville had left no stone unturned to obtain France's consent to the marriage, and when the Cardinal had given a friendly answer, strongly insisted upon his giving it in writing. He had further insinuated that, in case this matter should be gone into, Spain would not only agree to all necessary restrictions for the preservation of the balance of power, but all other points at the Congress would be made easy. Sinzendorff, too, had said something of the kind, but in such a hasty and careless manner, as if he affected to appear indifferent to the marriage; he even went so far as to say that it was entirely Bournonville's affair. He, however, desired at the same time, that the Cardinal should endeavour to get Elizabeth to postpone its conclusion for five or six years, and suggested to him some expressions he might make use of, if he would give his "compliment", as he styled it, in writing. And when Fleury persisted in his refusal, Sinzendorff did not appear to be at all discontented about it, whereas Bournonville continued to urge the Cardinal for a more decisive answer. [1]

Slingelandt now wanted to take advantage of this embarrassment of Sinzendorff's, to which his conduct testified. He wrote to Townshend that the Allies must now compel him to treat of the marriage with them, without, however, appearing to know what had passed between him or Bournonville and the Cardinal, but by basing themselves only on the reasons which could not but force the Hanover Allies to bring forward the affair. For that purpose they would have to make the Spanish plenipotentiaries aware that they were not opposed to the marriage, if only precautions were taken against its eventual consequences. The Emperor could not then refuse to discuss the matter without giving the Allies a plausible handle to render his intentions suspicious to the Queen of Spain. And should he agree, then at least the wrong consequences could be prevented, and perhaps even the marriage itself. "Plus ces précautions sont épineuses et difficiles à ajuster, moins cette proposition engagera les Alliés, plus elle embarrassera les Impériaux et plus elle est propre à rompre le mariage et l'union entre les cours de Vienne et de Madrid." Slingelandt supposed Fleury would the less object to this idea, since it might serve as an

---

[1] English plenipotentiaries to Newcastle, 20 June '28, B. M. Add. 32757; Townshend to Chesterfield, 18 June '28, R. O. Hl. 300.

expedient to extricate him from the difficulty he might feel as to the promised secrecy, and the Pensionary was most eager that the general pacification should be tried in this way. [1]

However, things had, in the meantime, taken an unfavourable turn in Paris.

II.

It was not only the question of the marriage that had immediately come up for discussion; there was also another point, viz: the restitution of Gibraltar. On this latter point Bournonville and Horace Walpole came into sharp opposition, the former demanding as strongly as the latter declined it. It being absolutely impossible to reconcile them, there was even danger of war. [2]

In this state of affairs it was an impossibility for the Cardinal to carry out his system. He was strongly opposed to Slingelandt's, but there was still a third, that of Sinzendorff's.

As we have seen, the latter differed from Bournonville on the question of the marriage. With regard to Gibraltar, although supporting him in some measure, he also differed from him. [3] Bournonville wanted these points to be finally settled, but Sinzendorff feared that this might put the Emperor into the dilemma of either having to give Maria Theresa to Don Carlos and going to war, or breaking with Spain. To get his Master out of this dilemma and retain his hold upon Spain, and further to prevent the introduction of German affairs at the Congress, Sinzendorff suggested to the Cardinal the putting of an end to it by a provisional treaty, such a one as would maintain the state of peace almost on the foundation of the Preliminaries, and which would suspend the definite adjustment of the pending differences. [4] The Ostend affair only should be finally settled. In this, however, Sinzendorff showed himself very reasonable. In conversation with Fleury, he did not contend that the Emperor was strictly within his rights, but merely stated that Articles 5 and 6

---

[1] Slingelandt to Townshend, 2 July '23, id. to Hop, 7 July '28, R. A. Hl. 2994, 2974.
[2] Baudrillart, *op. cit.* III, 430—'1.
[3] Baudrillart, *op. cit.* III, 430—'1.
[4] Although it is not quite certain, it is very probable that the idea of a provisional treaty originated with Sinzendorff. Cf. *Archiv für Oesterreichische Geschichte*, XLVI, p. 136; Townshend to Waldegrave, 28 Jan. '29, R. O. Germany 64.

of the Treaty of Munster were not clear. On this account, should his Master yield to the Dutch, he would be entitled to an indemnification, e. g. a limited trade to Bengal and China or to China alone, or else to a reduction of the annual charges which the Southern Netherlands were under to the States. [1]

Under these circumstances, the Cardinal thought fit, we do not say to agree to Sinzendorff's method, but still to take three steps in the Emperor's direction: he proposed that the Dutch should give some equivalent for the suppression of the Ostend Company, he agreed with Sinzendorff that none of the affairs of the Empire should be dealt with at the Congress, and, last but not least, he showed some inclination towards a provisional treaty.

The idea of such a treaty as Fleury had made mention of as early as June 25th., was by no means to the liking of Slingelandt. In his opinion it would be the very worst thing that could happen. At the best it was a "très mauvais pis-aller", only to be listened to in case of need, when everything else had been tried in vain to bring about a general pacification. He was afraid, however, that it would please Fleury only too well, as it would probably secure peace for his lifetime, he being always more inclined to postpone obstacles, rather than give himself trouble in overcoming them. As to the Emperor, Slingelandt understood very well that he desired it, for then none of the affairs of the Empire would come up at the Congress. Hence he would be able to bring the German Princes to complete subjection and to worry the Republic, either by invading her himself or by leaving her to the covetousness of the King of Prussia. What was of even far greater importance, the Emperor could go on keeping Elizabeth dependent upon him, for then the question of the marriage would not come up before the Congress either. [4]

This was the very thing Slingelandt wanted; not, however, in the manner of Hop, who, in one of his first conversations with Sinzendorff made the offer of consenting to the marriage, provided the Ostend affair were settled to the satisfaction of the States. [1]

---

[1]) Hop and Goslinga to Slingelandt, 1 July '28, R. A. Hl. 2985; cf. Huisman, *op cit.* 437 et seq.

[2]) Horace Walpole to Newcastle, 25 June '28, B. M. Add. 32755; Chesterfield to Townshend, 6 July '28, R. O. Hl. 301; Slingelandt to Hop, 7 July '28, R. A. Hl. 2974.

[3]) Hop to Slingelandt, 1 July '28, R. A. Hl. 2982; Townshend to Chesterfield, 25 June '28, R. O. Hl. 300.

He ought not to have spoken of it in order to gain a advantage for the Republic, and also without having first consulted the Allies. The connection between the interest of the States and the marriage was not a direct but an indirect one. The bringing up of the marriage ought to lead to the general pacification, and upon this the adjustment of the separate points depended.

So with regard to the Ostend matter, which was one of these points, the trend of general affairs had to be waited for. Slingelandt considered that it could not yet be an object of negotiations with the Austrians, without arousing prejudice, for if they acted as wise politicians, they would promise the Republic mountains of gold, if they could only separate her from her Allies by so doing, and so get her to lose sight of the main object of the Congress, whilst, once they had made her repugnant to her Allies, it was a question for themselves whether they would keep their promises or not. One of these Allies moreover, England, might consider herself as much interested in the Ostend affair as the Republic. This would appear when she brought her claims before the Congress. Should she also demand the suppression of the Ostend Company on the ground of its clashing with her treaties with Spain, and the Barrier Treaty, an equivalent for the suppression would concern her as much as the Republic, if not more so, on account of her larger trade with China. But she had not yet delivered her claims. This was another reason why Slingelandt did not wish for the present to enter into any discussion as to an equivalent. The Dutch plenipotentiaries were instructed to avoid it, and should the Austrian representatives press them upon this point, they were to represent to them that the Emperor was so heavily in debt to the Republic, which had ruined herself financially, to procure for him the Southern Netherlands, and the superiority that now oppressed and threatened her and her Allies, that she would be entitled to expect much more from him than the non-introduction of novelties, injurious to her trade, in a country that he could never have obtained without the help of the Republic. Having paid more than enough to secure herself against such novelties, the Pensionary did not think it equitable to make her pay again for the removal of them.

Neither could he comprehend how France could be the "entre-

SLINGELAND'S ATTITUDE TOWARDS FRANCE AND ENGLAND. 255

metteuse d'un marché si injuste." The allurement of an unconditional suppression had determined the Republic in the first
place to join the Treaty of Hanover, and only very recently France
had promised her support in obtaining it. Now, however, Fleury
spoke of the necessity of an equivalent. If the Republic had been
willing to agree to this, she might perhaps have obtained the
suppression as far back as five years ago. So the plenipotentiaries
had to disabuse the Cardinal of the idea, saying that it might even
give him the same amount of trouble to arrange an equivalent as
the making of the just cause of the Republic triumphant. [1]

Fleury's task ought to be to try and bring about the adjustment of
the Ostend matter, not by means of complaisance towards the Emperor, but by means of a general pacification. The way to this end
was to bring the question of the marriage before the Congress.
Slingelandt again endeavoured to get the English government to
induce the Cardinal to this, and for this purpose he left nothing undone. The Pensionary had noticed that they greatly objected to
guaranteeing the Pragmatic Sanction, so in a conversation with
Chesterfield he emphasised the fact that the bringing of the question of the marriage before the Congress was the most fitting
way to prevent it. The difficulties concerning the restrictions demanded by the balance of Europe's power would be insurmountable, and this would show to Elizabeth the impracticability of
her schemes. Apropos of this Chesterfield asked if the Republic
might ever be got to guarantee the Pragmatic Sanction; Slingelandt answered that he thought not, for the succession was sure
to be much contested. For that very reason it was all the more
desirable to introduce the marriage at the Congress. Fleury had
told Horace Walpole that France would not guarantee the Pragmatic Sanction, and he, Slingelandt, thought that the Republic
would not do so either, nor England alone. He therefore very much
questioned whether Elizabeth would be so eager with regard
to the marriage, when she became aware that the principal powers
were not willing to guarantee the succession, which made it so
greatly desired by her. [2]

Slingelandt's repeated appeals threw the English government
into great embarrassment. Their plenipotentiaries had spoken to

---

[1] Slingelandt to Hop, 7, 16, 21 July, id. to Goslinga, 7, 21 July '28, R. A. Hl. 2974.
[2] Chesterfield to Townshend, 6 July '28, R. O. Hl. 301.

Fleury of bringing the marriage before the Congress, and in some measure recommended it to him, but he positively declared against it, alleging that the Emperor would rather break up the Congress than allow this subject to be discussed there [1]). Instead of being a disappointment to the English government, this was rather a relief to them, "Now", Townshend wrote to Chesterfield, "we are in no danger of being carried further than we would." They were glad they could go along with the Cardinal in this respect: "The King is likewise far from determining that this affair ought to be brought thither." Still, Slingelandt's idea that the marriage could be taken advantage of, had not failed altogether in its effect. They were afraid of being looked upon as poor negotiators, if, such a secret having been lodged with them, they did not profit by their knowledge of it. For this reason they wished the marriage to be communicated to them in such a way as to allow of its becoming public. Then it would remain to be seen what public opinion upon it would be, and if the Electors and other Princes of the Empire would not rise up against it, and propose measures to prevent it, "It cannot be expected that we should, nor can we be blamed for not doing it, or for any of the consequences that may attend on this match." [2])

Slingelandt did not reject this idea altogether, but only wished to resort to it, if it should prove impossible to bring forward the marriage at the Congress. He remarked further, that the German Princes would hardly dare to take the first step. Upon this, the answer came than it was not by any means the intention that they should precede, if only there were certainty as to their following. It was added that the King was determined to support them in concert with his Allies in the strongest way, and to prevent their being awed into submission to the marriage. [3])

Thus he wished to take precautions against this danger, but outside the Congress. The uneasiness with which the English Government had looked forward to it had proved to be not unfounded. Spain energetically demanded the restitution of Gibraltar and a thorough discussion of commercial grievances. Any further nego-

---

[1]) Jorissen, *op. cit.* 279.
[2]) Townshend to Chesterfield, 25 June '28, R. O. Hl. 300
[3]) Chesterfield to Townshend, 9 July '28, Townshend to Chesterfield, 2 July '28, R. O. Hl. 301.

tiations could not but bring loss upon them. Hence they wanted
as soon as possible to come out of the difficulties; for this reason
they were, from the first, not averse to a provisional treaty. [1]
The only thing was that it would have to be safe and good, but
at present they did not see how such a treaty could be framed
so as not to leave them upon a worse footing than they already
were under the Preliminaries. For "If by it"—we now allow Townshend to speak — "no more is intended to be done than to turn the
"Preliminaries into a provisional treaty for a certain number of
"years, reserving to each of the parties concerned their several
"pretensions, when the said term shall have expired, the wr ong
"interpretations which the Imperialists and Spaniards have al-
"ready put upon the Preliminary Treaty itself, and the difficulties
"they have made in executing the most material parts of it, are
"strong objections to our consenting to this proposal.

"Secondly, by a fair interpretation of the words of the Prelimin-
"ary Treaty, all the important interests of the King and the States
"have already been determined, and therefore, strictly speaking,
"ought not to be brought any more into debate. However, as the
"Imperialists and Spaniards, after the conclusion of that treaty,
"have contested and continue so to contest the most important
"points of it, it will, in His Majesty's opinion, be impossible to con-
"vert same into a provisional treaty with the reservations above-
"mentioned in such terms as will not add great weight to the pre-
"tensions of the Emperor and Spain. And our rights, after having
"signed such a treaty, would stand upon an even less advanta-
"geous footing than they do at present, or even than they did at
"the commencement of these negotiations. For by reserving and
"leaving those points in suspense, we shall be construed to have
"given some kind of sanction to the pretensions of the Imperialists
"and Spaniards, and ourselves to have admitted them to be mat-
"ters worthy of being reserved and further considered.

"Thirdly, the Cardinal might soon die, and then France would be
"able to treat us after the expiry of the term just as she likes. Fur-
"ther if the treaty made at the Congress is not plainly decisive
"and strongly guaranteed; if we and the Dutch are left under un-
"certainty with the Emperor and Spain, and the great points under
"consideration are not perfectly secured, France may consider her-

---

[1] Townshend to Chesterfield, 18 June '28, R. O. Hl. 300.

17

"self fairly disengaged by what she has done, and our Hanover "Alliance will be forgotten.

"His Majesty, however", so runs the conclusion, "would be glad "to see a project of a provisional treaty, not liable to these objec- "tions, sufficient to content the Hanover Allies, and to secure us "that the Emperor and Spain will set the King and the States "entirely at ease. And if there be a short and sure method of doing "this by such a treaty, His Majesty has no inclination to spin out "matters, but will readily come into it." [1])

The idea of a provisional treaty had much to attract the English Government, but as they were by no means sure of France, it was too dangerous. It would lead to discord with Slingelandt, and they might then become isolated. At all events he had to be retained. With this object in view they again and again praised his ideas highly. They much applauded his expedient to draw Fleury out of the difficulty he had got himself into by his promise of secrecy. And by preference, they pointed out in his words what was agreeable to them, e. g. what he said with reference to the Pragmatic Sanction: he was right, England was no better disposed towards this than France or the Republic. [2]) But how little the trend of his ideas was to their liking would appear from Townshend's complaint uttered only a few days after the vacillations just mentioned: it would be harsh to absolutely decline a proposal that contained nothing against our engagements. [3]) In principle, England had already broken with Slingelandt's ideas; she was shortly to break with them altogether apropos of an effort of his to bring her to a more amenable frame of mind towards Spain, an effort which had been undertaken at the instigation of the Cardinal.

The latter was not yet fully determined in favour of a provisional treaty. He still had hopes of bringing about a reconciliation between England and Spain. He was not unacquainted with the disquietude of the English, and that they would much rather have preferred not to come to the Congress at all, if they could have stayed away with decency. [4]) Another thing, Broglie had written that

---

[1]) id. to id., 25 June '28, ibid.
[2]) id. to id., 28 June '28, R. O. Hl. 301.
[3]) id. to id., 2 July '28, ibid.
[4]) Secret instructions to the French plenipotentiaries, 30 May '28, A. E. Mem. et Doc. France 496.

for the past two years trade had been going very badly, and he expressed it as his opinion that if Spain would be more bending as to trade, England would do with regard to Gibraltar, just as she had done in the preceding century with regard to Tangier, which, after an occupation of some decades, she had abandoned. [1]) In order that she would the more readily come to this, the Cardinal wanted the Pensionary to try his influence with her. The latter had not entered into private correspondence with him, thinking it not proper for one in his position to do so, but he had let the Cardinal know that they could inform each other of their views through Goslinga. [2]) So through this channel Fleury communicated to him that in his opinion there were three ways of finishing the Congress, by a definitive treaty, by a provisional one, or by war. War did not suit any power, England being no exception. A definitive treaty was most desirable but this seemed impossible on account of the obstinacy of Spain and England. Hence nothing was left but a provisional treaty, unless Slingelandt should succeed in moving England to enter into expedients concerning her differences with Spain. [3])

The Pensionary did not look upon these as the Cardinal did. The latter took them for reasons why a definitive treaty did not come about. Slingelandt on the other hand took them for mere pretexts. This difference was not accidental; neither of them was able to judge otherwise. In Fleury's eyes they were essential, whereas in Slingelandt's they were only incidental. Slingelandt, however, was willing to comply with Fleury's request. That a person of such consequence as he was, should declare that these differences hindered a definitive treaty, was in itself a strong inducement to him. Further, although he did not think it likely that pacification would turn upon the restitution of Gibraltar, yet he was far from thinking it impossible. The Court of Spain was most pressing, and the restitution of Gibraltar was a popular point. So it might very well be that the King of England would have to face the dilemma of either giving it up or of going to war in order to keep it. It was his conviction that France would not go to war on this account only, and neither would the

[1]) Broglie to Chauvelin, 18 June '28, A. E. Angleterre 362.
[2]) Chesterfield to Townshend, 20 July '28, R. O. Hl. 301.
[3]) Slingelandt to Goslinga, 21 July '28, id. to Townshend, 16 July '28, R. A. Hl. 2974, 2994.

Republic. And even for England herself, he was of opinion, that Gibraltar was of too little importance to go to war about. Its possession even was prejudicial, and insisting on its retention was more a question of honour than one of interest. Should it now prove to be, which he did not believe, the only impediment to the pacification of Europe, he could not see why the King could not be prevailed upon, by the intervention of France or the Republic or of both, to bring the question of restitution before Parliament. His influence there was sufficient to make it pass. The public intercession of his Allies would save him on the point of honour. It would be a sacrifice made on behalf of general tranquillity, and one which would give him less pain, if at the same time France would get Spain to do full justice to the English nation's claims in matters of trade. [1]

Imbued with these considerations, Slingelandt, on July 16th., applied to Townshend. Their correspondence was of a confidential nature, but the former expressly entreated his addressee to regard his observations as those of a friend. He doubted very much whether matters were already in such a state as to enable a sure judgment being formed upon the manner of finishing the Congress. The Emperor wished to do so by a provisional treaty, but his position was not such that others could be compelled thereby to conform themselves to him. On his part there was no danger whatever of war, which otherwise would make the Pensionary very cautious. On the contrary, he seemed to be in much uncertainty as to Spain; the Allies, by means of the marriage, could very probably involve him in great difficulties. And besides, he (the Emperor) could not but perceive that he was losing ground in the Empire. Hence there was no necessity for adopting a provisional treaty; this latter was, on the other hand, fraught with so many objections that it ought only to be contemplated in the direst need.

According to the latest news from France, it was true that Fleury wished to prevent the consequences of the closer union of the Emperor with Spain, particularly such arising from the marriage, by means of two secret alliances, one between England and France, which would be communicated to the Pensionary, that the Republic would join at a proper time, and would have for its

---

[1] Chesterfield to Townshend, 3 Aug. '28, R. O. Hl. 301 : Slingelandt to Hop, 23 Oct. '28, R. A. Hl. 2974.

principal clause never to consent to the marriage or the Pragmatic Sanction, except by common consent; and the other, with the four Electors and other Princes of the Empire, to maintain their liberties against the encroachments of the Court of Vienna. But from either of these Slingelandt did not promise himself very much. With regard to the first, it could not be submitted to the Republic, before the circumstances against which it provided arose, and then it was very questionable whether she would join an alliance that would at once involve her in difficulties. Further, should it be mooted abroad it would give rise to strong jealousy towards England, in which case it would not be sufficient for this power to remark that Slingelandt was privy to it. Nor would England be able to justify the alliance to Parliament, if one of the Allies were not a party to it. [1]) And with reference to that with the Princes of the Empire he had very strong doubts as to whether it could be accomplished should the Emperor return as victor from the Congress and have prevented the settling of anything there to restore the balance of power and to prevent the marriage of at least to undo its evil consequences; for then the Princes would have no choice but to think that the Hanover Allies either despaired of opposing the union of the Emperor with Spain successfully, or that they neglected their chief interests.

The shortcomings of a provisional treaty would not by any means be retrieved by these alliances. It was to be feared, however, that such a treaty would be unavoidable, unless the great obstacles which inclined Fleury to it could be removed, viz., the feelings of Spain and England with regard to Gibraltar and matters of trade. Slingelandt did not think these matters would give so much trouble, the King being too just to suffer the abuse of the Assiento Treaty becoming the ruin of the Spaniards' trade, and even of that of his Allies and friends. But the question of Gibraltar was of quite another nature; it had become a point of honour, and for this reason might very well become a rock upon which the peace of Europe could founder, whereas to England it would

---

[1]) Poyntz to Chesterfield, 13 July '28, Chesterfield to Townshend, 16 July '28, R. O. Hl. 301. We have presented as Slingelandt's opinion those objections of Chesterfield against such an alliance which Slingelandt agreed with. The remark regarding the English government was made by the Pensionary himself. In another conversation with Chesterfield he said, such a treaty was at the best so much "waste paper" (Chesterfield to Townshend, 27 July '28, R. O. Hl. 301).

be a source of unlimited expenditure and of perpetual trouble in her trade with Spain and America. Slingelandt, therefore, took the liberty of asking Townshend: "Est-il absolûment impossible, Milord, de songer à des expédients pour sauver l'honneur du Roi et de la nation Britannique et procurer en même temps des avantages plus réels?" He recommended him to consider this question maturely and to take into account the repugnance of both France and the Republic against a war of which Gibraltar should be the cause or the pretext). [1]

Townshend was not very pleased at receiving this letter, the less so as he himself attached little value to Gibraltar. This was the current opinion among the leading English statesmen of those days. In 1718, James Stanhope had offered to surrender it. Horace Walpole once told Pesters in confidence that it would have been a good thing if it had never been ceded to England, while Townshend himself had more than once expressed his willingness to give it up for an equivalent. [2] At present however he considered it utterly impossible to do so. "A violent and almost superstitious zeal," so he had written to Poyntz some weeks previously, "has of late prevailed among all parties in this Kingdom against any scheme for the restitution of Gibraltar, upon any conditions whatever". [3] By it, he wrote to Chesterfield, the King was to lose the affection of the English nation to such a degree "as to make him so uneasy at home, that he could be of no weight or consequence abroad." "I have likewise," he continued, "for some time foreseen that the difficulties which might arise at the Congress in establishing the peace of Europe upon a lasting foundation, would be imputed to His Majesty's not gratifying Spain in this particular, but now we may justly expect, after what Sinzendorff has let fall, that there will be an end of that way of arguing." What was it that Sinzendorff had let fall? He had given Fleury to understand, that if the King of England were willing to consent to the marriage, he could keep Gibraltar. This was a hint which confirmed Townshend in his opinion that Elizabeth cared only for her own and her chil-

---

[1] Slingelandt to Townshend, 16 July '28, R. A. Hl. 2994.
[2] Leadam, *op cit.* 322, 337; *Eng. Hist. Rev.* XV, 266; Pesters to Slingelandt, 2 Nov. '27, R. A. Hl. 2981.
[3] Townshend to Poyntz, 3 June '28, in Coxe, *R. W.* II, 631.

dren's interests and not for those of the Spanish nation. [1])

When Townshend returned an answer to Slingelandt's letter on July 23rd., he referred him to this hint. After Sinzendorff's words it could no longer be said that Gibraltar and the English trade were points that rendered it impossible to finish the Congress by a definitive treaty. The source of the evil had to be looked for elsewhere, viz., in Fleury's weakness. Not that he himself was in favour of the marriage, but Chauvelin was not of his principles. The latter represented war to him as unavoidable, unless he were complaisant towards the Emperor and Spain; he prevented him from making the marriage public, by saying that the Congress would be interminable, as there would be no end to the restrictions for the safety of the balance of power in Europe, and he made him believe that, once he opened the door to the grievances and complaints of the Empire, he would become engulfed in them. From the beginning Horace Walpole had foreseen the dangers to which the machinations of Chauvelin would expose the Allies, but he had been very badly supported by Van Hoey; and recently, by his imprudent talk with Sinzendorff, Hop had also given cause for complaint. Still, how ever difficult it might prove to be, the Cardinal's eyes had to be opened to the fact that there was no danger of war, and how easily the method of bringing the marriage before the Congress, or at least, of having it publicly and authentically known, would bring in its train a sure and solid peace. For that purpose the English and Dutch plenipotentiaries had together to make the most serious, and, at the same time, the most cordial, representations to him. If the Cardinal could in this way be reasoned out of Chauvelin's ideas and brought to exhibit firmness, a definitive treaty could still be arrived at; if not, there was nothing left but a provisional treaty. This was indeed a "mauvais pis-aller," but if Fleury allowed himself to be persuaded to it, the Maritime Powers could do no more than turn it, as far as possible, to their own advantage. [2])

On receiving this letter from Townshend, Slingelandt, as he wrote in his answer of July 29th., was full of astonishment that his

---

[1]) id. to Chesterfield, 9 July '28, R. O. Hl. 301.
[2]) Townshend to Slingelandt, 12 July '28, R. A. Hl. 2994; cf. Townshend to Chesterfield, 9 July '28, R. O. Hl. 301.

question had been passed over in silence, but on reading the letter over a second time, he saw that he had to take the reply to it from the sentence that after Sinzendorff's hint the two points could no longer be considered as putting obstacles in the way of a general pacification. Slingelandt did not agree with this. The Chancellor's words were ambiguous to him, for they certainly referred to an unlimited consent to the marriage, but such a consent could not be looked upon as an expedient, as it would upset the balance of power, and besides, it would not remove the difficulties concerning trade, which were looked upon in Spain, and even in France and the Republic, otherwise than in London. Therefore Slingelandt felt himself called upon to repeat the question contained in his former letter, the more so, as he knew from a reliable source that only three weeks previously the Cardinal had pointed to the feelings of Spain and England on those two points as *the* obstacles that inclined him towards a provisional treaty.

At first, this additional reason of Slingelandt is not clear, but it must be taken in connection with what he said about Fleury either in this letter or in his conversations with Chesterfield. That the Cardinal was opposed to the marriage, as was thought in England, Slingelandt could not admit. Rottembourg's extraordinary conduct and his overcomplaisance with regard to Elizabeth was the first thing to raise suspicions in him about the relations of France and Spain, and he could but apply them to the marriage, now that he heard that Brancas, the new Ambassador of France at Madrid, made use of his influence to keep the King of Spain from abdication, under the miserable pretence that such an act on his part would interrupt or retard the Congress. [1]) To Slingelandt, the abdication was worth the whole Congress, for, as the failure of the marriage would be its natural consequence, it would at once bring about what the Allies wanted of this assembly. The conduct of the Cardinal himself was also very strange; he had given Bournonville and Sinzendorff a sort of consent to the marriage, whereas he obliged the Allies to keep it secret, and constantly refused to bring it up at the Congress. His long conferences with Sinzendorff were, according to himself, filled with vague conversations which led to nothing definite, as the Chan-

---

[1]) In the beginning, at the request of Elizabeth, Brancas did, indeed, counteract the abdication, but was soon ordered not to do so any longer, Baudrillart *op cit.* III, 417—8.

cellor spoke in so incoherent a manner, that he could not understand him. But Slingelandt told Chesterfield that as to himself, he had never been for an hour with Sinzendorff, but that he understood his intention very well. Besides, Fleury moved the idea of putting Don Carlos into immediate possession of some territories in Italy; it was too vague to frame a judgment upon, but the intention might be that this was a beginning, and that afterwards he should obtain the Emperor's other dominions. Should this be the case, it was anything but calculated to break the union of Elizabeth and the Emperor; on the contrary, it would only reinforce this union, as it would convince the Queen that the Cardinal was in earnest. Last, but not least, the latter's predilection for a provisional treaty was suspected by Slingelandt, as nothing was more fitted to facilitate the marriage, by removing the obstacles which the Congress might put in its way. Otherwise he did not understand why Fleury should be so much in favour of such a treaty; it was not out of aversion to war, for he (Fleury),was convinced that war was not the Emperor's object. Everything led to the conclusion that the Cardinal was in favour of the marriage. The prospect of the greatness of a Bourbon Prince seemed to blind him to the consequences.

Being face to face with this danger induced Slingelandt to repeat his question to Townshend. The provisional treaty, the sure precursor of the marriage, seemed unavoidable. Representations to inspire Fleury with vigour, would not do. The only way out was, that England would be willing for an expedient. In this case, the Cardinal, on account of his declaration of only three weeks previous, could not refuse to co-operate towards procuring a definitive treaty. [1])

Townshend was most astonished at seeing this question addressed to him again. He could not have believed that it sprang from Slingelandt, and had considered the matter as being cleared up when Chesterfield had written him that the latter had only put it at the strong instigation of Fleury and Goslinga, "so that I daresay you will hear no more of it from his quarter." [2]) Townshend had the less expected this, as he had ordered Chesterfield to make known to

---

[1]) Slingelandt to Townshend, 29 July '28, R. A. Hl. 2994; cf. Chesterfield to Townshend, 6, 9, 27 July, 3 Aug. '28, R. O. Hl. 301.

[2]) Chesterfield to Townshend, 20 July '28, Townshend to Chesterfield, 19 July '28, R. O. Hl. 301.

the Pensionary that it was impossible for the King to touch upon
the question of Gibraltar, and as the Ambassador had already
told him upon a former occasion, his Master did not desire to
keep up the abuses of trade. Besides, Slingelandt, who knew so
well the nature of the English Government, could not but realise
that it was impossible for the King to start his reign with the
restitution of Gibraltar. Since, however, he had repeated his
question, the Foreign Secretary, on the 3rd. of August, gave him an
answer the clearness of which left nothing to be desired:
"Sa Majesté se trouve obligée de vous dire de sa part, qu'elle ris-
quera tout avant que de rendre Gibraltar, et qu'elle réclamera les
engagements solemnels des Etats-Généraux, pris par tant de
traités faits et renouvelés, si Elle y est forcée par l'obstination
déraisonnable de ses ennemis, et qu'en cela Elle ne demandera pas
une grâce de la République, mais seulement qu'on lui fasse justice. A l'égard du commerce, le Roi ne refusera pas de faire ré-
former tous les abus qui se trouveront y être commis; mais pour
les droits et privilèges, qui sont clairement acquis à son peuple
par des traités solemnels, approuvés et garantis par ses alliés,
S. M. ne s'en départira jamais. Et S. M. a tant de confiance dans la
justice et dans l'équité de la République, qu'elle se promet d'en
être soutenu efficacement, surtout lorsque le Roi appuie si cor-
dialement de son coté les intérêts de l'Etat." [1])

On receipt of this letter, Slingelandt was extremely concerned at Townshend's having misunderstood his suggestion. As he
told Chesterfield, he had made it only in the event of the utmost
necessity arising, which he also thought was improbable; such a
letter he had not expected; Townshend's letters used to be in a
more friendly tone, and he felt he had not deserved such a reproof. He did not answer immediately. Knowing his own hasty
temper, he purposely allowed a week to elapse until August
13th., but Chesterfield wished he had allowed a longer time
to elapse, for his letter was none the less couched in rather
warm terms. [2])

"A la vérité," it ran, "je ne pensais rien moins, Milord, que
de m'attirer une lettre si forte par des instances, faites avec beaucoup de circonspection à un ministre, avec lequel j'ai l'honneur

---

[1]) Townshend to Slingelandt, 23 July '28, R. A. Hl. 2994.
[2]) Chesterfield to Townshend, 6, 13, 17 Aug. '28, R. O. Hl. 301.

d'être sur un pied de familiarité, simplement pour vouloir, en faveur d'un objet si souhaitable qu'une pacification générale, songer à un expédient pour en écarter un des principaux obstacles."

The reasons why he could not have expected such a letter were as follows: the Cardinal considered Gibraltar as being *the* great obstacle to a definitive treaty; therefore, Slingelandt had put his question, although he did not agree with the Cardinal, but thought that the question of Gibraltar was only a pretext, though certainly a most specious and popular one.

As Townshend himself called a provisional treaty a *mauvais pis-aller*, he did not imagine that he was sinning in the least when he submitted the consideration of an expedient for the purpose of preventing it. The less so, as he thought he was right in calling Gibraltar a nuisance for England, and as he had made no mention of any other expedient than one which would save the King's and the nation's honour, and procure for the latter more tangible advantages. If Townshend contested this view about Gibraltar, or if he considered it worth the breaking up of the Congress or a provisional treaty, then Slingelandt begged leave to say that he was only following the sentiments of the late King, who would never have written his famous letter to the Court of Spain if he had entertained the same idea of Gibraltar as the English government held nowadays, unless his letter were given a forcible interpretation, unworthy a great King.

Should difficulties again arise, Spain would certainly lose no opportunity of pointing to England's obstinacy as the sole cause of the disturbance and loss suffered by English trade.

Further, it was not necessary that England should herself propose an expedient; her Allies might very well bring one forward.

With regard to these, the Pensionary had not questioned whether France and the Republic were bound to support England as to Gibraltar. "Rien n'est plus clair. Mais avouons néanmoins, Milord, que ce serait un morceau de dure digestion pour nos provinces, si Gibraltar, après avoir été du temps de la Reine Anne la récompense de la dissolution de la Grande Alliance et d'une paix telle que la paix d'Utrecht, fut présentement la cause apparente d'une guerre."

The Pensionary brought his letter to a close with two questions. "Devais-je après tout cela m'attendre, Milord, à tant de vivacité que vous montrez dans votre lettre, pour avoir demandé non au Cardinal de Fleury, mais à Milord Townshend, à qui je suis accoutumé de m'ouvrir dans la dernière confidence, *s'il est absolument impossible de songer à des expédients pour sauver l'honneur du Roi et de la nation britannique, et procurer en même temps à celle-ci des avantages plus réels que Gibraltar ?* Et ne serai-je pas obligé d'être à l'avenir plus sur mes gardes, en écrivant a Votre Excellence, quoique cela rendra notre commerce moins utile?" [1])

There would be no need for him to be on his guard, for their correspondence ceased, as Townshend returned no answer to this letter. According to Jorissen, in so doing Townshend broke with Slingelandt. To him, what had taken place between the two statesmen who had been close friends for twenty years was a drama, ending with the breaking-off of the friendship on the part of Townshend. But, as often happens, history also steps in here and destroys the artist's illusion.

The reason for Townshend's not writing was not that he broke with Slingelandt, but rather because he feared a breach. This appears *luce clarius* from his correspondence with Chesterfield. "It would," thus he wrote to the latter immediately after the receipt of the Pensionary's letter, "be the most sensible mortification to me in the world, if I should have written anything to him that might lessen his friendship or break off the intimacy we have always had with one another." For the moment he did not write of it any more, for he intended by the next post to write to Slingelandt himself. That this intention was not carried out, was due to an accident. His colleague Newcastle had gone for some time to Sussex, and this had so much increased his occupations that he could not find time to write to the Pensionary; and that he did not do so by a later post was the effect of the advice which he, in the meantime, had received from Chesterfield. [2])

The Ambassador was so afraid of a coolness arising between Townshend and the Pensionary, "in whose friendship not only I, but the public is much concerned," that he took the liberty of advising Townshend that, in the event of his answering Slingelandts' letter, "which I own I could rather wish you did not at all,"

[1]) Slingelandt to Townshend, 13 Aug. '28, R. A. Hl. 2994.
[2]) Townshend to Chesterfield, 6, 13 Aug. '28, R. O. Hl. 301.

he should do so with as little warmth as possible. Chesterfield would the more regret any discord between them, as he did
not question Slingelandt's good intentions. When he had told him
that his letter was too warm, the Pensionary had expressed his
regret, and begged that it might be imputed to his constitution, and
not to his intention; he had thought it necessary to justify himself
with the King and Townshend, in again making mention of Gibraltar, which he feared had been misunderstood. At the same
time he had expressed both his deepest regard and friendship for
Townshend. [1])

Townshend thanked Chesterfield for his advice and took it.
Henceforth, what he wished to communicate to Slingelandt went
through the Ambassador's hands. There was the less objection to
this, as, in the few months of Chesterfield's stay at the Hague, a
great intimacy had sprung up between him and the Pensionary.
The latter took great pleasure in conversation with the talented
and witty man [2]) who was his junior by thirty years, and treated
him with the same familiarity he used towards Townshend. He
had allowed him to read his letters to the Foreign Secretary,
who on his part had allowed the Ambassador to peruse those
he wrote to Slingelandt. Hence there was no need whatever for
Townshend to continue a correspondence which was on the point
of leading to serious discord. [3])

Chesterfield's advice was most prudent. He had seen that there
was a profound difference in the views between them, which would
only be widened by a further exchange of letters. Now, however,
Slingelandt and Townshend did not become strangers to each other.
The next year Townshend, on his way to Hanover, as was usual
with him, touched at the Hague; he then, as we shall see more
particularly, conversed with Slingelandt upon state affairs. [4])
Once again, when Chesterfield was staying in England, they exchanged letters with each other. They did so, too, for the last
time, on Townshend's resignation, when they bade each other a
most cordial farewell. [5])

---

[1]) Chesterfield to Townshend, 13 Aug. '28, ibid.
[2]) Cf. Van Ittersum to Townshend, 25 May, 8 June '28, R. O. Hl. 296.
[3]) Townshend to Slingelandt, 9 Jan. '30, in Jorissen, *op. cit.* 123. Jorissen has put a
wrong construction upon this letter.
[4]) Chesterfield to Townshend, 3 June, 7 July '29, R. O. Hl. 304.
[5]) Jorissen, *op cit.* 122—5; Slingelandt to Goslinga, 27 May '30, R. A. Hl. 2974.

Thus a personal breach was prevented, and hardly anyone knew what had passed between them. The Court of France continued to regard them as intimate friends, and was under the impression that their correspondence was being carried on till Townshend's resignation. [1]) Of a breach between the Republic and England there was still less question. A suggestion by Fleury, made in conversation with Goslinga, that England's obstinacy with regard to Spain was a strong argument for the making of a permanent alliance between France and the Republic, did not meet with any success with the Pensionary. [2])

Still, what had happened had led to a breach, a breach on the part of Townshend with Slingelandt's system, which he at first appeared to have accepted. This was a breach of far-reaching effect upon the course of political events generally, and in particular upon Townshend, as we shall see later, as well as upon Slingelandt. The latter could only have succeeded if England had advocated his system at the Court of France. Now, however, at the same time that his system was declined by England, it was declined by France also.

III.

After having taken his three steps in the Emperor's direction, Fleury had still tried, in order to bring about a definitive treaty, to get Slingelandt to use his influence to gain England for an expedient. This was one of the two ways in which Fleury attempted to achieve his end. The other was to try to embroil Spain with the Emperor. This was the purpose underlying the Cardinal's answer to the overtures regarding the marriage. This was also lurking in the answer he gave regarding the introduction of Spanish garrisons in Parma and Tuscany. As we have already seen, the Emperor had hopes that this desire of Spain's would suffer shipwreck on the rock of opposition presented by France and England. Hence it was a disagreeable surprise for Sinzendorff when Bournonville brought to light an article of the Treaty of 1721, by which France and England had declared in favour of it; still worse for him was the fact that these powers now professed that they persisted in these same sentiments. The Cardinal, and Stanhope

---

[1]) Chauvelin to La Baune, 23 Dec. '28, 3 Apr., 1 June '30, A. E. Hl. 375, 379, 381.
[2]) Slingelandt to Goslinga, 7 Aug. '28, R. A. Hl. 2974.

too, did not confine themselves to this; they further told the Spanish plenipotentiaries that Spain ought to see that she regained the Austrian dominions which had formerly belonged to her. [1])

But Spain's conduct was no more promising than that of England; she did not show the least complaisance towards the Hanover Allies; on the contrary, she returned a most haughty reply to the representations made by them upon an exorbitant tax raised from a ship that had come from America, and Bournonville delivered some very strongly-worded notes. Moreover, Patiño worked might and main to make Spain as formidable at sea as possible. [2])

Although Fleury did not give up his endeavours to disentangle Spain from the Emperor, he nevertheless saw that at present his object could not be realised, and that this would take a good deal of time. In the meantime, a provisional treaty might be of use in preserving peace. Given the conditions, it suited France better than anything else, for should the Anglo-Spanish differences remain unsettled, the adjustment of the other differences, either beween Spain and the Emperor or between him and the Republic, could not be otherwise than to the prejudice of France. The leaning of this latter Power towards a provisional treaty might seem to be a step in the direction of the Court of Vienna: it was, however, determined by self-interest. The same may be said of the other steps which France took towards that Court, and first of all with regard to the Ostend affair.

This was among the few matters which had been brought forward officially at the Congress. On June 30th. the Dutch delivered the demand for the suppression of the Ostend Company. On July 5th. it was rejected, not, however, without a declaration to the effect that the Emperor would lend a willing ear to any reasonable expedients which the Dutch might propose. In a private conversation with Hop and Goslinga, Sinzendorff softened the refusal still more. He said that the answer could not be otherwise than general; the Emperor, however, was very well disposed, and expedients must be found. The Dutch plenipotentiaries, however, answered that on the part of the States, expedients could in no

---

[1]) Baudrillart, op cit. III, 435—7.
[2]) ibid., 431—2, 440—'1, 578—9.

case be proposed; in the event of the Emperor's being unwilling to agree to an unconditional suppression, which they demanded, then he would have to move an expedient himself. They remained unshaken in this attitude, even when Sinzendorff changed his tone and struck a menacing note. [1]

It was to the behaviour of the Dutch that the Austrian plenipotentiaries imputed the non-settlement of an equivalent; they were, however, not quite right. At least, Slingelandt was convinced that the suppression of the Company would not be obtained gratuitously, and therefore, although he thought the time was not yet ripe, he did not altogether reject the idea of an equivalent. Concerning Fleury's making mention of it, he wrote, "l'amour de la paix et l'envie de finir l'emporte *trop loin*, ou du moins le fait aller *plus vite* que je ne voudrais." He further gave his opinion upon the various equivalents that were being discussed in France. But any proposal of an equivalent had to come from the Austrians, either directly or indirectly through the Cardinal. On account of her constitution it could not proceed from the Republic. The stiffness of the Austrians in insisting upon this demand was, according to Slingelandt, a very considerable factor in the failure to realise an equivalent. [2]

Neither he nor the Austrians had yet seen this in its true aspect. On both sides they were not yet aware that the man who stood between them was not earnestly endeavouring to bring about an agreement. No sooner did the Cardinal make mention of an equivalent than he did his best to remove the uneasiness which this had caused in Goslinga, assuring him that he would not forsake the Republic, and that he would not do anything except in concert with her plenipotentiaries. Far from urging any particular equivalent on the Dutch, he advocated first one and then the other, but fixed on none. [3] His real intentions appear in the instructions given at the end of July to La Baune: time had not yet arrived for entering into negotiations as to an equivalent, but it was now no longer necessary to uphold the Dutch

[1] Hop and Goslinga to Slingelandt, 8 July, Hop to the same, 29 July '28, R. A. Hl. 2985, 2982: Baudrillart, *op. cit.* III, 440—'1.

[2] Slingelandt to Hop, 7, 16, 21 July, 5, 7 Aug. '28; id. to Goslinga, 7, 21 July '28, R. A. Hl. 2974.

[3] Chauvelin to Fleury, 17 June '28, A. E. Mem. et Doc. France 497, f. 230-32; Hop to Slingelandt, 1 July '28, R.A Hl. 2982; Hop and Goslinga to Slingelandt, 1, 4 July '28, Fleury to Hop and Goslinga, 8 July '28, R. A. Hl. 2985.

in their disposition to decline any sort of indemnification; he should confine himself to bringing into relief the fact that for the Republic there was nothing to be compared with the entire cessation of the Belgian trade with India, without saying anything more. [1] For France, circumstances might make it desirable that the States should give an equivalent, but, in the meantime, she would not make any serious effort to get the Ostend affair cleared out of the way.

Just as in this affair, so also with regard to those of the Empire, France's conduct was guided by her own interests. These interests contravened the action in the Empire into which Slingelandt had won George II.; for should this succeed, and should German affairs be brought forward at the Congress, France would have no choice but to concur with the Maritime Powers, whereas George II. would have the lead of it, and would at the same time increase his prestige through it. In the event of there being later on a resumption of friendship between him and the Emperor, the influence of France in the Empire would be reduced to nothing. Fleury's object, therefore, was to defeat this action. Its character was general, as it tried to embrace all separate points, East Frisia, Mecklenburg, Juliers and Bergh and others, and it was just this generality that the Cardinal combated. This he did, among other things, by ruling out of the Congress all matters of the Empire. In order, however, not to displease the Allies, he at the same time evinced a keen interest in each of the matters which concerned them particularly. Thus, he expressed his indignation at the Emperor's manner of acting with regard to Mecklenburg, and tried to move him to settle this matter to the satisfaction of George II. [2] He acted in a similar manner with reference to East Frisia.

Here the situation was becoming worse every day. The sub-delegates and the Prince were continuing their proceedings, although the Imperial decree was still being delayed. When the Dutch plenipotentiaries approached Sinzendorff concerning this dilatoriness, he excused it by saying that the deliberations of the Aulic Council were very slow, and assured them that both the Council and the Court were well-intentioned. [3] The States, however, were not

---

[1] Chauvelin to La Baune, 29 July '28, A. E. Hl. 375.
[2] Newcastle to Stanhope, 3 June '28, in Coxe, *R. W.* II, 629—30: Townshend to Chesterfield, 13 Aug. '28, R. O. Hl. 301.
[3] Hop and Goslinga to Slingelandt, 22 June '28, R. A. Hl. 2985.

satisfied with this assurance, and, on July 9th., decided on applying to their Allies. The plenipotentiaries were instructed to consult with the French and English Ministers as to how Sinzendorff could be induced, in the first place, to give a positive and specific answer with reference to the Emperor's intentions concerning the restoration of tranquillity in East Frisia, and particularly as to the redressing of what had been committed pending the deliberations of the Emperor, and with regard to the immediate stopping of all further proceedings; secondly, that the Emperor should mitigate the rigour of the decree, and, by disclosing to the States General on what basis he thought that tranquillity and order could be restored in the constitution of East Frisia, put them in a position to recommend to the Renitents an unlimited submission. The plenipotentiaries had also to ask the French and English Ministers whether, in the event of no satisfactory answer being returned or if in the meantime there should be hostilities against the town of Embden and its Dutch garrison, they could depend upon the Allies' taking it as a *casus foederis*.[1])

So far as the making of representations to Sinzendorff went, the plenipotentiaries met with complete success. Fleury and Chauvelin, although they had already done so, again urged upon Sinzendorff the necessity for the Emperor's giving a decisive answer to the Republic with regard to the East Frisian affair. The English Ministers were not behind the French in supporting her; they even admitted the *casus foederis*. The French did not, though declining in a very friendly way, saying that they would rather give the Republic assistance from goodwill than by virtue of any treaty. And Chauvelin dictated a strongly worded declaration to Hop, in which he said that France, if need be, would support her. He also again and again exhorted the Republic to show more firmness. [2]) It would be best, he wrote to La Baune, that the Dutch took up arms, but he added that this was not in the nature of advice, for then they would at once apply to France to guarantee them against the consequences, and of such an application there ought to be no question; but La Baune must not check them

---

[1]) Res. S. G. 9 July '28, cf. Slingelandt to Goslinga, 21 July '28, R. A. Hl. 2974.

[2]) Hop to Fagel, 29 July, 1 Aug. '28, in Rousset, *Recueil* V, 252 et seq.; Mémoire de Pecquet sur l'affaire d'Ostfrise, A. E. Hl. 375 f. 73—5; Chauvelin to La Baune, 29 July, 26 Aug. '28, ibid.

should they decide to do so of themselves. [1]) So France was ready to assist the Republic in this affair, provided it remained by itself and was neither classed under the engagements she was under, nor introduced at the Congress.

About this non-introduction there was much ado. It became known, not without Sinzendorff's aid, that the Cardinal had promised not to allow the introduction of German affairs at the Congress. This rumour also reached the Hague, and caused Slingelandt to immediately despatch instructions to Hop to make inquiries of Sinzendorff concerning this.[2]) The latter not only maintained that this was so, but even mentioned it in a letter to Koenigsegg-Erps, of which he gave Hop a copy. [3]) Thereupon the Cardinal was applied to for an explanation, first by the English plenipotentiaries and then also by Hop. In reply to this he wrote a letter in which he declared that Sinzendorff had given too free an interpretation to his words, as he had said no more to him than that affairs pertaining solely to the Empire would not be introduced at the Congress, and that he had always excluded those which might be a consequence of the Treaties of Westphalia, of which France was a guarantor, just as those which had close relations with the interests of the Allies, e. g., that of East Frisia.[4]) There is no doubt that, in making this promise to Sinzendorff, the Cardinal will have kept a loop-hole open, but, however this may be, the East Frisian matter did not come before the Congress. Neither did another matter, which, just as this, concerned one of the Allies of France, and had, moreover, relation to the Treaties of Westphalia, viz., Juliers and Bergh.

It was, of course, denied both to Hop and to Francken, the plenipotentiary of the Elector Palatine, that this matter would not be brought up at the Congress; but soon after Francken's arrival at Soissons, Chauvelin advised him, on account of the Court of Vienna, to make no mention at all of his master's object, for

---

[1]) Chauvelin to La Baune, 15 July '28, A. E. Hl. 375.
[2]) Slingelandt to Hop, 13 July '23, R. A. Legatie 84; Chesterfield to Townshend, 13 July '28, R. O. Hl. 301.
[3]) Sinzendorff to Königsegg-Erps, 26 July '28, Rousset, *Recueil* V, 260.
[4]) Hop to Slingelandt, 1 Aug. '23, R. A. Hl. 2982; Hop to Fleury, 29 July, Fleury to Hop, 30 July '28, in Rousset, *Recueil* V, 261—4. An error has crept into Rousset's translation of Hop's letter to Fagel of 1 Aug. 28 (*loc. cit.* 255 et seq.). On p. 256 he says: M. le Cardinal m'a d'abord repondu à ma lettre d'une manière qui *confirme* ce que la Comte de Sinzendorff avance. As appears from the Dutch original, *confirme* should be replaced by its opposite: *renverse*.

the time being. [1]) A considerable time before this the French Court had already made Count d'Albert, the Bavarian Envoy, who took a great interest in the affairs of the Palatinate, aware that France did not quite like the Elector's having two objects in view at one and the same time, i. e., to bring up the matter of Juliers and Bergh at the Congress, and, further, to obtain a guarantee from France, England and the Republic. The Count had been given to understand that the former matter ought, for the present, to be kept in the background. [2]) France intended, although she did not say so, that the guarantee from the Maritime Powers should also be kept in the background. For the present, she only wished that she herself should enter into negotiations with the Elector.

The final task that she had set herself to perform, was to bring the four Electors under a treaty which would oblige them to a full neutrality in the case of war between the Emperor and France, unless the Empire should take part in it, and in this latter case that they should then only give their compulsory contingent. To accomplish this end, the Elector Palatine had first to conclude such a treaty, and then he would be obliged to get the other three to join too.

France wanted to derive still further advantage from these negotiations with the Elector Palatine. She had some old differences to settle with him about some rights in Alsatia, the so-called Germersheim differences. The Elector objected to dealing with these now, and was not desirous of connecting them with the other objects of the negotiations, but France was inexorable: in addition to binding himself to a neutrality towards France, he had to lend himself to an adjustment of those differences.

To bring him to this, however, France needed some sort of a bait. This would be found by guaranteeing to the Prince of Pfalz-Sulzbach the succession to the two Duchies, first on the part of France, then by England and the Republic, and finally by the Congress. If the Congress, with the help of the Maritime Powers, should immediately comply with the Elector's wish, France would then no longer have a bait. [3])

---

[1]) Rosenlehner, *op. cit.* 381—2 :
[2]) ibid: 393—4, cf 375, 379.
[3]) ibid: Chapter VII.
Concerning the conduct of the French ministers as to the Juliers and Bergh matter, Hop wrote to Slingelandt: "Ils veulent l'employer comme un *motif* qui animerait les

With this object in view, therefore, she strained every nerve to defeat the negotiations with the four Electors set on foot by Slingelandt to bring about a general action in the Empire.

As we have seen, the Pensionary had been requested by George II. to sound Gansinot. It was the King's wish that the Electors should join the Treaty of Wolfenbüttel and Würtemberg. Being in ignorance, however, as to whether the original parties would approve of the treaty's being communicated to the Electors, Slingelandt did not feel that he was at liberty to make such a proposal to Gansinot. Chesterfield, who concurred in his opinion, but understood that his Court desired prompt steps to be taken, then suggested that Slingelandt should have an extract taken from the treaty, and that this should be offered to Gansinot as the foundation for a treaty to be made between the German Princes. This is what was done. [1])

Some weeks later, Gansinot informed the Pensionary that the Electors of Cologne and Bavaria thought well of the project, but before taking any further step they wished to re-consider it, and to submit it to the Elector Palatine and to the Elector of Treves. Slingelandt feared that the Electors would not venture on it, being afraid of the Court of Vienna. [2]) He was soon to hear that the reason was a different one. On July 20th. the Cardinal informed the English plenipotentiaries that the four Electors were to enter into a definitive treaty with France; the Duke of Wolfenbüttel and the other Princes of the Empire might also join it; he asked whether George II. wished to be a contracting party, or if he would join it later on; it might be of great use to the Hanover Allies, particularly should difficulties arise with reference to the Emperor's succession; he wished it to be concluded apart from the Congress, and also to be kept secret. [3])

---

quatre Electeurs à recourir aux liaisons avec eux *dont la principale raison cesserait si on fixait le sort de ces états*" (10 Sept. '28, R. A. Hl. 2982), and shortly afterwards: "Ce n'est pas tant la crainte des Impériaux qui empéche de parler dans le traité provisionel des affaires de Juliers et de Bergue que bien de ne pas ôter aux Electeurs *l'aiguillon* qui les fera aller plus vite pour s'adresser aux alliés d'Hanovre, *à quoi ils seraient peut-être moins portés si cette affaire était reglée d'une façon qui les interesse si fort*" (24 Sept. '28, ibid).

[1]) Chesterfield to Townshend, 24 and 25 June '28, Townshend to Chesterfield, 18 June '28, R. O. Hl. 300. Rosenlehner (*op. cit.* 422) is mistaken in thinking the four Electors were invited to join the Hanover alliance.

[2]) Slingelandt to Goslinga, 21 July '28, R. A. Hl. 2974; id. to Townshend, 29 July '28, R. O. Hl. 297; Chesterfield to Townshend, 20, 30 July '28, R. O. Hl. 301.

[3]) Stanhope and Walople to Newcastle, 20 July '28, R. O. Hl. 301

From this Slingelandt concluded that his action had miscarried. In a letter to Goslinga he complained of the conduct of France, in that she, having been informed that the Electors should be sounded, had still entered into separate negotiations with them. [1]

Just as in the affairs of the Empire, Slingelandt had failed to succeed in general affairs. The idea of a provisional treaty, which he detested, became in the course of July more and more fixed. Towards the end of this month Chauvelin told Hop that a draft of such a treaty could soon be expected. Slingelandt, who had already tried to reason the French Ministers out of it, not only indirectly, by means of the English, but also directly through Hop and Goslinga, now in the beginning of August decided upon a last effort.

He once more set out his principles. If the Allies would only firmly and immovably stand by them, they would, with just as little trouble, gain a definitive treaty as a provisional one — at least if the latter were such as to comprise a reasonable security, and not merely for the purpose of creating delay, of which the Vienna Allies would have all the advantage. He could not see that a Congress, which as yet could hardly be said to have started, should have to finish so soon, merely for the sake of those who feared it might throw obstacles in the way of their own ambitious views.

It is noteworthy that Slingelandt now mentioned both the Vienna Allies, and did not speak of the Emperor only. With regard to Spain, a rumour was in circulation that the King intended to abdicate, and the rest of Europe had for several weeks been groping in the dark as to that Prince's situation and intentions. This uncertainty had been another reason for the Pensionary why the Allies should not be in a hurry about anything, and why a provisional treaty should not yet be contemplated. [2] The latest news from Spain, however, made it quite clear that Philip V. held his seat on the throne, and that Elizabeth still had her hopes fixed on the marriage and therefore stood by the Emperor. [3] For this reason Slingelandt thought a provisional treaty all the more dangerous, for it rendered the union of the Emperor and Spain, in a

---

[1] Slingelandt to Goslinga, 21 Aug. '28, R. A. 2974.
[2] id. to Hop, 21 July '28, ibid.
[3] cf Baudrillart, *op cit.* III 418, 430 et seq.

sense, necessary, and both Courts would be obliged to consolidate this union by all sorts of ties. There would then be nothing further to hinder the marriage which would upset the balance of Europe and complete the servitude of the Empire. Further, the Vienna Allies would be able to continue to ruin the commerce and industries of those of Hanover. The haughty, almost insolent, answer which Spain had just returned to the memorial of the latter regarding the "indulto," was an example of what might be expected. There would be no remedy for this but war, the very thing that the provisional treaty was said to guard against. [1])

It was a source of great pain to the Pensionary that the negotiations should now already have come to such a point, to which the Hanover Allies ought never to have allowed them to come, before every means of arriving at a definitive treaty had been tried in vain. And taking into consideration the drawbacks of a provisional treaty, he could not dismiss from his mind the thought that they should make renewed efforts to unmask the Austrians by depriving them of hopes of coming off well, except by a definitive treaty, and by declaring at the same time to the Spaniards that they would be willing to consent to the marriage, provided they had the indispensable precautions necessary for their common safety. After such a declaration, would Sinzendorff have the courage, at the present juncture, to break off, rather than to enter into, negotiations about the marriage? Or if he did dare to do so, and the Allies considered it then to their interests to bring forward a provisional treaty, would he reject that overture and refuse to resume the negotiations? Slingelandt was of opinion that he would not. [2])

The French Ministers to whom these observations by the Pensionary were read, were not influenced by them to make such an effort; they declared against the marriage being brought forward in any way. There were two great objections, they said. The Emperor might consider the conditions proposed by the Allies as being too stringent, and lay it to their charge that it could not take place, and in this way Elizabeth would be driven still closer to the

---

[1]) cf Slingelandt to Hop, 13, 31 Aug., 3, 17 Sept., 7 Oct. '28, id. to Hop, Goslinga and Van Hoey, 19 Sept. '28, R. A. Hl. 2974, Legatie 84;
[2]) id. to Hop 5, 7, Aug. '28, id to Goslinga, 7 Aug. '28, R. A. Hl. 2974.

Emperor. Secondly, in that case the Emperor's succession would have to be settled at once, and this would estrange the German Princes and the Allies. Thus, for the present a definitive treaty was not possible. In support of this the French Ministers pointed to the strained relations existing between the Republic and the Court of Vienna, with reference to the Ostend matter, although they added that the relations between England and Spain, and in particular the point of Gibraltar, were the chief stumbling-block. Therefore there was nothing left but a provisional treaty. [1])

England also came to the same conclusion. She had had great sympathy for the idea from the beginning, but had not yielded to it at once, being afraid as she was of losing Slingelandt so long as she was not quite sure of the Cardinal. This latter, however, gave convincing proofs of his allegiance, not only by his intercession for George II. with regard to Mecklenburg, but also by his conduct regarding the Anglo-Spanish differences. In the draft of the provisional treaty, which was considered by the English and Dutch plenipotentiaries before it was settled, the possession of Gibraltar was expressly secured to England. A violent altercation, however, arose on the question of commercial privileges. Chauvelin wished them to be examined by a committee representing all the contracting parties, as a consequence of which both France and the Republic would have something to say on the differences between Spain and England. This was hotly opposed by the English plenipotentiaries, who asserted that a committee consisting only of the parties concerned should decide on the disputes between them. Although he was supported by Hop, Chauvelin did not prevail, the Cardinal yielding to the English. [2]) Fear that the latter would not support them on this point had caused them to lend an ear to Slingelandt's system as far as it had reference to general affairs, uneasiness with regard to Mecklenburg had influenced them in the same direction so far as the affairs of the Empire were concerned, but as soon as the fear and uneasiness ceased to exist, they went over completely to the Cardinal. This they did all the more readily, as it appeared that following the Pensionary any longer would be attended by the making of sacrifices for which they were by no means prepared.

---

[1]) Hop to Slingelandt, 14 Aug. '28, R. A. Hl. 2982.
[2]) Hop to Slingelandt, 14 Aug. '28, R. A. Hl. 2982.

Hence Slingelandt had lost; had he been the head of a powerful State he would probably have tried to assert his will, and the
plenipotentiaries instructed by him, would have tried to get into
touch with those representing Spain, in order to get the marriage
brought up at the Congress, but neither the position of the Republic nor his own position admitted of such a proceeding. [1]) He had
to acquiesce; the provisional treaty was unavoidable.

C. THE PROPOSED PROVISIONAL TREATY.

August 1728—August 1729.

I.

The draft-provisional treaty, or, as it was officially styled
"Idées Générales pour la Formation d'un Traité", which had been
drawn up by Sinzendorff and Chauvelin and somewhat modified
in the above-mentioned discussions with the plenipotentiaries of
the Maritime Powers, assumed a definite shape in the second week
of August.

This was the contents. The foundation was to be the Treaties
of Utrecht, Rastadt, Baden, the Triple and Quadruple Alliances,
in general the treaties and conventions prior to 1725, and moreover
the Preliminaries of Paris and the Convention of the Pardo. They
were to be binding on all parties to it, "chacun autant que cela
les regarde". The King of Spain declared that by the Vienna
Treaties he had never intended to grant any privilege that was in
contravention of those treaties and conventions, nor to grant to
the subjects of the Emperor any greater commercial advantages
than those enjoyed by other nations, which declaration was
accepted by the Emperor. The latter extended the suspension of
the Ostend Company for a number of years beyond the seven
fixed by the Preliminaries, the number being left blank.
As compensation for this concession, it was stipulated that the
new tariff for the Southern Netherlands, which, according to
Art. 26 of the Barrier Treaty, should be settled between the Emperor, the Republic and England, should come into force within
a period of two years, and this should be drawn up by Commis-

---

[1]) cf Slingelandt to Hop, 21 July '28, R. A. Hl. 2974.

saries of these three Powers. There were other matters which should also be settled by Commissaries in like manner and within the same period, viz., the question of Schleswig, the commercial differences between Spain and England, and those between Spain and France or the Republic. At the end there was a stipulation that if, within a certain period to be decided later, anything should arise that might cause hostilities among the contracting parties, or which might disturb them in the enjoyment of their privileges gained by virtue of the treaties anterior to 1725, then they should all of them combine to bring about a cessation of the hostilities and to redress any damage suffered [1]

The receipt of this project was a defeat for Slingelandt; it, however, speaks well for his practical sense that he was not cast down by it. Prior to its having taken definite shape, he had reckoned with the probabity of its coming about, and at the same time that he ordered Hop and Goslinga to make a last effort in favour of a definitive treaty, he had written that if it were not possible to avert a provisional treaty, then they were to see that they made it as good as possible. [2] In the deliberations on the settlement of the project, Hop made full use of his instructions, but with very little success. [3] This however did not discourage the Pensionary; now that the project lay before him, he did not cease his efforts to make it at least somewhat tolerable. It gave rise to a number of observations on his part, either in writing or in conversation with Chesterfield. [4]

With reference to the Ostend affair, he wished the suspension to be extended for a further twelve or fifteen years at least. He did not deem it a fitting moment to urge for a final settlement on this point now that the others remained unsettled. This might cause suspicion of the Republic to arise among the Allies. It would, moreover, certainly make England less ready to contribute to an equivalent, and on the other hand, it would cause the Emperor to demand a so much higher equivalent, to which he would be the more

[1] Idées Générales sur la Formation d'un Traité, R. A. Hl. 2982, cf. Baudrillart, op. cit. III, 442.

[2] Slingelandt to Hop, 5 Aug. '28; cf. Chesterfield to Townshend, 3 Aug. '28, R. O. Hl. 301.

[3] Hop to Slingelandt, 14 Aug. '28, R. A. Hl. 2982.

[4] Slingelandt's Remarks upon the Project, in Dutch, in Slingelandt to Hop, 21 Aug. '28, R. A. Hl. 2974; in French, in Chesterfield to Townshend, 24 Aug. '28, R. O. Hl. 301; Chesterfield to Townshend, 20 Aug. '28, ibid.

inclined, seeing that the only point which would be settled was
that in which his honour was most concerned. Further, the state
of affairs at the Court of Spain was still of such a nature, that
changes could be hoped for that might induce the Emperor to
become more easy. For all these reasons Slingelandt preferred an
extension of the time of suspension of the Company, rather than
suppression; the more so, as it would have the same effect if only
the period were long, and the Dutch and English East India Companies would take better precautions in the meantime than they
had done hitherto, against the detrimental competition of the
Ostend Company. [1]

Slingelandt did not make any objection to the article with
reference to the tariff of the Southern Netherlands, thinking, as
Chesterfield believed, that means would be found by which a new
tariff would not be concluded within the period prescribed, and
that consequently the old one would stand. He tried to guard
against any intention which the Emperor might have of settling
a new one on his own authority by a stipulation to be inserted at
the end of the treaty that should the differences regarding the
tariff of the Southern Netherlands and the commercial relations
with Spain not be arranged within the term, then all parties
should try in an amicable way to settle these differences, without,
however, coming to hostilities. Should these differences still be
unsolved at the termination of the treaty, then a Congress should
again meet for the purpose of settling at least a method by which
hostilities would be prevented and for the maintenance of public
tranquillity.

With regard to the commercial relations with Spain, the Pensionary desired that an article should be added with reference
to the trade with America, particularly that which was carried
on by way of Spain, that this should be restored to the same footing as that in operation during the life of Charles II. of Spain, without, however, any prejudice to the Assiento Treaty. As to this
treaty, the Republic was bound to guarantee England with regard to this, yet Slingelandt had always wished, and still wished,
as he wrote to Goslinga, that the Spaniards would demonstrate
the impossibility of preventing, otherwise than by a pecuniary

---

[1] Memorial on the Ostend Company, enclosed in Slingelandt to Hop, 21 Aug. '28,
R. A. Legatie 84.

equivalent, the frauds the English committed through the annual ship, to the ruin of the Spaniards' trade and that of the other nations, and that the French, together with the Dutch, would be able to support the Spaniards without injustice to the English or committing a breach of good faith. [1])

As to Schleswig, it was Slingelandt's desire that the Republic should not be concerned in any way with the affairs of the North. The last war in that part of Europe had been the cause of enormous losses to her merchants, without her having any share in the treaties. Nor was there a single advantage now to be expected from her concurrence in these negotiations It might even get her into difficulties with her friends. It was for the Princes, who had profited by the war, to give satisfaction to the Duke of Holstein, whom they had deprived of his patrimony, for no other reason than their mutual convenience, and to recompense the King of Denmark at the expense of a third. Now, these Princes would not like to have a duty preached to them which ran directly counter to their inclinations. [2])

All these objections had reference to the separate articles of the project, but Slingelandt's main objections were against the project as a whole. Nothing in it tended to dissolve the union between the Emperor and Spain, or to prevent the marriage, or at least its detrimental consequences. He tried to meet this defect by suggesting an article with regard to the Austrian dominions, excepting those that had belonged to Spain during the reign of Charles II. by which, during the term of the treaty, these should not be possessed, or held in any other way, by the Prince who might occupy the Spanish throne, nor by his wife or children; and that the parties to the treaty, should this article be violated, would oppose it with all their power.

Such an article was found in the memorial about the Congress drawn up by Horace Walpole in the preceding year, long before the communication of the marriage to the Cardinal, and when it was only thought to be likely. It was Slingelandt's opinion that the Cardinal, who persisted in his refusal to break the secrecy promised, could not object to the marriage being brought forward, by offering to the Emperor's plenipotentiaries in the name

---

[1]) Slingelandt to Goslinga, 21 Aug. '28.
[2]) cf. Slingelandt to Hop, 6 Nov., 1 Dec. '28; idem to Goslinga, 21 May '29.

of the Allies the part of that memorial which had relation to it. This seemed all the more necessary to the Pensionary, as it would serve to justify in advance any measures which the Hanover Allies might feel obliged to take in the interests of their common safety, and to set at rest the Electors and Princes of the Empire who had already declared for the Allies, or such as were on the point of doing so, they being uneasy on account of the Emperor's despotism and jealous of his relations with the King of Prussia, as well as of his design to transfer his succession, with the Imperial Crown, to a foreign Prince who "pourrait sans miracle la joindre à la couronne de France pour devenir non seulement un second Charles Quint mais un second Charlemagne". [1])

If this were not attended to, it was to be feared that the German Princes, who had been expecting great things from the Congress, would think themselves abandoned by the Allies, and would then return to the Emperor, the more so, as the treaty did not in any way look after the affairs of the Empire and made no provision whatever for the preventing of disturbances which might arise while the treaty lasted, either in East Frisia or in Mecklenburg, or in Juliers and Bergh.

With regard to the succession in these two Duchies, non-provision would be sure to lead to war, and therefore Slingelandt insisted on the insertion of an article by which the Prince of Pfaltz-Sulzbach should possess the Elector's succession until such time as the dispute should have been finally settled according to the Peace of Westphalia. He stood firmly by the insertion of such an article in the provisional treaty, even after France had proposed that the matter should be arranged by a private treaty among the four Electors. [2])

We have seen that on July 20th. the Cardinal had represented those Electors as being willing to enter into a treaty with France, but we also saw that the negotiations had no more than started, and that only with the Elector Palatine. The object of this communication was no other than the keeping of the Maritime Powers from entering into direct relations with these Electors, France desiring to be entirely master of the negotiations with them. To this end, she left no means untried to make those Powers be-

---

[1]) Slingelandt to Hop 5 Aug. '28; Chesterfield to Townshend, 3 Aug. '28, R. O. Hl. 301.
[2]) Slingelandt to Hop, Goslinga and Van Hoey, 19 Sept. '28.

lieve that she was really taking the Electors' interests very seriously to heart.

To begin with, she took advantage of the serious illness of the Elector Palatine in the second half of August. The French Ministers were convinced that, in the event of his death, no dispute would arise as to his succession, but that his brother, the Elector of Treves, would succeed. [1]) Still, on receipt of this news Chauvelin sent for Van Hoey and Horace Walpole. There was *periculum in mora*, he told them; it was to be expected that on his death the King of Prussia would seize the two Duchies, or it was possible that the Emperor would sequestrate them, both of which events would be prejudicial to the Republic. France was willing to furnish a number of troops, to act, if need be, in conjunction with the troops of the Republic and those of England. [2])

The despatch which Van Hoey wrote on this subject caused great uneasiness at the Hague. As regards Slingelandt, he was not angry that this alarm should come at this moment: "Le beau traité" he said to himself, "qui ne prévient pas des troubles capables d'allumer une guerre dans le temps même que l'on négotie" [3]) Apropos of the despatch, a resolution was passed expressing the wish to have the affair of Juliers and Bergh still settled at the Congress. The plenipotentiaries were further empowered by this resolution, to consider precautionary measures with the Allies that, in the event of a vacancy occurring in the succession, the House of Pfalz-Sulzbach should not be troubled (September 9th.). [4])

They did not, however, think it proper to carry out this resolution, chiefly because just then Chauvelin produced the project of a defensive alliance between France, England and the Republic, first with the Electors, and later also with other German Princes, to which a separate article had been added, assuring the succession to the two Duchies to the Elector's two brothers, and after their death, until a judicial decision or an amicable arrangement, to the Prince of Pfaltz-Sulzbach. Chauvelin handed this project to the plenipotentiaries of the Maritime Powers under the strongest injunction of

---

[1]) cf. Rosenlehner, *op. cit.* 393.
[2]) Van Hoey to Slingelandt, 28 Aug. '28, R. A. Hl. 2979.
[3]) Slingelandt to Hop, 9 Sept. '28, R. A. Legatie 84.
[4]) Secr. Res. S. G. 9 Sept. '28.

secrecy; this he declared was necessary, taking into account the constitution of the Republic (September 15th.). [1])

This was merely a pretext, and the whole project, as we shall see later, was a manoeuvre, but Slingelandt, who was ignorant of the secret intentions of the Court of France, could not do otherwise than take this project, just as he had taken the illness of the Elector, as being in earnest. In his opinion, it was a well-devised scheme, and might prove of great use to the Hanover Allies generally, and in particular to the Republic, which would have everything to fear from the Emperor, should he retain, and still further increase, his authority in the Empire, and which was also very uneasy about the extension of the territory of the King of Prussia on her frontiers. The object of the treaty, however, had been set out in such very general terms, and was so vague, that it could not do other than scare such a Government as that of the Republic. Through it she might be involved in matters which would fall under the Treaty of Westphalia, and these were matters in which she had never had any desire of being mixed up. The contracting parties might be considered to be bound to protect the Emperor against any attack, not even excepting an attack by the Turks, and also to interfere in all the domestic affairs of the Empire. The treaty would therefore have to be re-written, and would have to be directed more distinctly against the despotism of the Emperor, and also against the King of Prussia's violence.

Though not entirely approving of the project, still Slingelandt's attitude towards it was very different from what it had been towards a similar one in July. Then he still had hopes of attaining a definitive treaty; now, however, he considered a treaty with the Electors one of the most indispensable precautions for the gaining of reasonable security for the performance of the articles of the provisional treaty, and therefore he considered that the subject matter of this ought to be one of the principal articles of the convention into which he presumed the Allies would enter among themselves. This convention should have three objects: the guaranteeing to each other of the stipulations of the provisional treaty, the renewal and extending of the Hanover Alliance, and

---

[1]) Hop, Goslinga & Van Hoey to Slingelandt, 15 Sept. '28, R. A. Hl. 2985; (enclosed with this is the "Projet de Traité"). A summary of this project except the separate article is to be found in Rosenlehner, *op. cit.* 425—6.

the taking of the necessary steps against the consequences of the close union between Spain and the Emperor. Slingelandt also thought that the treaty with the Electors ought to be kept secret until the end of the Congress. For that reason it was not advisable to bring it before the Provinces, without which it could not be entered into by the Republic; he therefore proposed that it should be concluded by France and England without the Republic, and that she should join it later, as being an ingredient of such a convention of guaranty. [1]

Slingelandt informed Townshend of his opinions on this through Chesterfield, just as some weeks previously he had informed him of his Remarks on the Provisional treaty. Of these Remarks there was not one which found favour in Townshend's eyes. In the Observations which he wrote upon them, they were all rejected, even those of a formal character. Townshend wrote to Chesterfield, that the King had all possible regard for the sentiments prompting so great a Minister, but in his opinion, it was better to leave the project upon the footing on which the Cardinal had put it, because it answered the main objects of the Hanover Alliance. No mention at all of the marriage was made in it, it was true, but the King could not help it. He would fain have brought it forward, but as the Cardinal persisted in the opposite opinion, he thought it to be of no use to insist. He even thought it dangerous to insert an article on this point as proposed by Slingelandt, implying as it did an admission that a union of the Spanish and Austrian monarchies had not been provided against in previous treaties, thus should the proposed article be rejected, as it very probably would be, the Allies would be admitting that, although the Peace of Utrecht and the Quadruple Alliance were confirmed by this provisional treaty, they were not entitled to oppose that union. Later, means might more easily be found, and with less danger, of preventing evil consequences of matters which had not been sufficiently dealt with by this treaty.

The same thing applied to the affairs of the Empire. The King, just as the Pensionary, would have liked, something to have been done in particular to satisfy the German Princes, but he had not

---

[1] Slingelandt to Hop, Goslinga & Van Hoey, 19 Sept. '28, Slingelandt to Goslinga, Dec. '29; Chesterfield to Townshend, 21 Sept. '28, R. O. Hl. 301. With reference to the renewal and extension of the Hanover Alliance, cf. Slingelandt to Hop, 5, 7, 21 Aug., 23 Oct. '28, idem to Goslinga, 7 Aug. '28.

thought it necessary to lay any particular stress upon it. Certainly, a settlement of the Juliers and Bergh matter was most desirable, but it would not serve any useful purpose to continue the Congress, and to jeopardise the fruits of all the labours only because of that intricate question which could be settled much better at a time when the world was more tranquil. [1]

Townshend much applauded its being provided for by a separate treaty with the Electors, which other princes might join. He went so far as not merely to approve, as Slingelandt had done, the idea and the object of the scheme, but even its wording. He wrote to Chesterfield that it could not but be vague and general, as otherwise the Emperor would take offence. Still, however, he had an objection to it, one which, instead of decreasing the distance between him and the Pensionary, made it even greater-out of consideration for the King of Prussia he thought the article referring to Juliers and Bergh too strong, and more harsh and offensive than was necessary. [2]

Quantum mutatus ab illo! Only a few months earlier, he had exhorted Slingelandt to oppose with all his power the schemes of Prussia, and Imperial ambition, which words failed him to characterize, and against which he wanted not only the Republic and the whole of the Empire, but also France and the Scandinavian Powers to take action. Later, in the second half of July, when he already had a leaning towards a provisional treaty, he had still declared that this ought, in any case, to provide for the settlement of the affairs of East Frisia, Juliers and Bergh, Schleswig, and, last but not least, Mecklenburg "qui est une des plus criantes que l'Empereur a entreprise pour exercer un pouvoir despotique".[3] And now we find him agreeing that all the matters of the Empire should be left out of the provisional treaty.

Regarding this treaty as a whole, Townshend had also greatly changed. In the beginning he had himself thrown a strong light upon its drawbacks, while now he was singing its praises; at the same time he satirised the man who was so foolish as still to prefer a definitive treaty. His attitude is apparent from his letter to

---

[1] Townshend to Chesterfield, 6, 13, 20 Aug. '28; in the letter of the last mentioned date is enclosed "Observations on the Remarks upon the General Ideas for forming a Treaty", which document can also be found R. A. Hl. 2985.

[2] Townshend to Chesterfield, 17 Sept. '28, R.O. Hl. 302; Slingelandt to Hop, 7 Oct. '28.

[3] Townshend to Slingelandt, 12 June '28, R. A. Hl. 2994.

Chesterfield of September 6th. o. s., which might be called a verit-
able song, because it sprang from the sheer impulse of the soul and
without the least necessity. Had it remained unwritten, England's
interests would not have been injured at all, and it would have
been better for Towshend's reputation.

What prompted this outburst of feeling was a letter from Chesterfield in which he wrote him that on informing Slingelandt of his
(Townshend's) Observations, he had found him very firm in his
opinion, he still considering that a definitive treaty could have been
obtained if it had been insisted upon, and that his amendments
would be complied with should they be strongly and resolutely
demanded by the Allies. However, added Chesterfield, people in
general do not speculate, as do the Pensionary and the Greffier,
upon future and remote dangers. [1]) This communication caused
Townshend to express himself as follows "The King is glad to see
"that people in Holland did not run into speculations, but rather
"wished, and would be satisfied with, the removal of present and
"pressing inconveniences. Though having all possible deference
"for the Pensionary's opinion, *yet he cannot help thinking that there*
"*is more of name and sound than of substance and reality between*
"*a definitive treaty and a provisional and suspensive one as now*
"*proposed.* By the present scheme all our engagements are
"answered, our interests are secured, the previous treaties are re-
"newed, matters return to the same footing as before the dangerous
"Treaties of Vienna, and peace is certain for a good number of
"years. His Majesty does not apprehend what our vigour and re-
"solution would have procured more for our own particular inter-
"ests, and *to have been positive and risked the breaking-up the*
"*Congress because we could not model the scheme of Europe in*
"*every particular according to our taste* would have been in His
"Majesty's way of thinking an unseasonable and unjustifiable
"stiffness, and I fear it would have been much resented here even
"by the best intentioned, had His Majesty continued the present
"expense the nation is at and even ventured a war for the sake
"of coming to a definitive treaty and *nicely adjusting the balance*
"*of Europe according to the most refined notions,* besides His Maj-
"esty plainly saw how faintly his possessions and the rights of his
"subjects would have been supported, if he had tried that danger-

[1]) Chesterfield to Townshend, 3 Sept. '28, R. O. Hl. 301.

"ous experiment. These are His Majesty's thoughts which I
"send you only for your own information, *leaving both the Pension-*
"*ary and the Greffier to enjoy their opinions*". [1])

The last words are all the more remarkable as they are found
not in Townshend's letter itself, but in the draft of it in which
they have been erased. To this erasure of Townshend's a similar
one of Slingelandt's may be opposed. Some weeks later, the latter
wrote to Hop that Townshend, in his Observations, had rejected
all his Remarks for reasons "qui m'ont parues peu dignes d'un
ministre de la capacité de Milord Townshend," but the draft re-
veals something else: "qui m'ont parues *plus tôt d'un commis que
d'un ministre.*" [2])

Here we see two opinions opposing each other — Townshend's,
who thought that Slingelandt and Fagel, however greatly gifted
they might be, did not take realities into consideration, and were
visionary as opposed to practical statesmen: and Slingelandt's, who
considered that Townshend, though not lacking in powers, had
but the eye of a clerk which saw no further than the immediate
future instead of the broad, far-seeing eye of the statesman.

Which was right — the common-sense Townshend or the
thorough Slingelandt? The course of events will show us that
the latter was. For the time being, however, the Pensionary did
not meet with any success, and with the French as little as with
the English. The result was far short of his expectations, though
these had not been over-great; for, as he wrote Hop, he supposed
that the Cardinal would think his Remarks embodied more than
one point which he would be unable to obtain from Sinzendorff, yet to Slingelandt's mind there was none amongst them
which was not most necessary with a view to having a reasonable certainty; moreover, Sinzendorff must not think that, because he had gained the great point of clearing a definitive treaty
out of the way, he could slight the Hanover Allies to the extent of
prescribing them the terms of a provisional one in addition. [3])
Notwithstanding such representations, Slingelandt's Remarks
were practically all declined, both in private conversations with
Fleury and in further discussions upon the project. The safety of

---

[1]) Townshend to Chesterfield, 6 Sept. '28 (draft), R. O. Hl. 301.
[2]) Slingelandt to Hop, 7 Oct. '28 draft, R. A. Hl. 2974, original letter, R. A. Legatie 84.
[3]) Slingelandt to Hop, 21 Aug. '28.

the Allies and the tranquillity of Europe — so he was answered —
could be provided for in separate treaties. A renewal and extension of the Hanover Alliance was utterly rejected, as it might
displease the Austrians; [1]) and England and France, instead of
displeasing, wished to please them. This has the closest relation
with the conduct of Spain.

Queen Elizabeth's disposition was by no means such as these
powers wished it to be. They had held out to her hopes of Spain's
recovering the Italian countries which had formerly belonged to
the Monarchy, with the express purpose of embroiling her with
the Emperor, but she prescribed her plenipotentiaries to show
indifference to their schemes. [2]) She still had her heart set on the
marriage of Don Carlos and Maria Theresa. To gain this end she
now ordered her plenipotentiaries to insinuate to their English
colleagues, as they had previously done to the Cardinal, that,
should this point be facilitated on their part, the others should
be made easy on the part of Spain. [3]) No wonder that, being so
minded, she did not relish the provisional treaty much. The fact
that it implicitly confirmed the surrender of Gibraltar, and that
it transferred the discussion of commercial differences from the
Congress to Commissaries was of small account to her, but what
was most material to her was that the project, far from advancing
the marriage, suspended it, and did not even stipulate the introduction of Spanish garrisons, a proper preliminary towards that
end, in the eyes of Elizabeth.

Thus her answer (of Sept. 6th.) was tantamount to a refusal.
The project, such as it was, was in no wise admissible, but the
Court of Spain was willing to regard it as the rudiments of negotations which, by further demands and explanations, might be
brought to perfection. These demands and explanations were not
mentioned, except that the whole of the pending points should
not be referred to Commissaries, but that a great many of them
were still to be decided by the Congress, and in particular that
regarding the introduction of Spanish garrisons into Parma
and Tuscany. An ultimate decision would not be taken until

---

[1]) Hop to Slingelandt, 10 Sept. '28; cf id. to id., 14 Aug. '28, R. A. Hl. 2982.

[2]) Baudrillart, *op. cit.* III, 439.

[3]) Slingelandt to Hop, 7, 23 Oct. '28; cf. Baudrillart, *op. cit.* III, 480—1, and Hop to
Slingelandt, 19 Sept. '28, R. A. Hl. 2982.

Bournonville had been consulted, and he, for this purpose, was recalled to Madrid. [1])

Vastly different from the answer of Spain was that of her Ally, the Emperor. The idea of a provisional treaty was, of course, fully to his liking, to the realisation of which in this project he, however, raised several objections. As to the suppression of the Ostend Company, a limit of seven years from the conclusion of the new treaty was the farthest he was prepared to go. The article concerning the new Southern Netherlands Tariff had to be so formulated that the deliberations of the Commissaries could in no event exceed the term of two years, meaning that after the expiry of this term the Emperor would be free to settle it as he wished. By the omission of the clause "chacun pour autant que cela les regarde," he wished to make the Republic accede to the Quadruple Alliance indirectly in order to have more security against the introduction of Spanish garrisons. In addition, he asked permission to send an aviso to India to bring the Ostend Company's servants to Europe. [2])

Though most prejudicial to the Republic, the Emperor's answer was, on the whole, favourable, whereas that of Spain was most unfavourable. The French and English ministers considered that for the present nothing could be expected from Spain unless the marriage were brought before the Congress. As this was the last thing in the world they thought of — the English even avoiding [3]) giving the Spaniards an opportunity of explaining their insinuations — nothing remained but to take advantage of the good disposition of the Court of Vienna, and the even better disposition of Sinzendorff. A considerable point would have been gained if the Emperor could be brought to the signing of the provisional treaty without Spain. This might cause a coolness between them by which the Allies could profit. [4])

With this object in view the French and English ministers met

[1]) Baudrillart, *op. cit.* III, 444—6.

[2]) Hop and Goslinga to Slingelandt, 24 Sept. '28, with which is enclosed the "Remarques de l'Empereur", R. A. Hl. 2935; Höfler, *Der Congress von Soissons, Fontes Rerum Austriacarum*, Vol. XXXII, 69.

Huisman (*op. cit.* 441) is mistaken in ascribing the proposal concerning the aviso to the Cardinal.

[3]) of the references under note 3, p. 292.

[4]) Baudrillart, *op. cit.* III, 447—8; Townshend to Chesterfield, 24 Sept. '28, R. O. Hl. 302.

the Emperor's wishes as far as possible. This could not but be at the expense of the Republic. Not only that they declined practically all Slingelandt's Remarks, but they even went far towards granting the Emperor the modifications he demanded, e.g., "chacun" — etc., was left out. [1]) In connection with the Ostend affair, however, they did not entirely sacrifice the Republic. They insisted upon at least seven years after the expiry of the term settled by the Preliminaries. This Sinzendorff could not admit. Simultaneously, however, he expressed his regret at having so little scope, and undertook to write for new instructions. [2]) Thus, with his help, they hoped to get the better of this difficulty.

With his help, too, they hoped to induce the Court of Vienna to give her signature separately. After deliberating with Horace Walpole, the Cardinal, towards the end of September, proposed a project according to which both the Emperor and the Allies would accept, even though Spain should reject, the project of a provisional treaty such as had now been modified, and with the exception of Articles 7 and 8, which related to Spain. Pending this Power's ultimate decision, the Congress should continue, without, however, doing anything. [3])

The Cardinal met with success. Sinzendorff, it is true, declined this new project *qualitate qua*, but privately he approved of it, and promised to recommend it to his Court. [4])

It was, of course, kept from the Spanish plenipotentiaries. With them the negotiations concerning the provisional treaty were continued, and in particular the 7th. Article, which dealt with Anglo-Spanish relations. A formulation was eventually found, which satisfied the English plenipotentiaries, and which those of Spain hoped would satisfy their Court. [5]) Yet it was not on this Article that the expectations of France and England were built. No, these were built, on the one hand, on the new project, virtually an effort to embroil the Emperor and Spain in an indirect way, and on the other, on a new effort to embroil them in a direct way. When Bournonville, as late as October 20th., left

---

[1]) Höfler, *op. cit.* XXXII, 36, 112, 126, 244, 289, 338—9.
[2]) Hop & Goslinga to Slingelandt, 24 Sept. '28, R. A. Hl. 2985.
[3]) Baudrillart, *op. cit.* III, 448; Projet d'un traité entre l'Empereur, la France, la Grande Bretagne et la République à l'exclusion de l'Espagne, R. A. Hl. 2985.
[4]) Hop & Goslinga to Slingelandt, 26 Sept. '28, R. A. Hl. 2985; Syveton, *op. cit.* 263—4.
[5]) Townshend to Chesterfield, 15 Oct. '28, R. O. Hl. 302.

for Madrid, the Cardinal entrusted him with an Article in which France and England declared themselves willing to co-operate with Spain towards procuring more security for Don Carlos concerning the Italian countries appointed to him, and even to consent to the introduction of Spanish garrisons. [1])

II.

During the negotiations carried on in Paris in the course of September, France and England had been in the closest harmony with each other. Under these conditions the Republic had been unable to exert any influence. She had even been so much neglected that Sinzendorff had been informed of the new project before her plenipotentiaries. It is thus not surprising that when Slingelandt set himself to send instructions to these ministers — instructions upon both this project and upon the Emperor's remarks concerning the previous one — he asked himself why he should tire both head and hand over a subject upon which France and England — from whom the weak Republic could not sever herself without ruin — had visibly made their decision. So long as England agreed that the evil should be struck at its roots, he had had hopes of making the Cardinal depart, if not from a provisional treaty, then at least from this project, which was rightly called "idées générales." But he gave up his hopes now he saw that England, after having apparently obtained the promise of Fleury's support in her differences with Spain and in the affair of Mecklenburg, had entirely submitted to France concerning the provisional treaty, had not cared about the Republic further than her own interests necessitated, [2]) and had even so far removed themselves from his plan that her plenipotentiaries avoided giving their Spanish colleagues an opportunity of explaining their insinuations. Yes, now he even despaired of obtaining the slightest essential alteration or addition either in the project of a provisional treaty or in the new one.

In spite of that, Slingelandt's opinion was that the Republic ought not to give way to her Allies immediately, and without

---

[1]) Baudrillart, *op. cit.* III, 452—3; Chauvelin to La Baune, 21 Oct. '28, A. E. Hl. 375.
[2]) cf. Slingelandt to Hop, 3 Sept. '28; La Baune to Chauvelin, 24 Oct. '28, A. E. Hl. 375.

comment. With regard to Spain, the proposed step was very hard, for, once the new project was concluded with her Ally, she would have no choice other than acceptance or rejection without explanation. Now, should the Republic join her Allies in this, she would chagrin Spain unnecessarily, as it was highly probable that the Emperor would reject it. The difficulties made by the latter in connection with the points in the provisional treaty which affected his relations with the Republic even suggested his being in collusion with Spain. But even though this thought was suppressed, both those difficulties and the refusal, which, according to Slingelandt's tidings, Sinzendorff had accorded the new project, made it only too likely that the Emperor would reject it, and use this rejection to ingratiate himself with the Queen of Spain; and even should he agree to it, the Republic would run great risks, as the project left further steps in a state of absolute uncertainty. Whereas by the non-carrying out of Articles 7 and 8 the trade of the Maritime Powers was certain to be ruined, there was nothing in it to prevent the Emperor's supporting Spain in case of war, nor, on the other hand, was there anything to make Spain accede to it within a definite time.

The English Court to which these remarks of Slingelandt's were communicated by no means agreed with them. Such a clause would make a show of vigour and cause much empty clamour without being of any real use; while as to the Pensionary's opinion that the Emperor might support Spain even after signing, "such apprehensions seem to be founded more upon refined speculation than upon any reality." [1]) There, as at the Court of France, it was thought that the Emperor's acceptance would bring about a breach between Spain and himself. But Slingelandt thought differently. Although she seemed to be dissatisfied with the Emperor, yet Elizabeth had sons whose fortune she must make, while the Emperor had only great appanages and still greater expectations to endow his daughters with. She was certain to sacrifice her anger to her hopes of such a marriage! Such a powerful bait was more than sufficient to keep her in unity with the Emperor. Relying on this his advantage, the latter could safely sign the project, as the Hanover Allies had no equivalent to offer. These latter would, therefore, vainly flatter themselves that they would in

---

[1]) Townshend to Chesterfield, 11 Oct. '28, R. O. Hl. 302.

that case have one enemy less. The Emperor would, no doubt, find a means to pacify Elizabeth as soon as her first anger was past, and they would, in Slingelandt's opinion, join hands in ruining the trade and manufactures of the Hanover Allies (which would be as injurious to the latter as a war, if not more so) also after the conclusion of the provisional treaty, and whether Spain agreed or not.

Thus the acceptance of the project by the Emperor would be by no means to the advantage of the Allies. In one case, however, it might be; then it might even serve to bring the Congress back to its true object. The dissatisfaction or ill humour of Spain could not but be increased by it. The Allies might profit by this disposition of Spain's, and by her plenipotentiaries' desire to bring before the Congress subjects which the Emperor, in concert with France, kept as remote from it as he could, in order to compel these two powers either to consent to these subjects being dealt with and to the Spanish plenipotentiaries demonstrating in detail their grievances against English trade with America, and the damage they suffered from the Assiento Treaty, or at least to try and prevent this by a provisional treaty which should be nearer the principal object of the Congress than the existing project.

Both with a view to this possibility, a possibility heightened by Bournonville's journey, and on account of the danger to which the Republic exposed herself by proceeding rashly, Slingelandt thought it better that she should assume an attitude of expectation. She could all the better do so since Sinzendorff had been informed of the new project before even her own plenipotentiaries were. She could, therefore, decently await the Emperor's opinion before expressing hers upon it. Meantime she might bring to the fore her remarks upon the Paris discussions concerning the project of a provisional treaty.

To this end the Resolution of Oct. 23rd. was passed. By this the plenipotentiaries were empowered to lend themselves to a provisional treaty. In case of necessity they were permitted to admit the Republic's accession to the Quadruple Alliance, but not her being involved in the affairs of the North. The States were unwilling to put up with a term of seven years from the date of signing the provisional treaty, but insisted upon a further twelve or fifteen years. Should this be settled to their satisfaction, they would not object to the sending of an aviso.

The resolution was kept general. The plenipotentiaries could make such use of it as they thought proper; they could make remarks or depart from them as circumstances and the service of the State should require. This has relation to the uncertain state of affairs, in connection with which Slingelandt contemplated, in addition, the bringing forward of remarks on the new project once it should be brought to the deliberation of the States. This, it is true, ought to be done in a modest way, as the Republic had to avoid chagrining France and England. Still, these powers could not take amiss such conduct in her, for the step they planned with regard to Spain was so bold and extraordinary that it would not suit the Republic to have any save a reluctant part in it; while, in Slingelandt's opinion, the possibility that they might take an even more extraordinary step, viz., signing both projects with the Emperor and without both the Republic and Spain, was not to be feared. He could not imagine that France would be willing, and England daring enough to do so, and at the worst — so he asked himself — would the Republic lose much by it? She would certainly be allowed to accede still, she would offend Spain less, and "pour le fonds il serait ni plus ni moins." After all, the English would not lose common interests in the Ostend affair and in that of the tariff, and, though the Cardinal had frequently declared that, so far as it affected the Republic, he made the affair of East Frisia his, the Austrians had complicated it to such an extent that the Republic was unlikely to come out of it with other than generalities, or rather with a "pur verbiage."

So, at the risk of the treaty being concluded without the concurrence of the Republic, Slingelandt wished to await the course of events. The interests of the Republic did not prevent his doing so; on the contrary, he considered that nothing was pressing until it was known what might be expected from the Emperor regarding the suspensory term and the East Frisian affair. [1])

---

[1]) Slingelandt to Hop, 7, 23 Oct., 6 Nov. '28; with the first of these is enclosed Slingelandt's "Observations sur les idées générales sur la formation d'un traité provisionel et sur les remarques de l'Empereur" together with his "Observations sur le projet pour la signature du traité provisionel sans l'Espagne"; Secr. Res. S. G. 23 Oct. '28; Chesterfield to Townshend, 1, 15 Oct. '28, R O. Hl. 302.

This affair was still far from being in order, although the pressure exerted in July on the Court of Vienna by all the Hanover Allies, and particularly by France, had not entirely failed in effect. The Court had at last, on Sept. 13th., issued a new decree which gave the Renitents full amnesty provided they submitted unconditionally. They had to do so within a term of four weeks — this to be settled by the Sub-delegates. This decree was more favourable to them than any of the preceding ones, yet they wanted more. The restrictions upon the amnesty were of such a nature as to make it quite uncertain. Not only were two of their leaders excluded by name, but so were also all in general who had committed manslaugther, which might apply to any one who had been involved in the fighting. In addition, the sequestration of the Embden Seigniories was maintained, as was the obligation of the Renitents to indemnify all obedient subjects for the losses they had suffered during the disturbances, which would perhaps be so extended that all their possessions would not be sufficient to make good the others' losses. Finally, there was no indication whatever as to the base on which the constitution of the country would, for the future, be conducted. It is palpable that the Renitents could not submit on so uncertain a footing, and no less so that the States-General to whom they again applied, could not in honour advise them to submit unconditionally. They could do so the less, as the Emperor had not given them the necessary security as to the capital invested by their subjects in the East Frisian States nor with regard to their garrisons. They, therefore, on October 14th., resolved to ask for a more detailed explanation of the decree. Slingelandt did not expect much from this application. To him it was evident that the Emperor would impose upon the Republic with regard to the garrisons also. He, therefore, considered it desirable to make known to the Allies, who had been requested to support the application with the Emperor, that the Republic objected to signing the provisional treaty failing a more explicit and authentic declaration on his part. [1]

It was not only with respect to affairs in East Frisia that Slingelandt desired to safeguard the Republic as far as was possible

---

[1] Wiarda, *op. cit.* VII, 412—22; Rousset, *Recueil* IV, 509, V. 279 et seq.; Res. S. G. 14 Oct. '28; Slingelandt to Hop, 23 Oct. '28.

against an uncertain future. He also wished the Allies before signing the provisional treaty without the concurrence of Spain —
a power which could injure them more than any other — to
consider among themselves some expedient for remedying this
inconvenience and finishing with her to their mutual advantage. [1]) He also again urged the conclusion of a convention of
guaranty. In his opinion, the fact that Sinzendorff knew that the
Hanover Allies were taking precautions against becoming dupes
to a provisional treaty was no great obstacle. Should the Emper-
or's intentions be good, this could not arouse his suspicions;
otherwise, it would be all the more necessary, and in particular for
the Republic. [2])

The Pensionary's conduct was by no means accommodating,
but it did not prove to be imprudent, for, as he had thought
probable, the Emperor did not fall in with Sinzendorff: on the
contrary, he disowned him. The new project aspired to the breaking of his union with Spain, whereas his object was to keep
his hold on her. Besides, no compensation was offered for the extension of the suspension exacted from him. He therefore chose
to recall Sinzendorff and to remain loyal to Spain. [3])

The new project had miscarried, and so the hopes of France
and England of bringing about in this way a breach between
Spain and the Emperor vanished; and not only that, but the
success of the provisional treaty now became most precarious.

III.

When, at the beginning of November, the Court of France was
informed of the Emperor's decision, it at once developed great
activity. The situation was serious, as it was extremely probable
that, since the provisional treaty was on the point of miscarrying
through the Emperor's keeping to Spain, England would urge the
taking of vigorous measures without delay. Within a few months
Parliament was due to meet, and what would be in store for the
Government if things then were still unsettled? It was certain
that they would press the Allies to enforce a decision one way or

---

[1]) "Observations sur le projet pour la signature du traité provisionel sans l'Espagne",
cf. note p. 298.
[2]) Slingelandt to Hop, 23 Oct. '28.
[3]) cf. Syveton, op. cit. 264.

the other within that time. This was not to the liking of France, which power was opposed to war generally, and had, in addition, a particular reason against being in favour of vigorous measures: the galleons must first arrive. Now, had France wished the resignation of the English cabinet, she would have refused any vigorous measures and, for the rest, have left things in their unsettled state. However, she considered the present Cabinet to be bail for the union between the two countries. Should it be overturned its successor might unite with the Emperor by guaranteeing the Pragmatic Sanction, and with Spain by promising support with regard to the marriage, both of which contravened French politics Without proceeding to vigorous measures, France, nevertheless, desired to save the English cabinet. Thus no other course was left than to endeavour to still avert the miscarriage of the provisional treaty. [1])

It would now be utterly impossible to bring about an agreement between Spain and England, but perhaps, now Sinzendorff was still in Paris, something could be done between the Emperor and the Republic. This, of course, would have to be in connection with the Ostend affair. It was true that even though the parties concerned should agree, Sinzendorff would not sign, for his Court was unwilling to do anything without the concurrence of Spain. There was, however, a middle course. He might declare that the Emperor would content himself with a certain equivalent to be decided upon when the general treaty was signed and that in the interval he would stand by the inaction of the suspension. In that case he would at least have accomplished something, without, however, severing his master from Spain. The Dutch, for their part, would not lightly permit themselves to be dragged along by England once their own interests were provided for, which, moreover, would force England to depart from vigorous measures and make her more amenable with regard to Spain. [2])

This scheme, which was promising on all sides, was favourably received by Sinzendorff. He was prepared to finish the Ostend affair in this way, provided one ship annually be allowed to sail from Ostend to India, and to return to one of the Adriatic ports,

---

[1]) Baudrillart, *op. cit.* III, 480—1; Chauvelin to La Baune, 30 Dec. '28, A. E. Hl. 375; Hop to Slingelandt, 10 Nov., 3 Dec. '28, R. A. Hl. 2982.
[2]) Chauvelin, Memorial of 10 Nov. '28, A. E. Hl. 375.

say Trieste. Should this idea be agreed to, he would no longer insist upon a stronger article regarding the tariff, and the affair of East Frisia should be settled to the satisfaction of the Republic. [1])

This power had now to be gained. Up to this time France had never seriously tried to bring her to an agreement in the Ostend affair. [2]) Now, however, a real effort was made. This was kept from England, for, when Chauvelin informed the Dutch plenipotentiaries of the proposals settled in the conferences the Cardinal and he had held with Sinzendorff, he begged them to impress upon Slingelandt that he should not, for the time being, convey any news of them to Chesterfield. [3]) He was apparently convinced that England would like to proceed along other lines.

Chauvelin had a good idea of the state of the English Government, which was, indeed, most uneasy. Strong complaints were already heard concerning the uncertainty of peace or war. [4]) Under these circumstances they thought that nothing but a vigorous resolution on the part of the Allies would do. This alone would serve to hold back the Emperor from Elizabeth's wild ideas. A right spirit on their part would justify Sinzendorff's conduct, and would, perhaps, together with his representations, be successful in bringing the Emperor back to the disposition in which he was when he sent him (Sinzendorff) to France. Whether the King of Spain would, in conjunction with the Emperor, still accept the provisional treaty as it had recently been settled in Paris, remained to be seen. If not, the Allies ought to define a time-limit — say two months — for doing so, declaring at the same time that, after its expiry, they should themselves do justice. The English plenipotentiaries submitted this to the Cardinal, as did Chesterfield to the Pensionary. [5])

Had the latter been a vain man, the course of events would have given him more than one cause for satisfaction. He had expected the ill-success of the new project. He had foretold the obstacles which would attend the bringing-about of a provisional treaty, but, in spite of his frequent and solemn warnings, France and England had moved in that direction. They had acted

---

[1]) Hop & Goslinga to Fagel, 10 Nov. '28, to Slingelandt, 10, 11 Nov. '28, R.A. Hl. 2985.
[2]) cf. Chauvelin to La Baune, 7 Oct. '28, A. E. Hl. 375.
[3]) Hop & Goslinga to Slingelandt, 10 Nov. '28, R. A. Hl. 2985.
[4]) Villars, *Mémoires* V, 155—7.
[5]) Townshend to Chesterfield, 5 Nov. '28, R. O. Hl. 302; King, *Notes* 68 et seq.

in the closest harmony without taking any notice of his Remarks, and now that the success of the provisional treaty was precarious, their harmony was wavering, and each was obliged to appeal to Slingelandt, in this way making him the umpire of their decision. The conduct of England in particular might have given him cause for self-satisfaction. The desertion of his system and the abandonment of herself to France had so far done England no good, and whereas she had, only a few weeks previously, entirely rejected his remark that the new project ought to have contained a compulsive clause concerning Spain, she herself now urged the making of a vigorous declaration.

But, far from making any comments on what had passed, Slingelandt agreed with Chesterfield, when the latter informed him of the orders of his Court, that should Elizabeth, after the arrival of Bournonville, still make unreasonable and frivolous objections, the Hanover Allies ought to come to a vigorous resolution to intimidate, since they could not persuade. But in his opinion such a resolution could not be made speedily. Not only that it would be difficult to bring France to it, but Spain would not be in a hurry to cause the return of the galleons, for, by keeping them where they were, she would prevent the Emperor's leaving her in the lurch, and France's doing her any harm. Slingelandt did not agree with Chauvelin that the arrival of the galleons ought to be awaited before any vigorous resolutions were made, for if the Allies did so the Emperor and Spain would be in a better position to resist them.

As this reasoning did not satisfy Chesterfield he asked the Pensionary point-blank whether, should England and France resolve to restrict the Vienna Allies to a time-limit, the Republic would concur with them. "Not without some difficulty", was the answer. As Chesterfield very well knew, the provisional treaty had never been relished much in the Republic, so he questioned whether they would come to such a declaration in favour of it. In his opinion the answer to be returned by Spain would not be an absolute refusal, but she would probably offer to negotiate at the Congress on the base of the Preliminaries, a course which many in the Republic would prefer to the acceptance of the provisional treaty.

Not yet satisfied, Chesterfield pressed him further. Slingelandt then told him that, should the Republic be convinced that France

would act strongly in conjunction with England, she would certainly enter into the measures thought necessary by them both. [1]

So, though desiring of the Allies a strong attitude, the Pensionary did not want the Republic to run the risk of being involved
in a war because of the provisional treaty unless he were as
sure of France as of England. As this was not to be expected, the
reply was, under the prevailing conditions, tantamount to a
refusal.

Though not following England in her vehemence, Slingelandt,
on the other hand, was not minded to separate from her in any way.
One of the principal objections which he raised against the proposal coming from France was that it was incompatible with the
Republic's obligations, and also imprudent to act in the Ostend
affair without the knowledge of England. For the rest it was, in
his opinion, out of season to yield so much to the Emperor before
the effect of Bournonville's journey should be known and also in
how far Spain might be displeased with him (the Emperor). Nor
was it advisable to say one's final word to a Minister who was on
the point of leaving, and who would be pleased to effect something,
while perhaps being unable to make good what he might promise.

To these general objections the Pensionary added special ones.
The proposal to send a ship from Ostend to India, and which
should return to an Adriatic Port, there to have its cargo un-
loaded and sold, was so strange that it proved sufficiently the
design to have some pretext, of any kind whatever, of plying
between Ostend and India. In this way the Company would be continued and its navigation legalized for good. It was true that this
navigation would be put under restraint, but this, it might safely
be expected, the Company would evade in a hundred ways, and this
single ship would become an incessant source of complaint and
dispute, just like the Assiento ship granted by Spain to England.
This would be all the worse because, as Slingelandt foresaw, the
Republic would be little disposed to maintain her rights with vigour. To be sure, she had good guarantors, but rather than appeal to them, she would, just as she had done previous to her accession to the Treaty of Hanover, tie the hands of her East India
Company for fear of incurring a war. "Il faut peu connaître la fai-
blesse de notre gouvernement pour ne point convenir de tout

---

[1] Chesterfield to Townshend, 23 Nov. '23, R. O. Hl. 302.

cela". Therefore nothing would give the Republic the security she wanted save a suspension of long duration or a total suppression without reserve. To facilitate this, Slingelandt thought that the Republic would not be disinclined to reduce the subsidy or the interest which the Southern Netherlands annually owed her. Could the Ostend affair be settled in this way, Slingelandt would be delighted, but it could not take place in the way schemed in Paris. The Deputies for Foreign Affairs to whom only the affair was broken agreed with him, and so the proposal was declined. [1])

Thus France was unsuccessful in bringing about an agreement between the Emperor and the States. England, on the other hand, as we saw, did not succeed in bringing the States to a vigorous declaration. This conduct of theirs induced her to give up her project for the time being. If we are to believe her, she had a different reason for doing so — she averred that it was done on account of Fleury's representations which were that since Elizabeth was by no means satisfied with the Emperor's conduct it would be inadvisable to define a time-limit, which could not but irritate her and drive her closer to the Emperor, and of his assurance that he should bring things to more definitiveness before Parliament met. [2]) However, it is questionable whether England would have followed France so readilly, had the Republic been imprudent enough to follow England.

The efforts of both France and England to emerge into certainty having failed, the uncertainty remained. The provisional treaty was still on the carpet but its success remained equally precarious. From Vienna nothing reliable could be expected until Sinzendorff's arrival there, and from Spain no news arrived, but only bad omens.

Now that circumstances did not change, the policies followed by France and England did not change either. As to the former, she tried to keep the friendship of the Court of Vienna as far as possible. She hoped that the negotiations with Sinzendorff would sooner or later bear fruit. [3]) The Cardinal, in order to maintain the ascendancy he had gained over him, entered into correspondence

---

[1]) Slingelandt, Memorial of 15 Nov. '28, Slingelandt to Hop, 1 Dec. '28; Secr. Res. S. G. 17 Nov. '28.

[2]) Townshend to Chesterfield, 26 Nov. '28, R. O. Hl. 302.

[3]) Chauvelin to La Baune, 30 Dec. '28, A. E. Hl. 375.

with him after his departure. When, on Nov. 29th., Sinzendorff took leave of him, the Cardinal again recommended to him the proposal which had been rejected by the Republic: he no doubt made sure that he would eventually bring this Power to it. He continued exhorting her to be accommodating towards the Emperor, and prejudicing her against England's vehemence. This latter power, although having for the present relinquished the taking of vigorous measures, still continued to consider them, and would be glad to win the Republic over to her views.

The dispositions of France and England were, now that inactivity in general affairs had come, destined to show themselves in connection with the affairs of the Empire.

IV.

When Chesterfield informed Slingelandt of the King's resolution to delay making a vigorous declaration, the latter believed that while this might be very proper, yet eventually the Allies would have to come to it. The state of uncertainty was anything but to his liking. He looked for a way out. The Cardinal, we saw, thought that within a short time the Queen of Spain would break with the Emperor, but Slingelandt deemed this excluded, as by his late declaration that he should do nothing without Spain's concurrence, and by his disavowal of Sinzendorff, the Emperor had proved himself to be as closely united to her as ever. His conduct made her mistress of the situation: "Le Congrès de Soissons ou plus tôt le sort de l'Europe" — Slingelandt let fall in a letter to Goslinga, but the next moment deleted — "dépendra-t-il toujours des caprices d'un Roi imbécile et d'une Reine emportée et ambitieuse?." [1]) With her nothing could now be achieved by fair means. She would be most difficult to negotiate on the base of the Preliminaries only, and in no case depart from those claims which England would never agree to. The way out was thus not in the direction of Madrid; perhaps it would lie in that of Vienna. Thither had the Allies to turn all their efforts. They should concert to make a joint vigorous declaration to the Emperor. Could France, upon whose backwardness both he and Spain had all

---

[1]) 6 Jany '29, draft, R. A. Hl. 2974.

along counted, be brought to join vigorously in these measures, he would most probably be brought to reason.

On hearing these observations, Chesterfield remarked that Slingelandt attached too much importance to Spain's differences with England. They were not the real cause of the present difficulties, but rather the public pretences of which Elizabeth availed herself towards the Spaniards, whereas in reality she sacrificed that nation's interests to her own ends. Slingelandt here interrupted him. His reasoning, he said, would have been true some time previously, but the Queen had made use of these pretences so often, and the Spanish nation and even the King were so thoroughly convinced that they were to obtain satisfaction, that they had now become real obstacles which the Queen would never dare to ignore. If not to Slingelandt himself, then to Townshend at least did Chesterfield confess that he thought there was weight in this argument.

In addition he asked the Pensionary how far the Republic — so afraid of war — would join in a declaration to the Emperor on the lines he proposed. Slingelandt answered that he could not broach that point all at once: he wanted time to prepare the States who were always so cautious — often too much so. However, that same caution would carry them along with France and England, who alone could protect them, but they would require assurances on two points, viz., that France would act with frankness and vigour, and also the true intentions of England with regard to Spain, for here some jealousy of their being carried too far existed. [1]

Slingelandt perhaps came to his proposal of a joint declaration to the Emperor all the sooner because the latter had, in various ways, aroused the discontent of the Republic. "Si la Cour de Vienne"—thus the Pensionary exclaimed about this time—"avait formé le dessein de prévenir contre elle toute a terre, pourrait-elle s'y prendre autrement?" [2]) Her attitude in the Ostend affair and concerning the Southern Netherlands Tariff, as well as her connivance with the Ostend Company in its efforts to evade suspension were distasteful to the Republic. [3]) And so, more than all, was her conduct in relation to the affairs of East Frisia.

In virtue of the resolution of Oct. 14th., representations had

---

[1]) Chesterfield to Townshend, 14, 21 Dec. '28, R. O. Hl. 302.
[2]) Slingelandt to Goslinga, 31 Dec. '28.
[3]) Chesterfield to Townshend, 23 Nov. '28, R. O. Hl. 302.

been made to her concerning the absolutely unsatisfactory decree of Sept. 13th., but she had not as yet returned any answer. The situation became all the more serious, since the Sub-delegates were, in the meanwhile, making use of this decree to issue a time-limit which should expire as early as Dec. 29th., and before which date the Renitents must submit. The Renitents, most uneasy since they did not care to submit on so uncertain a footing, again applied to the States-General, who applied in their turn to the Allies. In the first place, so the representation ran, the time-limit must be extended. Should this be done, the States-General would be prepared to recommend the Renitents to submit unconditionally, provided that simultaneously a declaration was made to Fonseca by France, England, and the Republic, to the effect that the submission of the Renitents be understood in the sense that it did not entail the foregoing of their rights: that the Prince conduct no troops into Embden: that, as a result of the amnesty, the penal decrees be annulled, and that the Renitents be not bound to indemnify obedient subjects. Should one of these four points be encroached upon the Renitents would be maintained by the three Powers at the Prince's expense (Resolution of Dec. 2nd.). [1]

This application was most unwelcome to the Court of France. Under existing conditions she desired to spare the Emperor as much as possible. She gave very strong oral assurances, it is true, but at first she was not prepared to go farther than this. The Dutch plenipotentiaires, however, were so urgent that on Dec. 7th. Chauvelin gave them a written declaration. [2] This was far from satisfactory, for, as was said at the Hague, he had whittled down their four propositions to nothing. The declaration was so vague and equivocal that the States General, taking it as a base, could not urge the Renitents to submit nor promise them the guaranty of the Republic and her Allies in case their submission were taken advantage of. However strong the oral assurances might be, they failed to make any impression as a result of this declaration, which far more disquieted the States General than set them at ease. It made, for example, no mention of the accords, but, as Slingelandt expressed it, "Sans les accords, adieu à la gar-

---

[1] Res. S. G. 29 Nov., 2 Dec. '28.
[2] Chauvelin to Fénelon, 5, 8, 16 Dec. '28, A. E. Hl. 375; Hop, Goslinga & Van Hoey to Slingelandt, 8 Dec. '28, R. A. Hl. 2985.

nison d'Embden." The garrison served to secure the Magistrate
of this town the execution of the accords against the enterprises
of the Prince; but if they should now be deprived of the accords
and made more dependent on the Prince than was conformable to
them, what use would the garrison be to the Magistrate? Only in
case the East Frisian constitution were maintained more or less
on the old base, and the Renitents assured of life and property,
could the Republic have any security for her garrisons and
financial interests. [1])

The States resolved to ask for a more explicit declaration (Dec.
13th.). This was anything but relished at the Court of France. At
first Chauvelin flatly refused, as did Fleury. The latter, however,
thought better of it when the English plenipotentiaries pressed
him in favour of the States. It was to their efforts that the Dutch
plenipotentiaries ascribed Chauvelin's making a second and more
satisfactory declaration, though under the strictest injunction
of secrecy (Dec. 21st.). They were right, but right in a sense
totally different from what they thought. It was not for the sake of
England that Chauvelin proceeded to this step, but only to deprive this power of a weapon to counteract the influence of France
with the Republic. He even went so far in his suspicions against
England that he imputed the vehemence of the Dutch in this
respect to her suggestion.[2]) This was absolutely untrue, though it
was undeniable that at the moment the English were displaying
extraordinary zeal with regard to East Frisia. [3]) They did so, not
only so that the Republic should go hand in hand with them in
European affairs generally, but also for a particular reason — the
Mecklenburg affair.

As we remember, George II. had, the previous Summer, had
good hopes of coming favourably out of this affair by means of
France's intercession with the Emperor. These hopes had, however, not been realised, and he now became afraid that his troops
would be attacked under pretence of the Imperial decree. The
uneasiness which he suffered was the cause of his not declining

---

[1]) Chesterfield to Townshend, 14 Dec. '28, R. O. Hl. 302; Slingelandt to Hop, 14,
17 Dec. '28; Secr. Res. S. G. 8, 13 Dec. '28.

[2]) Hop to Slingelandt, 23 Dec. 28, R. A. Hl. 2982; Hop, Goslinga & Van Hoey to
Slingelandt, 23 Dec. '28, R. A. Hl. 2985; Chesterfield to Townshend, 28 Dec. '28, R. O.
Hl. 302; Chauvelin to Fénelon, 5, 23 Dec. '28, A. E. Hl. 375; Secr. Res. S. G. 27 Dec. '28.

[3]) Cf. Townshend to Chesterfield, 29 Nov., 3, 6, 10, Dec. '28, R. O. Hl. 302; Secr.
Res. S. G. 21 Dec. '28.

the opportunity of becoming friends with Prussia. This occurred in October, when the Queen of Prussia wrote a letter to Queen Caroline in which she proposed a match between the Prince of Wales and her eldest daughter. The King thereupon made his consort send an encouraging answer, but considering Frederick William's inconstancy, he could by no means count upon bringing the Mecklenburg affair to a favourable conclusion with the latter's help; and the less so since he was not inclined to request the hand of the Princess Royal of Prussia for the Prince of Wales unless Frederick William requested one of the English Princesses for the Prussian Crown Prince. The King of England, therefore, even as in May, applied to France as well as to Slingelandt. [1]

Once more the latter showed little inclination to involve the States in the affairs of Mecklenburg. [2] It was probably for this reason that, a short time afterwards, Chesterfield was ordered to represent that it was most necessary to bring the Emperor to reason — necessary to both the States and the whole of Europe. The Court of Vienna was establishing doctrines which, if not put a stop to, must soon enslave the whole Empire. The maxim of the Imperial Ministers was that the supreme authority of the Empire was vested in the Emperor. Previous to this it had always been vested in the Diet, but this was to become useless, as witness the affairs of Mecklenburg and East Frisia. The liberties of the Empire would soon be abolished now that the force of a resolution of the Diet was given to a decree of the Aulic Council, and now that the German Princes fell a prey to a set of councillors in Vienna wholly dependent on the Emperor. This did not affect the Empire only, for, should the Emperor become absolute there, the balance of power in Europe would be menaced. The King would be pleased to know how Slingelandt wished to limit the Imperial ambition.

As to the latter's opinion about affairs in general, the King entirely agreed with him that vigour and spirit were required, but he saw with concern that the Pensionary made no proposal of a vigorous step on the part of the States, but confined himself to saying that, should England and France precede, they would follow. This was a lifeless way of concurring in an alliance. Instead

---

[1] Townshend to Chesterfield, 12, 29 Nov. '28, R. O. Hl. 302; Coxe *R. W.* II, 526-7.
[2] Chesterfield to Townshend, 17 Dec. '28, R. O. Hl. 302.

of this the States, together with England, ought to inspire the Cardinal with firmness and spirit. [1]

When Chesterfield represented this to Slingelandt, the latter answered that, when he had told him that it would be difficult to induce the Republic to the taking of vigorous measures, he had told him what he believed and feared, and not what he hoped. He was as much convinced as everybody else of the necessity of showing vigour and spirit, but the States would not easily be brought to acting as they ought. The Republic was in a very miserable state, and though they knew it, they would take no measures of redress; they were loaded with debts which were on the increase rather than the decrease, so that how could there be any prospect that anything, short of necessity, would bring them to measures likely to cause additional expenditure? As, in this way, they were of no use to themselves, he did not see how they could be useful allies to others. However, he for himself would do his best to bring them to such measures as the King thought suitable, but he could not answer for success.

In addition to general affairs Chesterfield dealt with those of the Empire with Slingelandt. He asked him how a check could be put on the Emperor's despotism. The Pensionary knew of no other course than negotiation with the German Princes, unless, of course, an open breach should occur. If the Treaty of Wolfenbüttel and Würtemberg could be reinforced by the accession of the four Electors, or if these concluded a separate treaty of a like nature, it would be a very great curb upon the Emperor in his designs after absolute power. Just as in May, Slingelandt again desired a general action in the Empire. [2]

As then so now also did Gansinot happen to apply to him. He showed him one of the Elector-Palatine's letters in which the latter stated that there were good prospects of obtaining the guaranty of Juliers and Bergh at the Court of France, and requested that the Dutch Government give explicit instructions concerning this affair to their ministers in France, and that, in addition, she exhort England to enter into the same engagements. However, whereas on the former application Slingelandt had at once urged England to open negotiations with the four Electors, this time he left the

---

[1] Townshend to Chesterfield, 17 Dec. '28, R. O. Hl. 302.
[2] Chesterfield to Townshend, 4 Jany '29, R. O. Hl. 303.

the lead in the negotiations entirely to France. He answered Gansinot that the affair had to be concluded as it had begun, and that France would indubitably make England and the Republic enter the treaty to be concluded .[1])

Slingelandt was most astonished about this application of Gansinot's, with which one of Grevenbroch's to Hop correspond-ed. [2]) It was only some weeks previously that Goslinga had given him the communication that France was on the point of conclud-ing with the Elector Palatine, and now the latter asked that the affair be helped on by the Republic. There were other things bear-ing upon it which the Pensionary could not make out. He had heard no more of Chauvelin's project of a defensive alliance brought forward in September [3]) To be sure, some time after-wards La Baune had waited upon him and told him he was order-ed to declare that France persisted in her good intentions with re-gard to Juliers and Bergh, whereas the Republic seemed "s'endor-mir sur ses propres intérêts". Slingelandt, who understood nothing of this, asked Hop to solve the riddle, but the latter was even more astonished than he, for, whereas the French Ambassador at the Hague reproached Slingelandt with indolence, the French minis-ters in Paris had not even enquired after his sentiments about the project yet. [4]) However, though there was much that was not clear to him, the Pensionary did not for a moment suspect the good faith of France. Apropos of Gansinot's application, he now re-peated to La Baune what he had so often said during the previ-ous few months, that nothing was more advantageous to the Han-over Allies than tying the Electors to themselves; the Republic, however, could make no step in this direction: for the sake of secrecy the negotiations had to be carried on in France, but once let it be brought to a conclusion, the Republic would certainly ac-cede, as to which he was pretty certain of the province of Hol-land. [5]) From the frequent exhortations of La Baune that the Re-public evince interest in the cause of Juliers and Bergh, and even

---

[1]) Slingelandt to Goslinga, 31 Dec. '28, R. A. Hl. 2974; Copie d'un rescript de S. A. S. E. Palatine au Resident Gansinot, 16 Dec. '28, ibid.

[2]) Hop to Slingelandt, 7 Jany '29, R. A. Hl. 2983.

[3]) Chesterfield to Townshend, 4 Jany '29, R. O. Hl. 303.

[4]) Slingelandt to Hop, 8 Oct. '28, R. A. Legatie 84; Hop to Slingelandt; 15 Oct. '28, cf. 10 Nov. '28, R. A. Hl. 2982.

[5]) La Baune to Chauvelin, 4 Jany '29, A. E. Hl. 376; cf. the Same to the Same, 24 Oct. '28, ibid. 375.

reproaches of his as to her indolence in this respect [1]), Slingelandt could not but assume that France was fully in earnest.

However, she was not. These exhortations and reproaches were only intended to excite the idea that she was, and, far from indicating the real intentions of France, they were, on the contrary, meant to conceal them; for France did not intend to bring the Maritime Powers into a defensive alliance with the Electors, at least, not for the present. At the end of November La Baune was ordered not to proceed to formal negotiations as yet [2]). France did not desire that any negotiations be carried on between the Maritime Powers and the Electors so long as she had not brought her private negotiations with the Elector Palatine to a favourable termination. It was for this reason that she did everything to prevent their coming into touch. Higher up we saw that France imposed absolute secrecy on the Maritime Powers. She adopted the same course with the Electors [3]). In this way she, on the one hand, prevented her private views concerning the Electors from coming to the ears of the Maritime Powers, while, on the other hand, she could safely manoeuvre with the Maritime Powers in her negotiations with the Elector Palatine.

On Oct. 13th. these negotiations had advanced a step, for on that day a Treaty of neutrality between France and the Elector, one concerning the Germersheim difficulties, and, in return for the Elector's concessions in these, an Act of guaranty regarding the succession to the Duchies of Juliers and Bergh, were concluded. In the treaty of neutrality the Elector Palatine undertook to bring the other three to the same obligations, while France promised to do her best towards inducing the Allies to sign the Act of guaranty, even as she herself had done.

To further this, so it was said, France proposed a defensive alliance between the four Electors, France, England and the Republic, and at the conclusion of those treaties offered to the Elector Palatine the same project of such an alliance which she had offered to the Maritime Powers in September, that he should work in its favour with the Electors of Bavaria, Cologne and Treves. The Elector, however, would have been glad to see France herself

---

[1]) Chauvelin to La Baune, 26 Sept., 7, 21 Oct., 4, 28 Nov. '28, A. E. Hl. 375.
[2]) Chauvelin to La Baune, 28 Nov. '28, A. E. Hl. 375
[3]) Rosenlehner, *op. cit.* 445, 462.

enter into negotiations with the Electors of Bavaria and Cologne regarding this project, in which event only his brother, the Elector of Treves, would have to be dealt with. He would also have been glad if, considering it could not but take a good deal of time to make all of them agree, the Maritime Powers acceded in the meanwhile to the Treaty of neutrality and the Act of guaranty. But according to the French Ministers this was quite impossible, it having already taken infinite pains to obtain the promise of a guaranty for a defensive alliance from England and the Republic. These Powers would never put up with a simple treaty of neutrality, and they (the French Ministers) continued to insist that the Elector work with the other three [1]).

The object of France regarding the project of a defensive alliance was by no means what she pretended it to be, viz., to further the guaranteeing by the Maritime Powers of the succession to Juliers and Bergh to the House of Pfaltz-Sulzbach, but only to have, in the prospect of obtaining this guaranty, a stimulus for inducing the Elector Palatine to bring the treaties of Oct. 13th. to the completion desired by France. These treaties, is is true, had been concluded on that date, but they still required to be ratified. This ratification hung fire. The Elector desired some further modifications to be made in the act of guaranty. This, however, was not the principal reason which retarded the ratification. The principal obstacle was the fact that the Elector was not quickly successful in persuading the other three to agree to the treaty of neutrality. They were not accommodating, and least of all, Treves. The Elector Palatine therefore ardently desired that France should ratify the Treaty of neutrality, even in case they should not agree. France, however, avoided doing so, delaying it on all sorts of pretexts, and manoevring with the Maritime Powers, of which she represented England in particular as being little disposed for the guaranty the Elector desired [2]).

The year finished without the ratification taking place. Hence it is clear why the French Ministers were so absolutely silent towards the plenipotentiaries of the Maritime Powers concerning the project of a defensive alliance which they themselves had offered them. Negotiations on this project could not do otherwise

---

[1]) Rosenlehner, *op. cit.* 420—22, 428—9.
[2]) ibid. 249, 442—9

than confound the negotiations with the Elector Palatine. Hence it is equally clear why Gansinot applied to Slingelandt. Apparently the object for this was that the Pensionary should bring the Republic, and more especially England, into a more favourable disposition and should make them willing to give the desired guaranty without insisting on the defensive alliance, to which latter the other three Electors objected even more than to the Treaty of neutrality. In that case — so it was hoped — France, who had constantly made the unfavourable disposition of the Maritime Powers an argument for pressing the Elector would perhaps cease to resist, and ratify in spite of Treves' non-agreement. It was not once that Gansinot applied to Slingelandt, but repeatedly. He did the same with Chesterfield. They, however, relying on France, thought that Gansinot was not in the secret. [1]) However, they were out of it themselves. The Maritime Powers would again be played upon by France.

The affairs of the Empire, as they were at the end of the year, were not without danger to France. The Republic was uneasy concerning East Frisia, and George II. about Mecklenburg, while the negotiations with the Elector Palatine were still unfinished. Relations might very easily ensue between the four Electors and the Maritime Powers. Gansinot had already applied to Slingelandt and Chesterfield. Such relations might very well defeat the plans France had with regard to the Elector Palatine, and would moreover be quite out of season now that France wished to spare the Court of Vienna. France had to be on the alert to prevent such a general action in the Empire, just as in the Summer. She was wide awake indeed, though she took care not to show this. On the contrary, Chauvelin told Poyntz that it would be of great consequence if the Princes of the Union between Wolfenbüttel and Würtemberg could be brought into one treaty with the four Electors; a party of Protestants as well as Catholics strong enough to oppose the Emperor's arbitrary views at the Diet, and ready to join England in the event of a war, would in this way be formed. The King of England considered this scheme most prudent, but, because of the trouble which would attend the conclusion of a new treaty, he preferred that the four Electors should

---

[1]) Chesterfield to Townshend, 28 Jany. '29, R. O. Hl. 303; Slingelandt to Goslinga, 31 Dec. '28.

accede to the Union of Wolfenbüttel and Würtemberg, to which he had become a party in the meanwhile. Could they be brought to it there would be "more leisure to concert a complete system for preserving the liberties of the Princes of the Empire, and for keeping the Emperor's power within due bounds" [1]). The King was quite unconscious of the fact that France would be first to defeat such an action.

Having this aim, France showed great interest in the separate points that concerned the Maritime Powers, just as she had done in the Summer. We have already remarked it with regard to East Frisia. The same is applicable to Mecklenburg. France again advocated the cause of George II. with the Court of Vienna. Not only that, but on Jan. 13th. Chauvelin made a declaration in writing to the effect that, should the representations made to the Emperor fail, and should he abide by the decree of May 11th. the King of France was to support his British Majesty. In return for this the latter was demanded to promise not to enter into any negotiations with the King of Prussia concerning the succession of Juliers and Bergh [2]). The aim of France in demanding this was to prevent what was feared as a result of the negotiations about the mutual marriages, viz., that the Court of England would enter into too close relations with that of Prussia. It would exclude the possibility of the King's ever entering into relations with the four Electors. France, it is true, did not desire him to have any dealings with them, but the time might come when she would.

It was not only by showing interest in these separate points that France defeated a general action in the Empire: she did it in a totally different way also. George II. desired such an action purely in order to secure the support of the four Electors in the affair of Mecklenburg, and, in the very first place, at the Diet. France now let it be known that the Electors objected to giving such support. This was not true: it was said without their having any knowledge of it. France, however, could scarcely be suspected of insincerity, not only because she had recently made a declaration regarding Mecklenburg, but also because Chauvelin again and again, through Goslinga, pressed Slingelandt to induce the King of England to waive his demand for the Electors' support as to

---

[1]) Newcastle to Poyntz, 14 Jany. '29, R. O. France 193.
[2]) Declaration enclosed with Townshend to Chesterfield, 10 Jany. '29, R. O. Hl. 303.

Mecklenburg, which was the only obstacle to his entering into the treaty with the four Electors, in conjunction with France [2]).

Goslinga was ordered by Slingelandt to ask why the King might not have an advantage in return for his accession. Towards Chesterfield, however, the Pensionary adopted a different attitude. When the Ambassador said that if the Electors did not commit themselves as to Mecklenburg, it would be of no advantage at all to George II. to guarantee the succession of Juliers and Bergh to Pfalz-Sulzbach, Slingelandt answered that there was one, viz., that of not making Prussia greater. To this Chesterfield retorted that it concerned the Republic more than it did the King, his master. Just as in 1727, there was again a divergence of opinion about Prussia. The Republic was opposed to any increase of Prussia's power. When Slingelandt was informed of George II.'s acceptance of the declaration of Jan. 13th. he professed to be most pleased with the resolution the King had, in so doing, made concerning the succession to Juliers and Bergh; it was in the interests of no one's power to make a Prince who was so uncertain and unreliable, even greater. The King of England, it is true, declared that he likewise did not desire to make him greater, and that he was willing to enter into a project with France and the States to secure the tranquillity of those duchies, but on terms of reciprocity only; he could not defy the King of Prussia for the sake of his Allies, if he could not be certain that the Dutch and the four Electors would in their turn take his interests to heart and see that justice was done. He had set the mutual marriages on foot so as to place the possibility of being on good terms with Frederick William in his own hands; he wished to cause his Allies as little trouble as possible, but he had to safeguard himself should he see that they were not sufficiently favourably disposed. He had already committed himself to France concerning Juliers and Bergh, but he could not go any further unless France and the four Electors agreed to a scheme by which the mutual interests of all parties were secured, and to which the States ought at least to accede. [2])

---

[1]) Chesterfield to Townshend, 28 Jany., 15 Feby., 1 Mch. '29, R. O. Hl. 303. That this communication was made without the knowledge of the Electors, we infer from Rosenlehner's silence (op. cit.), and further from the circumstance that in the summer of this same year Bavaria and Cologn were ready to favour George II.'s views with regard to Mecklenburg (Jean Dureng, *Mission de Chavigny*, 89).

[2]) Chesterfield to Townshend, 28 Jany., 15 Feby. 1 Mch. '29, Townshend to Chesterfield, 28 Jany '29. R. O. Hl. 303.

Such a scheme was not formed. This was not Slingelandt's fault. He had, it is true, been rather reserved as to Mecklenburg, but this was caused by his considering it too risky to involve the Republic in this affair unless there were a general action in the Empire. It was not accidental that he was most reserved when the intelligence from France concerning the refusal of the Electors very much damped the hopes of such an action. This he would fain have seen as an accomplished fact. It was a "très bonne affaire," he wrote to Goslinga, that the treaty with the Electors was soon to be concluded with France; the Allies' interest in it was palpable; it was, therefore, a pity that England appeared to be less disposed for it than France, the more so as England's aversion might make the accession of the Republic all the more difficult. He would have been more than ready to exhort the English Government, but as their aversion proceeded from the Electors' refusal to side with the King regarding Mecklenburg, though this affair fell directly under the object of the treaty tobe made with them, he failed to see what could be done to remove this obstacle. [1]) We observe that Slingelandt to some extent imputed the miscarriage of the general action in the Empire to England, while he was of the opinion that France furthered it. This Power could not have been more successful, for whereas she gave the impression of furthering the general action, she nevertheless defeated it.

The game of France was the more difficult to penetrate as she did indeed attain something in connection with the separate points. On January 17th. the Emperor issued a new decree concerning Mecklenburg which, though not coming up to the wishes of George II. was, in Slingelandt's opinion, more reasonable than any of the previous ones. [2]). It deserves attention that, once France had attained this result, she dropped the affair of Mecklenburg for the time being. We do not know yet, Chauvelin wrote to La Baune, whether it is our interest to encourage or discourage the Dutch as to it; as long as we do not see clearer which way the general affairs will be going, we must suspend all decisive steps

---

[1]) Chesterfield to Townshend, 28 Jany. '29, R. O. Hl. 303; Slingelandt to Goslinga, the Same to Hop, 15 Feby. '29.

[2]) Townshend to Chesterfield, 4 Feby. '29, Chesterfield to Townshend, 22 Feby. '29, R. O. Hl. 303.

with regard to it; Mecklenburg has to follow the course of the general affairs. [1])

France adopted quite a different attitude with regard to East Frisia. As to this affair the Emperor had likewise done something. He let it be understood that the Renitents, in spite of the expiry of the term on December 29th., could still deliver in their submission, and, in a declaration on January 6th., made some explanations upon his decree of September 13th. [2]). This declaration was received with little relish at the Hague: people considered it as being little more explicit than the previous ones; in Slingelandt's judgement it was general, equivocal and, in the main points, unsatisfactory. Fleury and Chauvelin, however, thought the States could now very well advise the Renitents to submit, and strongly pressed them to do so [3]). Chesterfield crossed it. The Emperor seemed to him to be more accommodating with regard to East Frisia than to Mecklenburg, but he took care not to utter this opinion of his. From conversations with Slingelandt he had understood that it would be more difficult to engage the Republic in the affair of Mecklenburg should that of East Frisia be settled first. This Chesterfield desired to prevent — he wanted the two affairs to go hand in hand. Therefore at a conference which the Deputies had with Wenzel Sinzendorff, the new Austrian Envoy at the Hague, concerning the Emperor's declaration, at which he was present, he raised all possible objections; e. g., he passed censure on the following clause in the declaration: "il n'a jamais été et n'est *point encore* question de faire sortir d'Embden la garnison hollandaise". The expression "point encore" he said, seemed to imply that later there might be question of it, which remark greatly struck the Pensionary. Sinzendorff then offered to put instead: "nullement", but declined what Chesterfield proposed, much to the satisfaction of Slingelandt, "et ne sera jamais" [4]).

However, it was not Chesterfield, but the French Ministers

---

[1]) Chauvelin to La Baune, 17 Feby., 13 Mch. '29, A. E. Hl. 376.

[2]) Res. S. G. 24 Jany., 3 Mch. '29, in this latter the declaration has been inserted; Rousset, *Recueil* V, 299.

[3]) Chesterfield to Townshend, 28 Jany. '29, R. O. Hl. 303; La Baune to Chauvelin, 1 Feby. '29, Chauvelin to La Baune, 3 Feby. '29, A. E. Hl. 376; Res. S. G. 31 Jany. '29; Secr. Res. S. G. 15 Feby. '29; (Slingelandt's) Remarques sur la réponse de l'Empereur aux instances faites de la part de la France dans l'affaire d'Ostfrise R. A. Hl. 2985.

[4]) Chesterfield to Townshend, 1 Feby. '29, R. O. Hl. 303.

who prevailed. In order to conform to them, to put the Court of Vienna the more in the wrong, and on the other hand to prevent the Magistrate of Embden's taking a wrong step, Slingelandt thought it better that the States now advise the Renitents to submit. On March 3rd., after having applied once more to the Allies, they did so. This advice was not followed immediately. The Renitents distrusted the Emperor's intentions to such a degree that they could not yet decide upon taking this important step, a state of mind for which Slingelandt could very easily account. Too much incredulity — was his opinion — could be forgiven people in such circumstances. When, however, the States declared that they saw no other course open, they eventually (on March 24th.) submitted [1]).

The Renitents had at last taken the decisive step. This was apparently due to the efforts of the States. In reality, however, the strong pressure exerted upon these by France was responsible. This latter power wished to prevent the possibility of the Republic's finding some reason for following the vigorous policy of England, and to strengthen as much as possible her confidence in her other Ally.

The success of France would have been impossible had her peaceful policy not evoked some response from the Emperor. He, as we saw, had made a declaration as to East Frisia, and had issued a decree concerning Mecklenburg. In addition, after his return the same confidence was extended to Sinzendorff as he had enjoyed before his departure to France. This change in the Emperor's disposition has the closest connection with his relations with Spain.

As we remember, even before the Congress the harmony between the two Allies had left much to be desired. The Emperor had then referred Elizabeth, who pressed him both about the marriage and about the Spanish garrisons, to the deliberations with the Cardinal. These had not, so far as the marriage was concerned, led to any decision, the Cardinal's consent to it not being clear. The Emperor took advantage of this unclearness not to express himself decisively upon the marriage. As regards the Spanish gar-

---

[1]) Slingelandt to Hop, 15 Feby., 18 Mch. '29; Secr. Res. S. G. 15 Feby., 3 Mch. '29; Res. S. G. 3, 15, 19, 29 Mch. '29; Chesterfield to Townshend, 4, 18, 25 Mch. '29, R. O. Hl. 303; Chauvelin to La Baune, 17 Feby., 3, 13 Mch., 7 Apr. '29, A. E. Hl. 376.

risons, his calculations had entirely failed, but he now pretended that that was dependent, not so much upon him as upon the Empire. However, he did not succeed in permanently keeping the Queen of Spain dependent upon him, and the less so as something happened in his own family that provided her with a welcome opportunity of repeating her representations. The youngest of his three daughters died. Elizabeth's idea was that the two surviving Archduchesses were now *ipso facto* betrothed to two of her sons in virtue of the Convention of November 5th. 1725, and consequently she pressed the Emperor on that score. When he evaded a decisive answer, the energetic Queen, without delay, formally proposed the marriage of Don Carlos and Maria Theresa. The Conference of December 12th., to the judgment of which this offer was submitted, resolved to decline it in polite terms. Elizabeth once more applied to the Court of Vienna, but the Conference of February 15th. did but confirm the decision of December 12th.. [1])

From the time that she had first shown such impatience the Emperor had not disguised from himself the fact that a breach with Spain was more than possible. He wished to do nothing which might hasten this breach, and he therefore officially kept to Spain. He, just as this Power, returned no further answer concerning the provisional treaty, but at the same time he was intent upon restoring the old confidence with the Maritime Powers through private overtures to England and the Republic. He could not, however, take any steps in that direction so long as his negotiations with Prussia were unfinished. These lasted so long because of the Emperor's dislike to granting Frederick William's wishes concerning the succession to Juliers and Bergh. Should he now, in addition, be accommodating towards the Republic and England concerning East Frisia and Mecklenburg, the negotiations with Prussia were sure to end in smoke, the more so since the expectations of this Power aroused by the decree of April 1727 concerning East Frisia and that of May 1728 concerning Mecklenburg had by no means been realised. After the former Prussia had not been charged with the coercion of East Frisia, and the many restrictions added to that of May 1728 caused Prussia to derive scarcely any advantage at all. But no sooner had the Austro-

---

[1]) Syveton, *op. cit.* 260—1, 266—8.

Prussian Treaty been concluded (December 23rd. 1728) than the Emperor showed, in the declaration of January 6th. and in the decree of the 17th., more goodwill towards the Maritime Powers than could be comfortable for those at Berlin[1])

Moreover, at Vienna Schönborn, Vice-Chancellor of the Empire, showed an excellent disposition towards Waldegrave, [2]) and at the Hague Sinzendorff made overtures to Slingelandt (middle of January). His master, so he told him, was most desirous of resuming the old friendship with the Republic. The Ostend affair must, therefore, be removed by some means or other. It would be necessary to find a means of making up the decrease which would ensue in the revenues of the Southern Netherlands as a result of the cessation of the Company. These provinces would otherwise be unable to shift for themselves, and the Emperor was not in a position to support them financially from Vienna. The States must somehow supply the deficit which, however, was not unreasonable since they were as much interested in the defence of the Southern Netherlands and in the barrier against France as the Emperor himself, or perhaps even more. Should the States have any proposal to make in this connection, they need not to write of it to France. This Power, not being at all concerned in it, and England very little, it was unnecessary to inform either of them, but they could apply directly to him [3]).

If the Court of Vienna was of opinion that such overtures would have a friendly reception with Slingelandt, it was mistaken. Private overtures from that quarter he regarded with great suspicion. He told Sinzendorff plainly that a settlement of the Ostend dispute would be an insufficient ground for a resumption of the old friendship; that would require time and an attitude vastly different from that which the Emperor had of late years adopted towards the Republic; moreover, he added, even though the Emperor should entirely satisfy her, she would none the less perform her obligations towards her Allies [4]). A second overture in which Sinzendorff seems to have

---

[1]) Droysen, *op. cit.* II, 23—41, and particularly 48—9.

[2]) Townshend to Waldegrave, 3 Jany. '29, Waldegrave to Townshend, 5 Feby.' 29, R. O. Germany 64.

[3]) Chesterfield to Townshend, 18 Jan. '29, R. O. Hl. 303; Slingelandt to Goslinga, 15 Feby. '29.

[4]) Chesterfield to Townshend, 18 Jan. '29, R. O. Hl. 303; Slingelandt to Goslinga, 15 Feby. '29.

demanded an equivalent in money was likewise declined [1]).

Slingelandt was unwilling to deviate from the method of dealing with it in France and in concert with the Allies, hitherto
followed. He wrote Hop to the effect that the only thing to be
done, though it was a dangerous precedent to a weak Republic,
was for the Emperor, through Fleury, to mention the sum for
which he would be willing to give up his resistance to the suppression. Since from the various overtures it was apparent that
the Emperor realised the impossibility of his sustaining the
dispute, and that he now preferred a final settlement to an extension of the suspension, Slingelandt set into motion the idea
that France ought to press him strongly upon such an extension
in order to make him more tractable regarding an equivalent.
The Pensionary made this suggestion, because he considered a
final settlement so desirable that he would leave no stone unturned
to achieve this end, not because he believed in its success, for, as
regards the Emperor, his demand would be extravagant; he
would not rid the Republic of this thorn in the flesh so long as
she stuck to her Allies. And would France be pleased to see the
cause of the dispute removed so long as the Emperor kept to
Spain? The Ostend affair was not likely to terminate so long as
the prevailing system continued [2]).

Slingelandt had always looked upon it as being dependent upon
general affairs, which at present seemed hopelessly dark. He
expressed his joy when Hop wrote that the French Ministers had
realised that they would accomplish more along vigorous lines
than by placidity, but is it to be expected — so he asked — that
the vigour will extend to drawing the sword in the event of Spain
and the Emperor's declaration of their intention to keep to the
Preliminaries and the Convention of the Pardo, and their readiness to enter into immediate negotiations on that basis without
accepting the provisional treaty, and in case the Emperor at the
same time gave satisfaction as to East Frisia and Mecklenburg?
He believed not, and was of opinion that the year 1729 would pass
away in negotiations, just as the preceding year had done, and
perhaps also in reprisals against Spain. [3]).

---

[1]) Slingelandt to Hop, 3 Mch. '29; Chesterfield to Townshend, 11 Mch. 29, R. O.
Hl. 303.
[2]) Slingelandt to Hop, 3 Mch. '29.
[3]) Slingelandt to Hop, 15 Feby. '29.

It did not escape his attention that the Emperor was more peaceably disposed than had seemed to be the case in November and December, but, as he told Chesterfield, his opinion was that perhaps his disposition prevented Elizabeth from making war, and in the same way hers stood in the way of his making peace. In this way things might easily remain in a state of uncertainty for some time, only that — so he added — the necessity for England and the Republic to seize some Spanish ships might arise should these continue to make themselves a nuisance to the Maritime Powers in American waters, a course which, in his opinion, might be taken without risk of incurring a war. [1]) A vigorous attitude, towards the Emperor also, was to his taste; he expressed the hope that the firmness of France and the vigorous resolutions of Parliament would force him to act more openly than he had hitherto done [2]), but the Pensionary shrank from war because of the Republic's position. I do not see — he wrote to Goslinga — how to come out of the labyrinth; war does not suit us, a definitive treaty has been deemed impracticable, a provisional one will not make our situation any the better or surer: to make up with the Emperor and Spain and to sever from our Allies would contravene our safety and good faith; some great event has to take place which brings back quiet and confidence, and while we await such an event from the divine mercy, we must observe the rules of prudence [3]).

Such a great event was, as we have seen, approaching, but some time must elapse before it became an accomplished fact. Just now, it is true, events occurred which, in Slingelandt's opinion, might bring a speedy solution: Parliament took vigorous resolutions and the galleons arrived [4]). This arrival caused no change, however, as Spain was to detain the effects for months and months. The vigorous resolutions of Parliament did not actually determine the course of events, although, at the same time, they made themselves felt.

V.

Parliament met, and things were still in the greatest uncertainty. The Government thought they could do nothing better

[1]) Chesterfield to Townshend, 1 Mch. '29, R. O. Hl. 303.
[2]) Slingelandt to Goslinga, 15 Feby. '29.
[3]) Ibid.
[4]) Slingelandt to Hop, 18 Mch. '29.

than to admit the bad situation without hesitation. "It is with no small concern" — was said in the King's speech from the throne on February 1st. 1729 — "that I am again obliged to speak to my Parliament in this state of uncertainty; nor am I insensible of the burdens which my subjects bear, and that in our present circumstances some may be induced to think that an actual war is preferable to a doubtful and imperfect peace." However, it was very easy to make the exchange, and Parliament could depend upon it, that when a suitable occasion arose, he would not be backward in doing both himself and the nation justice [1]). Owing, at least to some extent, to this frank and vigorous attitude, the Government obtained a good majority in both Houses, but it was said unmistakably in the one as well as in the other, that the uncertainty had somehow got to come to an end.

Some Ministers, if not the whole Cabinet, endeavoured to get out of it by resuming friendship with the Emperor, and making an overture to Kinsky. [2]) But the principal hopes were set on the Allies. These were again applied to, the Cardinal in the first place. His promise to put matters in order before the meeting of Parliament had not been fulfilled. In spite of this Poyntz did not succeed in bringing him to resolution even now. He maintained that the provisional treaty had so far not been rejected by the Courts of Vienna and Madrid, and thought the Allies should take no open steps towards a war until after the arrival of the galleons, and until they could see whether the effects would be delivered, in accordance with the Preliminaries. He avoided explanation, however, with regard to the measures they would have to take, should this be refused and no satisfactory answer be given as to the concluding of the provisional treaty.

This conduct on the part of Fleury gave Townshend "more uneasiness than ever he felt in his life." He ordered Poyntz to apply to him again, and expose the situation of the Government. "We shall raise" he was instructed to tell him —" £ 3.500.000 this year, which is about £ 1.500.000 more than our ordinary ex-

---

[1]) Cobbett, *Parliamentary History of England*, VIII, 669.

[2]) It is an open question who took the first step as to this overture. Townshend later on contended that it was Kinsky: this was strongly denied, however, by the Court of Vienna. Most likely, Stanhope did so by order of the King and Queen, without the knowledge of Townshend, but not without the cognisance of Robert Walpole and Newcastle. Cf. Höfler, *op. cit.* XXXII No. 34, p. 302 et seq., and also pp. 26, 89, 117, 132—3.

penses in time of peace; and if we are not enabled to give assurances, at least privately, to the members of weight and interest in both Houses, before they are prorogued, that matters are agreed and concerted between His Majesty and France, in such a manner that they may depend either upon seeing an honourable end soon put to our present disturbances by negotiation, or that the Allies of Hanover have taken measures to do themselves justice by force of arms, the King's credit and influence in this Parliament will be entirely lost, which is an extremity the King must never suffer himself to be drove to. *The confusions and misfortunes that attended the reigns of King Charles the First, and the Second, and King James, in differing with their Parliaments, are too recent, and too notorious to be forgot.* If therefore His Eminency is not to be prevailed upon to open himself confidently to His Majesty, and to lay down such methods, as appear proper for bringing the Allies of Hanover out of this state of uncertainty (which is the only circumstance that makes the Parliament uneasy under the present burdens) the King must determine in that case, by lessening his expenses abroad, to ease the nation of the greatest part of the additional taxes they now bear." [1]

Townshend felt by no means sure that Poyntz would meet with any more success this time, for on the same day that he sent him these instructions, he instructed Chesterfield to strongly urge Slingelandt and Fagel to work hand in hand with the English Government to influence the Cardinal [2]

When Chesterfield obeyed, Slingelandt told him he was still in favour of strong measures, but it was difficult to persuade the Republic to take the initial steps; she would have to be drawn by the previous resolutions of England and France; people were convinced that France would do nothing, and so they had first to be sure that France would concur. Chesterfield replied that it was just as easy for the Republic and England to wake up France together as it was for England and France to arouse the Republic; his and Fagel's influence would be sufficient to bring her to such measures with England. Slingelandt said his arguments were strong and such as he could adduce with success if he had reasonable men to deal with, "but whom have I to deal with? Num-

---

[1]) Coxe, *R. W.* II, 638—40.
[2]) Townshend to Chesterfield, 21 Feby. '29, R. O. Hl. 303.

bers of people who, from utter ignorance of affairs, or blinded by self-interest, are equally incapable of either reasoning themselves or hearing it from others." Should he propose to go hand in hand with England in making a plan which would force the Emperor and Spain to become tractable, and to excite and press France to join in that design, their answer would be that he tried to involve them in dangerous measures without having first ascertained whether France, whose support was indispensable, would concur or not. As to his and Fagel's influence, "What does it amount to? We can do nothing. All the individuals compliment me, indeed, and tell me that I am a good patriot and that I am both able and desirous to serve my country and that they have the greatest deference for my opinion, but when it comes to the point, they do nothing that I propose; ever since I have been Pensionary, I have been endeavouring to retrieve the affairs of this province from visible and certain ruin, but you know I have not been able to advance one step yet; from this you may judge how considerable my boasted influence is." However, he would do his utmost, but before making one step openly, he wished to consult with Fagel and a few of the other chief men [1])

This did not cause any change. When, some days afterwards, Chesterfield asked him for a final answer, he said it was impossible for him to take such a proposal. People were so conscious of their own weakness, so persuaded of the inactivity of France, and so apprehensive of taking steps that might result in war, that he was sure it would be instantly rejected, and with a good share of indignation upon himself for having made it. Chesterfield exhausted all arguments to make him change his mind, and said in conclusion, that if the supposed indolence of France was to be the reason for the real indolence of the Republic, France could, with as much right, exculpate herself by means of the Republic's indolence, and then England would be in a hopeful situation between two such Allies. But it was all without success. Slingelandt told him that he was as much convinced of the truth of these reasonings, as Chesterfield could be himself, and as desirous to see the Republic take vigorous steps if possible, but that the weakness of the Government, the private interest of some, and the unreason-

---

[1]) Chesterfield to Townshend, 11 Mch. '29, R. O. Hl. 303.

able fears of others, made it impossible to carry it through, and consequently imprudent to attempt it.

Chesterfield did all he could; he had never had such heated conversations with Slingelandt and Fagel as upon this occasion. But he could not deny that the situation of the Republic was very bad. "It is impossible" — he wrote — "to describe the miserable situation of this Republic; the disputes between province and province engross both the thoughts and the time of the States General, as the disputes between town and town wholly employ the States of each particular province. Private interest or resentment is to be gratified at the expense of the whole. Present and imminent dangers are neglected from the fear of remote and chimerical ones, and I may venture to say with justice of this Government, that the utter ignorance of some, the notorious depravity of many, and the private views of all, render this Republic at present a most contemptible enemy and a most insignificant ally" [1]).

However, England could not do without her. This was so much the case that in order to keep her she withheld her support from the cause of the Prince of Orange. As we have previously noted, on account of representations on the part of Slingelandt, the King delayed bestowing the Order of the Garter upon him in the Spring of 1728. Here the matter rested until November, when it appeared in the press that the Prince was to be decorated with it. This made Slingelandt the more uneasy as the Prince was expected at the Hague. It had already caused alarm that he was going there, but this would be very much increased if it were accompanied with that mark of the King's favour and distinction. Therefore the Pensionary, in a conversation with Chesterfield, advised against bestowing it for the time being; he left the question as to whether it was more dangerous to have a Stadtholder or not unanswered, but this was not a time to determine either way [2]).

The English Court was not convinced of this. It was a severe affliction for the King and the Queen that at a time when one of the younger Princesses was hoping to marry the Crown Prince of Prussia, the Princess Royal was quite uncertain whether a match

[1]) Chesterfield to Townshend, 15 Mch. '29, R. O. Hl. 303. This letter and others exchanged between Chesterfield and Townshend in the second half of March have been inserted almost verbatim in King, Notes 71—84.
[2]) Chesterfield to Townshend, 30 Nov. '28, in Bradshaw, op. cit. II, 687 et seq; Jorissen, op. cit. 32 et seq.

between her and the Prince of Orange could ever take place. As
they thought that Fagel was more favourably disposed towards
him than Slingelandt, they ordered Chesterfield to sound Fagel
alone with regard to his prospects. Would he ever become a
Stadtholder of Holland? if so, when? and whether the match
would obstruct it?[1]) Chesterfield, however, took the liberty not to
obey. He saw it could only do harm as Fagel would immediately
tell Slingelandt. Should the match be mentioned — this was
what he thought — it had to be mentioned to both of them, but he
thought it better not to mention it at all. It was not the time for it
as long as the great question of peace or war remained undecided.
In time of peace England did not value the Republic's friendship
enough to mind a little grumbling, and in time of war the Republic would want England so much that she could not afford to
grumble at all[2]). This advice was taken in good part, and the garter
was not bestowed nor was the match mentioned. In the present
circumstances the Court did not like to do anything to displease
the Pensionary[3]).

The Prince's journey to the Hague took place in February. His
stay there was a period of triumph for the Orange Party which
had been kept under for so many years. The people followed him
wherever he went, calling out: "Long live our Stadtholder", and
uttering bitter invectives against the Government. His levée was
crowded with officers of all ranks who openly declared themselves
on his side; and even the Nobility of Holland, who, under the influence of Obdam and Van den Boetzelaar, were determined not
to wait upon him, seeing the enthusiasm of the people, finally
thought it best to do so, though they did it with a very ill grace,
five days after his arrival[4]).

Chesterfield was convinced that it would have taken very little
to cause a riot equal to the one in 1672, in which he thought Van
den Boetzelaar, who was openly cursed in the streets, would not
have fared better than the Brothers De Witt. But the Prince's
friends did not make the slightest attempt in his direction. It was
not their time yet, but they hoped to do a good stroke in May.

---

[1]) Townshend to Chesterfield, 29 Nov. 28, R. O. Hl. 302.
[2]) Chesterfield to Townshend, 14, 25 Dec. '28, R. O. Hl. 302; the former also in
Bradshaw, op. cit. II, 690 et seq.
[3]) Towshend to Chesterfield, 6, 17 Dec. '28, 11 Febr. '29, R. O. Hl. 302, 303.
[4]) Chesterfield to Townshend, 25 Feby., 15 Mch. '29, R. O. Hl. 303.

They wanted him to return to the Hague then, at the time of the
Kermis and when the troops were to be exercised. Their plan, however, was to come to nothing.

The Prince's stay had had a much better effect than either his
friends could have expected or his enemies apprehended. Everybody looked upon it as a forerunner of his match with the Princess Royal and upon that match as a sure forerunner of the
Stadtholdership. This persuasion gave the utmost uneasiness to
the prevailing party. Slingelandt mentioned this to Chesterfield
when the latter pressed him to make the proposition of arranging a
plan with England. The anti-Stadtholder party — he said — was
sure to oppose it, if it were only out of fear that a war would
facilitate the designs of the Prince; their uneasiness might be attended by very serious consequences at the present juncture, and
therefore he wished that some declaration could be made or something done on the part of England to quiet their fears. Chesterfield answered that he could not see what could be done to remove
such chimerical und unfounded fears, for Slingelandt could not
expect the King to declare that the match would never be made;
he himself knew nothing about it, but he thought the probability
of the match was great in view of the scarcity of suitable matches for
the English Princesses. Slingelandt said that he had never expected
such a declaration, and then came to the point. He had been informed that the Prince was to return in May; this would cause
general alarm and would possibly affect England very adversely
at the time, and in consequence he asked Chesterfield whether, in
case of his interference with the Prince's affairs, he would prevent
his return. The Ambassador denied — not according to truth —
that this had ever been the case, but was willing to transfer the
Pensionary's request to his Court.

When he did so, he emphasised, that the King had now to decide on the Prince's affairs. "The great point to be considered, and
by which the Prince, I think, is to direct his conduct, is, whether
His Majesty intends to bestow the Princess Royal on him or not:
and when? If His Majesty should think fit to make that match
this Summer, I think it is absolutely necessary that he should return to this place in May, both on account of the main view of the
Stadtholdership, and on account of his admission into the Council
of State in September, which is a very important point, and a lead-

ing card to the other." Should the match be made, and then the main object be pressed with vigour, Chesterfield had no doubts of success. But there was another side to the question. "On the other hand, it is certain that the match, the return of the Prince, and his admission to the Council of State will cause very great disorders here, both parties being now animated to the highest degree, so that it is to be considered how far the present situation of public affairs makes it advisable or not to venture those disorders that will inevitably happen" [1])

The consideration of this point did not require much time. At the present juncture there could be no question of risking such disorders, how ever much the Court might have desired to have advanced the Prince's interests. So Slingelandt's request did not meet with much opposition. At the same time, it was not immediately complied with. Though nothing could be done at present for the Prince, the uneasiness of his adversaries could at least be taken advantage of in some degree in behalf of English politics. The Government did not wish to be carried back to the Congress again under any circumstances. According to the 8th. Article of the Preliminaries it would only take four months, but now it had already taken twice as long, solely on account of Spain, who had not hitherto vouchsafed to give a final answer concerning the provisional treaty.They rather chose to abide by the Preliminaries for the remainder of the seven years prescribed by them as the term for the cessation of hostilities than to begin the Congress again. The plenipotentiaries would be ordered not to return thither unless it were to sign the provisional treaty. Now, Chesterfield had to ascertain the Pensionary's opinion as to the probability of obtaining from the Republic the same orders to her plenipotentiaries. If he thought it probable, Chesterfield had to show him a letter in which his request was granted; if not, he had, until he received further orders, to do nothing to prevent the Prince's return in May [2]).

Again Chesterfield was unable to obtain a favourable answer from Slingelandt. The latter said that the States could never be brought to give such orders without knowing first what part France was to take in that matter. The provisional treaty had never been much relished by them, so he thought it very unlikely

---

[1]) Chesterfield to Townshend, 15 Mch. '29, 2 letters, R. O. Hl. 303.
[2]) Townshend to Chesterfield, 10 Mch. '29, 2 letters, R. O. Hl. 303.

that they would agree to break up the Congress for the sake of it.
The argument drawn from the 8th. Article of the Preliminaries did
not hold water, for Spain could advance with some right that the
points, which according to the Preliminaries had to be discussed
and decided at the Congress, had not been brought before it, but
had been suspended by a provisional treaty without the participation and consent of Spain, so that to her there had virtually
been no Congress at all. Should he make the proposal, they would
answer him with such arguments and look upon the breaking up of
the Congress as the beginning of hostilities. They would certainly
take the proposal *ad referendum*, and consult their constituents
upon it, by which means the affair would become public, and if
not finally agreed to, as he was persuaded it would not be, the attempt having proved unsuccessful, he thought it would be attended by many very serious consequences, both with regard to His
Majesty and the Alliance. When Chesterfield continued to press
him, Slingelandt said he was prepared to propose it, provided he,
Chesterfield, accepted the responsibility of ill consequences, but
the latter did not consider it advisable to act contrary to his
advice.

Afterwards, Slingelandt told him that the most probable way
to get this proposition agreed to by the Republic, was for the
English Plenipotentiaries to communicate their orders to those of
the Republic and to press them strongly to join with them; they
would, of course, write this to the States and request instructions
concerning it, and he considered the probability of obtaining such
instructions greater in this way than in any other, especially
if France appeared to be coming into it, or even did not oppose it,
but even then he could not answer for success [1]).

Upon these conversations Chesterfield did not consider himself
authorised to give Slingelandt the letter concerning the Prince's
return. His Government, however, allowed him to give the letter or,
more correctly, another one much to the same effect. The Pensionary
had now, at least, — so Townshend wrote to the Ambassador — by
proposing an expedient, shown his willingness for co-operation. But
the true reason of their compliance was their desire to gain him entirely. They were very much afraid that if the uncertainty continued, the dissatisfaction of the nation would attain such a degree that

---

[1]) Chesterfield to Townshend, 25 Mch. '29, R. O. Hl. 303.

it would finally become uncontrollable. This could not fail to be the case, if the Allies should depart from the provisional treaty and allow themselves to be brought back to the Congress again; then they would be sure to return into the labyrinth from which they would not emerge without serious loss of time and under considerably less favourable conditions. The Government did not doubt in the least that the Allies had full right to such a course; the Pensionary's observation of what Spain could rightly say against the breaking up of the Congress, was entirely unfounded.

In order to convince him of this the Government even had a memorial drawn up, in which all the blame was laid upon the Vienna Allies. Since the departure of Bournonville and Sinzendorff no answer had arrived either from Madrid or from Vienna concerning the provisional treaty. Of the two Spain was the more to blame. In the answer of the 6th. of September she had said that the existing project could be perfected, but during the whole of the last seven months she had been silent as to how this should be done. Apparently, procrastination was her only object. But the Allies could take advantage of the 8th. Article of the Preliminaries in order to avoid their being delayed any longer, the more so as the restriction of the Congress to four months had been due to Fonseca.

Though strongly determined not to go back to the Congress, the Government did not intend to make this resolution public. Stanhope and Horace Walpole, who had left Paris in order to attend the Session of Parliament and were to return in a few days, would have to inform the Cardinal of it most privately [1]).

In conformity with Townshend's order, Poyntz had again applied to the latter. In spite of his exertions he did not succeed in tying him down to a fixed line of conduct. To be sure, Fleury was warmer than ever towards Spain and spoke a good deal about war, but he raised the objection that he could not believe the Republic would join in it [2]).

This was, of course, nothing more than an excuse, as he was not willing to go to war himself. This is evident from the instructions sent to La Baune that he was to oppose the idea of a war [3]), and

[1]) Townshend to Chesterfield, 18, 25, 28 Mch. '29, R. O. Hl. 303.
[2]) Same to Same, 14 Mch. '29, R. O. Hl. 303.
[3]) Chauvelin to La Baune, 13 Jany., 3 Feby. '29, A. E. Hl. 375, 376.

also from his efforts to remove everything that might cause the
Republic to go to war. These efforts, as we saw, were in matters
pertaining to East Frisia, and in no less a degree to the Ostend affair. Immediately the English Government began to press the
Cardinal again, he began to work in favour of an agreement in
the Ostend affair [1]). He explained himself in the above-mentioned
manner to Poyntz, but at the same time spoke quite differently to
Hop. Fonseca — so he told him — frequently pressed him to settle
the Ostend affair. He, the Cardinal, had always rejected his proposal of a limited trade, he would do nothing except what the Republic approved of, her advantage was his only object, but he
thought that a final settlement of the Ostend affair would be more
practical than if the Republic had to remain under arms and
perhaps have more expenses in a single year than the whole suppression would cost. Apart from this, he had learnt on good authority, that the Emperor was very desirous of concluding the affair in
order to be independent of the Queen of Spain whose only
thought was to impose the match upon him; it was only the Ostend affair that prevented him from breaking with her. The affairs
of East Frisia and Mecklenburg were now in a condition in which
it was easily possible to settle them, and if that affair should be
settled in addition, there would be nothing remaining to hinder the
reconciliation of the Emperor with the Hanover Allies. Horace
Walpole and Stanhope would return, as he expected, with the proposal either to give Spain a time-limit, or to break up the Congress.
Now, the Emperor would be better able to support this in Madrid
if he could give them to understand that he could rejoin the Hanover Allies, and, should Spain prove unwilling, he would undoubtedly leave her immediately. Therefore the Cardinal wished the
Republic to make matters easier, for only the obstinacy of the Hanover Allies could force the Emperor to continue following the fancies of Elizabeth [2]).

Shortly after Slingelandt had received the letter of Hop, in
which this conversation was recorded, Chesterfield waited upon
him. No sooner had the English Government been informed by
Poyntz that Fleury made the unwillingness of the Republic an
argument for not joining in the war himself than they ordered the

---

[1]) Slingelandt to Hop, 15 Feby. '29; Hop to Slingelandt, 24 Feby. '29, R. A. Hl. 2983.
[2]) Hop to Slingelandt, 22 Mch. '29, R. A. Hl. 2983.

Ambassador at the Hague to request Slingelandt to take action[1]). But when he did so the Pensionary silenced him by showing him Hop's letter. Chesterfield could clearly see the Cardinal's intention, and told Slingelandt that he hoped that the adjustment of the Ostend affair would have the good effect that Fleury expected it to have, but, if not, he feared it would only have an evil effect with regard to England, for it was most questionable whether the Republic, having settled her own affairs, would still support England. The Pensionary replied, that the tariff of the Southern Netherlands would be still outstanding, and this could be protracted as long as desired, but Chesterfield did not think that this alone would be sufficient to animate the Republic [2]).

Soon afterwards Chesterfield again waited upon Slingelandt. Poyntz had written him that the Cardinal had also said to Hop, that the States had to choose: if they desired war, and were in the position to undertake it, they could depend upon his support. Chesterfield now requested Slingelandt to see that the States were in a state of readiness equal to that of France and as the situation required. But the Pensionary answered, that he looked upon Fleury's declaration as a mere excuse to justify himself towards England by laying the blame upon the Republic; if he was indeed disposed for war, he would make arrangements with England, and then call upon the Republic to join in, which she neither could nor would refuse, instead of saying coolly that if the Republic had a mind for war he was in favour of it. Chesterfield retorted, that if he was only assuming this attitude it would be easy to disarm him by declaring that the Republic was willing for war in conjunction with the Allies, and then France would have to explain herself. Slingelandt agreed that this was true; and if it were dependent on him it would take place but he could not propose it [3]).

The question suggests itself whether the Pensionary was sincere in this respect. We have seen, ever since November, as often as England asked for his support, he had declined it referring to the impotence of the Republic and the inactivity of France. Did he make use of this to conceal his own unwillingness? The question is not whether the impotence of the one and the inactivity of the

---

[1]) Townshend to Chesterfield, 14 Mch. '29, R. O. Hl. 303.
[2]) Chesterfield to Townshend, 5 Apr. '29, R. O. Hl. 303.
[3]) Same to Same, 12 Apr. '29, R. O. Hl. 304.

other were causes or mere pretexts. They were indeed causes why
Slingelandt could not do what England asked him. But it might
be that he was not willing to do so either. He himself gave frequent and very strong assurances that he was willing, which fact
is no more to be neglected than the fact that Chesterfield was fully
convinced of his sincerity [1]). Still, it must be admitted, that his
sincerity towards Chesterfield was not unlimited. We remember
that Slingelandt had once made the concurrence of the Republic
conditional upon her being sure of the intentions of England with
regard to Spain, as there was some jealousy on the part of the
States of their being carried too far; Chesterfield had then answered him, that the King did not understand this jealousy. Thereupon Slingelandt had assured him that he himself had no such
jealousy, but that the people of Amsterdam even grudged the
English the advantages to which the treaties entitled them and
would be most unwilling to enter a war for the sake of a trade
which they looked upon as destructive to their own [2]). Upon a
former occasion when he spoke of this jealousy, shortly before the
Congress, the Pensionary had likewise laid the blame on Amsterdam; Hop — he had said then — would act more as Magistrate of
Amsterdam at the Congress than as plenipotentiary of the Republic, and so, should the Spaniards make any proposal in favour of
the Dutch trade in the West-Indies which, for the greater part,
was lost, he would not be able to prevent such a proposal having a
hearing [3]). Still, we have seen more than once what Slingelandt, in
his inmost-heart, thought of the English trade with Spanish
America. But apparently in order to have the more influence on
England, he dissembled his real meaning in this to her Ambassador. Now, it might be supposed that he acted in a similar
manner as regards England's request to incite the Republic to
act with vigour.

However, it is evident that this was not so from the expedient
he now suggested to Chesterfield. He told him it would be next to
impossible to bring France and the Republic to concur in breaking up the Congress under the pretence that the Vienna Allies had
not signed the provisional treaty, but he had found something. In

---

[1]) Chesterfield to Townshend, 4 Jany., 15 Mch., 12 Apr. '29, R. O. Hl. 303, 304.
[2]) Same to Same, 21 Dec. '28, 4 Jany. '29; Townshend to Chesterfield, 17 Dec. '28,
R. O. Hl. 302—3.
[3]) Same to Same, 25 Mch. '29, R. O. Hl. 303.

December the States had resolved to consult with the Allies as to
what should be done with regard to the encroachments made by
the Spaniards upon the treaties, even upon the Preliminaries and
of the Convention of the Pardo; apropos hereof the Hanover Allies had sent a joint memorial to their Ambassadors at Madrid in
February, instructing them to tender to the Court of Spain[1]). Now,
Slingelandt proposed that the English plenipotentiaries should
call upon the French ministers and the Dutch plenipotentiaries
without delay in order to consider vigorous measures with them
in case of the refusal of Spain to give immediate satisfaction
for the wrong that that memorial complained of. England
was fully entitled, not only to call upon the Allies, but also
upon the Emperor. This might have a good effect upon him, if he
were of the same mind that the Cardinal thought he was, and provide him with an excuse for either leaving Spain or adjusting the
affairs of Europe.

Slingelandt was extremely fond of this project. He thought
it would be the most likely to obviate all difficulties. The pretence was better than the non-subscription to the provisional
treaty and such to which the Allies of England could not deny
their concurrence. Besides, in his opinion, France would not object to it as the project was directed against Spain alone. The
Pensionary was convinced that the Cardinal would not, in any
circumstances, enter into a war with the Emperor which would inevitably involve the whole of Europe, but, on the ground of his information, he thought that as he was much provoked against
Spain, he could be persuaded to declare war against Spain
alone[2]).

The expedient shows that Slingelandt was not exactly unwilling to go to war, but, in the first place, the provisional treaty
did not justify a war, there must be a just and plausible
casus belli. Secondly, the Republic had to be sure of the co-
operation of France. Thirdly, the attack ought not be directed
against both of the Vienna Allies, but only against one of them, as
the object was to separate them from each other.

It was with a view to this object that Slingelandt suggested
in December making a vigorous declaration to the Emperor.

---

[1]) Res. S. G. 4 Dec. '28; Secr. Res. S. G. 24 Jany. '29; Baudrillart, *op. cit.* III, 497.
[2]) Chesterfield to Townshend, 5, 12 Apr. '29, R. O. Hl. 303, 304.

Now, again, he proposed to put him to the test. As to himself, he was willing to comply with the Cardinal's desire and meet him half way. So he did his best to make the Republic willing to observe facility in the Ostend affair. However, as he wrote to Hop, he abode by the principle that the Republic could make no offers of an equivalent. If the Emperor was in earnest, he ought to make them himself, and Fleury ought to transfer his ultimatum to both the Republic and England. As the Ostend affair affected England as well, this power ought also to contribute to an equivalent. If she happened to raise objections, Slingelandt thought, France could be of great service to the Republic in the matter. It might be, however, — so he continued — that the affair could be more easily brought to an end by bribing the Emperor's ministers, who perhaps would not be above it. In that event the English East India Company could be useful in procuring the money. Slingelandt wished the Dutch plenipotentiaries to submit this to their English colleagues when they had an opportunity, but he was afraid that these would have their heads so full of putting an end to the Congress that they would pay little attention to the Ostend affair. He hoped that they would, at any rate, not do anything which would more closely unite the Emperor and Spain, instead of endeavouring to separate them [1]).

However, although the English paid no attention to the Ostend affair now, they approved of Slingelandt's expedient, and the instructions of Stanhope and Horace Walpole were altered accordingly [2]). They were instructed to press the French ministers and the Dutch plenipotentiaries, in the manner schemed by the Pensionary, immediately they arrived in Paris. But when they arrived, general affairs had assumed new dimensions.

At last, a sign had come from Spain. When Elizabeth was informed that the Emperor had definitely declined the marriage, she began to turn from him. She did not break off from him at once, but she proposed that he should permit the introduction of Spanish garrisons into Parma and Tuscany. But her hopes to attain this end were far less on him than on the Hanover Allies, France in particular. On the 29th. of March La Paz wrote a letter to Fleury making the continuance of general negotiations conditional

[1]) Slingelandt to Hop, 14 Apr. '29.
[2]) Townshend to Chesterfield, 29 Mch. 29. R. O. Hl. 303.

upon the introduction of the 6,000 Spaniards. In that event the King of Spain was not to levy more than 14 or 15% of the effects of the galleons. This letter was handed to Fleury on the 11th. of April[1]).

VI.

La Paz's letter was destined to open a new stage in the negotiations which finally resulted in a treaty between the Hanover Allies and Spain. On the 11th. of April, however, there was not the slightest question of any alteration in the relations with this Power. On the contrary, Fleury was most incensed against her. By detaining the effects of the galleons she caused inestimable loss to the French merchants and, quite recently, she had returned a very unsatisfactory answer to the memorial concerning trade grievances which had been presented at Madrid by the ministers of the Hanover Allies. Besides, Spain had let him wait for months and months for her answer about the provisional treaty and about what he had sent with Bournonville. Now at last something came from Spain, but as it contained a clear demand for Spanish garrisons its method of execution was left entirely uncertain. Therefore, he thought it quite possible that the whole overture was only made to render the Emperor more easy to deal with. France was offered no advantage, even the delivery of the effects was made conditional upon the introduction of the Spaniards which would most likely lead to a war with the Emperor. So it was small wonder that he sent an answer to La Paz in which he bitterly complained of Spain's conduct (14th. of April).

The Cardinal, so far from being disposed to incur a war with the Emperor for her sake, continued negotiating with the latter, and did his utmost to bring the affair to a happy conclusion. He was aware that things had now come to a crisis. He therefore wrote to Sinzendorff on April 12th., that should the King of France and the Emperor come to an agreement with each other without separating from their Allies a reasonable peace could easily be arranged. Besides, he proposed an expedient to Fonseca which would finish the Ostend affair: the Company should once and for all send two ships to India, and the States should then give

---

[1]) Baudrillart, *op. cit.* III, 499—503.

the Company a certain sum under pretence of buying its goods and factories. Both he and Chauvelin urged the Dutch plenipotentiaries at the same time that the States should express themselves in connection with an expedient. He indeed eagerly desired to settle the Ostend affair in order to avoid a war which he feared Horace Walpole and Stanhope would urge upon their arrival[1]).

However, when they both arrived at Paris, on the 20th. of April, they immediately perceived that conditions had altered and, for the time being, it would not be wise to take drastic measures. It was not that they were, like Fleury, in favour of an agreement with the Emperor; they were not, and the less so as the latter had returned a most reserved answer to the overtures made to Kinsky in February.[2]) But they were inclined to seize the opportunity offered by Spain and to agree to the Spanish garrisons, provided that, at the same time, Spain was given to understand that she had to come to a decision without delay.[3])

Under the circumstances the Cardinal thought that it was the right time to approach Spain. Chauvelin seems already at this time to have decided in favour of the Spanish garrisons, but Fleury, far less anti-imperial than he and afraid of a war with the Emperor, remained inclined to come to an agreement with the latter, and could not get resolved to infringe the Quadruple Alliance. The instructions to Brancas and Keene upon which he agreed with the English plenipotentiaries did not go further than the assurance that France and England should try to obtain consent for the introduction of Spanish garrisons from the Emperor and the Grand Duke of Tuscany, provided that the King of Spain accepted the provisional treaty without delay. Should he refuse, the ministers should draw his attention to the fact that the breach was quite possible (instructions of the 9th. of May)[4]).

---

[1]) Baudrillart, *op. cit.* III, 497—9, 502—4; Chauvelin to La Baune, 28 Apr. '29, A. E. Hl. 376; Drafts to the Plenipotentiaries, 7 Apr. '29, R. O. France 193; Hop to Slingelandt, 18, 25, 30 Apr. '29, R. A. Hl. 2983; Hop, Goslinga and Hurgronje to Slingelandt, 30 Apr. '29, R. A. Hl. 2986.

Baudrillart has presented the Cardinal's letter to the Emperor of April 12th. as preceding receipt of that of La Paz (*loc. cit.* 499) which according to himself however (*loc. cit.* 502) took place on April 11th..

[2]) Beer, *Zur Geschichte der Politik Karl's VI, Historische Zeitschrift* 55 (1886) 53—4.

[3]) Hop, Goslinga and Hurgronje to Slingelandt, 30 Apr. '29, Hop to Slingelandt, 8 May '29, R. A. Hl. 2986, 2983.

[4]) Hop, Goslinga and Hurgronje to Slingelandt, 30 Apr. '29, R. A. Hl. 2986; Höfler *op. cit.* XXXII, 104, XXXVIII, 5; Baudrillart, *op. cit.* III, 512—4.

In these negotiations the Dutch plenipotentiaries had no part except that they were informed of the instructions. Still, Slingelandt, seeing the great significance it might have for general affairs, followed it most attentively. He was glad that Spain had now, through La Paz's letter to Fleury, made the proposal of the Spanish garrisons to the Hanover Allies as well as making it to the Emperor, for it was proof that her union with the latter had to a great extent decreased, if not entirely dissolved. On account of this, the answer that the Cardinal sent to this letter caused him considerable anxiety. It was too cold and was liable to deter Spain from further application: it ought to have been more obliging, for any discord between the Vienna Allies had rather to be encouraged than discouraged. So he was very pleased with the instructions of the 9th. of May, which were milder, and put Elizabeth to the test as to whether she indeed distrusted the Emperor or still remained faithful to him. Fagel feared the latter, but Slingelandt did not. He thought that her eyes had at last been opened, and that she would prefer to have something definite from the Hanover Allies than to remain in uncertainty any longer. To be sure, the success of a matter in which "le caprice et autres semblables conseillers" had been consulted, was doubtful, but he could not believe that the Emperor would send as favourable an answer regarding Don Carlos as the Hanover Allies [1]).

Slingelandt was pleased with the instructions of the 9th. of May on another ground: not only in respect of Elizabeth but also of the Emperor. In them both extremes had been avoided, for they estranged Elizabeth as little as they excluded an agreement with the Emperor. He had, as we noted, been preparing the way in the mind of the people for some time with the view to such an agreement. He had found some prominent men, especially Van Citters, the Grand-Pensionary of Zealand, favourably inclined. Van Citters declared himself in favour of a final settlement of the Ostend affair even though it should cost a considerable sum, provided the sum was not exorbitant, and was partly borne by the Dutch East India Company. Thereupon Slingelandt had sounded the English Government as to whether they were willing to pay

---

[1]) Chesterfield to Townshend, 29 Apr., 6, 13 May '29, R. O. Hl. 304; Chesterfield to the Plenipotentiaries, 24 July '29, in Coxe, *R. W.* II, 647 et seq; Slingelandt to Hop, 3 May '29, the Same to Goslinga, 21 May' 29.

half of it. Not being prepared to promote an agreement in the Ostend affair as long as their own difficulties remained unsettled, they refused. Slingelandt was afraid this refusal would make the regents of Amsterdam, several of whom were shareholders in the Dutch East India Company, still more backward than they already were, and therefore advised Fleury to be very cautious in his negotiations with Sinzendorff and Fonseca [1]).

Slingelandt himself also became less accommodating than he had been hitherto. This was a sequel to the Emperor's conduct. Now that the breach with Spain threatened, the latter was determined not to make any more concessions except in return for the guaranty of his Pragmatic Sanction. This was the true reason why he rejected the Cardinal's proposal to Fonseca. He did not in the least disclose his intentions to him, but continued to insist, before him, on a permanent equivalent, whether a limited trade, the suppression of the subsidy he yearly owed to the States in its entirety or by the half, or something else. [2]) But he acted otherwise towards Slingelandt. The Envoy Sinzendorff gave the latter to understand that, should the Republic guarantee the Pragmatic Sanction, the Emperor would go further in his concessions regarding the Ostend affair (2nd. half of May). However, this insinuation had the very opposite effect on the Pensionary. He understood from it that nothing could be expected from the Emperor unless the Republic went over to his side. He feared that his aim might be to give Fleury the impression that the Maritime Powers were negotiating with him to restore the old system. It was probably to prevent this impression that Slingelandt made the States of Holland declare, on the 4th. of June, that the limit of their compliance should be represented by their allowing one or two Ostend ships to ply to India once, which was still less than Fleury had proposed and the Emperor had already rejected [3]).

Slingelandt's increasing hope of an agreement with Spain rendered him the less amenable. Patiño said plainly that if the Han-

---

[1]) Chesterfield to Townshend, 3, 17 May, '29, Townshend to Chesterfield, 29 Apr. '29, R. O. Hl. 304; Slingelandt to Hop, 14 Apr. '29 (enclosed with this, Willem van Citters to Slingelandt, 8 Apr. '29), 13 May '29, the Same to Goslinga, 21 May '29.

[2]) Hop and Goslinga to Slingelandt, 31 May, 15 June '29, R. A. Hl. 2986; Huisman, op. cit. 450.

[3]) Slingelandt to Hop, 27 May, 27 June '29, the Same to Goslinga, 28 May '29, R. A. Legatie 84, Hl. 2974; Höfler, op. cit. XXXII, 36, 39; Secr. Res. Hl. 4 June '29.

over Allies agreed to the Spanish garrisons all their other affairs would be made easy [1]). To the Pensionary, no obstacle for so doing was represented by the Quadruple Alliance, for by it the Emperor had bestowed upon Don Carlos the eventual investiture of the Duchies of Parma and Tuscany, but though he had himself benefited by the Quadruple Alliance, his subsequent troubles with Spain had raised a strong and justified distrust about his intentions as to the destination of those Duchies. He could not, therefore, cry out about injustice, if the Hanover Allies, more in conformity with the indisputable purpose of the Quadruple Alliance than with the strict letter of it, lent a hand to Spain in the introduction of garrisons that depended upon Spain, and not entirely or in part upon the Emperor.

As regards the Princes of Parma and Tuscany, Hop compared the placing of foreign troops in their countries, by which they were virtually deprived of their power, with the taking possession of Naboth's vineyard [2]). But Slingelandt judged otherwise. Ever since their States had been pronounced fiefs of the Empire, they could not expect to dispose freely of them any longer. It was true, it ran counter to the ordinary law that Don Carlos, in a sense, took possession of the Duchies in their lifetime, but this irregularity was inevitable to extinguish a flame that had set Europe on fire since the death of Charles II. of Spain.

In the Pensionary's opinion no fear of the Emperor needed to refrain the Allies from agreeing to it, for, if they were to agree with Spain, he would not be able to help himself. And he would, no doubt, think twice before risking a war to prevent measures that tended to do nothing more than to secure for Don Carlos what the Emperor had formally promised him and to come, in that way, to a general pacification. On the other hand, the Hanover Allies might make it palatable to him by asking Elizabeth for a declaration to the effect that she wanted nothing more for Don Carlos than that which was conformable to the Quadruple Alliance. They might even guarantee the Emperor in his Italian dominions. All things considered, Slingelandt did not conceive how Fleury could be so scrupulous now about the introduction of

---

[1]) Secr. Res. Hl. 4 June '29.
[2]) Hop to Slingelandt, 13 Aug. '29, R. A. Hl. 2983.

Spanish garrisons which he himself had offered in October [1]).

It was in this strain that Slingelandt spoke to Townshend when the latter, on his way to Hanover, whither he followed his Master, called at the Hague, in the first days of June. In contrast to the preceding Summer, when their correspondence was broken off, there was a great measure of harmony between the two Statesmen, at least much more than between Townshend and his fellow-ministers. For, whereas Townshend, anti-imperial as always, wished to agree with Spain, Robert Walpole, whom Newcastle meekly followed, preferred, if it were impossible to be friendly with both the Emperor and Spain, then to be so only with the Emperor. People would then get rid of the disagreeable German disputes, and the war with Spain would, as a naval one, be less grave to England and, moreover, popular. The divergence of views that had existed in the Government for a long time had only recently made itself again apparent. Queen Caroline, who worked hand in hand with Robert Walpole, had still tried to reconcile Townshend to his colleagues, but in vain [2]). Under these conditions it was most welcome to the latter to find Slingelandt disposed to an agreement with Spain.

Their deliberations were not confined to the subject of the garrisons but also ran in another direction, which, in connection with the question of resuming friendly relations with Spain, was of great moment, viz. joint naval operations of England and the Republic. The latter had equipped a squadron of twelve ships during the Spring, with a view to difficulties with Denmark. She had intended to send these to the Baltic in the Summer, but in May it was thought better not to do so. The thought then suggested itself to Slingelandt to join that squadron with the strong English fleet at Spithead. Independently of him the same thought crossed the mind of Chesterfield. The latter mentioned it to Townshend, who much applauded it, and at once urged Slingelandt and Fagel to promote it. Owing to their influence the States forthwith unanimously agreed to the scheme. First of all the Pensionary had to give an assurance that there was no secret

---

[1]) Slingelandt to Hop, 22 Aug. '29; Chesterfield to Townshend, 11 June '29, R. O. Hl. 304; the Same to the Plenipotentiaries, 24 July '29, in Coxe, R. W. II, 647 et seq.
[2]) Newcastle to Stanhope, 22 May, 12 June '29, in Coxe, R. W. II, 641 et seq.

understanding which would commit the States any further, so that they would be free later on to send such instructions to the Vice-Admiral in command of the squadron as might please them. Slingelandt could give this assurance quite safely, for it was not, at least not with a view to the existing situation, his or Townshend's intention that the Anglo-Dutch fleet should bring Spain to reason, but on the contrary that, in case the Lords of the Council, without waiting for the final decision of Spain, should like to send the fleet to the Spanish coasts, the scheme should be retarded and rendered futile by the association with it of the Dutch squadron. It cannot be definitely said whether this scheme originated with Slingelandt, Townshend, or even Chesterfield, but one thing is certain, that this and nothing else was the object of the union of the fleets arranged at the Hague [1]).

By concurring in this, the Pensionary promoted an agreement with Spain. He did this in a more direct way by making first the States of Holland and then the States General agree to the introduction of Spanish garrisons. This was not his original intention. At first there seemed to be no reason why the Republic should interfere in negotiations that principally proceeded from the Quadruple Alliance. It was thought that it would be safe to wait for the outcome of those negotiations, and Slingelandt hoped that the Cardinal would conduct them in such a way that the Republic would participate in their fruits without being obliged to undertake an engagement so delicate. Van der Meer had caused him to change his mind. He had let him know that Spain would not take the indifference of the Republic in good part, that she would not feel under any obligation to her if she went with the stream after England and France had settled with Spain. Slingelandt, therefore, resolved not to wait, but would obtain merit by doing with a good grace what the Republic, who was in permanent need of her Allies, would not be able to refuse them. By his aid, as early as the 15th. of June, the States of Holland declared themselves in favour of the States General entering into the engagements which France and England might undertake to secure the eventual succession of Don Carlos to Parma and Tuscany, under the con-

---

[1]) Slingelandt to Goslinga, 21 May, 5 July '29; Chesterfield to Townshend or Newcastle, 27 May, 3, 4, 7 June '29, R. O. Hl. 304; cf King, *Notes*, 90—1.

ditions granted to the Republic in 1719, when her accession to the Quadruple Alliance was in treaty [1]).

The second part of the resolution contained the price to be asked for the first. It could be expected now — so was said in it — that the provisional treaty would soon be concluded as the opposition of Spain had always been the principal impediment. Now, upon that occasion, if the suppression could not be obtained, the States General ought to insist that the suspension should be prolonged for at least 12 or 15 years. This had first to be tried, and on account of the changed condition, it was thought easier now than at the time when the provisional treaty was drawn up. However, in the uncertainty whether the suppression or only the prolongation of the suspension could be effected, and in the general uncertainty as to how things would turn out in connection with the Emperor, France and England ought to commit themselves anew to what they had promised the Republic with regard to the Ostend trade and East Frisia.

Slingelandt did his utmost to get this resolution of Holland agreed to by the States General, but did not meet with immediate success. Some of the deputies wished to consult their constituents first. However, in order that the Republic should not lose the object and the fruit of the resolution through the scruples of these deputies, the Pensionary sent it to the plenipotentiaries so that they could inform the Allies of it in confidence without delay.

In doing so he seems to have meant, inter alia, to animate the Cardinal to agree to the Spanish garrisons. [2]) We saw shortly before that he had admonished him to be cautious as to an expedient in the Ostend affair. But neither the exhortation nor the dehortation were any longer necessary, for Fleury had entirely changed in the meanwhile.

One of the principal causes of this sudden turn was the attitude of the Court of Vienna. Sinzendorff had sent Fleury a reply that did not in any way come up to his expectations. Moreover, his expedient in the Ostend affair was, as has already been seen, entirely rejected. This coldness caused Fleury to relinquish the idea of resuming friendship with the Emperor. In his answer to Sinzen-

---

[1]) Slingelandt to Hop, 3 May, 11, 27 June '29; Secr. Res. Hl. 15 June '29.
[2]) Slingelandt to Hop, 17 June '29.
[3]) Hop to Slingelandt, 21 June, R. A. Hl. 2983.

dorff of the 30th. of May, he not only maintained his expedient, but settled the small amount of one million livres as the sum to be given by the States. He showed himself less easy, in addition, because he now questioned whether the Republic should adhere to the Quadruple Alliance, which was a point he had formerly admitted. The attitude of the Court of Vienna had another sequel. Unacquainted, as he was, with its true motive, viz., not to make any concessions except in return for the guaranty of the Pragmatic Sanction, the Cardinal inferred from it, that the Emperor still entertained hopes of keeping his hold upon Spain, and this, more than anything else, was liable to make him easy towards the latter. There were still other inducements to lead him in that direction: the strong uneasiness that the French nation displayed on account of their belief that the effects of the galleons would be seized, and, not least in importance, the conduct of the English. Now that, according to letters from Madrid, it could be expected that the proposals of the 9th. of May would be entirely rejected, the English were most vehement. In their judgment those proposals amounted to an ultimatum, and so they now insisted upon an immediate expedition to the coasts of Spain. The Cardinal succeeded in allaying the storm by giving up his reluctance to consent to the introduction of Spanish garrisons. The joint instructions of the 14th. of June allowed Brancas and Keene to go, if need be, to that limit. [1])

It was principally a desire to maintain peace which had brought Fleury to make that concession. He was, therefore, very uneasy when he saw that at this very time, on the 16th. of June, a Dutch squadron set out for Spithead to join the English fleet. It was feared in France that the joint fleet was going to blockade the Port of Cadiz, a scheme regarded as both dangerous and rash, as it would make Spain detain the effects of the galleons and drive her closer to Austria. The Court of France was very dissatisfied that the Republic lent a hand to this scheme, and Chauvelin did not conceal his opinion from Hop that Townshend had persuaded Slingelandt into the union of the fleets, nor his indignation that France had not been consulted about it. In conformity with Slingelandt's

[1]) Baudrillart, *op. cit.* III, 518—21; Höfler, *op. cit.* XXXII, 25, 36, 206, 234, XXXVIII, 5, 38—9, 69; Hop and Goslinga to Slingelandt, 31 May '29; Hop. to Slingelandt, 31 May, 7 June '29, R. A. Hl. 2986, 2983; Chauvelin to La Baune, 15 May '29, A. E. Hl. 377; Drafts to the Plenipotentiaries, 5 May '29, R. O. France 193.

directions, Hop answered him that the sending of the squadron
to Spithead was by no means the fruit of a secret understanding
with England, and there was no further mystery at the bottom
of it than to keep the adversaries in the same uncertainty as to
the use of the squadron in which the Republic herself was. This
was perfectly true, although Chauvelin did not believe it at all
and even ordered La Baune to complain. This became obvious
through Slingelandt's conduct when the Lords of the Council
urged the despatch of definite instructions to the squadron. [1])

The Lords, we saw, preferred to become friendly with the
Emperor. They were encouraged in this by the overtures of
Kinsky, which corresponded to those which Wenzel Sinzendorff
made to the Pensionary in the latter half of May. To be sure
they did not withhold their approbation of the conduct of the
plenipotentiaries as to the instructions of the 14th. of June,
principally because of the turn in the disposition of the French
Ministers, but at the same time they advised the King to fix
a day on which, if in the meantime no satisfactory answer had
come from Spain, a part of the fleet would leave for Gibraltar
and another for the West Indies. It was probably owing to the
Queen's influence that the King consented to this scheme. In any
case it was directly opposed to Townshend's ideas. The latter,
however, had already taken his measures. He had written to
England saying that the last time the English and Dutch
fleets were united, all orders for the English fleet had been
sent to the States for their concurrence, and he must insist
upon the same being done in this instance. Robert Walpole was
very uneasy at the union, as he felt that it would not facilitate,
but retard, the operations. But taking things as they were,
he wanted immediate orders for Chesterfield to deliberate with
the States; however, this only referred to that part of the fleet
that should be sent to Spain, for, in his judgment, whatever
was to be done in the West Indies should be done solely by the
English. But he did not obtain his wish. Chesterfield was directed by Townshend to sound the Pensionary as to what share
the Republic would prefer to take in the projected operations

---

[1]) Chauvelin to La Baune, 16 June, 7, 14, 24 July '29, La Baune to Chauvelin, 21,
24 June, 15 July '29, A. E. Hl. 377; Hop to Slingelandt, 16 June '29, R. A. Hl. 2983;
Slingelandt to Hop, 11 June '29, the Same to Goslinga, 5 July '29.

both in Europe and America. The States— so Townshend wrote to London — would never agree to leave the operations in the West Indies to His Majesty alone, even should the proposing of it to them most certainly break the union which existed between them and the King, which would be fatal at this juncture. [1])

The Foreign Secretary did still more to defeat the intentions of his colleagues. In addition to the letter to Chesterfield which contained the above-mentioned order he wrote him a private one. In this he condemned the step the Lords had taken as unnecessary, they went on "pretty fast" notwithstanding the fact that they had good reasons to expect a settlement with Spain, "to which the steps the States lately took will very much contribute". However, he was glad that the orders fell into Chesterfield's and Slingelandt's hands, who "will take care at least that they shall do no harm at this critical juncture" [2])

Townshend was not disappointed. Most astonished at the Lords' hasty resolution, the Pensionary raised several objections against the despatch of the requested instructions: it would be difficult to persuade the States to it before an answer had come from Spain. Spain's answer was likely to be satisfactory, but if not, the projected operations would drive her closer to the Emperor, and war with the latter would be a most serious thing for the Republic, besides she ought to know what France thought of it first. [3])

In promoting an agreement with Spain, Slingelandt and Townshend worked hand in hand with each other. Slingelandt did the same in warding off any particular negotiation with the Emperor. The latter was greatly disquieted by the course of events. He heard that Spain was negotiating with the Hanover Allies and that a joint Anglo-Dutch fleet was lying at Spithead. The last mentioned fact especially attracted his attention as he suspected these ships might transport the Spanish garrisons to Italy. The situation was made the more serious as the information received from Fonseca was that France could

---

[1]) Newcastle to Stanhope, 22 May, 12 June '29, in Coxe *R. W.* II, 641 et seq.; King, *Notes* 90—8; Townshend to Chesterfield, 1 July '29, R. O. Hl. 304.

[2]) Townshend to Chesterfield, 1 July '29, in Coxe *R. W.* II, 645—6.

[3]) Chesterfield to Townshend, 7 July '29, R. O. Hl. 304 cf. the Same to the Same, 7 July '29, private, in Coxe, *loc. cit.* 646.

no longer be depended upon. For a long time, ever since the end of 1726, the Emperor had depended upon the Cardinal's desire for peace, but Fonseca was now persuaded that the latter would eventually be drawn along by Spain. Fleury's letter to Sinzendorff, dated the 30th. of May, confirmed the same opinion. The only remaining course, therefore, was to prevent the Maritime Powers from concluding an agreement with Spain, and to induce them to join him, the Emperor, or, in other words, to revive the old system. So he instructed his plenipotentiaries to declare to those of England and the Republic that if they would guarantee the Pragmatic Sanction and commit themselves either for the first time or anew as the case might be to the Quadruple Alliance, the Emperor would give them every satisfaction they desired each in their own particular points(instructions of 11th. July). [1]

The Austrian plenipotentiaries did not meet with any success. Those of the Maritime Powers answered that they had no instructions as to the Pragmatic Sanction. It was true that they did not doubt that their Masters would favour this point, but the affairs of the Congress must be settled first and in particular their differences with the Emperor must be removed, according to the rule: *spoliatus ante omnia restituendus*. The Austrians had such small success that they advised their Court to apply direct to England and the Republic. This had already been done. Philip Kinsky had left London for Hanover. He met with no more success. Townshend declared that the Pragmatic Sanction affected general affairs too much to be discussed anywhere but at the Congress and after deliberation with the Allies. Slingelandt quoted his answer when he received an application for opinion from Sinzendorff. He added that the conduct of the Court of Vienna towards the Republic ever since the Peace of Utrecht had been such that she could not safely engage in negotiations with it, for even though these should result favourably to her, the result would be most dangerous as the Republic's Allies would not guarantee it, and the guaranty of Prussia and of the the Czar would not satisfy her. [2]

---

[1] Rescript to the Austrian Plenipotentiaries, 11 July '29, Sinzendorff to St. Kinsky, 11 July '29, in Höfler, *op. cit*. XXXII, 35 et seq. 67 et seq.; Hop to Slingelandt, 22 July '29, R. A. Hl. 2983.

[2] Relations of the Austrian Plenipotentiaries, 6, 27 July, 3, 22, 24 Aug. '29, in Höfler, *op. cit*. XXXII; cf. ibid., 139; Coxe, *loc. cit*. 528—30; Slingelandt to Hop, 22 Aug. '29.

In this way Slingelandt utterly declined to make a separate agreement with the Emperor. In his judgment the overtures had probably no other object than to make strained relations between the Republic and her Allies and give the Emperor an opportunity of agreeing with these at her expense. Besides this, it would make the fruit of the negotiations with Spain lost to her, which fruit would be at least the renewal of commercial advantages.

The Pensionary was also opposed to the Emperor's admission to the general negotiations as long as the Hanover Allies did not separate him definitely from Spain, and come to an agreement with Spain themselves. He was persuaded that until this had come to pass it would be impossible to treat with him. Necessity would only bring him to reason, and as long as there was a possibility of his hampering the negotiations he would do so rather than make them general by accepting reasonable terms himself [1]).

In all this Slingelandt wholly agreed with Townshend. How was this? Had he become friendly with him whose policy he had so mercilessly condemned in the preceding year? Not at all. Thus far he agreed with him but not a single step further. They agreed that now, before anything else, an arrangement with Spain had to be achieved, but differed *toto coelo* as to what should happen afterwards. Townshend cared little for that. His only care was, that Elizabeth, after obtaining all she desired from the Hanover Allies, might turn to the Emperor again, still with a hope of arranging the marriage between Don Carlos and Maria Theresa. His first idea was to demand a declaration from her stating to whom she intended marrying her son, but if that could not be, he would like to deter the Emperor from this marriage by threatening him with the guaranty of his hereditary dominions to Saxony and Bavaria. Slingelandt did not at all favour this idea. He did not think it advantageous to the Maritime Powers to dismember and weaken the Empire; France would so greedily accept the proposition on purpose to weaken the Empire, and in particular the House of Austria, that it would be difficult to turn her from it later on; besides, the Emperor knew only too well that such a division of his dominions would be against their interest, and so that threat would have no effect upon him. Still, the Pensionary agreed

---

[1]) Slingelandt to Goslinga 22, 23, 28 July '29, the Same to Hop, 2, 22 Aug. '29; Chesterfield to the Plenipotentiaries, 24 July '29, in Coxe, *loc. cit.* 647, et seq.

with Townshend that the marriage had to be prevented. The latter therefore requested him and Fagel to suggest another expedient. Fagel said he thought it better that a hint should be dropped by the ministers of the Hanover Allies to the effect that in the event of no security being given that the marriage of Don Carlos would not take place, they should make other arrangements to prevent the marriage. A hint of this description was preferable to a threat which would only hurt the Austrian pride, but it if was necessary to threaten the Emperor, he ought at the same time to be offered the guaranty of the Pragmatic Sanction on condition that he married his daughter to a Prince to whom they did not object. [1])

The Greffier as well as the Pensionary had the best intentions towards the Emperor. He even expressed the fear that on account of the Emperor's unreasonable conduct the Allies might have to be more severe with him than it was their interest to be.[2]). Townshend had no such fear, it was immaterial to him whether Spain reconquered all the Italian dominions which were formerly hers, but Slingelandt adhered to the Treaties which had adjusted the affairs of Europe after the war of the Spanish succession, and more especially to the Quadruple Alliance. In promoting the introduction of Spanish garrisons he only meant to secure for Don Carlos what the Alliance had promised him. From the outset his opinion had been: "qu'on n'irait pas jusqu'à donner à la Reine le moindre sujet de se flatter que les Alliés pourraient souffrir que l'Espagne contrevînt à la Quadruple Alliance, moins encore qu'ils pourraient prêter les mains à cela" [3]). It was anything but immaterial to him what was to happen after the agreement with Spain. In his judgment, it was necessary to admit the Emperor to the negotiations on reasonable terms before the final conclusion, viz., as soon as the decision of Spain became definitely known.

Slingelandt's striving for the general peace of Europe was responsible for his taking this view. The pacification would not be general as long as the Emperor would not be included in it. But his desire for the Republic's interests also influenced him. For if an agreement came about with Spain, in which the Emperor was

---

[1]) Chesterfield to Townshend, 11, 21, 28 June '29, Townshend to Chesterfield, 14 June '29, R. O. Hl. 304.

[2]) Coxe, *loc. cit.* 649.

[3]) Slingelandt to Chesterfield, 17 Jany. '30, B. M. Add. 32765.

not included, he would become much more difficult to handle regarding his differences with the Republic, especially in the Ostend affair. This was then to become a great stumbling block, and Slingelandt did not see how to remove it. A seperate agreement with the Emperor was, in his estimation, as we have seen, as dangerous as it was unfair. To keep in with the Allies and to make a favourable treaty with Spain seemed to him to be the best means for attaining the end. He hoped that the support of the Allies would procure for the Republic what he despaired of obtaining from the Emperor's free-will, but whether these hopes would be realised or not was most uncertain. The Pensionary, therefore, thought it advisable to spare a Prince who might go to extremities if he thought his honour or greatness were at stake, and could flatter himself that his adversaries would rather come to loggerheads with each other than consent to the overthrow of the balance of power. The Emperor ought not to be given the slightest offence, if it were at all possible to avoid it; the Allies ought even to be considerate of him in every possible way [1]).

In their conversations with Sinzendorff, Slingelandt and Fagel had constantly been so considerate. It was true that when he enquired they did not dissemble towards him their inclination of furthering the introduction of Spanish garrisons, still less that, at all events, they intended keeping firmly to their Allies. Their attentions to the Emperor, had, as Slingelandt expressed it, less relation to the substance of affairs, which as far as the Republic was concerned had been settled by the Resolution of the 23rd. of July, than to the method of treating them. But ever since the moment when Sinzendorff had broached the subject of the Pragmatic Sanction to them (2nd. half of May), they had expressed themselves most favourable to it, providing always that there would be no question of Spanish marriages [2]).

Those attentions had, however, very little effect. It was not that Sinzendorff did not incessantly boast about the Emperor's inclination to give satisfaction to the Republic, but he went no further. Fagel complained in his letter of the 6th. of September to Hamel Bruynincx, that whenever he passed from generalities he put his demands so high that it was utterly impossible to comply with

---

[1]) Slingelandt to Goslinga, 23, 28 July '29, the same to Hop, 22 Aug. '29.
[2]) Höfler, *op. cit.* XXXII, 36, 39, 130, 138, 351—3; Slingelandt to Hop, 22 Aug. '29.

them. As regards the Ostend Company, he declared that his Master would never acquiesce to the prolongation of the suspension or to the suppression, unless he were indemnified by a sum of money; how much, he did not say, but expressed the hope that eight million guilders would suffice, which, however, he could not answer for. [1]

Such attentions, sighed Slingelandt, were of no effect at all in the affairs of East Frisia. [2] These were still in a very bad condition. The Renitents' submission had not brought any relief. It had been rejected immediately by the Sub-delegates (March 28th.). And, though, pending the Emperor's final decision, everything ought to have remained *in statu quo*, the Sub-delegates and the Prince continued their hard proceedings. Slingelandt suspected them of being prompted by secret orders and hints from Vienna. Very probably he was right, at any rate the Emperor's excuse for delaying his decision for such a long time, was suspicious: he had accepted the submission on the 3rd. of May, but owing to the neglect of the Chancellory this had not been published. However this may be, the situation of the poor country grew still more serious. The States General, to whom the Renitents again applied in their distress, could not stand it any longer. The Renitents would consider themselves relinquished and misled by them if they did not oppose force to force. They did not hesitate one moment more, when the Sub-delegates to whom they had remonstrated entirely denied what was laid to their charge. So then, on the 20th. of July, they ordered their Commander in Emden to give the assurance that, should any more proceedings be taken against the Renitents, pending the Emperor's decision, the States General should come to their assistance in virtue of their guaranty of the East Frisian accords concluded under their intervention. [3]

This resolution, which, in order to save time, had not been submitted to the Allies, roused the anger of Chauvelin to a high degree. One of the causes of this anger was the fear that in the existing European crisis the step might be attended by grave consequences. Chauvelin suspected Chesterfield's consent to the resolution, and praised La Baune for having represented to Slinge-

---

[1] Höfler, *op. cit.* XXXII, 351—3, cf. 86; Slingelandt to Goslinga, 21 Aug. '29.
[2] Slingelandt to Hop, 2 Aug. '29.
[3] Res. S. G. 14 Apr., 6, 12, 16, 20 July '29; Slingelandt to Hop, 12 Juli '29, R. A. Legatie 84; Höfler, *op. cit.* XXXII,95—6; Chesterfield to Townshend, 5, 12 July '29, R. O. Hl. 304.

landt that England was glad, on account of her own interest, if one of the Allies took a step that could lead to war. He was not far wrong. Chesterfield rejoiced in the firmness of the Republic because if the Allies became more necessary to her she would become more useful to them [1]).

It must be borne in mind that Chesterfield was still urging the despatch of orders to the Dutch squadron. It was not *pro forma* that he did so, but first of all because the King had instructed him so to do; besides, should the proposals of June 14th. be refused, even Townshend would be in favour of the sending of the joint fleet to Spain. Nor would Slingelandt have opposed it under those circumstances, but, as he told Chesterfield, he could not bring the States to a decision as long as Spain's answer was not known. This was delayed for a long time. But happily a provisional answer, dated July 9th., arrived at the Hague on the 25th. of that month. It only contained the promise that the effects of the galleons should be delivered. People wished it had been clearer and more to the point. Still they looked upon it as a good sign. Chesterfield, therefore, wrote to London that if the Lords desired the immediate departure of the English fleet, they had better send it alone, as it would be imprudent now to press the States strongly; it would be better to do so if the final answer was unsatisfactory. The Ambassador apparently thought that the Lords were unwilling to wait any longer, but at the same time the provisional answer was rather pleasing to them and they decided to wait for the final one [2]).

This came fairly soon. It was dated July 30th. and arrived in Paris on the 13th. of August. There was much to say against the project of which it consisted. The Lords called it crude, obscure and unsatisfactory. Yet, even in their opinion, it was such as might, with sufficient alterations and amendments, be made the means of arranging a peace with Spain, and for the present they delayed the departure of the fleet. They did so because they felt, as also did Slingelandt, that Spain had broken entirely with the Emperor[3]).

---

[1]) Hop to Slingelandt ,29 July 29, R. A. Hl. 2983; Chauvelin to La Baune, 26 July, 7 Aug. '29, La Baune to Chauvelin, 2 Aug. '29, A. E. Hl. 377; Chesterfield to Townshend, 12 July, 1 Aug. '29, R. O. Hl. 304.

[2]) Chesterfield to Townshend, 7, 19, 23, 25, 25 July, 2 Aug. '29, R. O. Hl. 304—5; Newcastle to Stanhope, 17 July '29, in Coxe, *loc. cit.* 650.

[3]) King, *Notes* 99—100; Chesterfield to Townshend, 19 Aug. '29, R.O. Hl. 305.

This was indeed the case. As soon as Elizabeth saw that the Allies did not immediately show an inclination to favour the introduction of 6,000 Spaniards, as mentioned in La Paz's letter of the 29th. of March, she immediately applied to the Emperor again for his permission for the introduction of these troops. This request was refused, just as the offer of marriage was a few months previously. Then the Queen did not hesitate any longer, but she broke loose from the Emperor and turned to the Hanover Allies[1]). The breach of those who had been united since 1725 was inevitable.

The breach was not the work of the Hanover Allies, at any rate not in the first place. Slingelandt, if he had had his own way, would have provoked it a year previously, but France and Enggland then thought it best to side with the Emperor, who suggested the idea of a provisional treaty in order to prevent a breach. The Pensionary saw very well that, through this, the solution had been retarded instead of promoted. It was impossible as long as the great question of the marriage and the Austrian Succession was not taken in hand. But Elizabeth did what the Congress did not do — and the Alliance, which was based on the marriage, fell through. As a matter of course the provisional treaty also fell through. After the breach the interest of the Emperor ceased. The same applied to France, who now need not fear that Spain would declare war on England, as well as to Enggland, who could now hope that Spain would yield in the points of dispute. Both in the proposals of the 9th. of May and the 14th. of June the provisional treaty had been made mention of, but in the project which would be returned to Spain in answer to hers of the 30th. of July, it was not to be spoken of. The provisional treaty was done with.

D. Negotiations preceding the Treaty of Seville.
August—November 1729.

I.

French politics had, at the end of May, turned from the Emperor. This had immediate influence on the Empire. As we have

---

[1]) At this time Elizabeth no longer, as some authors think, pressed the Emperor as to the marriage, but only on the question of the Spanish garrisons (Höfler, *op. cit.* XXXII, 33; Arneth, *op. cit.* III, 238—9).

seen, France had twice frustrated a general action in the Empire, both in the Summer of the preceding year and in the Winter. She had done so, on the one hand, out of regard for the Emperor, and on the other because of her private negotiations with the Elector Palatine. These negotiations had occupied many months. The Elector Palatine had a far from easy task in making the other three Electors adhere to the Treaty of neutrality, which was the condition France had exacted in return for the guaranty so eagerly wished for. Though the Treaty of Marly, which was the eventual result of the negotiations, was dated February 15th. 1729, it was not before the end of April that it received its final signature[1]. Once it had been concluded, obstacles against the instituting of a general action in the Empire by France no longer existed; on the contrary, the treaty which to some extent bound the four Electors to her, secured her the leadership in it.

Her first aim now was to dispose George II. in its favour. In that way not only might England be gained, but also the union of Wolfenbüttel and Würtemberg which had recently been strengthened by the accession of the King of Sweden, in his capacity as Prince of the Empire [2]), and of which George II., as Elector, was the principal member. It was in order to make him enter into a union with the four Electors that France, during the latter half of June, sent the cunning Chavigny to Hanover [3]).

In the Winter the King had refused to do so because the Electors were said to be unwilling to undertake any obligations with regard to the Mecklenburg affair. Thereupon, as he had told his Allies in advance, he had made a proposal to the King of Prussia to the effect that they settle this affair between themselves, but in May the effort had miscarried [4]) It caused him continual uneasiness, the more so when in June the Emperor brought it before the Diet. This was one of the subjects of the deliberations which were held at Hanover in the Summer of 1729, in which, in addition to Townshend and Chavigny, Plettemberg and Bevern took part, the former for the Elector of Cologne, the latter for the Elector Palatine. Its principal subject was the project of a treaty between the Hanover Allies and the four Electors, which had been drawn

[1]) Rosenlehner, *op. cit.* Chap. VII, particularly pp. 460—1.
[2]) Townshend to Chesterfield, 14 June n. s. '29, R. O. Hl. 304.
[3]) Dureng, *Mission de Chavigny en Allemagne* (Paris 1911), Chap. III.
[4]) Droysen, *op. cit.* II, 51—3.

up by D'Albert, the Bavarian Envoy at Paris. Concerning these negotiations and the discussions of the Diet about Mecklenburg, we know but little [1]). Nor do we know how far the conflict between George II. and Frederick William which arose at this very time, is connected with these questions. Perhaps Dureng is right, ascribing it to the Mecklenburg affair: [2]) perhaps it originated in a mere outburst of George II.'s passion.

As is generally known, the King-Elector disliked his Prussian brother-in-law. On the other hand, the latter provoked him, and indeed, all his neighbours, by enlisting soldiers on his territory. Not being prepared to suffer it, George II., a few weeks after his arrival in Hanover, resolved on reprisals He gave in charge some Prussian soldiers who happened to be on Hanoverian soil. Another trifling hostility was added to this. Frederick William became furious. He had several Hanoverian subjects apprehended, and exacted the liberty of his own subjects without delay. This George II. refused unless the Hanoverians were simultaneously liberated.

The two Kings could not agree. In the course of July and August their discord became increasingly serious. Each equipped himself and appealed to his Allies, George II. in particular doing so. He had brought great trouble upon himself, and felt by no means safe in his Electorate. He probably would not have admitted Robert Walpole's description of Hanover — that it would be no more than a breakfast to a Prussian army — though he knew quite well that it was open and unprotected by any fortress. He turned to all sides for help — to Wolfenbüttel, to Hesse-Cassel, to Denmark, to Sweden, to the Lords of the Council in England, to France, and last but not least, to the Republic [3]).

Here Chesterfield met with complete success. The States immediately wrote a "dehortatory" letter to the King of Prussia, and, shortly afterwards, one to the Emperor, whom they suspected of inciting him. Not only that, but in a few days, with unheard-of speed, they came to the vigorous resolution of September 3rd.. Holzendorff, Chesterfield's secretary, who had at first been rather

---

[1]) Dureng, *op. cit.* 73—4, 82—92; Rosenlehner, *op. cit.* 463; Matthias, *Die Mecklemburger Frage im* 18ten *Jahrhundert* (1885) was not accessible to me.
[2]) Dureng, *op. cit.* 86.
[3]) Droysen, *op. cit.* II, 55—74; Schilling, *Der Zwist Preuszens und Hannovers* 1729—30. (Halle, 1912).

sceptical about their assistance, felt obliged to admit that "in short they have done wondrous things, and their former lethargy is now turned into the quickest vigilance".

Particular zeal was displayed by the province of Holland. She at once proposed considerably exceeding, if necessary, the obligatory contingent of troops, and, contrary to all rules, voted the quota of the expenses she would have to bear immediately upon the reading of the petition of the Council of State. The credit of this conduct is due to her Pensionary, who, though confined to his bed by his usual illness, worked indefatigably to secure the Republic's greatest possible assistance to George II.. He summoned influential members of the States to his bedside, and animated them. Meynertshagen, Prussian Envoy at the Hague, complained to him of the extraordinary zeal developed by the Republic, and particularly that orders had been given to exceed the obligatory contingent, whereas she had not the least right to interfere in the dispute, this being of a strictly German character. Slingelandt answered that, had it depended upon him, a body of troops twice the size should have been sent; the Republic had nothing to do with the dispute itself; the knowledge that George II. was attacked was sufficient reason for her assisting him [1]).

The Republic cut a fine figure; a finer — so Slingelandt wrote to Hop — than would have been the case had the dispute resulted in war [2]). This, however, did not happen. At the moment of action, Frederick William shrank from the responsibility of a war with Hanover which might easily result in general hostilities, in the existing crisis. He agreed to the mediation of the Dukes of Brunswick-Wolfenbüttel and Saxe-Gotha, as a result of which the affair which had seemed likely to cause a European conflagration suddenly sank down to a somewhat insignificant German law-suit. This mode of action may reflect honour on him, but it is certain that his reputation suffered greatly as a result. He appeared to have yielded to the menaces of the Hanover Allies.

Of these, France also had shown great interest in the affairs of George II. The French Envoy at Berlin had openly declared that

---

[1]) Res. S. G. 29 Aug., 1, 3, 7, 8 Sept. '29; Slingelandt to Hop, 6 Sept. '29, R. A. Legatie 84; Townshend to Chesterfield, 23 Aug., 2 Sept. n. s. '29, Chesterfield to Townshend or Newcastle, 30 Aug., 2, 3, 6, 9 Sept. '29, Holzendorff to Tilson, 30 Aug., 3 Sept. '29, R. O. Hl. 305.

[2]) Slingelandt to Hop, 13 Sept. '29.

his master would support him. The aim of this declaration was, in the first place, to intimidate the King of Prussia, for France by no means desired a conflict between them, if only for the reason that by so doing she would have procured a strong ally for the Emperor, and just at a time when she was exerting herself to isolate the latter. The aim of the declaration was at the same time to get into George II.'s good graces, and to make him the more willing to agree to the projected treaty with the Electors. This is evident from Chavigny's emphasising the advantages which the King might derive from the union with the Electors, in the event of hostilities with Prussia [1]).

The French ministers also wanted the Republic to assist in bringing him to it. At least, as we take it, this intention underlay what they said to the Dutch plenipotentiaries on this point: England adduced as excuse for her non-accession that the Republic was not disposed to guarantee the succession to Juliers and Bergh to the House of Pfalz-Sulzbach [2]); or, at another time: this succession seemed to mean far less to the Republic than it had previously meant. Slingelandt utterly repudiated this reproach [3]). It was, indeed, totally unjust. In spite of his efforts, the guaranty of this succession by the Maritime Powers and a general action in the Empire, had twice miscarried. It had been good news to him when, in May, the Anglo-Prussian negotiations came to nothing, since from it he inferred that it would render George II. all the more inclined towards a treaty with the Electors. [4]) And now he attentively followed what was occurring in Hanover as in his judgment the Republic had a great interest in it [5]).

II.

From the time that France turned from the Emperor, she strove all the more to gain Spain. What was her object now? — to unite with Spain alone, or in conjunction with the rest of the Hanover Allies, and in particular England? The crisis through

---

[1]) Droysen, *op. cit.* II, 62—3; Schilling, *op. cit.* 78; Dureng, *op. cit.* 86, 88—9.
[2]) Hop to Slingelandt, 15 Sept. '29, R. A. Hl. 2983.
[3]) Slingelandt tot Goslinga, 8 Sept. '29.
[4]) Chesterfield to Townshend, 17 May '29, R. O. Hl. 304.
[5]) Slingelandt to Hop, 22 Aug. '29; cf. Chesterfield to Townshend, 25 July '29, R. O. Hl. 304.

which France passed in August ran on this question. The Spanish project of July 30th. showed little regard for English trade, and maintained the pretensions to Gibraltar [1]). By no less a person than Chauvelin was this project advocated. In his opinion it was not prudent to free England of all her difficulties, nor was it to the interest of French trade. For a moment Chauvelin seems to have prevailed upon Fleury, but his influence did not last. The latter considered that he could not depend upon Spain, who again retarded delivery of the effects [2]). Especially was he convinced that should he not procure satisfaction for the English amicably they would themselves procure it by war. For these reasons he yielded to Horace Walpole's energetic remonstrances. It was not made easy for him, as the English put their claims very high, but for the sake of peace he went as far towards them as he could. The counter-project which was sent to Spain on September 11th. was in the end such as to make Robert Walpole fear it was too good [3]).

One point the Cardinal did not yield: the confirmation by Spain of the cession of Gibraltar. He wished the English to content themselves with an implied confirmation. To persuade them to this, he also made use of the Republic. He begged Slingelandt through the medium of both La Baune and the Dutch plenipotentiaries to influence the English government. The Pensionary was perfectly prepared to accede, and strongly urged Chesterfield to dissuade the Government from insisting on this point, but even before they were informed of this, they had abandoned the demand [4]).

France, it is true, preferred to make use of the Republic in order to induce England to moderation in her demands, and she intended to do so should Spain raise objections to the counter-project but she ignored Dutch interests. The time for taking care of them had now arrived, as on July 23rd. the States General had adopted

---

[1]) Townshend to Chesterfield, 21 Aug. '29, Chesterfield to Townshend, 26 Aug. '29, R. O. Hl. 305; King, *Notes* 99.

[2]) Baudrillart, *op. cit.* III, 532: Villars *Mémoires* V. 190 et seq.

[3]) Lavisse, *Histoire de France* 8, II, 118—9; Bourgeois, *Manuel*, I, 479—480; Coxe, *H. W.* 167—9; idem, *Memoirs of the Kings of Spain* (London, 1813) II, 425; King, *Notes*, 109—10; Baudrillart, *op. cit.* III, 530 (3rd footnote), 535; Chauvelin to La Baune, 21 Aug., 11 Sept. '29, A. E. Hl. 377, 378.

[4]) Baudrillart, *op. cit.* III, 531, 2nd footnote, 535, 537 et seq.; Coxe *R. W.* II, 651, 653; Chesterfield to Townshend, 6 Sept. '29, very secret, R. O. Hl. 305; Slingelandt to Goslinga, 8 Sept. '29.

the resolution passed by Holland on June 15th.. However, the
desire to participate in the negotiations with Spain which this expressed, had a cool reception at the Court of France, and in spite of
the promises made both when the instructions of May 9th. were
dispatched and when Spain's provisional answer of July 9th. arrived [1]), the Republic's interests were neglected and she was excluded from the negotiations. For the sake of secrecy — so was
pretended — she could not yet engage herself in it [2]).

What caused France to act in this manner? As we have seen,
she took the combining of her squadron with the English fleet
very badly in the Republic as also the resolution of July 20th. regarding East Frisia. Her principal motive of this indignation was
not fear of war. At all events not in the latter case. For, apropos
of this, Chauvelin wrote to La Baune, that it was not for the sake
of the matter itself that France so bitterly complained of her not
having been consulted before the resolution was taken; on the
contrary, it was in itself most proper that the Republic should
give the Court of Vienna to understand that she was not satisfied
with fine words, but that *France ought not to permit the passing
of resolutions without consulting her to become customary* [3]).

That is the point. France wished to retain the Republic's depend-
ency. She would be of especial importance to her once the treaty
with Spain had been concluded. For then the question of the relation to the Emperor, and, in close connection with this, that of
peace or war would immediately present itself. Under these circumstances France would be glad to manoeuvre with the Republic at discretion, and in consequence did not consider it wise to
secure advantages for her too soon.

Not only France, but England, too, disregarded her interests. At
the very time that the Republic took up the cause of George II. in
the Prusso-Hanoverian conflict so cordially, his plenipotentiaries
did not pay any attention to Ostend and East Frisia. The principal motive of this conduct appears to have been dissatisfaction
at the Republic's having wished to become a party to the treaty
on the favourable conditions granted her in 1719, when, however,

---

[1]) Plenipotentiaries to Slingelandt, 7 May, 29 July '29, R. A. Hl. 2986; Chauvelin to
La Baune, 26 July '29, A. E. Hl. 377.
[2]) Hop to Slingelandt, 19 Aug., 8 Sept., 18 Oct. 29, R. A. Hl. 2983; Baudrillart, *op cit.*
III, 533.
[3]) Chauvelin to La Baune, 26 July '29, A. E. Hl. 377.

her accession to the engagements on behalf of Don Carlos was far more important than now. The English particularly disliked the demand that the Republic should not be required to supply more than 3,000 men in the event of a war in Italy. It was for this reason that they did not advance her accession to the treaty, for they expected that, should she accede to it at a later date, she would have to bear a greater share in its burdens [1]).

France and England — it must be admitted — were more easily able to neglect her interests as her own plenipotentiaries were not awake. Shortly before the counter-project was dispatched they were informed of it and asked whether they desired anything adding to it. They then replied that since it had not yet been communicated to the States they could not have been instructed; they could only declare that their Masters were most willing to enter into the same engagements as their Allies and would be most pleased if they would bring this under the notice of Spain. That they could speak in this way was the result of their supposing that the treaty would not be signed in Spain, but returned to France and before its conclusion communicated to the States [2]). But this turned out to be an error. France and England sent together with the counter-project full powers to settle matters. And Stanhope, formerly ambassador at Madrid, left for Spain in order to help forward the conclusion by his personal influence.

Slingelandt was anything but pleased with the attitude of the plenipotentiaries. "If it could have been foreseen" — he wrote — "that things would take such a turn, the resolution of July 23rd. would have been worded so as to empower the plenipotentiaries to act more directly in the name of the Republic. They have been too scrupulous; they knew that the object of the negotiations as well as of the resolution was to detach Spain from the Emperor, and as to the Republic in particular, to take upon herself the credit of a step to which she would have to come sooner or later and so ingratiate herself with Spain and the Allies. It is most difficult to procure an alteration in a resolution, once it has been passed, but not, to obtain approbation of what has been done according to its spirit though it may exceed its letter; there is little risk in conforming one self to powerful allies to promote in that way the

---

[1]) Hop to Slingelandt, 19 Aug., 8, 15 Sept., 18 Oct., 21 Nov. '29 R. A. Hl. 2983.
[2]) Plenipotentiaries to Slingelandt, 8 Sept. '29, R. A. Hl. 2986.

Republic's interest if otherwise, as in the present case, this would be exposed to neglect." Had Slingelandt had his way the pleni-potentiaries would have prepared everything so that the Republic would engage in the treaty as a contracting party and so that once it had arrived in Spain Van der Meer would have nothing to do but to sign [1]).

The Pensionary was no better pleased with the English. "The English" — he wrote to Goslinga — "who do not stand in good repute here either with the Republicans or with the magistrates of our large towns run the risk of losing all their credit if they continue to neglect our interests in the negotiations with Spain, while in compact with France they formally exclude us from it and desire to be supported by us even to the disadvantage of our trade which suffers greatly from the Assiento Treaty and the use they make of it. If you speak of it to Horace Walpole, *"je vous prie de lui faire mes très humbles compliments"* [2]).

Regarding France, Slingelandt also vented his indignation. He did so particularly when this Power — after having insinuated that the dispatching of the squadron to Spithead and Holland's resolution of June 15th. had been suggested by England — also showed that she was offended at the resolution of July 20th. Then he wrote to Goslinga who to a great extent agreed with the feelings of the Court of France, as follows. "If upon a step so necessary so compulsory, so tardy, so justified by all that has passed between us and our Allies, especially France, we cannot rely on the cordial and real assistance of our Allies, who have reproached us a hundred times with timidity, I think we had better renounce our alliances and abandon ourselves as humble supplicants to the discretion of the Emperor. Nor do I comprehend" — so he continues — "that it needs to rouse the anger of Chauvelin because we sent a squadron to Spithead without first consulting him, though there was no understanding about it with England and it followed naturally from the advices of France. I doubt whether such a way of acting has a good effect here and reinforces the confidence, so greatly necessary amongst allies. We are willing to go great lengths in our compliance, but we cannot but reflect upon the cool

---

[1]) Slingelandt to Hop, 8, 13 Sept. '29; Chesterfield to Newcastle, 13 Sept. '29, R. O. Hl. 305.

[2]) Slingelandt to Goslinga, 13 Sept. '29.

reception our scheme to take part in the negotiations with Spain has met with, notwithstanding that, in the proposals made to this Power as upon other occasions the Republic has been engaged indirectly without her knowledge, and even her name made use of as of a contracting party, just as if she were under guardianship" [1]).

The way the Allies treated the Republic will indubitably have made Slingelandt rejoice the more at the proposals made by the Emperor at this juncture.

III.

The Emperor's position was a most critical one. He had no longer anything to hope for from Spain; on the contrary, he had to fear that she would join the Hanover Allies and that, consequently, he would become almost isolated. He was fully aware of the delicacy of the circumstances. This is evident from his attitude towards the Prusso-Hanoverian conflict. He was, to be sure, wise enough to make use of it to bind Frederick William more closely to him, but did not — as people thought in the Republic — incite him; on the contrary, he exhorted him to be amenable to reason [2]). Far from aiming at a war, he did his utmost to win over his adversaries. It was for this reason that he allowed the Mecklenburg affair to lie dormant at the Diet [3]), and for this that he disowned the Sub-delegates' proceedings in East Frisia [4]), and, on September 12th., issued a decree accepting the submission of the Renitents, and allowing them two months in which to deliver *gravamina* against the decrees of the Aulic Council and the ordinances of the Sub-delegates. It was, finally, for this that, on August 31st., he ordered his plenipotentiaries to make the following proposals:

1. L'abolition de la Compagnie d'Ostende, moyennant l'envoi pour une seule fois de deux vaisseaux.

2. Abandonner l'excédant des revenues des Pays-Bas, déduction faite des frais civils et militaires qui seraient compris dans une liste de même que toutes les dettes et dépenses des dits Pays-Bas.

---

[1]) The Same to the Same, 21 Aug. '29; cf. the Same to the Same, 5 July '29, and the Same to Hop, 2 Aug. '29 ib.

[2]) Höfler, *op. cit.* XXXII, 99, 143—6, 251.

[3]) Dureng, *op. cit.* 96.

[4]) Chesterfield to Townshend, 19 Aug. '29, R. O. Hl. 305; Chauvelin to La Baune, 28 Aug. '29, A. E. Hl. 377; Res. S. G. 19 Sept. '29.

Le dit excédant abandonné pour tenir lieu de 500 mille écus
stipulé par le traité de barrière, qui moyennant cet excédant
restent à la charge des Etats-Generaux.

3. Commissaires nommés par l'Empereur, l'Angleterre et la Hollande en exécution du traité de barrière pour convenir d'un
   nouveau reglement de tarif, Sa Majesté Imperiale promettant
   pendant une année la continuation du tarif présentement établi, et si le nouveau tarif n'est pas reglé dans l'année, l'Empereur rentrera dans les droits de souveraineté pour établir tel
   tarif qu'il jugera à propos.

4. L'exécution de la Quadruple Alliance sans y rien changer n'y
   innover, comme une condition sine qua non, sauf à convenir
   ensemble des mesures, qui pourraient être prises pour l'execution du dit traité de la Quadruple Alliance sans en pouvoir
   changer ni le sens ni la lettre.

5. Reconnaissance publique et formelle avec guarantie par toutes
   les puissances contractantes de l'ordre de la succession établi selon la Pragmatique Sanction de l'Empereur, pour en
   faire un article du traité. Cette garantie proposée comme une
   condition sine qua non [1]).

The significance of these proposals lies, not in the fact that they
made great concessions to the Republic — in Slingelandt's opinion
they were, so far as her interests were concerned, even more prejudicial than previous offers — but in the fact that they were made
to each of the three Hanover Allies [2]). This is evident in comparing
the instructions of August 31st. with those of July 11th., which
latter prescribe silence towards France concerning the Pragmatic
Sanction, but advocacy with the Maritime Powers. This, however,
had led to nothing. In Paris the plenipotentiaries of England and
the Republic had referred the Austrians to London and the
Hague, and there people had refused to negotiate upon so important a point with France excluded. Because of this attitude adopted
by the Maritime Powers, the Emperor resolved to apply to
France as well [3]). As a result of this decision his proposals ceased
to bear the character of private overtures; one might say that he

---

[1]) Rescript 31 Aug. '29, Höfler, *op. cit.* XXXII, 117 et seq; Précis des propositions
faites verbalement par. M. M. de Kinsky et Fonseca de la part de l'Empereur, ib. 350,
and Secr. Res. Hl. 12 Oct. '29.

[2]) Slingelandt to Hop, 27 Sept., 25 Oct. '29.

[3]) Rescripts 11 July, 31 Aug. '29, in Höfler, *op. cit.* XXXII, 35 et seq., 117 et seq.

now brought the affair of the succession before the Congress.

"Voilà — Hop wrote to Slingelandt — "la négociation au point où il m'a paru que vous avez toujours cru qu'elle devait venir pour en espérer une bonne issue" [1]). He was right. From the outset it had been Slingelandt's wish that the succession should be discussed, and now the man who had previously done his utmost to suppress the affair not only ceased his resistance, but even introduced it himself. It was a fine opportunity which could not be neglected. The principal concern now was to secure the concurrence of France and England, both of whom had, at the beginning of the Congress, assisted the Emperor in keeping the question remote from it. To this end the Pensionary took up his pen and wrote a memorial, dated September 28th., which he sent to the Dutch plenipotentiaries, in addition to Townshend — to the latter by means of Chesterfield.

For two centuries — it ran — the Emperor's hereditary dominions have served as barrier to Christendom against the Ottoman power and at the same time as counterpoise to preserve balance among the principal Powers of Europe, on which their mutual security depends. Christendom and Europe would lose these two equally important advantages if, on the death of Charles VI., his succession should be rent asunder in wars against the pretenders kindled by foreign Powers, and in the end be divided just as happened to the other branch of the House of Austria after the death of Charles II. of Spain.

To prevent this there seems to be a no more efficacious and proper remedy than that the guaranty which the Emperor demands. The demand as it has been made is, to be sure, too general to be complied with in an unmodified form and without certain elucidation. Still, the Hanover Allies will be wrong if they do not make use of it, it being evident that the Emperor will pay their guaranty, a thing he cannot expect them to give merely upon such a vague demand.

In this matter there are three important difficulties to be faced. The first is that the succession to the various Austrian dominions may have been regulated in a manner incompatible with a guaranty which would extend over the whole of them indiscriminately. The second is that this guaranty will put the entire seal to the

_____
[1]) Hop to Slingelandt, 15 Sept. '29, R. A. Hl. 2983.

Emperor's despotism in the Empire by discouraging the Electors and Princes who began to oppose it, and who showed willingness to take measures among themselves and with the Allies of Hanover to reduce it to within the reach of the Treaty of Westphalia. The third is that the Austrian dominions, which have of late years considerably increased, might by marriage fall into the hands of a Prince who, by acquiring them, would obtain such a position as would enable him to overthrow the balance of Europe's power.

The first difficulty might be removed by the application of the judicious remark of an ancient: *omne magnum exemplum habet aliquid ex iniquo, quod utilitate publica compensatur,* and the maxim of the jurists that the rules of ordinary law are not applicable to the succession in monarchies, consisting of several parts which had each its own settlement of succession while they were by themselves, but follow a common rule after being united into one body, as witness the French and Spanish monarchies. It will be sufficient, however, to guarantee merely possession, and not the right of possession, and, by so doing, to leave the path of justice open to the parties concerned.

And as the Elector of Bavaria and the Prince Royal of Pologne are the only presumptive pretenders, it would be proper to advise the Emperor to promise them one or more provinces bounded to Bavaria and Saxony, in case he died without male issue. In addition to which, he might even settle the succession to his dominions in the House of Bavaria in case his daughters should likewise die without male issue. These princes, on the other hand, then ought to be made aware that they cannot force their pretensions unless by a war of which the success is most uncertain, and that consequently it is in their interests to be satisfied with what the Allies can procure for them by agreement.

The second difficulty would be of far less importance if the Elector of Bavaria gave ear to the idea just mentioned, since, in order to be sure of the effect of what had been stipulated in his favour he would of necessity be compelled to retain his attachment to the Allies. And as to the other Electors and Princes of the Empire, to encourage them to support German liberty and their own rights and prerogatives against the encroachments of the Court of Vienna, it appears sufficient that the Hanover Allies — upon the occasion of the guaranty of the Emperor's succession — insist upon the renewal of the guaranty of the Treaty of Westphalia by France and Sweden, and, considering that that of the latter power has lost much of its value, demand in addition the adjunction of the guaranty of England That the King of England is a Prince of the Empire, cannot be an obstacle, for the King of Sweden was no less so when his guaranty was accepted than he is at the present time.

The third difficulty is the more considerable as it may be looked upon as the principal motive of the Hanover Alliance. However, since fear of the union of the French and Spanish monarchies was the motive of the last war, it seems prudent to apply to the present case the remedy then resorted to after a bloody and expensive war, and to stipulate clearly that the dominions of which the guaranty is to be given cannot become the possession of the Kings and Queens of France or Spain, or of their immediate and presumptive heirs or heiresses, in any way whatsoever. It must be upon the understanding, however, that this stipulation will have no relation to the Italian countries that formerly belonged to Spain, an exception necessary to spare the feelings of Spain and to prevent the ill use the Emperor might make of that stipulation to the prejudice of the Allies.

Apart from this stipulation, without which the third difficulty appears absolutely insurmountable, it will be necessary to settle in favour of France the permanent confirmation of the Act of neutrality granted by the Emperor and France to the Duke of Lorraine for his Duchies of Lorraine and Bar, which Act was intended , in the event of a war between the Emperor and France, to prevent either of them passing through these countries, or making use of them in any way whatsoever. One may expect that, either on these terms or on others in which France finds his income equally with the rest of Europe, this Power will be ready to contribute to the settlement of the Emperor's succession, or at least to refrain from opposing it. For has not she thought better of certain maxims which, ever since the ministry of Richelieu, have disquieted the other Powers of Europe, and is not she ruled by a Prince who, satisfied as he is with having nothing to fear from his neighbours, finds his greatness in the happiness of his subjects and the maintenance of the tranquillity of Europe?

The author does not pretend to have entirely removed the difficulties that present themselves, and there may be others on which he has not even touched, but he feels confident that the impartial reader will admit that the remaining ones are not comparable with the consequences, either of a refusal to enter into negotiations upon the Emperor's demand, or of delays that the Emperor could take as a refusal.

It is not necessary to specify these consequences here. Those for whom this memorial has been written are too clear-sighted not to perceive them and too well-intentioned not to pay due regard to them. Moreover, some of them, and perhaps the principal ones , are too delicate to be trusted to paper, but none the less disquiet, not only the speculator but everybody who dispassionately compares the experience of the past with the possibility of the future.

In any case, whatever may be the success of this affair, it will be prudent, to say the least, to conduct it on the part of the Hanover Allies, and especially of England and the Republic, who, after all, think somewhat differently from France upon the subject of the Emperor's succession, in a manner capable of convincing the world that, if it miscarries, it will not be their fault, but only that of the Emperor.

Yet, however great a facility the Allies have to show, the author does not wish them to neglect their own interests. On the contrary, while granting to the Emperor a guaranty which he has so much at heart, they must insist, in the first place, that the does them justice *simul et semel* on the points brought before the Congress, that, secondly, he lends himself to the measures taken or to be taken with Spain for the security of the succession of Don Carlos to Tuscany and Parma in the manner laid down in the counter-project, and, finally, that he agrees with the Allies regarding the method most proper for preventing the public tranquillity from being troubled by the King of Prussia's pretentions upon Juliers and Bergh, and to secure their possession to the Palatine House until the dispute be finished either by way of justice or by an agreement. Since the latter is preferable, it will be expedient to work at it jointly without delay, and to make the two parties aware that they can do nothing better than finish the dispute as soon as possible by a division to be guaranteed by the Emperor and the Hanover Allies. [1])

To this memorial, Slingelandt gave the name: — "Pensées impartiales et pacifiques." In a letter to Goslinga, he justifies these epithets. "The second," he wrote, "has a right to existence, for the object of the memorial is to prevent, on the one hand, the disasters that menace Europe if the Emperor retains his competency to bring, by marriage, his dominions into one of the great reigning houses, and, on the other hand, the disturbances in case he dies without male issue and without measures having been taken in his lifetime between him and the principal Powers to impede them. The first epithet is not so easily justified, but after considering the means and expedients I suggest, you will admit that I am not better disposed towards the Emperor than the object of the memorial absolutely requires, nor shall I 'stipulate anything about him, either in favour of Powers whose guaranty he wishes for, or of any other except what he must consider as a just return for the guaranty of the one and the acquiescence of the other, and what he may be expected to concede if he takes the guaranty so much to heart as it deserves in its present circumstances and if he does not conceal other designs under that demand. One may reasonably suspect him of this on account of his conduct after the Treaty of Vienna. It is indeed very probable that not only, perhaps not even in the first place, does he make the Pragmatic Sanction a *conditio sine qua non* of the success of a congress of which he has proudly maintained that his succession *had nothing to do with it.* But after all the Emperor is father, and so the disasters that menace his family cannot be immaterial to him. This is what must render him more amenable and disposed towards expedients. [2])

The long and the short of Slingelandt's reasoning was that the Allies had to discuss the Emperor's proposals. There was nothing that contravened the intentions of France more. This is evident from the draft-answer to them composed by Chauvelin and to be made jointly by the Hanover Allies. It ran as follows:

[1]) "Pensées impartiales et pacifiques que L'Empereur demande aux Alliés de Hanovre comme une condition sine qua non de la réconciliation générale, ou de l'accommodement, auquel les principales puissances de l'Europe travaillent au Congrès de Soissons", Jorissen, *op. cit.* 273—8.
[2]) Slingelandt to Goslinga, 11 Oct. '29; Memorial quoted in preceding reference.

1 & 2. La première proposition paraitrait se rapprocher de ce que l'on peut prétendre selon les traités, mais la seconde proposition qui regarde le changement de 500 mille écus stipulés par le traité de barrière dans la seule perception de l'excédant des revenues des Pays-Bas, déduction faite des dettes et dépenses, renverse totalement ce que l'on parait abandonner gratuitement.

Les stipulations qui regardent les garnisons de la barrière et des Pays-bas, et les subsides stipulés pour leur payement sont clairement établies par le traité de barrière, et ne peuvent qu'être étrangères aux affaires destinées au congrès.

3. On conviendra de nommer des commissaires pour former un nouveau tarif, en exécution du traité de barrière, l'on fixera même un temps, mais jusqu'à ce que l'on soit convenu autrement par un traité de commerce à faire, le tout doit rester, continuer et subsister sans aucun changement, conformément à l'article 26 du traité de barrière.

4. Les Alliés de Hanovre ont été fidèles au traité de la Quadruple Alliance, et s'il y a eu quelque contravention, ce n'est pas de leur part.

5. C'est une proposition *absolument nouvelle et étrangère aux négociations présentes*, et qui ne doit pas être une condition pour exécuter les traités antérieurs; d'ailleurs comment répondre sur une proposition aussi vague et qui a tant de branches différentes? [1])

The articles 1 to 4 were in an unfriendly style, and the last was excessively so. The draft was unmistakably a refusal to discuss the guaranty. The principal argument France adduced in recommending it to the Maritime Powers was, that the undertaking of that affair would endanger the success of the treaty with the Electors. The object in setting this treaty on foot was to form a party in the Empire capable of constituting a counterpoise to the despotism exercised there by the Emperor, but this could not pos-

---

[1]) Réponse concertée par les Ministres de France, d'Angleterre et des Etats-Généraux à faire verbalement à M. M. de Kinsky et Fonseca sur les propositions faites de la part de l'Empereur, in Höfler, *op. cit.* XXXII, 350—1, and Secr. Res. Hl. 12 Oct. '29.

sibly be attained should the Hanover Allies enter into negotiations with him upon such an important point as the guaranty. It was, therefore, better not to disquiet the Electors, but to conclude a treaty that had lingered on too long.

France strongly pressed the Maritime Powers to contribute towards this end. She did so, not in the first place, as she pretended, in behalf of the formation of such a party in the Empire, but for the sake of the 7th. article of the project as it had been drawn up by D'Albert and certainly not without the knowledge of the French Government. This article forbade the contracting parties making any concession, treaty, alliance or agreement except in concert with and upon the approval of all of them. In that manner France could prevent England and the Republic at any time from guaranteeing the Pragmatic Sanction, a thing she might do without appearing openly in it herself — by inducing the Electors, especially the one of Bavaria, to be against any plan of that nature. So, not only for the present, but also for the future, France endeavoured to render the guaranty of the Emperor's succession by the Maritime Powers impossible [1]).

The Dutch plenipotentiaries understood her intentions very well. Hop was of opinion that, in this way, the treaty with the Electors might become, instead of a means of checking the Emperor, one of securing the supremacy to France, who seemed to look forward to the Emperor's death in order to gain such a superiority both in the Empire and in Europe that there would be no Power capable of counter-balancing her [2]).

As to Goslinga, he considered the recommendation of the guaranty of the Austrian succession in its entirety to France, purposeless. But perhaps — he supposed — she would be less averse to giving it exclusively for his Italian dominions. This would be immaterial to the Electors; it would check Elizabeth in her ambitious views, and show the Emperor that he had nothing to fear from them and could, in consequence, permit the introduction of Spanish garrisons [3]). But this expedient could only come under dis-

---

[1]) Hop to Slingelandt, 5 Oct. '29, R. A. Hl. 2983; Slingelandt to Goslinga, 11 Oct. '29; H. Walpole to Poyntz, 4 Nov. '29, Coxe, *R. W.* II, 659 et seq.

[2]) Hop to Slingelandt, 5 Oct. '29, R. A. Hl. 2983.

[3]) That Goslinga moved this idea is nowhere expressly reported but it is most probable, cf Slingelandt to Goslinga, 11, 25 Oct. '29; Höfler, *op. cit.* XXXII, 373; Jorissen *op. cit.* 282—3.

cussion after the guaranty of the whole succession had been rejected, and that was a matter on which England would have
something to say.

France was opposed to it while Slingelandt was in favour of it.
The decision lay in the hands of the English Government. As to
Townshend, his sentiment is clear from the following observations
which he made upon the memorial of Slingelandt. He forwarded
them through the same channel as that by which he had received
the latter document.

"I agree entirely with the Pensionary in opinion as to the ne-
"cessity there will be of preventing a division of the Austrian do-
"minions upon the decease of the Emperor and that getting the
"chief Powers to guarantee his succession would be the most effec-
"tual method of preventing such a division, and likewise any dis-
"turbances in Europe that might arise on account of the said succes-
"sion. But I am clearly of opinion that this is by no means a proper
"juncture for stirring that question on our part. Because I am per-
"suaded from the nature of the thing itself as well as from what
"passed between the Cardinal and Count Sinzendorff when he was
"in France that nothing but necessity or the fear of being engaged
"in a war with the Maritime Powers against them will bring the
"Court of France to consent to it. Secondly because it is to be ap-
"prehended that any such proposal to the Court of France on the
"part of the King and the States would lose them all trust and con-
"fidence there and might make the French run more strongly into
"all the views of the Court of Spain and perhaps bring them, if they
"found there was any danger of their being involved in a war with
"the Emperor and thought they could not depend upon our assist-
"ance, not only to consent to the match with Don Carlos but even
"to encourage it, choosing rather if they found that the succession
"to the Austrian dominions must be guaranteed to have it done in
"favour of a branch of the House of Bourbon than in that of any
"other house.

"We ought therefore to see how we can settle our matters with
"Spain before we enter into any considerations about the said guar-
"antee, and I am firmly of opinion we ought not even then to stir
"this affair on our parts unless the Emperor will himself offer to
"comply with what we shall stipulate with the Queen of Spain in
"favour of Don Carlos, declare to whom he intends to give the

"Archduchess and give not only to the Empire but also to the
"neighbouring powers sufficient security that neither he nor
"his successors will torment and plague them in the manner he
"has of late done with the Aulic Council, for unless some bounds
"are set to the proceedings of that judicature, the Emperor must
"be absolute master in Germany, and even the Powers whose
"territories join to those of the Empire will never be at peace or
"quiet.

"What the Pensionary proposes on this last head will not, I fear,
"be found practicable for the Popish Princes in the Empire will
"scarce be brought to consent that the Crown of Great Britain
"should be added to the Powers who are at present guarantees of
"the Treaty of Westphalia, neither do I know whether the parlia-
"ment here would approve of the King's entering into so extensive
"an engagement.

"Lastly, as the Emperor is on the one hand not old and of a very
"strong constitution and lives very regularly, and as on the other
"hand the Empress by the accounts we have is very much broken in
"her health, and, according to the opinion of her physicians, not
"likely to hold out long, if she should happen to die before the Em-
"peror, His Imperial Majesty would without doubt marry again,
"and might then have issue male, wherefore on this account there is
"no necessity of being pressing or forward of entering into such a
"guaranty; and if the case should fall that the Emperor should die
"before the present Empress and without leaving issue male, those
"Powers who are now inclinable to give their guaranty would
"naturally from the same principle endeavour to assist the Arch-
"duchess in preserving the Austrian dominions united, and the
"present treaties with the Emperor would give a sufficient handle
"for interposing in her favour.

"The three objections which are made in the Pensionary's paper
"to the giving the guaranty required are stated with great strength
"and clearness, and the solutions which are given to them are like-
"wise solidly explained, and no doubt will be of great use and force
"when that business shall come to bear. But I am still of opinion
"that matters are not yet ripe enough to enter upon any negotia-
"tions concerning the point of this guaranty; our taking more and
"earlier care of the House of Austria than they have thought fit to
"take care of themselves, has, for many years past, cost the

"Maritime Powers great sums of money, and we have had but "very ungrateful returns" [1]).

This document of Townshend's contained a refusal no less unequivocal than that of Chauvelin's. However, the time when the Secretary for the Northern Department voiced the whole Cabinet was gone. As has been seen, Robert Walpole and Newcastle were by no means in accord with his sentiments towards the Emperor. To be sure, they, too, were of opinion that the latter's succession ought not to come under discussion at present, and they therefore approved of Chauvelin's draft-answer. They, too, supposed the Emperor's sole object to be the overthrowing of the negotiations with Spain, which power would have to abandon the illusion of rejoining her lost dominions should the Hanover Allies enter into deliberations upon the guaranty. In respect of France, too, they considered it imprudent to appear well disposed towards it, so long as the negotiations with Spain were not happily concluded. This latter must first take place, and they therefore detained the delivery of the answer to Austria as long as possible. Once let things reach this stage, however, they would no longer be opposed to negotiations with the Emperor [2]).

It was in accordance with their intentions that Stanhope, when leaving for Spain, told the Austrian plenipotentiaries that though it was impossible for the King of England to enter into the guaranty for the moment, since Spain might be suspicious of such a course and refuse to conclude a treaty, yet what he was going to do in Spain would not be derogatory to the Emperor's interests nor prevent the complete reconciliation of the last named and his master at a later date [3]).

The majority of the Cabinet were absolutely unprepared to exclude this possibility by entering into the treaty with the Electors. Townshend, however, was, and he had already done everything in his power to persuade his colleagues to this course. In July, he had sent them the project from Hanover, provided with Plettemberg's marginal notes. In order to evade giving a direct

---

[1]) These observations are enclosed in Townshend to Chesterfield, 10 Oct. '29, R. O. Hl. 305, and R. A. Hl. 2994.

[2]) Hop to Slingelandt, 18 Oct. '29, R. A. Hl. 2983; H. Walpole to Poyntz, 4 Nov. '29, *loc. cit.*

We have taken the liberty of representing the opinion of H. Walpole as that of R. Walpole cum suis.

[3]) Höfler, *op. cit.* XXXII, 222.

answer, they, at that time Lords of the Council, wrote that since the project and the notes were contradictory, and since they did not know what had been agreed upon, they would refrain from expressing an opinion. However, when Townshend, in the King's name, reverted to this subject, they could no longer delay an expression of opinion upon it. They then passed such a censure on the 7th. and other important articles as clearly showed their dislike to the project. Nevertheless, the King, when in danger of attack from Prussia, was on the point of agreeing to it. To prevent this, the Queen, who worked in absolute unison with the Lords, caused him to make a hurried return from Hanover, where he had been totally overborne by Townshend and Chavigny.

The latter, who had seen his efforts almost crowned with success, felt that George II.'s precipitate departure on September 19th. boded little good. He did not lose courage, however. In concert with Plettemberg he gave a new redaction to the project; he then sent it, along with an appeal to his promises of September, to Townshend. The Foreign Secretary would doubtless have given ear to Chavigny had it been dependent on him, but his colleagues forced him to return an answer which was expressly silent concerning the 7th. article but which raised several objections to other articles, and in particular to such as stipulated subsidies in favour of Cologne and Bavaria, and concerned the succession to Juliers and Bergh [1]).

That answer was sent to Chesterfield to be handed to Bellanger, who had come to the Hague in order to further the treaty for the sake of the subsidies. Chesterfield, as may only reasonably be expected, spoke of the project to Slingelandt. The latter, of course, objected to the 7th. article in a preponderant degree. Moreover, the fact that only two Electors instead of four would be parties to the treaty, affected him in a disagreeable manner. The one of Treves who had become Archbishop of Mainz in the beginning of the year had refused to join, while the one of Cologne was unwilling to bind himself for more than three years, and on account of the lay of his countries he was the one who could be of the greatest use to the Republic [2]).

[1]) King, *Notes* 101—5; Dureng, *op. cit.* 83—96; Coxe, *R. W.* I, 336; H. Walpole to Poyntz, 4 Nov. '29, ib. II, 659 et seq.; Townshend to Chesterfield, 3, 7 Oct. '29, Chesterfield to Townshend 7, 21, 25 Oct. '29, R. O. Hl. 305.

[2]) Chesterfield to Townshend, 7 Oct. '29, R. O. Hl. 305.

But Slingelandt also objected to it apart from the particulars of the treaty. We remember that, in the beginning of the Congress, when he was still in hopes of a definitive treaty which would also provide for the affairs of the Empire, he had rejected the Cardinal's idea of a secret defensive alliance with the Electors. Later on, when the provisional treaty seemed unavoidable, he had changed. Then he had looked upon such an alliance as one of the most indispensable precautions for the execution of the provisional treaty. And wherever France had given him an opportunity he had permanently furthered it. However, now that the hope of a definitive treaty had revived, owing to the breach between Spain and the Emperor and of the latter's proposals, the Pensionary reverted to his original idea, and again wished, as his memorial clearly shows, to make the affairs of the Empire a component part of the general pacification. Only in August, he had called the treaty with the Electors an obstacle to guaranteeing the Pragmatic Sanction, [1]) but now that France did likewise after the Emperor's proposals, Slingelandt put the question as to whether there were no means of putting a check to the Emperor's exorbitant power in the Empire other than this treaty, and whether this power was so dangerous as to compare with the consequences of his death, without precautions having been taken to prevent them [2]).

It was also with a view to the private interest the Republic had in the treaty — the matter of Juliers and Bergh — that Slingelandt wanted the affairs of the Empire to be settled in concert with its Head. As has been seen, he had even insisted that this affair should be provided for by the provisional treaty, in contradistinction to all other German affairs. In his conviction that it had to be a component part of the general pacification he was further strengthened by the Prusso-Hanoverian conflict. It had come off well, thanks to the quick and cordial interference of France and the Republic, yet the King of Prussia was and remained a dangerous neighbour. The guaranty of Juliers and Bergh to Pfalz-Sulzbach without the concurrence of the Emperor as had been conceded by France in the Treaty of Marly, and which was also proposed in the treaty that was under discussion, gave, in his opinion, no security whatever against what would result from the death of the Elector

[1]) Slingelandt to Hop, 22 Aug. '29.
[2]) The Same to Goslinga, 11 Oct. '29.

Palatine, yes, it would even lead directly to a war upon the frontiers of the Republic. To prevent such a war the Pensionary had
conceived the idea of making up the matter with the King of Prussia during the Elector's lifetime, the former of whom would perhaps permit the Republic to garrison Wesel, as she had done previous to 1672, and leave her Ravenstein if, in return for these concessions, he would be sure of success. But no sooner had the Emperor shown himself willing to enter into a general pacification
than Slingelandt suppressed the idea, and wished for nothing better — as witness the close of his memorial — than to finish the
matter in concert with the Emperor [1]).

For all these reasons he was opposed to concluding the treaty,
and, very differently from his conduct on previous occasions, he
now, when requested by Gansinot to exhort England to enter into
it, excused himself. [2]).

Small wonder, for the fact that England did not go so far was
a comfort to him, and his only one. His observations regarding
the Pragmatic Sanction had not received a hearing in England,
while as to France, the draft-answer, her Ministers' expression of
opinion upon the guaranty of the Emperor's succession, and their
pressing the treaty with the Electors, all greatly aroused his uneasiness. Should France plot towards her own aggrandisement and
the overthrowing of the balance of power upon the Emperor's
death, what — so he asked — would be the fruits of the Alliance
with her in the long run? [3])

He did what he could to avert the impending danger. He understood very well that England, now she required all the help
France could give her in order to come out of the negotiations
favourably, would only express herself vaguely upon the guaranty,
but there was no necessity for haste so long as the success of the
negotiations with Spain should remain uncertain. For the present
it would be sufficient not to estrange the Emperor by a too
haughty and a too decisive answer; time could be gained by asking for explanations. The resolution of October 14th. ran on these
lines. It approved of Chauvelin's draft except on the last point.
The guaranty did not appear to be "*strange to the present ne-*

[1]) The Same to the Same, 8, 13 Sept., 25 Oct. '29.
[2]) The Same to Chesterfield, 17 Nov. '29.
[3]) The Same to Goslinga, 11 Oct. '29.

gotiations" to the States, since pursuant to the 6th. Article of the
Preliminaries their object was not only to procure satisfaction for
the Hanover Allies, but in particular to establish a general pacification. That object might be served by discussing this point, and
to this end the answer was not to give the impression of a refusal,
but to elicit a clearer and more detailed proposal, and in this
way to discover the true intentions of the Emperor without any
committal on the part of the Allies [1]).

By chance, Chesterfield went to England shortly afterwards,
for some months. Slingelandt then charged him to recommend his
ideas to his Government in the strongest manner [2]). In addition,
he sent him the continuation of his memorial: "Suite des Pensées
impartiales et pacifiques." This document, characterised by the
Pensionary himself as a sort of commentary upon the resolution of
October 14th., was likewise sent to Hop and Goslinga, whose letters had evoked it [3]). According to Slingelandt it had been written
with more vivacity than the first, a fact which he ascribed to the
importance of the matter, and the way in which it was dealt with
both in London and Paris, though from different points of view [4]).
Its contents were as follows:

The more one considers the consequences of the Emperor's
death without male issue, the more one feels the necessity of the
settlement of his succession between him and the Hanover Allies.

Those consequences menace the Republic far more and more
immediately than they do France or England, and so it is natural
and she cannot be blamed for thinking that it is not at all proper
to allow such a favourable occasion to slip by as that which presents itself of coming to a settlement of that succession as well as
of an equitable agreement of her differences with the Emperor.

That succession having been the principal object of the uneasiness that has led to the Hanover Alliance, the great point for a
congress, met, in the first place, to effect a general pacification
seems to be its settlement. As those for whom this memorial is intended know, at the beginning of the Congress, there were some
persons who endeavoured to have that matter introduced there

---

[1]) The Same to Goslinga, 11 Oct. '29; Secr. Res. S. G. 14 Oct. '29.
[2]) Chesterfield to Harrington, 14 Feby. '31, *Hist. MSS. Comm. Rep.* X App. I, 247.
[3]) Chesterfield to Slingelandt, 28 Oct. '29, R. A. Hl. 2994; Slingelandt to Goslinga, the
Same to Hop. 25 Oct. '29.
[4]) Slingelandt to Hop, 25 Oct. '29.

on the part of the Allies. The author does not reprove those who thought differently then, and put forward as their chief argument that the Emperor would rather have broken up the Congress than have entered into discussion upon it. But now that he agrees with it, leaving his principle or design absolutely out of the question, it appears indisputable that it is to the interest of the Allies to make use of this occasion to procure a lasting peace for Europe and a just and rightful satisfaction to each of the Allies. The author even goes so far as to say, it is so clear that without having other and even suspicious views, it is impossible to think otherwise. He admits that the Allies are not equally interested in the settlement of this succession, and that is it natural to balance one's eagerness with one's interest, but that inequality of interest must not make them follow diverse or even opposed lines. They must not lose sight of the connection between the Emperor's demand and the great aim of the Hanover Alliance and the Congress of Soissons on the one hand, and the danger of regarding that demand *as strange to the present negotiations,* on the other.

Indeed, though England too is interested in the preservation of the balance, yet she would suffer far less from its downfall and other consequences which might result from the Emperor's dying without male issue, than the Republic would. On account of her fortunate position and by the means of subsistence and the extensive trade she finds in her isle and in her rich and numerous colonies, she would not fail in commanding respect and even having her alliance sought for. Consequently, she cannot have the same zeal as the Republic, and might, in case she did not scrupulously attach herself to the great aim of the Alliance and the Congress, even prefer other objects to this for the present, how ever greatly important it might be.

But matters would be much worse if France, forgetting that aim, planned to overthrow the balance and to aggrandize herself at the expense of her neighbours, and then refused the guaranty. However, judging from her invariable conduct since the death of Louis XIV., and the disposition of the present ministry, one cannot refrain from admitting that she has no such design in view and it must be expected that she will consider it in her own interest to grasp the present opportunity to round off her frontier rather than to await the death of the Emperor.

Everyone knows that it is defective on the side of Lorrain and
Luxemburg. It may be that the perpetual neutrality of Lorrain
and Bar, which has been recommended in the preceding memorial
will be considered insufficient to remedy this defect, but in that
case, the Emperor, who recognises so well the consequences to
himself, of the concurrence of France in this matter, will, without
doubt, consent to other expedients regarding these Duchies and
even to the razing of Luxemburg rather than refusing to buy at
this price the guaranty of France.

In consequence, it appears that the repugnance which France
shows to the guaranty, is anything but insurmountable, and that
the plenipotentiaries of the Republic, — a country which is so
interested in the preservation of peace and of the balance of power, in making up her differences with the Emperor, and in maintaining her independence towards her Allies, the latter of which
would be impossible after the Emperor had lost all hopes of
obtaining the guaranty — would err greatly in not taking all the
advantage possible of the access they have to the Cardinal to
make the latter realise that the guaranty, as modified in the first
memorial or in some other way, is naturally part of the aim of the
Hanover Alliance, and of the Congress of Soissons; and that, not
only is it an absolute necessity to Europe and particularly to the
Republic — for whom he shows so much tenderness — but
also most conform to the real interests of France.

The principal and most specious objection raised against the
guaranty, is that the Emperor only makes his demand to thwart
the negotiations with Spain, and that this guaranty is so deliber-
ately opposed to the latter's views that she might break off the
negotiations, how ever much they might be advanced, on hearing
of any inclination on the part of the Hanover Allies to place it
under discussion. This objection, however, falls to the ground,
since, in the first place, the demand for the guaranty has been on
such general and vague terms that it is easy to keep the Emperor
in suspense by putting questions and refraining from expressing
oneself too positively until Spain has been finished with. Secondly,
in case Spain is satisfied with what she demands, viz., the introduction of 6000 Spaniards, it will not be difficult to bring her to
understand that the demand for the guaranty may efficaciously
contribute towards her aim, for the Emperor has it so much at

heart that, in order to obtain it, he will undoubtedly consent to the treaty that is being concluded with Spain, recognising the fact that there is no other course left. Thirdly, in case Spain, which is only too probable, has other views and intends to engage her Allies in a war with the Emperor to reconquer her former dominions in Italy, France and England — who according to the third article of the Quadruple Alliance have formally guaranteed to the Emperor his Italian as well as his German countries and the Southern Netherlands — cannot but oppose Spain quite apart from the question of their entering into the guaranty of the Emperor's succession or not.

To meet the difficulties which are encountered by the guaranty the expedient of not giving it in its entirety for the succession, but only for the Italian dominions, has been suggested. But it may be taken for granted that it will not have any chance of success with the Emperor. For, can it be expected that he will consent to leave his patrimony and the Southern Nederlands a prey to the various pretenders to his succession, while the Archduchess could not in any way profit from former guaranties, how ever secure they might be? Moreover, is it in the interests of Europe, France excluded, if she should unfortunately return to her old maxims, while Italy were tranquil, that Germany would be rent by wars and the balance of Europe overthrown, much the same as if there had been no guaranty for the Italian dominions? We are not even considering the question as to whether such a guaranty would be far less proper to alarm and to pique Spain than one of a more general character.

In conclusion, those who read this and the preceding memorial are requested not to draw conclusions before making the following reflections.

If the demand of the Emperor is refused, the Congress will end without any treaty with him either provisional or definitive.

Despair may drive him to most extraordinary resolutions and measures, which are especially to be feared from a Prince "qui a en main de quoi tenter et d'ébranler la vertu et la constance même" (Maria Theresa).

There is little chance of satisfying Spain without a war, the aim of which clashes with the engagements of France and England, and so the regard for Spain in this matter must, and can only

consist in conducting the management of the negotiations
prudently.

One cannot hope for a more favourable opportunity of obtaining the concurrence of France in the guaranty than under the
present ministry, and for the sake of the general pacification, and
to allow this opportunity to slip by without urging France to
one's utmost, and to flatter oneself that this Power will be easier
after the breaking up of the Congress would only be to intention-
ally deceive oneself.

The Republic will not only leave all her differences with the
Emperor unsettled, but will also be exposed to incessant extor-
tions and chicanes which the neighbourhood of the Southern
Netherlands and even the Barrier Treaty will furnish abundant
matter. We are not considering here the disturbances which may
be brought on by the Emperor through the King of Prussia, whose
avidity and whims and whose military forces also render him a
most dangerous neighbour. In the midst of this perpetual unrest
the Republic will be compelled to consume the remainder of her
forces as though it were in the thick of war, while she can rely on no
assistance except that of France, since England is not armed in
time of peace, and since neither the Emperor nor Prussia stand
much in fear of the latter's naval forces. The Republic might
even be overwhelmed by a sudden invasion before England could
come to her help.

The author might extend his reflections still further and extract very evil consequences from them. He prefers to conclude
by asking whether it would not be hard for the Republic to see
the guaranty rejected or, in milder terms but to the same effect,
declared *strange to the present negotiations*, not because the Emperor refuses to give reasonable explanations and restrictions or
to grant what the Allies might, with justice, demand from him,
but because Spain desires war with the Emperor, because France
is determined to keep herself free to, if she thought proper, profit
by the Emperor's death, and because England, under present
circumstances, will avoid anything which may retard her agreement with Spain, or throw the least obstacle in its way; and
whether the right thing would not be to keep the Emperor in suspense, a thing made easy by the very nature of his demand, until,
after the conclusion of the treaty with Spain, which seems near

at hand, the Allies might speak openly with his ministers [1].

When this second memorial arrived in Paris, the conference for settling the answer to the Austrian plenipotentiaries had just taken place. Here Chauvelin's draft passed without any difficulty. How ever strange it may seem, the Dutch maintained silence, too. Before going to the conference Hop had proposed to his colleagues that the Allies be informed of the resolution of October 14th., but Goslinga, whom, according to Hop, Hurgronje followed blindly [2], was extremely opposed to it. However, some time elapsed between the conference and the communication of the answer to the Austrians, for, though the latter had already waited for six weeks, Horace Walpole succeeded in still further delaying the communication until the next courier should have arrived from Spain [3]. In that interval Hop was successful in persuading Goslinga and Hurgronje to propose some further mitigation in the answer, viz., instead of "étrangère aux négociations présentes": *"jusqu'ici étrangère"*, etc. [4] It was in vain. The article was not vitally changed. To be sure, it underwent a change, but only a formal one. This was caused by the substitution of another 2nd. article on the part of the Emperor. It read like this:

Comme les revenues des Pays-Bas Autrichiens ne suffisent point pour les charges qu'ils doivent supporter et qu'il ne serait pas juste que l'Empereur y suppléât des revenues des dits Pays-Bas pour régler là-dessus un pied fixe et un système nouveau pour trouver le supplement de ce qu'il faut pour les fraix des dits Pays-Bas par la diminution des troupes, par le reglement du tarif et par d'autres moyens que l'on pourrait trouver, de manière que ces pays ne soient point à charge en temps de paix aux autres pays héréditaires de l'Empereur [5].

The difference between this second article and the original one is, that it left undecided from what quarter the relief of the Southern Netherlands was to come, and that the third article, instead of being co-ordinate with, was subordinate to the second. This

---

[1] "Suite des pensées impartiales et pacifiques sur la garantie que l'Empereur a demandée aux Alliés de Hanovre", 25 Oct. '29, in Jorissen, *op. cit.* 279—85.

[2] Hop to Slingelandt, 15 June, 7 Dec. '29, R. A. Hl. 2983.

[3] The Same to the Same, 28 Oct. '29, R. A. Hl. 2983.

[4] Plenipotentiaries to Slingelandt, 7 Nov. '29, R. A. Hl. 2986; Secr. Res. S. G. 26 Nov. '29.

[5] Secr. Res. Hl. 16 Nov. '29.

showed considerable compliance on the Emperor's part. In making his proposals he had acceded to the Republic's desire that he should apply to each of the Hanover Allies; now he met her other wish that he should moderate his high demands. Indeed, Sinzendorff was entitled to say that, should matters not proceed now, the Emperor was not to blame [1]).

The fault lay with France and England, who carried through the disagreeable answer to the Austrian plenipotentiaries which was made to them on November 3rd.[2]) and whose representatives in Spain concluded the treaty of Seville a few days later, on November 9th.

IV.

The Treaty of Seville would certainly have been concluded at an earlier date if Stanhope had not been sent to Spain. His arrival was first awaited. Contrary to the expectation of the Court of France, it then came about with very little trouble.

By this treaty the treaties and conventions of France and England with Spain were renewed. This stipulation confirmed England's possession of Gibraltar without its being specified. The treaty, moreover, reinstated both France and England in the commercial privileges they had formerly enjoyed. The commercial disputes between England and Spain, and those, too, between France and Spain, should be settled by Commissaries. In return for these advantages France and England engaged to contribute towards introducing 6000 Spanish soldiers, to be paid by their own King, into Livorno, Porto-Ferrajo, Parma and Piacenza.

In the separate and secret articles this introduction was regulated. The contracting parties should endeavour to obtain within four months the consent of the present Possessors, and notify the Emperor of their invariable determination to effectuate the introduction. This had to take place within six months. Should it encounter any opposition — so the 6th. of these articles enacted — on the part of either the Emperor or the Possessors,

---

[1]) Rescript 8 Oct. '29, in Höfler, *op. cit.* XXXII, 241 et seq.; Sinzendorff to Kinsky, 12 Oct. '29, ib. 253.

[2]) Höfler, *loc. cit.* 324 et seq.; Hop to Slingelandt, 4 Nov. '29, R. A. Hl. 2983.

the contracting parties should go to war and conclude a treaty with each other, the object of which would be not only to overcome the obstacles against the introduction but also to establish a just equilibrium in Europe [1]).

Of the States no mention was made other than that they should be invited to accede. Nobody expected their accession would take up less than two months. However, it took place within twelve days of the conclusion of the principal treaty, viz., on November 21st., thanks to the eagerness of Van der Meer. When the plenipotentiaries informed him that the counter-project did not provide for the Republic's interests, Slingelandt expressed the wish that they would still redress the omission, [2]) but this Van der Meer accomplished, not they. When the counter-project arrived in Spain, he ascertained whether Brancas and Keene were empowered to sign together with him; they proved not to be so empowered, whereas he could not sign except in conjunction with them. Thereupon he appealed to the States for power enabling him to sign independently. This authorization, sent to him on October 25th., arrived only two days after the conclusion of the treaty, viz., on November 11th. He then resolved to urge the accession forthwith, the more so as he had perceived some inclination in France and England to prevail upon Spain not to grant to the Republic the favourable conditions which Slingelandt, to have a better chance of success, had taken from resolutions passed by the States in 1719, and then accepted by the Allies [3]), and to which conditions Patiñino in conversations with Van der Meer had already assented. The Ambassador met with complete success: within a few days the Act of the Republic's Accession was signed.

Among its stipulations was a point which had particularly excited the displeasure of the Allies, viz., that 3000 men would suffice as the contingent of the Republic for a war in Italy. For the transport of the Spanish garrisons she had, in addition, to keep two ships and one battallion ready. In return for these engagements on her part, the King of Spain pledged himself to redress her grievances and to restore trade according to the previously concluded treaties. Pursuant to these the Dutch should enjoy the most-favoured-

---

[1]) Baudrillart, *op. cit.* III, 540 et seq.; Secr. Res. Hl. VIII, 190 et seq.
[2]) Slingelandt to Hop, 13 Sept. '29.
[3]) Cf. the Same to the Same, 17 June '29, the Same to Goslinga, 21 Aug. '29.

nation-treatment, and this even in the sense that, if in future His Catholic Majesty might grant any advantage to some other nation, he should grant it simultaneously to them. To the States General he accorded the title of "Hauts et Puissants Seigneurs", even as France and England had done by means of the Triple Alliance. These two powers renewed their engagements with regard to the affairs of Ostend and East Frisia, and Spain entered into them for the first time. Should the case present itself that on account of her accession the Republic should be attacked or troubled, the Allies should send her the assistance specified in the treaty without delay.

The Republic had forestalled France. Brancas was not yet acquainted with the intentions of his Court. Had he opposed Van der Meer, Stanhope and Keene would certainly, in Van der Meer's opinion, have sided with him, but they did not dare to take the lead for fear the Dutch Ambassador might do them an ill turn with Patiño regarding their trade [1]).

It was in this manner that the Republic joined her Allies in associating herself with Spain. The Triple Alliance of Hanover had been replaced by the Quadruple Alliance of Seville.

---

[1]) Secr. Res. S. G. 22, 25 Oct., 11 Nov. '29; Van der Meer to Fagel, 23 Nov. '29, in Secr. Res. Hl. VIII, 184—6; ib. 190 et seq.

APPENDIX.

THE OPPOSITION OF THE DUTCH TO THE OSTEND TRADE.

In two principal points our conception of this opposition deviates from that of Huisman (*La Belgique Commerciale et l'Empereur Charles VI. La Compagnie d'Ostende*. Bruxelles/Paris, 1902). In the first place with regard to the share the Dutch had in it, and, secondly, concerning their right to act in the way they did.

I.

We shall deal first with the opposition to the Ostend trade before the establishment of the Company. Apropos of this, we find the following observation by Huisman, *op. cit.* p. 229: — "Les Provinces-Unies et la Grande-Bretagne, aussitôt que notre mouvement d'expansion commerciale s'etait dessiné, avaient convenu d'unir leurs efforts et d'enrayer le développement du trafic flamand. Mais, chaque fois qu'il avait fallu concerter un plan d'action commune, les compagnies des deux Etats, jalouses et défiantes l'une de l'autre, s'étaient reproché mutuellement leur indifférence et leur absence d'énergie."

Is this observation right? Did the United Provinces and Great Britain, directly the Belgian enterprises began, agree on a combined action against them? If they did, Huisman ought to have demonstrated it more amply, particularly as his account of the hindrance of the Ostend trade cannot be said to tally with it. But for these remarks he does not speak of this agreement anywhere, and what he has related on pp. 135—138 makes clear beyond doubt that the English Government did not enter into it when such a combined action was proposed by the States in 1720.

These very pages may be quoted against the latter part of the passage. From them it does not appear, that as often as a plan of common action had to be settled, this was frustrated by the mutual jealousy between the Companies of the two States. In that

case at least, the two Companies pulled together. And had they
not also agreed on a common line of conduct previously, when
the India House deputised Decker to the Hague (p. 124)? These
instances do not testify to that mutual jealousy; and where are
those that do?

To this observation of Huisman's we prefer the facts adduced
by him to build our opinion upon. According to these, speaking
generally, the Companies of the two countries were at one with
each other, but the Governments were not, cf. above pp. 66—70.

There is another passage in Huisman's book that we must quote
in this connection. On pp. 225—226 we read: "Aussi longtemps
que le commerce transocéanique des Pays-Bas autrichiens avait
été livré à l'initiative de quelques particuliers, les Puissances
Maritimes avaient laissé à leurs compagnies des Indes le soin de
prendre toutes les mesures offensives et défensives que compor-
taient leurs intérêts. Les gouvernements, les diplomates anglais et
hollandais n'étaient intervenus dans les contestations soulevées
par les iniques captures des vaisseaux ostendais que pour inti-
mider l'Empereur et l'engraver dans d'interminables négociations."

Here the two Governments are represented to have acted in the
same way. This is what we contest.

The English Government interfered but very little with the
Ostend trade. At the instigation of the India House they remonstrated against the engaging of Britons in Belgian ships, and,
when they were satisfied on this point, they again, at the request
of the Company, delivered a note advocating the Court of Vienna
not to issue any more patents whatever. That note, though
aiming at the destruction of the Ostend trade, was nevertheless
"de forme courtoise, amicale même" (p. 123). We find why this
note was so mildly worded explained at the bottom of the same
page: "Sollicité par la compagnie des Indes d'intervenir près du
cabinet de Vienne, George I. y avait consenti, mais *avec l'intention de ne pas pousser les choses à l'extrême, pour le moment du
moins.* Il venait, en effet, de demander le secours de six batail-
lons belges contre les menaces de débarquement de la flotte
espagnole et d'un retour du Pretendant Stuart. Si les entreprises
lointaines de l'Autriche devaient amener des conflits coloniaux,
il préférait laisser aux Provinces-Unies le soin de livrer les premiers

engagements." We see that the English Government gave some satisfaction to their East India Company, but were by no means inclined to go to any further lengths. As appears from the words "pour le moment du moins", Huisman restricts that disposition of the Government to the particular juncture when they were apprehensive of an invasion on behalf of the Pretender. He has, however, as it appears to us, himself felt that it was not only then that they cared little for the Ostend Company. This is obvious from some few words of his on p. 195.

He had previously stated that when, about the middle of 1720, the negotiations concerning the Dutch or Belgian seizures of ships by way of reprisals were still pending, the Dutch took another vessel which was on the point of sailing for India. Seeing that the Austrian Government did not take strenuous measures, the States allowed the sale of it. But this time Prié resolved on reprisals. The States then hesitated and proposed to reopen the negotiations. To this Prié agreed. De la Bassecour, one of the lawyers of the West-India Company, was sent to Brussels. His offers were quite unacceptable, but the Company attained its end, and in this way things dragged on. (pp. 191—194).

And now Huisman proceeds as follows (p. 195) "Les Provinces-Unies, après le retour de Mr. De la Bassecour, se montrèrent d'autant moins accommodantes qu'elles voyaient l'Angleterre, *jusque-là hésitante*, disposée à s'unir effectivement à elles et à s'opposer de vive force à notre commerce d'Orient." So until then (1721) the English Government were hesitating.

As we understand, they hesitated still longer; for the attack on the Flandria, that Huisman adduces, cannot satisfy us that they then became disposed to join the United Provinces effectually and to oppose the Ostend trade by main force. This particular attack occurred in the following manner: — In 1721 an Ostend ship sought shelter at Benkoulen in Sumatra, at that time an English possession. But instead of finding it, the captain was taken prisoner and the cargo was forwarded to Madras. Notwithstanding the most strenuous reclamations of the Austrian Ambassador in London, no satisfaction was given. "Le cabinet de Saint James en fit retomber la responsabilité sur la Maison des Indes, qui, elle même, assura que le gouverneur de Bencoulen avait agi sans mandat ni pouvoir." Further remonstrances were ineffectual (p. 195). We cannot see that this event shows a change in the disposition of the English Government. They refused to allow the Company to give satisfaction, that is all. They did not in the least try to justify it; the Company itself even disavowed the fact. As before, the Government once more confined themselves to some complaisance towards the Company which they could not dispense with, but vindication of its rights and claims was quite out of the question.

This conduct made a bad contrast with that of the Dutch Government. From the outset the latter made the cause of their Companies theirs. As early as in 1717 they issued a severe edict prohibiting their subjects even under penalty of death from enlisting in Belgian ships (p. 104). When the agents of the Companies committed cruel acts of violence upon the Ostend sailors, the States exculpated them (p. 128); when a Belgian ship was taken, they justified it with a reference to the Treaty of Munster (pp. 129—130). To this they referred again, when they claimed satisfaction for the capture of a Dutch ship that the Belgians had taken by way of reprisal for one of theirs (pp. 133—134). It was on this occasion that the States, on behalf of their Companies, applied to the English Government and proposed to them a plan of combined action (pp. 135—136).

As we have seen, this proposition was supported by the English East India Company. Ever since the beginning of the Ostend trade this Company was aware of the dangers menacing it from that quarter. And no less than the Companies in the Republic did it endeavour to avert them. [1]) But, unlike them, it was not fortunate enough to obtain a hearing with the Government.

This disposition of the English Government is evident from the behaviour of the Austrian authorities perhaps more than from anything else; for the latter did not fail to make use of it. In 1720 it was to be feared, as we know, that the union of the two Maritime Powers would come about. But Prié was convinced that the Dutch "n'oseront rien entreprendre s'ils ne se voyent pas appuyés par l'Angleterre" (p. 136) and therefore tried to give as much satisfaction as possible to the English Government; in this way he succeeded in preventing that union. This disposition of

---

[1]) Huisman, *op. cit.* 92, 102, 2nd. footnote, 118, 123, 124, 135, 137, 195; *Engl. Hist. Rev.* XXII, 257, 265.

the cabinet of St. James appears also from the further conduct of
Prié. It is a known fact that he was against the formation of a
Company. He was fond of his own authority and, in addition, the
system of extending patents to private people was most profitable
to him. So when he was requested to supply all kinds of informa-
tions and elucidations concerning the best shape to be given to
the future Company, he delayed it by means of various pretexts
for nearly two years. One of the arguments he put forward was
the difficulties made by the States with regard to the prizes (pp.
161, 191—192). Now if he could have pointed at the opposition of
the English Government too, is it possible to imagine that he
would have neglected it? We think not. We even do not fear to
contend that in that case the Ostend Company would never
have been established. For when, after its establishment, St.
Saphorin protested against it, Eugene of Savoy emphasized
again and again; "pourquoi si le roy de la Grande-Bretagne vou-
lait s'opposer à ce commerce ne s'est-il pas expliqué plus tôt de la
même manière qu'il fait à présent, et pourquoi ne se déclarer que
lorsque nous ne pouvons plus rétrograder sans la plus grande pro-
stitution". [1]

Thus we may say that previous to the establishment of the
Ostend Company the Republic was the only Power that opposed
the Belgian trade, whereas England did no more than she was
obliged to do out of regard for the India House.

Passing on to the period after the establishment we again find,
when we examine things closely, that the general views of Huisman are not confirmed by the facts he himself relates. He has only
looked at the object attacked, his Company of Ostend, but has
failed to discern between the attackers. So he tells us, (p. 313):
"Elle trouvait devant elle, dès son installation, s'opposant à son
activité et à son développement, une coalition d'intérêts puissants,
la ligue des sociétés des Indes anglaise, hollandaise et française,
protégée ouvertement ou sous main par leurs gouvernements
respectifs." If this had been true, the Company could not have
held out even for a year; it would at once have sunk under such an
opposition. Moreover, this contention is not confirmed by facts:
for where are the instances of the opposition of the French Com-

---

[1] Pribram, *Oesterreichische Staatsverträge. England* I, 446 note.

pany and of the protection of the English and French Governments given to their Companies to be found in Huisman's book? It is true that in 1724 three Ostend captains were taken prisoners at Dunkirk and not released until some months afterwards, but this arrest was ordered by the French Government at the instigation of the Republic (pp. 281—282); while, as to the English Government, what they did in this respect, was done either by the pressure brought to bear upon them by the India House or for the gratification of Spain.

Besides omitting to discern between the attackers of the Ostend Company, Huisman has attributed too much significance to it in the negotiations of those days. He continues the passage we quoted in this way: "Cette situation créait non seulement un danger constant pour l'existence de notre compagnie de navigation; elle *menaçait la paix du monde.*" (p. 313). Somewhere else (pp. 322—323) he speaks of the situation of the Emperor, when Ripperda arrived at Vienna: "He was isolated, every day hostilities might break out in Italy or in the Southern Netherlands; *à chaque instant un conflit pouvait se produire à propos de la compagnie d'Ostende.* It was to be feared that the Maritime Powers would pass on from menacing notes to acts of violence. These were already being committed in India, and the ill-will of the English was evident from their refusal to give satisfaction for the insult to the Flandria, but *lately* surprised at Benkoulen."

We admit that at that time the peace of the world was menaced, also that the Emperor was in a bad condition, for it was by no means impossible that England and France would at last be prevailed upon to join Spain in a war, but then the succession in the Italian Duchies would have been the *casus belli* and not the Ostend affair, which those three Powers had agreed only some months before not to introduce at the Congress of Cambrai. And as to the acts of violence in India, these had been committed ever since the beginning of the Ostend trade both by the English and Dutch Companies, but, as it seems to us, instead of increasing they had very much decreased of later years — at least Huisman does not mention any after that inflicted on the Flandria, the defence of piloting Ostend ships (p. 284) being at the most an indirect act of violence. And that had not *lately* taken place ("*naguère*"), but in August 1721, more than three years before!

Huisman has come to these mistaken notions, as he was of the opinion that England and France were really opposed to the Ostend trade. But from the reception the applications of the Republic met with on their part, he might have gathered that this promise was erroneous, cf. above pp. 72—79, which have almost wholly been built on Huisman, *op. cit.* 229/35, 246/7, 314/5, 319/21. With regard to the first application, we note that in the beginning the English Government would give no more than a "simple promesse de bons offices," which was "justement ne rien faire du tout", but were then once more forced, as had occasionally been the case previous to the establishment, to take some measures (pp. 229—231). When the Republic applied for the second time, the reception was almost as cool. That upon the third application it was not the Ostend affair itself which caused them to interfere with it, has been set forth above (pp. 75—79). While as regards the French Government, their proceedings against the Belgian trade were rather indifferent. In Vienna, the Regent was considered not to be an adversary [1]), and Morville's attitude towards it was even less unfriendly than his [2]). France was not prepared to remove that which seemed to definitely embroil the Emperor and the Maritime Powers [3]).

After the conclusion of the Vienna Treaties she continued acting on the same lines (pp. 336—337). To be sure, she then guaranteed to the Republic the suppression of the Ostend Company, but she imagined she had done enough for her in bringing about its suspension. France only made serious efforts to settle the affair definitively when England strongly urged her to take vigorous measures, as was the case in November 1728 and in the Spring of 1729.

As to England, her attitude towards the Ostend trade underwent a great change in 1725. From that year its destruction was a part of her programme. It was expressly stated in the private instructions of Waldegrave, who was to go to Vienna that: "that stumbling-block must be unquestionably removed". [4]) And, with England's assistance, in 1731 it was removed.

However, she had not the principal share in it. That she took the matter up in 1725 was — as has been set forth above (pp. 83, 88,

[1]) Syveton, *Une Cour et un Avanturier au 18me siècle* 120—1, note.
[2]) Huisman, *op. cit.* 320—1, cf. 315.
[3]) Dureng, *Le Duc de Bourbon et l'Angleterre* (Paris 1911) 54—5, 82, 186—7.
[4]) 26 Oct. '27 o. s., R. O. Germany 62.

89) — only in some measure for her own sake, but principally since she wanted the Republic. The course of events confirms the correctness of this opinion. England always considered it of far less importance than the preservation of Gibraltar and of the commercial privileges. She refused her concurrence as often as there was any question of taking it in hand previous to these points, cf. Hop and Goslinga to Slingelandt, July 1st. 1728, R. A. Hl. 2985; Hop to the Same, Nov. 10th. 1728, ib. 2982, and above p. 342; and even neglected to settle it together with them in the negotiations preceding the Treaty of Seville, cf. above pp. 362—4. It was then considered to concern England so little that in the famous protest raised against it by the Lords in the Opposition, no mention was made of it at all [1]). Only after this Treaty, in the course of 1730, when England began to seek the Emperor's friendship, did she earnestly take it up, almost solely because she desired the Republic to come into the Treaty to be concluded with the Court of Vienna.

We can, in addition, point to a number of places taken from the original documents, either directly or indirectly, where the Ostend affair is said to concern the Dutch without any mention whatever of the English, or to concern the Dutch in the first place. It is spoken of as if it concerned only the Dutch, by the Court of France in her instructions to Chavigny, [2]) by Fleury [3]), by Morville [4]), by Villars [5]), by St. Saphorin [6]), by the English plenipotentiaries at the Congress of Cambrai [7]), by the Austrian plenipotentiaries at that of Soissons [8]). It is spoken of as principally interesting the Republic and to a minor extent England by Fleury [9]), by St. Saphorin [10]), by George II. [11]), by the plenipotentiary Hop [12]), by Slingelandt [13]).

As to the last named we must mention that upon several occa-

---

[1]) Cobbett, *Parliamentary History* VIII, 775—7.
[2]) *Recueil des Instructions* XVIII, 171—3.
[3]) Baudrillart, *op. cit.* III, 325.
[4]) Dureng, *op. cit.* 187.
[5]) Villars, *Mémoires* V, 235.
[6]) Dureng, *op. cit.* 296.
[7]) Dureng, *op. cit.* 187.
[8]) Höfler, *op. cit.* XXXVIII, 191.
[9]) Pesters to Slingelandt, 25 Sept. '27, R. A. Hl. 2984.
[10]) Dureng, *op. cit.* 520.
[11]) Hop to Fagel, 12 Sept. '27, R. A., S. G. 7348.
[12]) Hop to Slingelandt, 10 Nov. '28, R. A. Hl. 2982.
[13]) Chesterfield to Townshend, 18 Jan. '29, R. O. Hl. 303.

sions he expressed it as his opinion that the Ostend affair concerned England and the Republic equally. It must, however, be remembered that he did so on purpose, his object evidently being to
establish the principle that England ought to bear an equal share
in the equivalent to be paid for the Company's suppression [1]).

This, therefore, need not prevent us from drawing the general
conclusion that the Ostend affair itself was rather immaterial to
the English Government, and that their opposition was principally owing to indirect reasons, in particular that they wanted the
Republic to go along with them. She it was to whose tenacious
antagonism the ruin of the Ostend trade must be ascribed in the
very first place.

We had already drawn the above-mentioned conclusions and
written our second chapter when we saw an article referred to,
that had hitherto escaped our notice. It spoke of "England and
the Ostend Company", the author being G. B. Hertz (*Eng. Hist.
Rev.* XXII, 225 et seq.). We became rather nervous in consequence,
as it might possibly impair the conclusions we had already
arrived at.

From the very first perusal of the article we perceived that, in
the opinion of Hertz, England, and not the Republic, was the real
destroyer of the Ostend Company. He complains that "historians
have attached more weight to Dutch than to British resistance to
the Company in determining the causes of its ruin" (p. 264) or,
as he expresses elsewhere (p. 271): "To foreign authorities like
Huisman, England's part is always secondary and Townshend's
foreign policy has been treated as less determinate than that of
the States General". This he tries to account for by continuing:
"The insularity of the British dialectic of the day deprived it of
recognition abroad, while the official memorials of the Dutch at
once required most eager criticism and reply." The same explanation he had already stated in other words: "Continental critics
were far more familiar with the Dutch pamphlet literature of the
day, which was either composed in or translated into French or

---

[1]) Secr. Res. Hl. VII, 848: Fénelon to Chauvelin, 30 Sept. '27, A. E. Hl. 371; Slingelandt to Hop, 7 July, 5 Aug., 7 Oct., 6 Nov., 15 Nov. '28: cf. above p.

Latin, than with that of England, which never passed out of the vernacular" (p. 264)

This "never" is erroneous, for at least two of those English writings were translated into French (cf. Huisman, *op. cit.* 399—401). Besides, it is hardly conceivable that those historians will have judged of the share each of the Maritime Powers had in the Company's destruction only by the writings published on either side.

But in whatever manner Hertz accounts for this, in his opinion, wrong notion of other historians, is less interesting than to know what he thinks himself. This can be derived from several expressions of his. On p. 265 he says: "To the jealousy of the country more than to any other agency is to be ascribed the downfall of the Ostend Company." "The country" or "the nation" (p. 266) is rather vague, but on p. 271 he expresses himself more clearly. "It is however" — thus he sets his opinion against that of the "foreign authorities" — "reasonable to believe that the defeat of the Ostend Company was really due to the relentless energy of the middle-class Whigs". "It is clear", he goes on, "that they won for Townshend the lingering support of Walpole." Townshend himself won France. "The adherence of that State indeed was decisive of ultimate success and it was far from being caused by the attitude of the dilatory and pacific United Provinces. *England, and England alone was determined to kill the Ostend Company at all costs.*"

It must be admitted that Herz represents things as nobody else has done. He is himself so well aware of it that he would have done better had he but endeavoured somewhat more to convince his readers of the correctness of his opinion. It is not enough that he *assures* them that "the jealousy of the country" was the principal agency in bringing about the Company's downfall or that he *thinks* it is *"reasonable"* to ascribe this more particularly to the middle-class Whigs, of whom, moreover, it is *"clear"* that they won Walpole's support for Townshend.

One is less inclined to be satisfied with such arguments, considering that the English Government have not always allowed themselves to be influenced by the ill feeling against the Ostend trade. We came to the conclusion above that previous to 1725 the English Government did not care much for it. In this, our opinion is confirmed by a particular Hertz himself provides us with. He tells us that the Jacobites, who had at first accused the Government of "apathy towards the danger of Belgian competition, and who had asserted that George I. was working for England's impoverishment, were forced to strike a different note of antagonism in view of the strong diplomatic pressure brought to bear on Charles VI., after the Treaty of Vienna" (p. 265).

Hertz further informs us that in 1725 and ensuing years the Government strongly opposed the Ostend Company. But how was this brought about? Considering their former conduct, it is hardly likely that the Company itself roused their anger, and consequently the change will principally have been determined by other motives. To be sure, Hertz could not draw this conclusion, as he did not start from the premise of this change, although he knew that the Ostend Company was not the only question at issue, for the public were certainly no less interested in those of Gibraltar and of the commercial privileges in Spanish America. Consequently, when speaking of the influence exerted by the nation, or, more particularly, by the middle-class Whigs, Hertz would have done better to have examined how far the enmity against the Ostend Company entered into this opposition.

But Hertz has doubtless allowed himself to be led astray by the connection that, for some time after the Vienna Treaties, the English nation placed between the Ostend Company and those commercial privileges in Spanish America; for those treaties roused their anger solely as they supposed that that Company had been endowed with privileges detrimental to their own (cf. above pp. 83, 90—91). Hertz considers this supposition the right one (p. 263)[1], but, however this may be, the connection did not last for any length of time: this he should at least have noticed. For by the Preliminaries of 1727 the commercial privileges of the English nation were restored to them as they had been before 1725, and in addition, two years afterwards Spain was detached from the Emperor, and entered into a treaty with England. Disentangled from the connection with the commercial privileges in the Spanish Indies, the English opposition against the Ostend Company

[1] On the authority of Huisman we have averred that this is not correct (p. 83), but afterwards we found that both Ranke (*Zwolf Bücher Preuszischer Geschichte* III —IV, 44 note) and Hertz (p. 263) disagree with him. Compare also the account of the general meeting of the Ostend Company of Dec. 4th. '25, in Hertz's article (263 at the foot of the page) with that in Huisman (*op. cit.* 537—9).

nevertheless continued until 1731, when the Emperor suppressed it.

How is this to be accounted for? The conduct of the Government before 1725 seems to prove that the interest of England was not sufficiently affected by the Ostend trade to explain her strong opposition, from the Treaties of Vienna until the very suppression of the Company. We are confirmed in this opinion by the following words of the elder Pitt, quoted by Hertz (p. 278): "The abolition of the Ostend Company was a demand we had no right to make, nor was it essentially our interest to insist upon it."

This is perfectly right. Not their own interest, but something else, decided England's share in that abolition. It was the deference that the English Government were obliged to entertain for the Dutch in 1725 and ensuing years. Next to the excitement of the nation, principally produced by that idea concerning the privileges in Spanish America, this factor has determined their conduct After the conclusion of the Austro-Spanish Alliance they absolutely needed the Republic, and so they were obliged to take up the struggle against the Ostend Company on account of their Ally, apart from any considerations of their own. And these considerations ceasing to a great extent, they none the less persisted in that struggle.

Deference for the Dutch, that is the key to the problem. This is the very last thing Hertz could possibly have imagined. He has understood, to be sure, that in the destruction of the Ostend trade the Dutch were also concerned, but he has not known what to do with them. He allows "that the first alarm reached London from the States General" (264), he recognizes the effect of the Dutch pamphlet literature of the day (264), written by "more learned writers" (270) than that of the English, he even admits that "a story of this least worthy of British triumphs would be very partial if it minimised the effects of the assistance of the Dutch" (271), but that these last words have been written only "pour acquit de conscience" is evidently proved by the immediately preceding: "England and England alone was determined to kill the Ostend Company at all costs," which are too absolute to permit of any mitigation.

However, historical questions are not decided by high sounding words like those. Hertz ought to have understood that England's share cannot be determined without making due allowance for that of the Republic. The share of the one depends on that of the other. But Hertz appears to have thought that the Republic was then of only very little importance. Speaking of Townshend's efforts to persuade France against the Ostend Company, he says: "The adherence of that State was indeed decisive of ultimate success and it was far from being caused by the attitude of the dilatory and pacific United Provinces" (271). Though the former part of this sentence is open to criticism, the latter is perhaps even more so. The United Provinces may have been dilatory and pacific, but they were, nevertheless, by no means to be neglected. Both England and France sought their friendship. Utilizing this position, they brought about that which they would have been incapable of, had they acted alone, viz., the suppression of the rival Company of Ostend. This is principally due to them, and not to England.

In this conviction we have not been shaken by Hertz's article. We have rather been confirmed in it, for both the accusation of apathy, directed against the Government by the Jacobites previous to 1725, and the words used by Pitt some years after the Company's suppression, speak in its favour.

II.

In the second chapter we have maintained that it is unreasonable to absolutely condemn the conduct of the Dutch towards the Ostend trade. But we have not done so without promising that we should try to justify our opinion.

We cannot start better than by taking into consideration the juristic arguments that the Dutch set against the efforts of the Belgians. They were to this effect. According to the Barrier Treaty, between the Belgians and the Dutch, matters of trade were to continue on the footing of the Treaty of Munster. Hence the Dutch deduced that the Emperor had engaged himself not to alter in any way the commercial system, to which the Spanish Government, by virtue of that treaty, had submitted the Southern Netherlands.

Huisman has weighed this argument and found it erroneous in three respects. In the first place, the Austrian Belgians could not be put on a par with the Spaniards spoken of in the Treaty of Munster. Secondly, this treaty had, in matters of colonial trade, no relation whatever to the Emperor. Thirdly, there was no ground at all for the pretension to a monopoly, by which the Ostend Company was even denied the trade with China, though the Dutch had no factories left there at all.

Of the last point we shall not treat. We heartily admit that Huisman is right in this respect. And as regards the first, we also think he is right. But not as to the second. It is in connection with this point that we intend to protest against the general opinion of Huisman. According to him, the Dutch were led by sheer greed and hate; he ascribes only mean motives to them. When reading Huisman one gets the idea that when they opposed the Ostend trade, the Dutch cannot have acted in good faith.

And yet they certainly did act in good faith. At least we can point to the opinions of some of their best men, men of good repute all over Europe. Some years afterwards the Court of Vienna was willing to agree to a limitation of the Ostend trade, but Fagel said: "This stood on a par with entering by force into a man's room and then telling him that for friendship's sake one would be content with a corner of the room". [1] According to Goslinga the Ostend trade altogether clashed with the drift of the treaties [2], Slingelandt also spoke of "the evident injustice" [3] done to the Republic by the Emperor. He believed in her right, based on the treaties [4], though, with regard to that of Munster, allowing that there was "something to say against it." He used this expression in the following connection: "As to the indemnification or equivalent for the suppression of the Ostend Company"—which at that time was under discussion — "the Emperor is so heavily in debt to the Republic, which has ruined herself financially to procure for him the Southern Netherlands and the superiority that now oppresses and threatens her and her Allies, that she would be entitled to expect much more from him than the non-introduction of novelties, injurious to her trade, in a country which he could never have obtained without the help of the Republic more than of any other Ally, even though there was something to say against the Treaty of Munster, confirmed by a possession of nearly eighty

[1] Huisman, *op. cit.* 349.
[2] Goslinga to Marshal de Huxelles, 26 Mch. '27, A. E. Hl. 368.
[3] Slingelandt to C. Hop, 3 Mch. '29.
[4] Slingelandt to Townshend, 11 Aug. '23, R. O. Hl. 280; idem to C. Hop, 27 June '29.

years", [1] "an immemorial possession", as he called it somewhere else [2]).

Slingelandt's defence is an appeal to history. "Les articles 5 et 6 du Traité de Munster (the commercial ones) font la partie la plus considérable du prix auquel l'Espagne acheta alors la paix et nous détacha de la France; le prix auquel nous sommes entrés l'année 1701 dans la Grande Alliance, toute minutée pour l'avantage de la maison d'Autriche, a été l'avantage qui en reviendrait à notre commerce" [3]). But the Emperor — thus Slingelandt complained in a letter to Townshend — "n'a pas pour les Puissances Maritimes les égards que méritent les signalés services qu'il en a tirés, et dans les affaires du commerce il semble avoir oublié une des principales fins de la Grande Alliance" [4]).

It is the Grand Alliance Slingelandt refers to again and again. To understand the character of this Alliance well, we must glance backwards. At the end of the Eighty-years-war the power of Spain was broken. This result was not only due to the exertions of the United Provinces, but also to the support given to them by France. But in the common struggle against Spain the power of this Ally rose to such a height that they grew uneasy. In 1635 they had concluded a treaty with her, according to which neither of the parties would be free to put an end to the war with Spain unless the other agreed to it. On seeing the remarkable progress of the power of France, however, they became more and more sceptical as to the use of reducing Spain still more. At last they were prevailed on by the latter to conclude a separate peace in contravention of the treaty with France. Spain succeeded principally by engaging herself not to extend her trade with the East-Indies any further, and by closing the Scheldt, which excluded Antwerp from oversea trade to the advantage of Amsterdam. (Treaty of Munster, Articles 5, 6, 14).

After detaching the Dutch from France, Spain did everything in her power to keep them at her side. Being unable to defend the Southern Netherlands any longer, she saw that she could only save them from falling into the hands of Louis XIV., if she had

---

[1] Slingelandt to C. Hop, 7 July '28: "al viel schoon iets te seggen op het Tractaat van Munster, geconfirmeert door een bijna tagtigjaarige possessie".
[2] Slingelandt to C. Hop, 27 June '29.
[3] Slingelandt to Goslinga, 21 July '28.
[4] Slingelandt to Townshend, 11 Aug. '23, R. O. Hl. 280.

recourse to the Republic. The latter was willing to help, provided
she was paid for it. This payment took the form of commercial advantages, in the first place in the Spanish Netherlands themselves. To Spain these provinces had no value other than political—
they offered an opportunity of exerting some influence in Central
Europe. Thus she did not object to the granting of those advantages, though — more than they had been already by the closing of
the Scheldt — the Belgians were in this way economically subdued
to the Dutch, who, later on, were joined by the English [1]). Apart
from these privileges the Maritime Powers were granted others
concerning Spain herself and her trade to the West Indies. As
early as 1650, two years after the Peace of Munster, the Dutch
were exempted from certain duties, which Spain continued raising
even from her own subjects in the Netherlands, and were granted
"the treatment of the most favoured nation", rights extended to
the English seventeen years afterwards [2]). They also obtained a
share in the "galleons", the Spanish commercial fleet, for the cargoes of which the Spaniards had to resort to other nations. Every
time Spain wanted their help, she had to grant some new privilege, and as in the second half of the 17th. century the Southern
Netherlands were constantly in danger of falling into the hands of
France, a kind of system developed between Spain, on the one
hand, and the Republic with — to a minor extent — England, on
the other.

Of this system, antagonism against France was a *conditio sine
qua non*. But this condition might cease to exist with the extinction of the Spanish Habsburgs. On this account, no less than on
others, did the Maritime Powers occupy themselves with the future
of the Spanish monarchy. The Italian portions of it they did
not care so much about; they might be given to a French Prince
or even to France herself; but Spain, the colonies and the Southern
Netherlands, viz., those parts they were especially interested in,
had to be kept out of the hands of France. This is evident from
both treaties of partition concluded by them with Louis XIV. [3]).

As we know, these treaties had not the desired effect, a grandson of the King of France being appointed heir to the whole of the

---

[1]) Huisman, *op. cit.* 9, 24.
[2]) Huisman, *op. cit.* 14.
[3]) Cf. Pribram, *Oesterreichische Staatsverträge. England* I, 211—12.

Spanish monarchy and his grandfather accepting it for him. What had to be the line of conduct of the Maritime Powers now? As to William III., he understood quite well the danger resulting from the union of the French and Spanish crowns in one house. It would be a danger equally to the trade as to the liberty of the two nations, for the French would most probably make themselves masters of the entire lucrative trade with Spain and her colonies; and the Southern Netherlands would perhaps be annexed to France: their economical dependence at least would soon be put an end to. William III. did not hesitate as to what was to be done, but the two nations who were not so clear-sighted as the King-Stadtholder hesitated. The profits obtained in the above-mentioned manner were so considerable that they were afraid of losing them by a war. They were not against the succession of a Bourbon prince in Spain if only France and Spain were kept apart and the commercial privileges continued. [1]) They preferred therefore to exhaust all means of diplomacy previous to engaging in a war. By and by, however, principally owing to the imprudent proceedings of Louis XIV., they changed their minds and lent willing ears to the requests of the Emperor for help. Negotiations with him led to the Treaty of the Hague of 1701, the "Grand Alliance". As stands to reason, they took especial care of their trading interests in this treaty. All the commercial rights and privileges the Maritime Powers had enjoyed under the reign of Charles II. in the whole Spanish monarchy should be restored to them, and the countries and cities that might be occupied in the Spanish Indies should remain theirs. As to the Southern Netherlands, it was expressively stipulated that they should be conquered to be a rampart and a barrier for the security of the States as they had been formerly (*ut sint obex et repagulum, vulgo Barrière, Galliam a Belgio Foederato removens et separans pro securitate Dominorum Ordinum Generalium quemadmodum ab omni tempore inservierunt donec rex Christianissimus nuper eas milite occupavit.*). [2])

Yet the aversion of the Maritime Powers to the war was still so strong that they insisted on an article that two months should be spent in efforts to obtain the object in a peaceable way. These were not made, however; for when, on the death of James II., a

---

[1]) L. von Ranke, *Englische Geschichte* VIII, 15.
[2]) Articles 8, 6, 5. (Pribram, *op. cit.* 229—30).

few days after the conclusion of the treaty, Louis XIV. at once recognized his son as King, all hesitation came to an end. [1])

This act of Louis XIV. provided the Maritime Powers with a
casus belli of a political and religious nature. There were, besides,
others of a similar nature, but the economical ones prevailed. Seeley has called the war of the Spanish succession the most businesslike of all English wars. Whether this is exactly true, we do not decide, but according to Heinsius and Marlborough it was only *spe
praemii vel lucri,* that the nations could be prevailed on to go to
war [2]).

To be sure, they did not enter into the war without informing
the Emperor what they intended fighting for. He knew it quite
well. His ministers complained that only the Dutch and English
commercial interests appeared to be concerned in the affair of the
succession, and he understood that Belgium would be to him a
possession, the advantage of which was to be entirely counterbalanced by its burdens [3]).

We could not have spoken our mind more clearly. Once the Alliance had been concluded on that footing, we, i.e., the Dutch, did
what was within or rather what was far beyond our power. Large
armies were organized, millions and millions spent on behalf of
the Austrian cause. To us the unfortunate results of the war
could not be imputed.

Nevertheless, we were the dupes. The English excluded us from
a share in the trade with the Spanish Indies and from new profits
acquired from Spain or France. Our only advantage had to be
found in the Southern Netherlands. But with regard to them we
were also disappointed: on the one hand by England, on the other
by Austria. What England alone did in this respect need not be
mentioned here, but with the assistance of both, the King of Prussia made himself master of Spanish Upper-Guelders [4]). This was
entirely inconsistent with the stipulation that the Spanish Netherlands should be henceforth a barrier for the Republic. But far
from scrupling to cede a part, the Emperor would have liked to

---

[1]) Pribram, *op. cit.* I, 240 et seq.; Srbik, *Oesterreichische Staatsverträge, Niederlande* I,
334 et seq..
[2]) Pribram, *op. cit.* I, 218; Srbik, *op. cit.* I, 356 et seq.; cf. Blok, *op. cit.* VI, 3—4,
36—37 and Bourgeois, *Manuel* I, 238, 243—5.
[3]) Pribram, *op. cit.* 220, cf. 216, 215.
[4]) Rive, *op. cit.* 72—79, especially 78.

cede the whole of them. It was his aim to exchange them for Bavaria[1]). In that case the Dutch barrier would have been devoid of any sense, as the Elector of Bavaria was a satellite of the French Crown. What happened to the Dutch garrisons in the Belgian fortresses in 1701 — when that Elector was Governor of the Southern Netherlands — is proof of it.

Not succeeding in his aim, the Emperor was obliged to take possession of the Southern Netherlands himself; however, as we have formerly related, not on the conditions proposed by the States. Though allowing that the States were right in as far as former negotiations always ran on such a footing, the Emperor, nevertheless, rejected their claims. They had to yield on several points. And even that was not enough. The Barrier Treaty had scarcely been concluded, when new concessions were exacted from them, and three years afterwards, in 1718, they had to acquiesce in a convention which altered that treaty to their disadvantage.

In their opinion that treaty was already so detrimental. They would never have agreed with Huisman, who thinks it was very favourable to them. It is true, that they received a subsidy of 1.250.000 gulilders annually, but this by no means served to "alimenter les caisses de la République", as Huisman says (p. 71); for this amount was insufficient by far for that "corps de troupes, qui mange l'argent de l'Etat". [2])

As the military stipulations of the Barrier Treaty could hardly be said to be profitable, the commercial ones, set down in the XXVIth. article, constituted the only advantages acquired by the war. They were two. In the first place, the import and export duties should continue on the same basis as they actually were at the conclusion of the Barrier Treaty; with this restriction, however, that as soon as possible a new treaty of commerce should be settled by the Emperor in conjunction with the King of England and the States; and secondly, between the Belgians and the Dutch matters of trade should remain on the very same footing as that established by the Treaty of Munster.

Of the advantages these clauses contained or were considered to contain, the Dutch were very tenacious. As to the first, we shall

---

[1]) Huisman, *op. cit.* 57.
[2]) Slingelandt to Townshend, 11 Aug. '23, R. O. Hl. 280; cf. Fénélon, *Mémoire* 141 and Fruin, *Geschiedenis der Staatsinstellingen* (edited by Colenbrander) 302, 308.

afterwards see that they delayed the conclusion of a commercial treaty as much as possible, in the settlement of which they had promised to take part. This was a downright transgression of the Barrier Treaty. Yet we cannot judge of it so severely as does Huisman. Why? In 1680 Spain granted the Maritime Powers a tariff that was most profitable to them, but on account of Belgian dissatisfaction, it was only in force for some months. By means of the "Grand Alliance", however, these Powers secured the renewal of that tariff; for it was settled that all rights which they used and enjoyed during the life of Charles II., or which they might use and enjoy by some right obtained before his death, should be restored to them. As a matter of course, this tariff was revived during the Anglo-Dutch administration. Thus, so much the more did the Maritime Powers feel it as an injustice that they were obliged by the Barrier Treaty to co-operate for the settlement of a new one.

The second clause was always referred to in order to prove the unlawfulness of the Ostend trade. As we have shown, Huisman has tried to refute this argument. Three objections he has opposed to it: the first and second concern the Treaty of Munster, and it is the latter of these we want to consider now more particularly.

It is to the effect that with regard to colonial trade the Treaty of Munster had no relation to the Emperor. Huisman's reasoning is as follows: Suppose, he says, that under Spanish rule the Belgians had been absolutely 'excluded from trade to the far countries, could they be excluded simply on that account also now that they had been put under Austria? No, for the Emperor did not possess the Southern Netherlands as general heir to Charles II. of Spain, but as his particular successor in the Southern Netherlands; consequently, he was only bound to the Treaty of Munster as far as it related to that part of the Spanish monarchy, not on those points regarding other parts of it, e.g., the colonial traffic. Secondly, the Barrier Treaty did not ratify the Treaty of Munster as a whole, but only the mutual commerce between the Southern and Northern Netherlands; so it was not applicable to the trade with the Indies, which were not spoken of, and where the Emperor did not possess anything; besides, that trade was carried on between the Belgians and free and independent nations. The third is an *argumentum e silentio :* neither in the negotiations resulting in the Barrier Treaty nor in those that led to the Convention of 1718 had the diplomats of the Republic spoken of the exclusion of the Southerns from transoceanic traffic, though several ships had already set sail for India and Guinea, and several had even returned before the Convention was concluded. [1]

In Huisman's demonstration this last argument may have some additional force; it is not compulsive, however. Beyond any doubt, at that time the colonial traffic of the Belgians was generally understood in the Republic to be quite unlawful, and so there was no reason to embarrass the barrier-negotiations with this affair.

By his second argument Huisman has tried to break the connection between the Barrier Treaty and that of Munster with regard to the Indian trade. According to him the former did not ratify the Treaty of Munster as a whole, but only the mutual traffic between the Southern and the Northern Netherlands. We agree to the former, but not to the latter part of this sentence. The whole Treaty of Munster was not confirmed by the XXVIth. article, only the commercial articles of it — but these without any restriction. This is evident from the wording of the article: "demeurant au reste *le commerce et tout ce qui en dépend entre les sujets de Sa Majesté Imperiale et Catholique dans les Pays-Bas Autrichiens et ceux des Provinces-Unies* en tout et en partie sur le pied établi et de la manière portée par les articles du traité fait à Munster le 30 de Janvier 1648 entre Sa Majesté le roi Philippe IV de glorieuse mémoire et les dits Seigneurs Etats Généraux des Provinces-Unies *concernant le commerce, lesquels articles viennent d'étre confirmés par le présent article*". [2] It is undeniable that at the end of this clause all the commercial articles of the Treaty of Munster are confirmed. But, referring to the beginning, Huisman thinks this confirmation was limited to the mutual trade of the Belgians and the Dutch. This would be inconsistent, for the beginning is not allowed to disagree with the end; it is, moreover, incorrect. If Huisman were right, the wording ought to have been different, not: "demeurant au reste le commerce et tout ce qui en dépend entre les sujets de S. M. I. et C. dans les P. B. A. et ceux des P. U." but: "demeurant au reste le commerce entre les sujets de S. M. I. et C. dans les P. B. A. et ceux des P. U. et tout ce qui en dépend." Everything pertaining to trade should remain among Belgians

---

[1] Huisman, *op. cit.* 387.
[2] Pribram, *op. cit.* I, 319; Srbik, *op. cit.* I, 497.

and Dutch on the same footing as had been established by the commercial articles of the Treaty of Munster. [1])

"Le commerce et tout ce qui en dépend", consequently the relations between the Belgians and the Dutch with regard to colonial trade. So we reject the outcome of Huisman's first argument. The starting point we cannot accept either. It is to the effect that the Emperor did not possess the Southern Netherlands as general heir to Charles II. but as his particular successor in that part of his monarchy. But what about the Grand Alliance? A question such as this must not be dealt with in the abstract, but in the light of history. Now, the Grand Alliance did not allot the whole Spanish monarchy to the Emperor. Nevertheless he had agreed to several clauses in behalf of the Maritime Powers concerning the whole monarchy in general, and the Indies and the Southern Netherlands in particular. In as much as the Maritime Powers were committed to procure for him satisfaction, he was to procure for them security with regard to their territory and their trade. Now, it had been expressly stipulated, that no peace should be concluded except in behalf of the subjects of His British Majesty and the States the faculty was obtained of using and enjoying all the same commercial privileges, rights, immunities, and liberties by land and sea in Spain, in the Mediterranean, and in all the countries and places that Charles II. had possessed in Europe and out of it. These privileges etc., were either those which at that moment were being used and enjoyed or those which they could use or enjoy by right, obtained before the death of the said King, by means of treaties, conventions, consuetudes, or in some other way [2]). It is indisputable that the trade to the East Indies was included by this article, as ic speaks of the countries out of Europe and refers to custom in case formal right should be deficient. Confronted with these clauses the first argu-

---

[1]) Our argument is confirmed by the fact that in the preface to the Barrier-Treaty the commerce of the Belgians, English and Dutch is made mention of, not the mutual trade, cf. Pribram, *op. cit.* I, 298, Srbik, *op. cit.* I, 476.

Owing to a mis-reading of this article, Huisman accuses (p. 334) the States of a notorious infraction of the Barrier-Treaty, although there is no question of any such. In that case the States did no more than what they had previously done (cf. ib. 24): they regulated their own tariff, independently of that of the Southern Netherlands. Of course this was not very friendly, but to the States this was more of the nature of measures of reprisal against the cruel injustice done to them by the Emperor, and did not in any way clash with any treaty whatsoever.

[2]) Article 8 of the Grand Alliance (Pribram, *op. cit.* I, 230; Srbik, *op. cit.*, I 347—8).

ment is no more — as it seems to us — than a lawyer's subtlety. It
falls to the ground when the Grand Alliance is taken into consideration.

Not only here, but in general it has been a fault of Huisman's to
neglect that Grand Alliance. He has not been fully awake to the
fact that according to that Alliance Belgium was to remain what
it had been in the second half of the 17th century: an object of
transaction between the Sovereign on the one hand and the Maritime Powers, the Dutch especially, on the other. He has looked
at things from a purely Belgian point of view. Consequently, he
could not do justice either to the Emperor or to the Dutch. The
former he has accused of timidity towards the Maritime Powers,
the latter of greed, envy, selfishness and so forth. But to judge
properly of their conduct one must start from the Grand Alliance,
by which they for the first time entered into relations with each
other concerning the Southern Netherlands.

It is not our aim to exculpate our ancestors in their dealings
with the Belgians. In several respects they did not act as behoves
the one sister-nation towards the other. With regard to their opposition to the Ostend trade, we repeat that the Treaty of Munster was not a solid base. We understand quite well that the Belgian lawyers availed themselves of this deficiency and of all the
arguments their inventive genius could adduce to protect the
promising enterprises to the Far East from the soft and forcible
means by which the Dutch tried to crush them. Still more, we
cannot but express sympathy for those poor Belgians who suffered so much and who could not overcome their sufferings notwithstanding the admirable exertion they displayed.

During that period it was their fate to be merely disposed of.
This was hard, very hard for them. But let us be just. They not
only suffered from, but also profited by, the transaction of which
they were the object. Is it not owing to the Dutch in the very first
place that the Southern Netherlands never fell a prey to the covetousness of Louis XIV., either in the 17th. or in the beginning of
the 18th. century?

The Dutch — it must be admitted — accomplished what they were
paid for. First of all with regard to the Spaniards, afterwards concerning the Emperor. On his behalf the Republic dislocated her finances
most alarmingly, never to be retrieved as long as she existed.

Nevertheless the Peace of Utrecht was for her a cruel deception, the Barrier Treaty another. And after all — "rupture totale du Traité de Barrière, déjà très onéreux à l'Etat"[1] — the Emperor promoted the Ostend Company, which, according to Goslinga, would entirely ruin the Republic in the long run [2]). Was it a wonder then that she tried to prevent that blow from him "from whom she considered she was entitled to expect much more than the non-introduction of novelties, injurious to her trade?" No matter how she may have wronged the Belgians, was she not right with regard to the Emperor?

He felt this himself. He scarcely ever dared to defend the Ostend trade. Huisman adduces several instances showing that the Belgian lawyers were forced to abate the expressions they had made use of in their memorials or to strike out some passages; others, that the writings defending the good right of the Company were publicly disavowed, this even in 1723, in the same year in which the charter was published. Huisman constantly ascribes this conduct of the Emperor to his desire to be good friends with the Maritime Powers. We doubt, however, whether this desire can account for all his weakness and faintheartedness. We doubt among other things on the score of a fact which Huisman himself has provided us with, who — it must be admitted — with all his partiality is an impartial historian, as he relates facts as they are, and so allows his readers to interpret them in their own way. That fact is that the Austrian plenipotentiaries at the Congress of Soissons once said, the right of the Emperor was clear, but a "droit de convenance" was entirely in favour of the States and of no consideration for the Belgians [3]). Does not this "droit de convenance" refer to the state of things in the 17th. century which was confirmed by the Emperor in the Grand Alliance?

----

1) Slingelandt to Townshend, 11 Aug. '23, R. O. Hl. 280.
2) Goslinga to Huxelles, 26 Mch. '27, A. E. Hl. 368.
3) Huisman, *op. cit.* 396—7, 437—40.

Printed in Great Britain
by Amazon

29885608R00236